Sun Yat-sen: *Frustrated Patriot*

Studies of the East Asian Institute
Columbia University

SUN
YAT-SEN

C. MARTIN WILBUR

FRUSTRATED PATRIOT

C. 1

Columbia University Press   New York   1976

B
SUN, Y.

Library of Congress Cataloging in Publication Data

Wilbur, Clarence Martin, 1908–
  Sun Yat-sen, frustrated patriot.

  Bibliography: p.
  Includes index.
  1. Sun, Yat-sen, 1866–1925. I. Title.
DS777.A595W55   951.04′1′0924 [B]   76-18200
ISBN 0-231-04036-9

Columbia University Press
New York   Guildford, Surrey
Copyright © 1976 by Columbia University Press
Printed in the United States of America

The East Asian Institute of Columbia University

The East Asian Institute of Columbia University was established in 1949 to prepare graduate students for careers dealing with East Asia, and to aid research and publication on East Asia during the modern period. The faculty of the Institute are grateful to the Ford Foundation and the Rockefeller Foundation for their financial assistance.

The Studies of the East Asian Institute were inaugurated in 1962 to bring to a wider public the results of significant new research on modern and contemporary East Asia.

Preface

Among all of China's modern leaders, Sun Yat-sen probably is the most universally revered by his countrymen all over the world. During his lifetime, hard-working Chinese abroad contributed millions of dollars to his causes. His death in March 1925 was widely mourned, and he was later canonized as *Kuo Fu*, the Father of the Country. This nearly universal respect is due to the memory of his leadership in the struggle to overthrow the Manchu dynasty, his subsequent opposition to military factions exploiting the people and dominating governments in Peking, and the antiimperialist stand he embraced during the latter years of his life. To the Chinese he has become a symbol of the virtuous patriot.

Indeed he was a patriot, deeply concerned for the fate of his country. This study develops the thesis that Sun Yat-sen was an enormously frustrated patriot, but frustrated in part by an overweaning confidence that he could surmount all obstacles. He dreamed great dreams for the betterment of his people and for the restoration of his country to its just place in the modern world—a world he knew much better than most of his Chinese contemporaries. Yet he identified his country's good with his own prescriptions in a singularly insistent way. Lured on by his dreams and seeing himself as the instrument for their fulfillment, he was repeatedly thwarted by intractable realities within China and the outer world. He died a disappointed man.

This book grew out of a study of the Chinese Nationalist Revolution during the years 1922–28. Dr. Sun launched that revolution with the help of a few colleagues in the Kuomintang. Then Soviet Russia, the Comintern, and the small Chinese Communist Party joined in the effort to unify the country, end warlordism and foreign domination, and set the nation on a course of social and economic reform, though not all collaborators had the same objectives. The more deeply I became engaged in this study the more I wished to understand this fascinating, enigmatic man. The quest leads in many directions and raises puzzling questions.

This is not a full biography. It emphasizes the last years of a revolutionary career. Yet it tries to disclose the major influences shaping Dr. Sun's personality and to sketch out the main lines of his frustrated political life. We then turn to two interesting topics: his endless search for funds with which to finance his revolutionary work, and his world-embracing quest for foreign support. Having set this stage, the book then turns to his "alliance" with Soviet Russia and his last burst of revolutionary activity with Russian assistance. This final phase of his career bore great consequences for the Chinese nation, and the world, after his death.

I have piled up many obligations during years of studying the Nationalist Revolution and wish here to express my gratitude for help that is related to this book. Many Chinese friends aided me in the Republic of China when I was privileged to spend a year of study in Taiwan. The late Professor Lo Chia-lun arranged for me to consult the Kuomintang archives, of which he was the director. He was also the principal editor of two important works that I have used extensively. Mr. Huang Chi-lu became the next director and was always helpful during my subsequent visits to Taiwan. Two scholars, then staff members of the archives, Mr. Chiang Yung-ching and Mr. Li Yün-han, were particularly helpful and became my good friends. The late Professor Kuo Ting-yee, then director of the Institute of Modern History, Academia Sinica, opened many academic doors for me; he also wrote a long and rigorous critique of my preliminary study, *Forging the Weapons,* for which I am most grateful. I also remember the assistance given me by Professors

Chang Chi-yun, Shen Yi-tsen, Shen Yun-lung, Sung Shi, Tao Hsi-sheng, and Wu Hsiang-hsiang.

I am deeply indebted to the late Mrs. Lydia Holubnychy for many abstracts and translations of recent Russian scholarly work on Sun Yat-sen and the National Revolution. She was writing a book on Borodin in China when she died.

My main indebtedness for library assistance is to the General Library of Columbia University, its excellent East Asian Library, and its extensive microfilm collection. In connection with this book, I have also used the New York Public Library, the collections of the Hoover Institution at Stanford, and, through the assistance of Professor Ichiko Chūzō, the Toyo Bunko collection in Tokyo. Much of what may be new in this study arises from research in archival collections. I recall with pleasure many hours spent in the Public Records Office in London, the Library of the British Information Service in New York, and the National Archives in Washington. Keepers of manuscript collections in the Library of Congress, the State Historical Society of Wisconsin, and Stanford University Libraries assisted me by providing copies of documents related to Sun Yat-sen, and I have used material preserved in the manuscript collections of Columbia, Cornell, Harvard, and Princeton.

Several students and former students who have pursued subjects similar to mine were helpful, and I wish to thank Mrs. Carol Andrews, Professor Gilbert Chan, Mr. Joshua Fogel, Professor Bernadette Li Gentzler, Mr. Gary Glick, Mrs. Bonnie Lawrence, Miss Edith Lim, Mrs. Carol Reynolds, and Professor Odoric Wou. I also thank many friends and colleagues for information and ideas: Dr. Dorothy Borg, who gave me copies of important manuscripts; Professors Edmund Clubb, Eto Shinkichi, Josef Fass, and Thomas Ganschow; my revered teacher, Emeritus Professor L. Carrington Goodrich, who participated in Dr. Sun's Christian funeral service; Professor Walter Gourlay, Dr. Richard C. Howard, Professor Chun-tu Hsüeh; Mrs. Julie How Hwa, my collaborator in another study; Professor Marius B. Jansen, Mrs. L. Kisselgoff, Professor Donald W. Klein, Dr. V. K. Wellington Koo, Professor George A. Lensen, Mr. Lu-chao Li, Mr. John Ma, Miss June Y. Mei, Dr. Morty Rozansky,

Professor Harold Z. Schiffrin, Mr. John S. Service, Professors Minoru Shinoda, Paul Sih, Tong Te-kong, and Ezra F. Vogel, Capt. Marvin Williamson, and Dr. David C. Wilson.

I also wish to thank my skillful editor, Ms. Agnes B. McKirdy, who used her sense of style to improve my exposition and her sharp eye to detect many errors.

During the course of my study and writing I was fortunate to receive a Fulbright award for study in the Republic of China, a Senior Specialist Fellowship for writing from East/West Center in Honolulu, and a grant from the East Asian Institute of Columbia University for a semester's research leave and travel funds, derived from Ford Foundation support. The Bancroft Fund provided cost of some manuscript typing. I am grateful for the help in many other ways that attended these grants. For Columbia University, where I have enjoyed most cordial relations with colleagues and students during many years of teaching, I feel a profound sense of obligation.

My wife, Kay, despaired that I would ever emerge from my Sun Yat-sen syndrome. I hope she is pleased that I have—at least temporarily.

March 1976   C. Martin Wilbur

Contents

Sun Yat-sen: *Frustrated Patriot*

Introduction

There are many difficulties in discovering the "true" Sun Yat-sen.
During his lifetime he was a controversial figure, and much that
was written about him has a hostile bias. After he died, a process of
sanctification began. The literature about him by writers of all political persuasions is enormous, and there is a large body of scholarly
work about him in Chinese, Japanese, Russian, and other European
languages.[1] There are twenty-two different editions of Dr. Sun's
collected works in Chinese, and recently eighteen of these were
analyzed for their inclusiveness.[2] The popular edition of Sun's writing, speeches, letters and telegrams which I have used, and which
is the second most extensive, numbers 2,600 pages. Sun, himself
wrote at least six autobiographical accounts, while many Chinese
colleagues in his several revolutionary organizations have written
reminiscences about him.[3] Where in this mass of materials should
we find the real Sun Yat-sen?

The canonization of Dr. Sun has created a legendary figure and
distorted historical reality. It obscures his personality and leaves
most of his revolutionary associates in the shadows. In addition it
blurs our perceptions of the events with which he was connected
and sometimes magnifies their importance.

Paradoxically, the canonization does have some benefits. Dr.
Sun's followers in the Kuomintang have assembled an enormous
record of his activities, writings, and speeches; they have published
chronological biographies and collections of reminiscences; and

they have written adulatory books and essays on many aspects of his career and teachings. Few Western scholars can claim to have absorbed this vast literature, which is indispensable for the reconstruction of his revolutionary activities.

What has been published, however, is by no means enough to reveal the totality of Sun's lifework. A great deal of his correspondence, particularly with foreign friends, has been lost. Evidently part of the documentation, especially that concerning his relations with Soviet Russia, is still considered too sensitive to release. Only fragments of his financial records are available. Much important information, some of it undoubtedly disconcerting, probably remains in archives, personal papers, obscure journals, and bank and police records in many parts of the world.[4] In spite of all that has been accomplished, serious biographers still have much searching and absorbing to do in order to reveal the intimate and esoteric aspects of Sun Yat-sen, the man.

In this situation it seems only too easy to make false judgments and reach conclusions that may be disputed by facts unknown to the commentator. We are trying to understand a person from a different culture who was born more than a century ago and whose life ended in 1925. The China he knew is not easy to reconstruct. Thus, what we piece together from artifacts can present only an exterior view of the man and his time.

In trying to write about Dr. Sun, one skirts a delicate area—the emotional attachment of the Chinese people to their national hero. Chinese readers may think it presumptuous for an outsider to comment upon so treasured a person. Yet the search for the man in his times must go on.

Sun Yat-sen was very often photographed after the successful revolution of 1911–12, though seldom before. Pictures of the younger Sun show him of slight build and natty dress, sporting a well-groomed mustache, his black hair carefully parted on the left, pomaded, and swept back in a slight wave. He had a somewhat dark complexion, but it was his "comely features" and "diminutive stature" that struck one reporter, who was present at Dr. Sun's dramatic release from the Chinese legation in London in 1896 when

[2]

Sun was just under thirty years of age. In studio portraits taken in his mid-forties, when he was provisional president of the new republic, Dr. Sun gazes out with open look and friendly smile. In group pictures he usually occupies the front center position, standing erect, sometimes in military uniform, a little shorter than most of his Chinese companions. With advancing age Dr. Sun grew portly, and later pictures show his receding hairline above a kindly but very careworn face.

Many have tried to describe his personality. One can read not only laudatory descriptions from those who knew him well, but also remarks that are most disparaging. Some point to his personal magnetism, his courage, his sincerity, or his indomitable will; others comment on his vanity, his obsessions, and his pathetic folly.

Dr. Wellington Koo, while yet a student, met Dr. Sun at Columbia College in 1909 and still remembered the occasion vividly some six decades later.

> I was at once impressed by his geniality, approachableness. He was quite different from some of the other leaders either then or since. . . . When he talked to you, you immediately felt you were on an equal footing with him. He treated you as an equal, just like one of you. He talked a lot, and would also say, "What do you think of my plan?" and so forth. But, he said it with no air. He never put on airs. I suppose that was one of his great qualities, which attracted his followers. . . . I don't think I have ever seen anyone like him in all my life, so amiable, yet he was such a great leader.
>
> He was certainly a very amiable person and a very democratic man and very warm-hearted and he showed a great deal of enthusiasm when explaining his plan of military strategy. He was the kind of personality that would naturally arouse enthusiasm and gain friends to his cause, if not all of them to his party.[5]

Dr. James Cantlie, Sun Wen's teacher in Hong Kong, rescuer in London in 1896, and warm friend thereafter, regarded him as "a truly noble character." He wrote the following description on the basis of a twenty-five-year acquaintanceship:

> Charity in the true sense of the word is Sun's outstanding characteristic. An unkind thought, far less an unkind word, is foreign to his nature; a keen regard for the feelings of those around him is apparent in his every

word and deed; unselfishness to a degree undreamt of amongst modern men; a living example of the Sermon on the Mount. . . . The secret of his success is unselfishness—seeking only his country's good, not his own advancement . . . ready and anxious to stand aside when the interests of his country are to be benefited thereby. . . .

I have never known anyone like Sun Yat Sen; if I were asked to name the most perfect character I ever knew, I would unhesitatingly say Sun Yat Sen. In our house he was the most welcome of visitors: children and servants alike conceived a deep regard for him; his sweetness of disposition, his courtesy, his consideration for others, his interesting conversation, and his gracious demeanor attract one towards him in an indescribable fashion, and have led me to think of him as a being apart, consecrated for the work he had in hand.[6]

Mr. Li Lu-chao, who met Dr. Sun in 1910 and then served as his secretary for much of the time from 1916 to 1924, recently wrote me the following description of his mentor:

Dr. Sun was soft spoken, calm and friendly; democratic, straightforward and sincere. In conversation he would frequently show a pleasant smile. He was never seen in anger or in violent agitation. Broadminded and sympathetic, he was a congenial man to work with. He rarely "cracked a joke," but was appreciative of a good one and would show approval with a smile. But no joke however rollickingly funny could draw from him a burst of loud laughter.

In public speaking, he was a ready and eloquent speaker. He could get up before an audience and speak for hours on a stretch. His speeches were not flowery like those of Wang Ching-wei that were emotionally touching and soul moving. His were inspirational and stirring in grass roots language, a quality easily understood and appreciated by the masses. . . . I have to add that in his speeches he never used strong and abusive language and on issues of politics he never exhorted his audience to use violence. Neither would he start the shouting of slogans such as are so commonly resorted to at most political gatherings and demonstrations of the present day. Very rarely would he use stereotype terms as "imperialism," "capitalism," "exploitation of the masses" and "class struggle" in his speeches.

Dr. Sun was a dreamer. He dreamed of Utopia, of establishing a sane and orderly government, a government that was benevolent to the people. For his dreams of such high ideals, which were hardly possible, he was dubbed by the Cantonese as "Big Gun," synonymous to being idealistic and impractical. For his conservatism and moderate views he was

[4]

regarded only as a "revolutionist" by the communists, but not as a "thorough revolutionist" as the extremists and radicals would have it.[7]

In an article written during the last year of Dr. Sun's life, Nathaniel Peffer tried to unravel "the enigma of Sun Yat-sen"—the reasons not only for his continuing prestige as a revolutionary but also for the disdain in which he was held as a political figure. On the latter aspect, Mr. Peffer thought him obsessed with the idea of a republic and occupied with the forms rather than with the content of government.

> Dr. Sun is gullible beyond imagining and credulous past understanding in a man of his experience, his keenness of intellect and his learning. . . . His desperation and his two most pronounced weaknesses—his vanity and his hunger for flattery—subject him to imposture and betray him into squandering his energy.

Yet Mr. Peffer described him as a man of undeniable integrity:

> However serious Sun's mistakes and however blind his egotism, his patriotism, in the larger sense, and his dedication to the welfare of his people cannot be challenged. The Chinese may be tired of him and his political incapacity, but they do not class him with officialdom. They respect him as a man. . . . He has irresistible magnetism.
>
> I have never known anybody who has been face to face with Dr. Sun who has not been impressed with him. . . . Nothing about him strikes you till he talks—in a low and uninflected tone with rapid flow of words. Then his poise, his dignity, his enthusiasm and, above all, his utter sincerity record themselves on your memory forever.

This is how Mr. Peffer summed up his observations in the spring of 1924:

> What made Sun Yat-sen win renown and write his name in history in his younger days is what distinguishes him yet—force of character, a high quality of soul, the element of greatness that marks men for the world's note in all ages and climes. . . . He is one of the great men of Asia, perhaps the greatest Chinese in this generation.[8]

Here, then, are four favorable views of Dr. Sun, but others that are quite negative might easily be quoted. One observes a clear difference between accounts of him as the planner and dreamer, and accounts of him as the man engaged in practical politics and administration. This difference may be one clue to the enigmas of his personality and career.

The records of Dr. Sun's political activity give the impression of a man whose vision of himself, and whose ambitions for the reform of China, far outreached practical reality, given the society in which he lived and the power he could muster. The discrepancy between his hopes and the objective situations which so repeatedly thwarted him raises questions about the personality structure that drove him to pursue unrealizable goals.

One is struck by the disparity between form and substance that characterized many of his actions. For example, in 1921 he claimed to be the president of China and to govern six southwestern provinces—a pure fiction; he asserted that his was both the de jure and de facto government of China, and he thereupon sought international recognition—without any success; he appointed hundreds of officials, most of whom never took office; and he issued bonds that had virtually nothing to back them up. When he was a refugee he offered treaties to foreign powers, and several times he mounted military campaigns with put-together armies which had to live off the countryside, but they had little effect on the national scene. It is as though he believed that his assertions were equivalent to reality.

Perhaps there is an explanation. Dr. Sun spent sixteen years as an exile scheming to overthrow the Manchu regime. Then suddenly, with no governmental experience at all, he was elevated to the position of provisional president of the republic. To a Chinese in this position, proper form would be essential even if there were no substance to the office. Removed from the provisional presidency in about three months, Sun was soon back to planning and scheming. In the last eight years of his life he had three more brief periods in which he attempted to govern in Canton, either as a self-styled generalissimo (he had no military training) or as the would-be president. Sun always went in at the top without the benefit of practical administrative experience. But this explanation only raises another question: was he driven by a psychological compulsion always to be top man?

Sometimes his actions seem inexplicable. But our view is always that of outsiders; no one can get inside Sun Wen's psyche to appreciate particular circumstances as he perceived them.

In pursuit of his goals, Dr. Sun did some things which seem unscrupulous, but were they so in terms of his own moral standards and those of his contemporaries? He was, after all, a revolutionary. As a political figure he was counted out many times, yet somehow he always won another chance. Shortly before his death from cancer, he may have believed that the moment of triumph had finally come.

The mature Sun Yat-sen may be described as a marginal man. He was fairly well at ease in three cultures: Chinese, Japanese, and Anglo-American. He made the unusual transition from a humble peasant background to the cosmopolitan treaty-port world where he lived by no other occupation than that of political leader. Yet he maintained connections with all he had left behind: rural Kwangtung; the overseas Chinese; Hong Kong and Macao; the secret-society underworld; England and America; Christian missionaries; and the world of Japanese *ronin* and political dissidents. His dominant ideas were derived from Western political thought, particularly the theories of republicanism and socialism, but they were definitely colored by ethical Confucianism.

Sun's reformist prescriptions seem at all stages of their development to reflect the ideas currently fashionable among the then-radical Chinese intellectuals; in short, he absorbed and popularized more than he innovated. The ideas that he advocated—that the hated Manchus must be overthrown, that China must become a modern republic with a socialist economy, that the country's natural resources should be rapidly developed and its goods be more equitably enjoyed by all—were his major capital. Although he sought influence through the politics of ideas and through propaganda, he was regularly frustrated by the politics of material power, both military and financial. Yet by the end of his career he had articulated a systematic plan for China's political modernization and an ideal scheme for its governance.

In historical terms, Dr. Sun is a transitional figure, reflecting the great Chinese passage from a decaying imperial tradition to an in-

[7]

dustrializing, nationalistic society. He played a political role in this transition, helping to bring about a republic and to prevent a monarchical restoration. Yet in historical perspective, he was only one among many figures swept along on the same tide.

Sun's conduct in foreign matters seems mercurial. During most of his political career he could not operate without the good will, or at least the tolerance, of one or more foreign powers. He repeatedly appealed for sympathy, money, or recognition of a government he headed. He was constantly concerned about his image abroad. At various times he would announce his affinity for Great Britain, Japan, or the United States; at other times he would denounce them. One can understand his occasionally passionate outbursts because he was so regularly disappointed, frustrated, or even insulted by some foreign government or individual. As a patriotic and cosmopolitan Chinese he was distressed by the foreign economic and political domination of his country. Yet he believed that foreign investment was advantageous to China, and he offered, in exchange for financial or military support, concessions and privileges that actually would have increased foreign domination. Toward the end of his life, he even proposed intervention by foreign powers, led by the United States, to enforce unification upon the country. He clearly looked abroad for solutions to China's problems.

Dr. Sun spent an adult lifetime trying to reshape his country's political system according to his particular vision. He also drafted imaginative plans for China's economic development, plans which were impossible to achieve in his own day, but which foreshadowed recent schemes for international cooperation in assisting underdeveloped countries. He also had a compassionate concern for the poor and oppressed, though his ideas for changing their condition were essentially those of a reformist rather than of a social revolutionary. He clung to this reformist position even when under the influence of Russian advisers and when Chinese Communists were active and articulate in his party.

There was one matter in which Dr. Sun was very practical: the raising and controlling of money. Funding was essential to his own plans, and he strove to prevent monies from reaching his rivals. Dr. Sun wanted money not for himself but for his political purposes. He needed funds to support agents, pay secret-society leaders, buy and smuggle arms, recruit troops and suborn officers, subsidize journals, lure members of Parliament, and for a variety of similar purposes. His schemes to attract gifts, loans, and investments were ingenious, and though most of his grander ones failed, occasionally he had a striking success, and he did raise and handle millions of dollars. He learned early that he must control the funds raised either in his own name or in the names of organizations he headed. His treasurers were always those closest to him. Apparently he used money as fast as he raised it, and thus was always quickly out after more.

The strongest impression of Dr. Sun that I have derived from my study of his career is that he was a man persistently devoted to a single cause—the political reform of his country. Reform was his life's ambition, and it was a goal he pursued by many different means, some highly impractical and some irresponsible. In spite of enormous frustrations and repeated defeats, he wavered only occasionally from this pursuit. He conveyed the impression of being sure he was right both in his goal and in his various methods. Indeed, he seems to have been a man obsessed with the conviction that he alone was right and that he alone must direct the course of political change to its appointed end. Perhaps this obsession explains some of the anomalies of his behavior.

CHAPTER ONE

Molding Influences and the Career Line

The complexity of Sun Yat-sen's personality may be ascribed in part to the variety of contradictory influences which helped to mold him. The culture of a Kwangtung peasant village during his childhood was replaced by the regimen of a British missionary school in Hawaii. From adolescence to maturity cosmopolitan influences constantly impinged on him. He lived most of the time either in Hong Kong or in foreign countries, thus his education consisted of a combination of Chinese and Western thought; his intellectual inspiration came through reading Chinese classical and historical literature, modern reformist journals, and a wide variety of books and articles in English. He adhered to a foreign religion, Christianity.

Early Influences

The child, first named Ti-hsiang, was born on November 12, 1866 in Hsiang-shan County, in a village of farmers and fishermen some fifteen miles from the Portuguese colony of Macao. He attended various village schools for a few years and gained a traditional elementary education. When not yet thirteen, he was taken to join his emigrant elder brother in Hawaii, where he attended missionary schools in which English was the language of instruction. After four years in Hawaii and with a good beginner's knowledge of English, he was sent by his brother back to China. By then, however, the young Sun's horizons had been broadened, and he could not adjust himself to the restricted life of his native rural community. In 1883, at the age of seventeen, he went to the British colony of Hong Kong where he continued his education in English. He formally embraced Christianity in 1884 after having been influenced by an American missionary and a native pastor, who gave him a new name, Yat-sen. In the same year he married a girl who had been selected by his family in the traditional fashion. After a brief return to Hawaii, Sun Yat-sen enrolled in the Canton Hospital Medical School headed by an American physician and then transferred to the small College of Medicine for Chinese in Hong Kong. Here he spent five more years, from 1887 to 1892, under British and foreignized Chinese instructors, and earned a "Licentiate in Medicine and Surgery of the College of Medicine for Chinese, Hong Kong." [1] During some of his years in Hong Kong, Sun studied classical Chinese under a tutor, reading the dynastic histories. Thus by the age of twenty-seven he was equipped with a fair Chinese education, an extensive but disrupted Western education, and a modern profession. He had spent twelve years in either Hawaii or Hong Kong.

During these maturing years, while surrounded by Western influences, Sun Yat-sen developed an intense concern for the state of his country. These were the years of the humiliating Sino-French War of 1884–85 and of the thrust toward national "self-strengthening" led by the viceroys. The influences of Sun's semi-Westernized Chinese mentors, who were advocates of reform, seem to have left an indelible impression. His closest Chinese friends were, like himself, caught up in the reformist ideology prevalent among professional and commercial people residing in China's partially Westernized port cities.

While still a young man in medical school, Sun demonstrated his concern for the nation; there he also revealed a lasting personality trait—a rather brash self-confidence. From 1890 to 1892 he presented rather conventional proposals for reform to two progressive officials, both from his native district; and in 1894 he journeyed to

Tientsin to present a similar proposal to Li Hung-chang, a grand secretary and one of the most influential Chinese officials, who had long been directing China's "self-strengthening" movement. With the failure of these efforts to impress those in power, Sun began to organize his first anti-Manchu revolutionary society. Many years later, in a speech describing how he became a revolutionary, he said it was the contrast between the orderly and progressive British administration of Hong Kong, under which the Chinese prospered, and the conservatism and corruption of officials in his nearby native county, in the provincial administration, and particularly in Peking, which drove him to plan for the replacement of the Manchu regime by a modern republican form of government.[2] During the remainder of his life he reached for power so he might lead China to "a position of strength and honor among the nations of the world."[3]

Becoming a Revolutionary

The two years from November 1894 to October 1896 marked a decisive turning point in Sun Yat-sen's career. He organized the Hsing Chung Hui in Honolulu, attempted his first revolutionary uprising in Canton, and, as a consequence of these activities became a fugitive on three continents. He then gained international notoriety from the attempt by the Chinese legation in London to kidnap him.

The Honolulu Hsing Chung Hui, or Society to Restore China's Prosperity, was an insignificant organization in itself: its membership of little more than 100 was comprised of Chinese small businessmen, traders, cooks, clerks, tailors, laborers, farmers, and local governmental employees. Most were from Sun's native district.[4] However, in its first few months it produced some $288 in dues and $1,100 in "shares" of The Commercial Union of China. Dr. Sun's brother and a close friend contributed $5,000. Virtually all the money went to Sun on his return to Hong Kong.[5] The young revolutionary had found one source of financial support to which he would appeal continuously thereafter—the overseas Chinese. Yet

[13]

the amount he collected would not go far toward financing revolution.

Sun Yat-sen immediately organized a Hsing Chung Hui in Hong Kong and was soon plotting—together with several like-minded conspirators—the first of a series of efforts to spark a revolt that would overthrow the Manchu dynasty. Professor Harold Schiffrin has provided a brilliant reconstruction of the attempted uprising which was to have broken out on October 26, 1895. It seems that Sun was the true leader in Canton, and that he and his closest associates were the link among overseas Chinese adherents, Triads and local bandits, Christian workers, and some Ch'ing naval officers. In the Hong Kong base, the chief fund raiser, arms procurer, and recruiter of local toughs was Yang Ch'ü-yün, who was Sun's rival for leadership of the movement.[6] When the ambitious and well-prepared plot was exposed and hence fizzled, Sun barely escaped. The authorities, on discovering his central role, placed a much higher price on his head than on the heads of the other escaped leaders. Thus he was irrevocably cast in the role of a rebel.

Two aspects of Sun Yat-sen's personality were particularly evident at the time of the 1895 revolt. One was his courage. He exposed himself to great danger for at least twenty days by organizing the revolt from within Canton itself. In fact, he was betrayed to the officials a few days before the date set for the uprising, but luckily the governor-general did not take him seriously. Had the facts been fully uncovered, he probably would have been captured, tortured, and executed. The second aspect revealed was his will to lead, which was evident in the competition with Yang Ch'ü-yün. On October 10, just sixteen days before the scheduled uprising, an election was held to select the president of the provisional government if the revolution succeeded. Apparently the election also determined the chairmanship of the Hsing Chung Hui. It was a bitter contest which Yang won. He was five years older than Sun and, because of his better connections, a much more effective fund raiser. According to two friends of Sun, the defeat was a "great blow" to him, and one that "always rankled in his breast."[7] The contest nearly split the movement, and Sun continued the battle until January 1900, when Yang resigned his chairmanship of the Hsing Chung Hui as a result of Sun's scheming.[8] Thereafter, except for one special circumstance, Sun headed each of "his" revolutionary organizations.[9]

Soon after the 1895 revolt, the young plotter was banished from Hong Kong. During the next sixteen years he did not set foot on Chinese soil, except for three surreptitious and fleeting stops at Shanghai and one day in December 1907 when he crossed the Indochinese border into Kwangsi to observe an attempted revolt.[10] In Japan, his first stop in exile, the fugitive adopted a new guise: nicely cut and parted hair in place of the shaven forehead and queue, a moustache, and a Western business suit. He was the picture of an up-to-date Japanese. This was the Sun Yat-sen known to the world until about 1912, when he adopted the Chung-shan uniform.[11]

The kidnapping episode in London revealed not only Sun's reckless streak but also his ingenuity—he persuaded the English housekeeper and porter in the Chinese legation to help effect his release. However, he was a very lucky captive in having two influential friends in London, his former teachers, Dr. James Cantlie and Dr. Patrick Manson. When they heard of his detention they forced his release by appealing to the British Foreign Office and to the press. On October 23, 1896, amid a swarm of reporters and police, Dr. Sun was handed over by his captors who had meant to spirit him back to China and certain death. Thus, a few weeks before his thirtieth birthday, Sun was suddenly propelled onto the international stage as a celebrity. Enhancing the worldwide publicity that attended this dramatic escape, Sun gave interviews, wrote an autobiography in Chinese for the leading British sinologue, H. A. Giles, and with the help of an editor wrote a colorful account of his detention entitled *Kidnapped in London.*[12]

Such publicity must have increased the young man's self-esteem. He received numerous congratulatory letters and admiring visitors. His name was mentioned in Parliament. In a letter to the Christian pastor who had participated in his baptism, he reported that his detention "shook the entire country, agitated Europe and every country in the world." His imprisonment seems to have strengthened his Christian faith and his confidence in his revolutionary destiny. In his account of the kidnapping he reported praying constantly for God's aid. He pleaded for help from his English guard on the grounds of Christian fellowship. In his letter to the pastor he wrote, "I was saved by God. . . . Now I believe in God more than ever. . . . I owe everything to the great favor of God. Through the Way of God I hope to enter into the Political Way. . . ." [13]

In an article which he wrote for an influential journal, Dr. Sun appealed for British support—or, "benevolent neutrality"—toward the cause of the "Reform Party," that is, support for himself and his hopes to overthrow the Manchu regime. This article was probably his first effort to influence a foreign government's policy by appealing to public opinion. The appeal contained several ideas that would appear frequently in his later efforts to win foreign aid and conveyed a sense of confident optimism: the cause was on the verge of success and "the whole people" were behind it. [14]

Sun Yat-sen stayed on in London till July 1897, spending considerable time reading in the British Museum's library, where he became acquainted with the ideas of Karl Marx, John Stuart Mill, and Henry George. He observed the slums and learned about labor unions, strikes, and social legislation. China, he came to believe, need not go through the social turmoil that attended the Industrial Revolution in Europe. It could step to the front of the procession toward social reform.

The young revolutionary had earlier been influenced by the reformist ideas of the scholarly comprador, Cheng Kuan-ying, whom he had first met in 1894. Cheng was about twenty-five years Sun's senior and was from Hsiang-shan County also. Near the zenith of his career, he was noted for his essays urging China to change its institutions and develop its economy. These essays were gathered and reprinted in 1893 under the title *Sheng Shih Wei-yen* [Warnings to a Prosperous Age]. [15] Another influence upon Sun was Yen Fu, the translator of such important Western social philosophers as Herbert Spencer, Thomas Huxley, Adam Smith, and John Stewart Mill. [16] A later influence came from Sun's competitor, Liang Ch'i-ch'ao, the scholar-journalist with a wide following. Early in the new century, at the time he was formulating his Three Principles of the People, Dr. Sun lived much of the time in Japan. Chinese journals published there were filled with articles on socialism, anarchism, and other theories of social reform. In his principle called The People's Livelihood, he emphasized the importance of avoiding the social inequities arising from unregulated capitalism, and attempted to specify how this might be achieved—by state socialism in the area of railways, utilities, and other large-scale industries, and by a rather vaguely defined taxation theory derived from John Stewart Mill and Henry George—the taxation of future rises in land values. Although termed "equalization of land rights," this scheme was essentially urban rather than agrarian, and preventative rather than remedial.[17]

Most of the revolutionary student leaders who joined Sun's cause in the T'ung Meng Hui (Revolutionary Alliance), and edited or wrote for the *Min Pao* [People's Journal], also championed socialism, a fashionable doctrine. Later, Sun turned his support to labor unions, and several of his co-workers were active in organizing unions and labor welfare plans. Until the last years of his life he seems to have been little concerned about China's problems of rural poverty. What centrally interested him was the modernization and revitalization of his country.

We cannot trace all the influences that impinged upon Dr. Sun and impelled him towards his supreme goal, the remaking of China according to his own expanding vision. We shall mention briefly several important incidents in his expatriate years. First was the well-known attempt by Liang Ch'i-ch'ao to cooperate with Dr. Sun in 1899, an attempt which degenerated into bitter rivalry between the Hsing Chung Hui and K'ang Yu-wei's Pao Huang Hui (known in English as the China Reform Association) for influence with and the financial support of overseas Chinese.[18] This rivalry taught Dr. Sun the importance of directly controlling overseas organizations which could be solicited for funds, so far as it was within his ability to do so. A second incident was Sun's involvement in the Filipino uprising against American control in 1899–1900, which fore-

[17]

shadowed his later pan-Asiatic and antiimperialistic positions.[19] Another event was the ill-fated Huichow (Waichow) revolt of October 1900, a Triad-style uprising commanded by Cheng Shih-liang with the help of some Japanese adventurers and with Sun's distant direction. Yang Ch'ü-yün was also closely involved and afterwards was assassinated for the Ch'ing government's promised reward.[20] A final incident was the well-reported organization of the T'ung Meng Hui in 1905, of which Dr. Sun, the senior revolutionary leader, was elected president. This organization battled the constitutional monarchists for leadership among the nationalistic youth and for contributions from the overseas Chinese. It attempted several uprisings in the South, and then seems to have fallen apart during the years from 1908 to 1910. On the basis of recent studies, it seems clear that shortly before the revolution of 1911, Dr. Sun, always abroad, was being bypassed by rapid developments in China and was slipping in his leadership of the revolutionaries.[21]

One wonders at the compulsion which, during sixteen years, drove this opponent of the Manchus to wander the globe, establishing branches of revolutionary societies, begging for funds, battling rivals, and plotting uprisings in Kwangtung, Kwangsi, and Yunnan. This rebel was actually at the scene of only one of these revolts, and he was successively banished from Hong Kong, Japan, French Indochina, Singapore, and the Malay States. Yet he kept his hopes for revolution alive and spurred on his confederates. In Professor Schiffrin's estimate,

> Utimately Sun's major contribution to the Revolution was his optimism. While even stalwarts like Huang Hsing, Hu Han-min and Wang Ching-wei at times despaired of the Revolution's chances, Sun continued to plug away, boosting the morale of the fighters with promises of funds and luring Overseas Chinese with talk of imminent victory and promises of investment opportunities. . . . If Sun's unrestrained optimism did not prepare his followers for a decisive struggle in 1911–12, it nevertheless energized their repeated attempts which eventually overthrew the Manchus. And when the Revolution did break out, he was recognized as "undoubtedly its prime mover." [22]

The victory, however, was the cumulative result of the work after 1903 of many activists who published revolutionary journals, propagandized against the Manchus, conspired with indigenous secret societies, raised funds among the overseas Chinese, subverted army units, and assassinated officials.

The Brief Period of Triumph

The years from late 1911 to mid-1913 marked another turning point in Dr. Sun's career. He reached the pinnacle when he was chosen the first, though provisional, president of the Chinese Republic; he then resigned in favor of the experienced administrator and politician, Yuan Shih-k'ai. He served in Yuan's government for less than a year and then turned against him to pursue once more the career of rebel. During this brief episode, Sun tasted the pleasures of public adulation and was commissioned to plan for railway development. Little actually came of his work, but he had found another role, that of constructive planner for his country.

There was pathos in this situation, too. Dr. Sun was in the United States when the Wuchang revolt broke out unexpectedly. He learned of it in Denver, Colo. through a newspaper. This uprising was the result of a new strategy, which involved concentrating on the Yangtze provinces instead of those in the remote South, a plan probably worked out independently of Dr. Sun. It is not clear whether or not Sun contributed financially to the Central China plotters before the event, and it is uncertain how much the fund-raising organization he had developed in the United States could contribute after the revolt broke out. Instead of speeding across the Pacific to China when he learned of the uprising, Dr. Sun went to England and then to France, where he attempted to prevent the execution of loans to the Manchu government. For two and a half months—while decisive battles were fought in China, provinces and cities being declared for the republic one after the other, and the leaders on the spot beginning to negotiate with Yuan Shih-k'ai for an end to the fighting—the itinerant chief seemingly had no influence on decisions made by men on the scene.[23]

Then there is the matter of the presidency. For years Sun Wen had been selling bonds in the name of the Chinese Republic and signing them as "President." After the Wu-Han revolt broke out, as

Dr. Sun later recalled, while he was passing through St. Louis on his way from Denver to Chicago, he read in a newspaper that in the proposed republic he would be president.[24] At the least, this newspaper story must have planted the expectation in his mind. When he reached London he received a telegram from Canton; the telegram, he told Dr. Cantlie, "was asking me to be President of the new Republic." [25] While he was in London, the *Times* carried a dispatch from Shanghai, dated November 16, 1911, on "The Revolutionary Program," which mentioned that the capital would probably be at Nanking, with Sun Yat-sen as president. Provincial revolutionary leaders were gathering at Shanghai to hold a national convention.[26] But Dr. Sun must have learned some different news, for he telegraphed to the *Min-li Pao* in Shanghai, for the attention of the military government, saying he was happy to learn that Li Yuan-hung was to be elected president, and that he also had heard Li would resign in favor of Yuan Shih-k'ai, which would be appropriate and good.[27]

We may imagine what his true feelings were! Yet here one confronts the Chinese habitude which requires a person to decline a time or two before accepting an honored position. Dr. Sun may have been showing proper humility, while at the same time calling attention to himself. Whatever was the case, not until a political struggle between the supporters of Huang Hsing and Li Yuan-hung for the generalissimoship became deadlocked did the leaders in Shanghai find a compromise solution to their conflict in the return of Sun Yat-sen.[28] He arrived in Shanghai on Christmas Day. By then, however, it was virtually settled that if Yuan Shih-k'ai brought an end to the Manchu dynasty and committed himself to a republic, he would be chosen president. Sun Yat-sen's election as provisional president on December 29, 1911 probably was well understood, and by Sun himself, to be only a temporary measure.[29]

The deal was consummated on February 12, 1912 with the Manchu abdication. On the next day Dr. Sun offered his resignation and recommended that Yuan Shih-k'ai be made provisional president on three conditions: that Nanking be the capital, that Yuan come there to assume the presidency, and that Yuan observe the provisional constitution then being drafted. The third condition is significant. Dr. Sun later became the upholder of constitutionalism, as he interpreted it. This position was the rationale for two revolts and the establishment of several rival governments in which he was a prominent figure. Neither of Sun's first two conditions was met, but Yuan was elected anyway. Then, after a political struggle in which the revolutionaries were completely outmatched, he was inaugurated on March 10, 1912 in Peking. On April 1, Sun Yat-sen gave up his post.[30] His great dream, the ending of the imperial system and establishment of the Chinese Republic, had been fulfilled.

Rarely in history has one ambitious man been willing to step aside for another. It is commonly asserted that Dr. Sun's ambitions were not personal. Perhaps he realized that his provisional presidency had little substance to it (although during his tenure he busily issued mandates and appointed officials). He eventually described his position as that of a puppet.[31] Probably he had no choice but to resign. Later he came to believe that his stepping down in favor of Yuan Shih-k'ai was the worst mistake he ever made.[32]

At the time, it was different. Dr. Sun seems to have been filled with optimism about the new republic, but he was also impressed with the amount of constructive work that needed to be done. In a letter to Mrs. Cantlie, dated March 12, 1912, he said:

> It is true that the Tai Ching dynasty is "a thing of the past" but the dethronement of the Manchus does not mean the complete salvation of China. We have an enormous amount of work ahead of us, and it must be accomplished in order that she may be ranked as a great power among the family nations. . . .
>
> I am going to Canton shortly and there try to convert the old city into a new and modern one. . . .[33]

Dr. Sun went on a speaking tour, first to Wuchang, where the revolution had broken out, and then to Fukien and Kwangtung, where he was received with great honors. To enthusiastic audiences he gave lectures on the development of industry as the prescription for ending poverty, on the equalization of land rights, on local self-government, on love of the country and its people, on promoting women's education, and other subjects to which he wished to direct the nation's efforts. On his return to Shanghai, his favorite theme became a vast program of railway development, an idea which soon became a fixation.

In August 1912, the former provisional president went to Peking on the invitation of Yuan Shih-k'ai, against the advice of some of his colleagues, and at the possible risk of his freedom.[34] Far from doing him harm, President Yuan ordered the most elaborate reception for his former rival. A special train brought Dr. Sun from Tientsin to Peking on Saturday, August 24; the station was crowded with notables, and Dr. Sun rode in a handsome carriage with mounted outriders through the streets lined with smartly dressed troops. He was lodged in the new building housing the foreign ministry and was offered one of the palace parks for his pleasure. The next day Yuan and Sun conferred for many hours, and afterwards both declared their perfect agreement on all questions. Dr. Sun was received at the Summer Palace by the empress dowager, was tendered banquets and receptions, and he gave many speeches.[35]

On August 25 he attended the formal inauguration of a new political party, the Kuomintang [National People's Party] formed from a union of the old T'ung Meng Hui and several lesser groups. He was elected with the highest number of votes to its nine-man executive committee, and on September 3 he was elected by the committee to be its head, but he delegated this position to Sung Chiao-jen, the main architect of the new organization.[36]

Yuan Shih-k'ai, who was still only provisional president, seems to have charmed his predecessor. In all, they met thirteen times. On the day after their first conference, in a speech before the two leading political groups, Dr. Sun expressed his personal desire that Yuan be elected president and stated that he, himself, had no intention of entering the political arena.[37] On September 5, at Yuan's request, he telegraphed Huang Hsing, urging him to come north speedily.

> Have talked with Yuan twice since my arrival in Peking. Regarding industries and related matters, his ideas are the same as mine. As to de-

fense and foreign policy, our views are also quite similar. According to my observation, he is in a situation beyond suspicion and deserves our sympathy. . . .[38]

In a speech delivered on October 5 before the Shanghai bureau of the Kuomintang, he spoke of Yuan as "really a man of ability. . . . Some people in the South still distrust him, but I definitely believe in his sincerity. . . . In order to govern the Republic one must have a combination of new ideas, old experience, and old-fashioned methods. And President Yuan is just the right man." [39]

Dr. Sun's charitable view of Yuan Shih-k'ai was shared by other revolutionary leaders at the time, including Huang Hsing and Sung Chiao-jen, though not by all, for Yuan was a wily politician.[40]

Dreams of Modernizing the Country

Probably one reason why Dr. Sun favored the new provisional president was that Yuan listened to his plans for railway development and, on September 9, appointed him director of national railway planning, with full powers "to consider and draft plans for a national system of railways," and to "submit and discuss the same with international financiers." He was to report his negotiations to the government for approval.[41] He was also authorized to organize a railway corporation through which to seek foreign capital, apparently independently of the government.[42] Yuan not only gave Dr. Sun this fine position, he also allocated 30,000 taels per month for his expenses. The *Republican Daily News* quickly attacked Dr. Sun for accepting the position and the stipend, which, it argued, Yuan had no authority to grant. Dr. Sun defended himself to members of the National Assembly, explaining that he would accept the expense money as a loan from the government, to be repaid by the railway corporation when it had been formed.[43] He then plunged into his new work with characteristic enthusiasm.

It is embarrassing to recall Dr. Sun's preliminary ideas for railway development, but he was not an engineer and had a very limited personal knowledge of China's terrain when he began his dreaming. His first articulated plan called for three trunk routes: a southern route from Kwangtung and Kwangsi through Kweichow, then running between Yunnan and Szechwan, across Tibet and along the southern edge of the T'ien-shan Mountains; a central route starting at the mouth of the Yangtze, passing through Kiangsu, Anhwei, Honan, Shensi, Kansu, and thence through Sinkiang to Ili; and a northern route beginning at Tsingtao, skirting Liaotung, winding through Inner and Outer Mongolia, and terminating in Urianghai.[44] He spoke on July 22 at a meeting of the Chinese Railway Association in Shanghai, first mentioning the 200,000 miles of railways in the United States, equivalent to 700,000 *li*. He reasoned that since China was five times as large as the United States, she should try to build 3.5 million *li* of trackage, whereupon she would become the most powerful country in the world. To accomplish this, China would have to borrow abroad just as the United States had done when it was a poor country. He hoped that in ten years China's railways could be completed so the nation would profit and the people become wealthy.[45]

This was an era of foreign investment in Chinese railways, and foreign competition for mining concessions. Only a few years earlier there had been widespread agitation to prevent outside investment in China's railways and mines for fear of foreign control; in fact, the agitation was one of the elements in the background of the revolt which brought down the Manchu dynasty. As an advocate of foreign-financed economic development, Dr. Sun was opposing the nationalistic current.

In speeches in Peking he reduced his objective to 200,000 *li* (some 70,000 miles). To construct this would require $6 billion of capital, and Sun argued that China should welcome foreign loans, for there was no hope of building railways otherwise. He had now settled upon three trunk routes: from Canton through Kwangsi to Yunnan, and thence to join the Burma railways; from Canton through Hunan and Szechwan to Tibet; and from the mouth of the Yangtze northwestward to Ili, as in the earlier plan for a central route.[46] It was with such ideas in mind that he toured China's northern railways; set up an office in Shanghai; and telegraphed Wang Ching-wei in Paris asking him to discuss loans with French capitalists for railway development in China's southwestern provinces, and then to go on to New York for discussions with Mr. Mo-ken—i.e., J. P. Morgan—whose support, Sun said, would be crucial.[47]

On October 14, Sun Yat-sen informed Yuan Shih-k'ai that he had established a Chinese General Railway Corporation, with himself as president. He engaged George Bronson Rea as an adviser, and they developed a plan for 10,000 miles of trunk railway, at an estimated cost of $500 million. He then dispatched Mr. Rea to Europe and the United States to negotiate for loans to finance the plan. Mr. Rea first consulted Sir Charles Addis, chairman of the board of the Hong Kong & Shanghai Banking Corporation and head of a British group of bankers. According to Mr. Rea, Sir Charles expressed the willingness of his group to undertake the entire financing, but upon the urging of J. P. Morgan and Company, Mr. Rea went to New York late in February 1913 to lay the plan before the American consortium. President Woodrow Wilson opposed American participation in the proposed reorganization loan to Yuan Shih-k'ai's government, and he also opposed investment of American capital in Chinese railways. Wilson's attitude effectively foreclosed Dr. Sun's hopes for American assistance.[48]

In February and March 1913, while his American agent was exploring possibilities in England and the United States, Dr. Sun was on a five-week tour of Japan, studying Japanese railways and seeking financial assistance for China's economic development. It was a triumphal tour, for Sun was now an international celebrity. Besides enthusiastic receptions given by Chinese students in Japan and reunions with old Japanese helpers, he met high government leaders and important capitalists, and there were discussions about the possibility of establishing a Sino-Japanese firm that would use Japanese capital to develop China's raw materials. Several months later, the formation of the China Industrial Company was announced, with Sun Yat-sen as president, Viscount Kurachi, as vice-president, and capital to be provided by the greatest Japanese firms.[49]

Dr. Sun also appointed Wang Ch'ung-hui, an old friend, to negotiate with Lord French, the representative of Pauling and Company, Ltd., for a contract to build the Canton-Chungking-Lanchow Railway. The negotiations apparently reached a conclusion early in July, 1913, but by then it was much too late for any governmental enterprise connected with Sun's name to bear any results.[50] No sooner had he completed his triumphal tour of Japan than he suffered a series of shattering experiences climaxed by his flight from China.

The Dashing of All Hopes

The first blow was the assassination of Sung Chiao-jen on March 20, 1913. Yuan Shih-k'ai's prime minister was implicated as the man behind the assassination, and it was widely believed that Yuan himself was involved.[51] Soon after the assassination came the consummation of the reorganization loan with a face value of £25 million offered by the Five Power Consortium, accepted by Yuan Shih-k'ai, and signed by his government on April 27, without the agreement of Parliament.[52] In a declaration addressed to the governments and peoples of foreign powers, Dr. Sun warned that the loan would bring on civil war, and he begged that the funds be withheld in order to force Yuan to compromise with his republican opponents.[53] Apparently the plea had no effect, and with large funds available, Yuan's position became invulnerable. He was soon bribing parliamentarians and splitting the Kuomintang. In June he dismissed Li Lieh-chün, Hu Han-min, and Po Wen-wei, the revolutionary military governors of Kiangsi, Kwangtung and Anhuei. This action brought on the "Second Revolution," which lasted barely two months, from July 12 to September 12, and was a disaster for the revolutionary side.[54] Sun Yat-sen and scores of other revolutionary leaders fled to Japan.[55] By coercing Parliament, Yuan Shih-k'ai secured his election as president on October 6, and he was inaugurated on the second anniversary of the outbreak of the Wuchang revolt. On November 4 he then revoked the credentials of all Kuomintang members of Parliament; his troops beseiged Kuomintang headquarters and searched the houses of members. Parliament could not muster a quorum and adjourned for an indefinite period. It was formally dissolved on January 10, 1914.

The positions which Sun Yat-sen took *at the time* on Sung Chiao-jen's murder, the loan agreement, and the Second Revolution, have been subject to much historical controversy and to later reinterpretation by Sun himself.[56] But the results of these events, so far as Sun's personality is concerned, seem clear. He became a very bitter man, disillusioned by China's first experiment with democracy and filled with hatred for Yuan Shih-k'ai; he repeatedly indulged in recriminations against revolutionary comrades who, he claimed, had opposed his ideas. In human terms his reaction is understandable. The forty-seven-year-old patriot saw nineteen years of effort to establish a Chinese Republic destroyed by a northern autocrat. He was even denied the prospect of working constructively for his country's economic modernization and social reform. With accustomed single-mindedness he set out to rescue the country by whatever means he could find.

The Later Years

The previous twenty months of triumph and disillusionment seem to have left an indelible impression on Dr. Sun's beliefs about solutions to China's political problems and to have shaped his later career. As it turned out, he had less than twelve years remaining, and there is a pattern to his use of them. The strongest theme was his active opposition, most of the time, to whatever government sat in Peking, on the grounds of the flagrantly unconstitutional acts by those in power. But there was a fluctuation between periods when he schemed in exile without any real power and periods when he attempted to build a military base in South China from which to overthrow the rulers in Peking. He presided over three separate administrations in Canton during a total of four years, but experienced two intervals of defeat while he regathered strength in Shanghai. By establishing rival governments he was partly responsible for an eleven-year division of China, north and south, though this was not his intention: his purpose was national unity, apparently under a government headed by himself. He was ever-willing to participate in national unity conferences if he thought the conditions were right; and he yearned for foreign assistance in order to bring the country together.

During these remaining years Dr. Sun and his close colleagues created two successive revolutionary political organizations, which are linked by Chinese historians because Dr. Sun was their Leader—*Tsung-li*. The second of these political organizations went through three reorganizations. Yet it appears that Dr. Sun's bursts of attention to party organizing came during his periods of political impotency in Japan or in the French Concession in Shanghai. Political parties seem to have been important to him primarily as the means for raising funds and disseminating propaganda. When he held office in Canton he rather neglected the party except during its final reorganization in late 1923 and early 1924, when he became convinced that the Kuomintang could, like the Bolshevist Party, become in itself an important instrument of political power.

I shall now briefly outline the fluctuating pattern of the latter years of Dr. Sun's life as an introduction to two interesting topics— his financial efforts and his relations with foreign governments and foreign helpers.

August 1914 to April 1916: Exile in Japan. The main feature of this period was Dr. Sun's unflagging effort to overthrow Yuan Shih-k'ai and to redress the errors of the first revolution, as he perceived them. In July 1914, he created a new secret society, the Chung-hua Ke-ming Tang (Chinese Revolutionary Party), of which he was to be undisputed leader: all those who joined had to swear an oath to obey him in revolutionary work. Many of the principal leaders in exile refused to join this party, and there were bitter contests between Dr. Sun's followers and other revolutionary factions for financial support from the Chinese in Southeast Asia.[57] Dr. Sun strove to gain support against Yuan Shih-k'ai from the Japanese government, even when nearly all other Chinese political leaders supported Yuan in his resistance to Japan's Twenty-One Demands. Thus, Sun's actions were widely condemned as unpatriotic, and his image was compromised. When Yuan attempted to make himself emperor, Dr. Sun—with Japanese help—became part of a many-sided opposition, although his role in the defeat of the monarchical movement was not central.

It probably was on October 25, 1915—and not 1914—that Dr. Sun married his English language secretary, Miss Soong Ch'ing-ling, who also used the name Rosamonde.[58] Thereafter, this young and beautiful woman was his constant companion and helper.

May 1916 to July 1917: A period of lecturing and writing in Shanghai. Sun treated the problems of governmental organization that had arisen after the death of Yuan Shih-k'ai in June 1916. With Li Yuan-hung's succession to the presidency and the reconvening of Parliament constitutional government seemed to have been restored in Peking. Then the request of the American government in February 1917 that China sever relations with Germany, followed by pressure from the Allies for China to join their side in the war, precipitated a serious debate among Chinese political and intellectual leaders. Dr. Sun vigorously opposed China's involvement in the war, a minority position. Upon the dissolution of Parliament on June 13, 1917 and Chang Hsün's subsequent effort to restore the Manchu monarchy, Dr. Sun became a leading champion of constitutional republicanism. He led a movement to create an alternate government.

July 1917 to May 1918: The "Constitution Protection Movement" in Canton. An "extraordinary session of Parliament"—that is, about 100 members out of a necessary quorum of 580—approved a Military Government and on September 1 elected Dr. Sun grand marshal (*Ta Yuan-shuai*) with 84 votes. (The number of Parliament members in Canton gradually increased to about 230.) The effort to protect the constitution was supported, in varying degrees, by a number of national political figures and by Dr. Sun's more personal associates such as Hu Han-min, Chu Chih-hsin, Wang Ching-wei, and even by Ch'en Chiung-ming. Real power, however, lay with the Kwangsi clique led by Lu Jung-t'ing, whose troops largely controlled Canton. The Military Government existed only on paper at first, although the grand marshal made hundreds of appointments and issued many official orders from his headquarters in the cement works on Honam Island. Despite much frustration, the government gradually began to take on substance when the Kwangsi clique permitted Ch'en Chiung-ming to command thousands of local troops for an expedition against Fukien, and as the grand marshal succeeded in gaining control over salt revenues and partial control over revenues from two railway lines in Kwangtung. Then, in April 1918, Dr. Sun's opponents in the "Extraordinary Parliament," backed by the Kwangsi clique, effected a governmental reorganization by which a seven-man directorate replaced the grand marshal. Although Dr. Sun was one of the seven, he resigned and left Canton, again taking up residence in Shanghai.[59]

May 1918 to November 1920: Retirement in Shanghai. During this period Dr. Sun programmed the rejuvenation of the Kuomintang and schemed to return to Canton. He also wrote both *The Memoirs of a Chinese Revolutionary (Sun Wen Hsüeh Shuo)*, in which he analyzed the causes of the defeat of the republican revolution and developed his political philosophy, and *The International Development of China (Shih-yeh Chi-hua)*, a scheme for vast railway, highway, harbor, and mining development with foreign capital. Dr. Sun was involved in warlord politics and negotiations to reunite the North and the South. He also had indirect and sporadic contacts with the Bolshevist regime in Russia. He seems to have had little or no role in the May Fourth Movement,[60] but he and his associates were galvanized by it to create two journals of opinion, *Hsing-ch'i P'ing-lun* [Weekly Critic] in June, and *Chien-she Tsa-chih* (The Reconstruction) in August 1919. They also began the creation of an open political party, the Chung-kuo Kuomintang, organized officially on October 10, 1919 in respect to overseas branches, and a year later as a party in China, its constitution being adopted on November 9, 1920. By this time Ch'en Chiung-ming, Hsü Ch'ung-chih, and Teng K'eng had led the Kwangtung Army (*Yüeh Chün*) from southern Fukien in a drive to recapture their province from the Kwangsi clique. With Dr. Sun's political assistance they liberated Canton on October 26, 1920. Sun was invited back, arrived late in November, and resumed the military government.

November 1920 to August 1922: The second administration in Canton. During his second administration Dr. Sun attempted to influence national politics by a northward military expedition. There had been a long rivalry between him and Ch'en Chiung-ming, and, of course, between their respective adherents. Nominally Ch'en was the subordinate, but in fact he was the most powerful of the commanders of the provincial army and as governor of the province had at least titular control over provincial revenues. Governor Ch'en wished to concentrate upon the reconstruction of Kwangtung and opposed expensive military involvement in national affairs, but Dr. Sun was eager for national reunification. Early in 1921 it became evident that he hoped to be elected president by the "Extraordinary Parliament." Despite Ch'en's opposition, the election was carried out on April 9, Dr. Sun being elected "Extraordinary President" (*Fei-ch'ang Ta-tsung-t'ung*), receiving 213 votes from a rump group of 221 parliamentarians. Inaugurated on May 5, he organized a national government, appointed ministers, and appealed to the foreign powers for recognition, calling himself President of the Chinese Republic.

In the summer of 1921 Kwangtung troops invaded Kwangsi and crushed the Kwangsi Army. Dr. Sun then planned his northern military campaign to start from Kweilin near the Hunan border. From mid-October until his return in April 1922 he was in Kwangsi, absorbed with this project. While in Kweilin he met with J. F. M. Sneevliet (pseudonym Maring), a Dutch representative of the Comintern. Opposed in his military plans by Ch'en Chiung-ming, Dr. Sun had great difficulty with finances, munitions, and supplies. After a fruitless winter in Kweilin, he brought his troops back to Kwangtung in hopes of settling his problems with the governor. Meanwhile, Dr. Sun had allied himself with Chang Tso-lin against the Chihli clique led by Ts'ao K'un and Wu P'ei-fu.

The next four months were stormy. Dr. Sun "dismissed" Governor Ch'en, who withdrew to Huichow (Waichow). Then on May 11, Sun launched his campaign into Kiangsi from Shao-kuan, which was the head of the railway from Canton northward. The campaign began, however, just after Sun's ally, Chang Tso-lin, had been defeated by Wu P'ei-fu. After sending his troops off toward Kiangsi, Dr. Sun returned to Canton on June 1 to deal with a dangerous situation: the city was invested by the rebellious troops of General Yeh Chü, a subordinate of Ch'en Chiung-ming. Dr. Sun attempted to bluff the troops into submission by threatening them with an attack of poison gas shells. Instead, Dr. Sun was himself driven from the presidential palace on the night of June 15–16; he fled to the sanctuary of a gunboat. This experience was a deep humiliation. Dr. Sun then directed a naval bombardment of the city and called on his expeditionary army to return and subdue the rebellion, but Ch'en's forces defeated Sun's army, which scattered. Efforts to negotiate a settlement failed and, in an impossible situation, Dr. Sun was taken on a British gunboat to Hong Kong where, on August 9, he boarded *The Empress of Russia* for Shanghai.

August 1922 to February 1923: In Shanghai, organizing for the recapture of Canton. Dr. Sun was just as determined to punish Ch'en Chiung-ming as he had been earlier to drive out Yuan Shih-k'ai. From Shanghai he negotiated with greater and lesser militarists to revitalize a combine against the Chihli clique and, more particularly, to organize a military campaign to retake Canton. He collected money and arranged for arms to be smuggled to his adherents. Yet at the same time he negotiated secretly with Wu P'ei-fu for his own return to Peking as president, a project encouraged by Soviet Russia. It failed. Dr. Sun's alternative effort brought part of Fukien under control of friendly forces, while concurrently his agents enlisted various Yunnanese and Kwangsi troops, and units of the Kwangtung Army, for a drive down the West River route to Canton, which they captured in mid-January. During the same months Dr. Sun kept himself in the public eye by issuing declarations and statements to the press; in addition he negotiated with emissaries from the USSR and leaders of the Chinese Communist Party; and he made another effort to revitalize the Kuomintang.

The beginnings of Dr. Sun's Soviet alliance and his admission of a few Communist leaders into his party appear in the historical afterlight as the major events of this period, but at the time they were merely part of his effort to get to Peking and extraneous to his drive to retake Canton. The Sun-Joffe conversations came just after the armies in Dr. Sun's pay had captured Canton and while he was preparing to return there. But scarcely had he and Adolf Joffe issued a manifesto on January 26, 1923 signalizing Russian sympathy for the Chinese Revolution and Sun's support for the Russian position regarding Outer Mongolia and the Chinese Eastern Railway, than one of the generals who had joined the drive on Canton staged a coup and drove Dr. Sun's political appointees out of the city. Dr. Sun had to cancel his passage back to Canton. Then, the wheel turned once more, and he sailed back to Canton on February 15, stopping in Hong Kong for a few days of public courtesies and private reconnaissance. He arrived in Canton on February 21 with a fanfare of welcoming receptions. Would he be able to govern or was he to be a figurehead for the "guest" armies?

February 1923 to November 1924: In Canton, building a power base. We shall deal with this period in detail later. In the present sketch, and viewing it from Sun Yat-sen's position, we can distinguish two main phases. During the months till October 1923, Dr. Sun and his associates reestablished the military government and extended the area of its control in the delta region around Canton, along the West River and northward along the railway. Yet the hold on Canton was endangered by Ch'en Chiung-ming in the East. Finances were a pressing problem, the cardinal issue being whether the Military Government would collect and dispense revenues or whether the revenues would be collected and spent by commanders on their own. The municipal administration of Sun Fo, mayor of Canton, Dr. Sun's son, produced large amounts of money for the grand marshal's war chest; in order to obtain these funds, extra taxes were levied, which created strong discontent.

In October Michael Borodin arrived in Canton to act as Soviet Russia's instrument through which aid and guidance should be given to the southern revolutionary movement. Borodin's arrival marks the beginning of the second phase, during which there were developments of far-reaching importance. One was the reorganization of the Kuomintang along Bolshevist lines, although the party retained much from its own past. After its First Congress in January 1924, the Kuomintang moved toward becoming a national, five-tiered organization with strong direction from the top and with a definite political program that was more radical than before. Its great propaganda themes became antiimperialism and antimilitarism. Dr. Sun lectured on the *San Min Chu-i* and was now more militantly nationalistic than before. The party congress agreed to the admission of Communists and the Leader gave a number of them places in the Central Executive Committee and posts in the central apparatus. With Russian assistance the Kuomintang also established a military academy to train junior officers who would be politicized and dedicated to the revolutionary movement.

The growing influence of young Communists within the Kuomintang, and, to some extent, the growing Russian presence in Canton, created problems for Dr. Sun: disaffection among some of his old followers and fears of bolshevism among the propertied Cantonese. There was a strong move within the Nationalist Party to drive out the Communists, but Dr. Sun and his leftist-inclined associates rejected this challenge to the new Russian orientation. The merchant leaders of Canton and nearby cities tried to protect themselves from the depredations of the mercenary armies supporting Dr. Sun by expanding their protective corps and arming them with weapons from Europe. Discovering this, Dr. Sun ordered a large shipment of European arms confiscated, and this act brought on a protracted crisis, which was settled by force on October 15, 1924 on Dr. Sun's orders. In the process of crushing the Merchants' Corps, the troops supporting the generalissimo burned and looted much of Canton's commercial quarter. Their actions blackened Sun's image among Cantonese communities in China and abroad.

In fact, the aging revolutionary was not in the city during the incident; he was off near the northern border of Kwangtung about to launch another northern campaign. He had reallied himself with Chang Tso-lin and the Anfu clique against the current masters of Peking. His involvement in this military campaign ended when Feng Yü-hsiang overthrew Wu P'ei-fu in Peking on October 23. Dr. Sun saw a golden opportunity to participate in the reorganization of the Peking government, hastened back to Canton, and on November 13 departed on his ill-fated journey to the capital. He died there four months later of cancer.

Reflecting upon the fluctuating pattern of Dr. Sun's life after 1916, as he alternated between Shanghai and Canton, we see a steadily growing determination to replace the government in Peking with

[34]

one of his own. In 1917, Shanghai became his planning ground for a rival government in Canton, but later Canton became the base from which Sun hoped that, by allying with other power factions, he could overthrow whatever government sat in Peking. Dr. Sun's determination was fuelled by his disillusionment with the republican experiment and by personal ambition. There were grounds for disillusionment; all men of conscience were disillusioned. Presidents and parliaments became the playthings of militarists—four presidents in sequence forced from office; Parliament bribed and coerced or arbitrarily dissolved and a new Parliament created. By forming rival governments in Canton, Dr. Sun claimed to be upholding constitutionalism, but the constitutional basis of his own regimes was questionable indeed. His alliances seem purely alliances of convenience, and he admitted this. In the last years he claimed to be antimilitarist, but he allied himself with the Fengtien and Anfu military cliques and even in his own base was dependent upon militarists. This behavior might seem anomalous in light of the Sun legend, but it was a common pattern among power contenders at the time, and a power contender was what Dr. Sun really was.

This sketch has said little about the development of Dr. Sun's political theories which probably are his best-known attributes.[61] This neglect is not meant to discount the importance of Dr. Sun's ideas as a motivating force; we shall deal with them later. Dr. Sun seemed confident that his political theories and prescriptions for governmental organization, if applied, could solve China's pressing social and political problems. But he had little opportunity to test them in practice and thus they remained abstract conceptions.

The Private Man

What of Dr. Sun's personal life about which we have said little? Several who visited his home speak of the modest two-storied house in the French Concession in Shanghai, with its book-lined study and simple furniture, and a lawn large enough for croquet. Even at his headquarters in the Canton cement works on Honam

Island, he and his young wife lived in modest rooms. This simplicity of personal life contrasts with the impression of pomposity in Dr. Sun's behavior as an official; the private and public man seem very different persons.

Dr. Sun had warm friends among his classmates at the Hong Kong medical school, among members of the Shanghai Christian community, some among his revolutionary associates, and a few among his Japanese, British, and American acquaintances. He also knew a vast number of people in all walks of life: wealthy Hong Kong compradors and rural secret-society leaders, humble workmen among the overseas Chinese, troop commanders, labor union leaders, foreign political figures, and a generation of Chinese intellectuals who came to maturity during the first decade of the present century. He kept an enormous correspondence. Some of his friends and revolutionary associates stuck by him through all adversities; others came in and out of his life as he needed them to carry out revolutionary work. "As he needed them. . . ." This raises a question: did he see others primarily as agents to serve his cause? Some evidence points in that direction.

What of Dr. Sun's relations with women? In thinking of this we must bear in mind the several cultural outlooks he absorbed. As a young man—only seventeen—he dutifully married a girl selected by his family; she bore him three children. He lived very little with Lu Mu-chen. His elder brother cared for her during most of the time that Sun was an itinerant revolutionary. Yet when Sun became provisional president he brought his wife to Nanking, and he took her to Japan in early 1913 on his triumphal tour. Later he settled her comfortably in Macao but probably rarely saw her again. She lived till 1952. The culture that Dr. Sun absorbed in Yokohama and Tokyo had a different outlook on the relationship between men and women. It seems likely that he consoled his loneliness in relationships with lower-class Japanese girls, but little is known of this. Finally, there was his second marriage to a spirited and beautiful daughter of a Chinese Christian friend. This marriage was in the Western tradition of romantic love, happy and devoted. Soong Ch'ing-ling never bore him children, but apparently she adored her husband, was always by his side, and gave him strong psychological support.

Of the three children by his first marriage, all raised in Hawaii, Dr. Sun seems to have been closest to his son. Sun Fo had a Christian upbringing and a good Western education, graduating from the University of California at Berkeley in 1916, and earning a Master of Arts degree in economics from Columbia University the next year. His father gave him a position in his first Canton administration, and later Sun Fo displayed administrative and political talents as mayor of Canton during most of the time from 1921 to late in 1924. During these years he effectively backed up his father's work. Four letters from Dr. Sun to his son, dated in July and August 1918, and written from Shanghai, and in June 1923, when Dr. Sun was at the East River front directing a campaign against Ch'en Chiung-ming, have recently been published.[62] In the earlier missive the father is full of advice to his son to use his time profitably, to read serious books, and even to translate certain books into Chinese for the public benefit. The doctor also prescribes medical treatments for his son's ailing wife. In the first letter from the war front, he exhorts his son, the mayor, to patch up a breach between himself and Hu Han-min, who was threatening to leave Canton. In the second letter, Dr. Sun pleads urgently for money and shows his anger over associates who have failed to fulfill their financial pledges. He urges his son to ask all the colleagues to cooperate closely to overcome the present crisis. These are among the few family letters from Dr. Sun that have been revealed.

Dr. Sun's second child, a daughter, died in 1913 at the age of eighteen. The youngest daughter married Tai En-sai in 1921, after his return from graduate study at Columbia University (M.A. 1915, Ph.D. 1918). Tai served in Dr. Sun's southern regimes and later represented China as minister to Brazil. This brief summary conveys very little about Dr. Sun's family life. What more may be said of the private man?

Sun Yat-sen was a voracious reader, preferring English works in economics and politics. He also read Chinese classics and history, as well as contemporary works. He practiced calligraphy, and there is a charming photograph of him in scholar's dress with brush in hand. One who knew him well wrote that,

> He was an avid reader. He could read for hours poring over books for study and research. He played a little chess at home and occasionally a home movie was shown for his benefit. As for out-door recreation, Madame Sun was resourceful in arranging picnics and field trips to interesting places. What he enjoyed most was playing croquet with Madame Sun. My wife and I were often invited to see them play and have tea with them. When playing croquet Dr. Sun would swing his mallet with force and send Madame's ball to far away distances at the first chance he got. On such occasions and anticipating the worst treatment, Madame Sun would turn to us on the side lines and yell out, "Watch that Bolshevik." Dr. Sun never smoked. He never imbibed alcoholics. Neither did he drink tea or coffee. But he was a ravenous eater of fruits. . . . On the dinner table a big platter of fruits in season was always placed for his convenience. He was very careful about his diet. He was not keen on meat as he was on fish and vegetables. Early in the morning he would start the day with a bowl of steaming hot bird's nest soup.[63]

Others have said Dr. Sun preferred American style breakfasts and was devoted to milk—a most unusual taste for a Chinese.[64]

Was there an aesthetic side to his life? Did he admire Chinese painting or poetry? Was he a connoisseur of porcelains or jade? Did he paint or compose purely literary pieces? Did he enjoy Chinese opera or Western music? About such aspects of the private man little is known. A sense of fun or humor is not evident in his published writings, which seem purely political and dead serious.

"Dead serious" are suitable words for his entire life, from the youngster in Hawaii earning a high place among his classmates in English, to the man who set off for Peking on the morrow of his fifty-eighth birthday in pursuit of the illusive presidency of China.

Let us now consider several aspects of Dr. Sun's public life in more detail: his constant quest for funds; his attempts to use foreign wealth and power for domestic political purposes; his interest in Soviet Russia; and the final years when he fought his way triumphantly back from a humiliating defeat and then, with Russian help, began a new kind of revolutionary movement, which he did not live to see victorious.

CHAPTER TWO
Financing Revolution

It is difficult to get more than an episodic picture of Dr. Sun's financial activities, since information is mainly about specific fund drives and is much clearer on income than on expenditures. In a pioneer study, the late Dr. Shelley Hsien Cheng pieced together much obscure detail to present a coherent account of T'ung Meng Hui fund-raising efforts during the period from 1905 to 1912; but even this excellent study does not disclose much about expenditures.[1] A lack of records about expenditures is a defect inherent in the nature of revolutionary activity: specific evidence of bribery, arms smuggling, and payoffs is not likely to be kept around long! Nevertheless, some accounting probably was necessary, at least by category of payments, in order to maintain mutual confidence within the revolutionary leadership. Income records were important because donors and lenders had to be honored or remunerated, yet inevitably many records were lost. Fund raisers worked in many different countries, sometimes with the police on their heels. In all his moves and travels, Dr. Sun never had a permanent and secure headquarters; only in the last ten years of his life did he even have a home of his own.

Fund raising clearly was a cardinal occupation during most of Dr. Sun's mature life—he was almost perpetually on the trail of cash and rather ingenious in acquiring it—so we should at least sample his methods and gain some sense of his difficulties. His main, and continuing, source of support was the overseas Chinese, but he was assisted by some foreign backers and even by foreign governments that wished to use him. Of course, he did not work alone; many associates raised gifts and loans for the revolutionary cause, and there were not a few rivals soliciting in the same fields.

The Variety of Fund-Raising Schemes

A few wealthy patrons helped before the 1911 revolution. Foremost among them was Dr. Sun's elder brother, Sun Mei. Without his help, the young doctor could scarcely have begun his revolutionary career. Sun Mei cared for Sun's wife and children, helped him to organize the Hsing Chung Hui in Hawaii in 1894, and was an important source of funds for nearly ten years.[2] Defending himself in 1909 from charges that he had grown wealthy from political work, Dr. Sun countered that, except for something over $10,000 raised in Honolulu and Hong Kong, his brother and he had contributed all the funds for the 1895 Canton revolt, and that he had collected all but about $25,000 of the more than $100,000 spent on the Huichow revolt of 1900. His brother had become bankrupted and he, himself, had contributed nearly all the earnings from his medical practice. Apparently after 1904, however, Sun Mei was no longer able to contribute much to his brother's cause.[3]

Early in his revolutionary career, Dr. Sun made two important Japanese acquaintances, Inukai Ki and Akiyama Teisuke. Without Inukai's patronage and protection, beginning in 1897, it is difficult to imagine how the impecunious fugitive could have maintained himself in Japan.

The most steadfast of Sun's wealthy Chinese patrons was Chang Jen-chieh (Chang Ching-chiang), scion of a well-to-do Chekiang family and owner of a prosperous business in Paris. The two men met in Saigon late in 1905. Mr. Chang, eleven years younger than Dr. Sun and already showing progressive tendencies, was so impressed with the revolutionary leader that he offered him financial support. They set up a code so Sun Yat-sen could report his needs, "A" standing for $10,000, "B" for $20,000, and so forth. Mr. Chang made a number of contributions before 1911; later Dr. Sun credited him with having sold a factory to send $60,000 or $70,000, but probably that was only a fraction of Mr. Chang's total assistance.[4]

There were many wealthy Chinese in Southeast Asia but before the revolt of October 1911 showed signs of being a success, few of them contributed anything substantial.[5] On the whole Sun and his collaborators depended upon a great number of small contributions.

Before 1900 the main sources of funds from Chinese were Hong Kong, Hawaii, and Japan. Not until after the formation of the T'ung Meng Hui in 1905 did Dr. Sun and his associates begin to cultivate the Southeast Asian Chinese communities successfully. Chinese migrants were mostly from Kwangtung and Fukien and so were Dr. Sun's solicitors. They worked within the institutions which overseas Chinese organized—common speech-group fraternities, benevolent associations, and lodges of the Hung Men society. Dr. Sun formally joined the Hung Men in Hawaii in 1904 in order to gain access to its members.[6] However, until about 1909, his faction faced stiff opposition from the much more illustrious Emperor Protection Society (also known as the China Reform Association), established by K'ang Yu-wei in 1899. Mr. K'ang and his followers probably raised more money than did Sun's party, and they used similar methods.[7]

Supporters of Dr. Sun's movement who joined a revolutionary society abroad normally paid a small initiation fee and annual dues of $1 or so. However, Dr. Sun recruited only about 500 persons into the Hsing Chung Hui and the total number of people in the Tung Meng Hui before 1911 probably was not even 10,000.[8]

The more important sources of funds were contributions and loans. To tap these sources was the main purpose of Dr. Sun's seemingly endless tours. It was discouraging work most of the time: sometimes he would gain only enough money at one stop to cover his travel to the next. Yet when seeking funds for specific revolts between May 1907 and October 1911, Sun and his colleagues raised nearly HK$600,000, most of it abroad, according to Dr. Cheng's reconstruction.[9] This amount came in gifts, loans, and from the sale of bonds.

The bonds were essentially promissory notes; after the establishment of a republican government the purchaser would be repaid many times his investment. An early version of these bonds is found in the regulations of the Hong Kong Hsing Chung Hui of 1895, where members were invited to buy shares worth $10 in silver to be redeemed at $100 after the establishment of the Chinese Republic.[10] In 1904 Dr. Sun had bonds printed in Hawaii; they were to be sold for $1 each and be repaid by $10 when the Manchu regime was overthrown. He is said to have sold about $4,000 worth in San Francisco, but had to spend all of this on his further travels.[11] A variant account says he issued paper notes of "The Chung Hua Republic," which promised the bearer $10 in gold on the formation of the Chinese Republic at its treasury or from its agents abroad. Reportedly, these notes were exchanged for coin by Dr. Sun and his agents in many parts of the world.[12]

After the formation of the T'ung Meng Hui, Dr. Sun's financial ambitions were much higher. He had bonds printed in Japan with a face value of Ch$1,000, to be repaid in five installments with interest; the bonds were to be sold at only $250. Hopeful of raising $2 million from the sale of these bonds, Dr. Sun tried them out in October 1905 in Indochina, where he became acquainted with some wealthy Chinese and where he again attempted to merge the Hung Men and the T'ung Meng Hui. He may have been somewhat successful in the sales.[13] Wishing to test the chances in Singapore he wrote his follower, Ch'en Ch'u-nan, about the thousand-dollar bonds, asking him to sound out Chinese merchants as to their interest in this "good investment," but there was little enthusiasm in Singapore at that time.[14] Early in 1911, Dr. Sun had bonds printed in San Francisco in denominations of US$10, $100 and $1,000, hoping to raise funds for the scheduled Canton uprising. After the establishment of the republic the bonds were to be legal tender in China. Apparently they were offered at half the face value.

Finally, the revolutionary leader was successful. By 1911 he had a strong following among the ranks of the Hung Men, and revolution was in the air. In several cities in Canada Hung Men members mortgaged their clubhouses to buy bonds. The equivalent of more than HK$70,000 was subscribed in Canada alone and subsequently sent off to Huang Hsing in Hong Kong where Huang was master-minding the planned spring revolt. Dr. Sun raised an additional HK$15,000 in Hawaii and the continental United States.[15]

There were several sweetening devices to induce gifts and loans for the cause. One was the promise of special honors, on a gradu-ated scale, after establishment of the republic: Ch$100 guaranteed citizenship, $1,000 held out the promise of business preferences, and so on upwards to $1 million, which would earn the patriotic donor statues and parks named for him.[16]

The offer of business preferences was another device. For ex-ample, in September 1907, when in Hanoi trying to raise funds for a revolt in southern Kwangsi, Sun Wen wrote his friend Teng Tse-ju asking the comrades in Singapore to appoint a fund-raising commit-tee. "All those who help with money will be repaid with high inter-est to show our gratitude while those who pay very substantial amounts shall be given special privileges to open up the country and to exploit its natural resources. . . ." [17] The next year, now ex-iled from the French colony and desperately in need of funds for a revolt planned in Yunnan, Sun visited Singapore, but with very little success. He wrote Mr. Teng urging him to persuade a wealthy Chinese businessman in Kuala Lumpur "to save the situation." "If he does give us this $100,000 then we promise him the monopoly rights to all the mineral resources of the province of Yunnan for ten years." Apparently this inducement did not move the prospective donor.[18]

Another plan was to establish a Chinese industrial corporation, with headquarters in San Francisco. It was to be capitalized at $1 million and limited to 10,000 shares at $100 each. Dr. Sun held out the prospect that Chinese investors would be in on a company enjoying monopoly rights in China for ten years.[19] This scheme failed. Then he organized a fund-raising bureau with the help of the leaders of the Hung Men. The bureau's leadership was drawn from the secret society and the T'ung Meng Hui, but the money raised was to go for the operating expenses of the latter organiza-tion. According to the charter only "Elder Brother Sun" was allowed to withdraw funds raised and deposited in local banks. Whoever made a contribution prior to the revolution would be listed as a "preferential citizen" and would not be subject to whatever conditions for citizenship the new military government might create. He who contributed $5 or more would receive bonds of the Chinese Republic worth double the contribution.[20]

The line between contributions, loans, or purchases of bonds was somewhat artificial since the prospects of a return were speculative in the extreme, particularly during the period of abortive uprisings from May 1907 through April 1911. Nevertheless, taken in the aggregate, the amount Dr. Sun raised for his cause is impressive. In the sixteen years before the Wu-Han revolt broke out, he must have collected personally several hundred thousand dollars, calculated in Hong Kong currency. (The Hong Kong dollar, the Chinese silver dollar and the Japanese yen were each valued at about fifty cents in American currency during this period.) Much more money than that probably passed through his accounts.

Discouraging Times and Times of Elation

The itinerant revolutionary was often broke and for long periods dependent on others for his maintenance. Late in 1904, his friend Dr. Charles B. Hager found him in New York "careworn and oppressed with anxiety."[21] This was at the end of a discouraging effort to create a new revolutionary organization, since the membership of the Hsing Chung Hui in the Hawaiian Islands had practically been taken over by the Emperor Protection Society. During that entire year Dr. Sun had raised only a few thousand dollars in America.[22] It was at the end of this discouraging year that he issued his little pamphlet, *The True Solution of the Chinese Question*, in which he turned his attention to the American public and asked for their moral and material support.

Another period of deep discouragement for Dr. Sun consisted of the fourteen nearly fruitless months he spent in Singapore and the Malay States from March 1908 to May 1909. Six attempted revolts during the previous year had failed. As reconstructed by Professor Wang Gungwu, largely from Sun Wen's own letters, "They were months of a thousand little problems and months that were frustrating to his great plans." [23] In April 1909 he wrote his loyal supporter, Teng Tse-ju,

> Chung Hsing Daily News has nearly exhausted its money. The 1,000 dollars you sent me has gone to pay its debts and other bills, and we are desperately in need of cash again. . . . My resources are exhausted. As for helpers, we have only just over ten people around us. . . . Before the money from Siam and Burma arrives, I need 300 dollars for the rest of the month. [24]

Toward the end of his stay he could barely raise enough to begin his travels once more.

There were times for elation as well. In November 1910 Dr. Sun called some of his closest revolutionary comrades to a conference in Penang to plan another uprising at Canton. Those who attended were Huang Hsing, Chao Sheng, Hu Han-min, Teng Tse-ju, and Dr. Sun's elder brother, as well as several leaders of the T'ung Meng Hui in Malaya. They planned to raise HK$130,000 among the overseas Chinese in Southeast Asia. By persistent effort the colleagues were able to come very close to their goal, and Dr. Sun had his great triumph in Canada and fair success in the United States, raising about HK$85,000. The revolt, later known as the "Huang Hua Kang Uprising" of March 29 (or April 27, 1911, by Western reckoning), failed. Again the comrades were in deep gloom. [25]

When the revolt broke out at Wuchang in October 1911, Dr. Sun was in the midst of his American money-raising campaign. On his way back to China, he visited Chicago and New York, London and Paris, Penang and Singapore, but in spite of his reputation as a fund raiser and the anticipation of his revolutionary comrades, he arrived in Shanghai virtually empty-handed, according to his own account. [26]

The Basis for Financial Success

Who were these Chinese who helped finance Dr. Sun's dream, and what were his appeals to them? Most of them were Kwangtung migrants, which meant humble folk with little formal education,

[45]

who went out in search of opportunity to better themselves and to support parental families back home. Through unremitting toil, penny-pinching, or luck, some of them accumulated a stake with which to start a business of their own. Hu Han-min stated that most contributors in Malaya, Indochina, and Siam were people of the middle and laboring classes; by middle class he meant store clerks, salesmen, and small business men.[27] There were also tailors and barbers, waiters and peddlers. Out of their modest incomes day laborers gave Dr. Sun his strongest financial support. A few overseas businessmen of middling wealth upheld the cause, but before the October 1911 revolt there were few wealthy contributors.

Dr. Sun did reach other groups, however. An important one in the last few years before the revolution was composed of Chinese students in Japan, the United States, and Europe. They were from all over China and usually came from educated families that were fairly prominent in their localities. Many of these students made small contributions from their allowances. Another group that supported Dr. Sun consisted of Chinese Christians living in a few cities in the United States. They tended to be professional people of long residence or even second generation.

There were several million migrant Chinese living in those countries worked by Sun and his colleagues. The revolutionists appealed to their patriotism, to their pride in being Chinese. One important aspect of this patriotic appeal was racist: drive out those Manchu barbarians who have lorded it over us Chinese for more than 200 years. This appeal, which Dr. Sun used ardently, touched a strong emotional chord among Kwangtung men—the province had a long tradition of hatred and resistance—and it went straight to the original raison d'être of the Triad Society, which had lodges throughout Southeast Asia. Although it was easy to arouse Chinese passions against the Manchu barbarians, the situation was not simple. Until about 1909, the Emperor Protection Society probably outdid the revolutionists in influence among the overseas Chinese: it had the stronger chain of newspapers, more power in Hung Men lodges, and apparently more support among the big shots in Chinese communities abroad.[28] If one were a person of substance it was safer to favor constitutional monarchism and gradualism as espoused by K'ang Yu-wei and Liang Ch'i-ch'ao, both Kwangtung men of high status. Humbler folk could be less inhibited in backing up their anti-Manchu feelings.

Another of Dr. Sun's appeals to patriotism was the promise of a glorious, modern China of which all could be proud. To migrants who remembered the poverty of their tradition-bound home communities, prosperity and modernity were strongly appealing. In Hong Kong, Singapore, Penang, and Saigon they saw how European colonial administrations made material improvements and created a climate for business. In Japan and Siam they saw modernizing Oriental countries. In England, France, Canada, and the United States they lived as observers in a world of democracy and material progress. To these knowledgeable Chinese, Dr. Sun held out the promise that with the establishment of a republic—the latest thing in Western governments—and the elimination of corrupt and antiquated officials, China would enter the bright world inhabited by the Western democracies.

Dr. Sun also played on the wounded pride of the migrant Chinese, emphasizing the humiliation of being second class, and insecure at that, in colonies or in Western countries and Japan. He reminded them that the Manchu government could not protect them and promised that a new Chinese government would.[29]

Another explanation for Dr. Sun's ability to persuade many tight-fisted overseas Chinese to part with their money emphasizes his personal magnetism. He was a fellow provincial, who knew about the life of overseas Chinese from the inside, yet had acquired both a Western technical education and a respectable Chinese education. He was widely traveled, a world figure. From many accounts it is clear that he could exercise a strong personal attraction: it seems he had charisma. His manner radiated sincerity, dedication, and optimism.

Did he appear to his fellow Kwangtungese as a self-sacrificing redresser of wrongs in the Chinese chivalric tradition? Did they think he really could repay their loans and redeem the bonds he sold? Chinese often make gifts under the guise of loans with no expectation of repayment. It is the considerate way, much easier on the recipient's self-esteem. Also, it is not surprising that the notoriously gambling Cantonese were willing to take a shot on bonds which had an outside chance of a handsome payoff someday.

We may wonder whether the revolutionary fund raiser ever tried to repay the loans and to redeem the bonds which he and his associates sold. Professor Harold Schriffin believes that Dr. Sun took his debts seriously, and quotes Sun's friend Chung Kung Ai to the effect that some of the bonds were redeemed at their very high bonus. They were, in effect, claims against the republican government, when established. Yet when the revolutionaries set up their provisional government at Nanking they were desperately trying to raise more money by borrowing abroad and were offering a hundred-million-dollar bond issue, which went poorly. Such a government could scarcely repay the debts to former supporters.[30]

It is alleged that some of Dr. Sun's creditors dunned him repeatedly after he was elected provisional president and that just before he gave up the office he instructed the minister of finance at Nanking to issue receipts for the amount agreed upon with the creditors, promising repayment just as soon as the government obtained the money.[31] Part of the agreement of transfer from Dr. Sun's provisional presidency to that of Yuan Shih-k'ai was that Peking would take on $5 million of obligations incurred by the revolutionary regime. The Peking government tried to raise the money by a foreign loan,[32] but whether that government ever paid Dr. Sun's bondholders is still unclear.

Later Efforts at Financing

During a few hectic months between October 1911 and March 1912, the revolutionary leaders were determinedly searching for funds, primarily to pay troops that had joined the revolutionary side and masses of new recruits. And, from the first of the year, they also had a government to run. For example, Chang Chien, the eminent scholar and industrialist, borrowed some 140,000 taels (about Ch$200,000) from various chambers of commerce on the security of Liang-Huai salt revenues in order to pay off extraprovincial troops so they would leave Nanking, the new capital. He declined the post of minister of finance because he believed that, even with the lucrative salt revenues and Shanghai customs receipts, the government would run an annual deficit of 80 million taels. He proposed that the provisional president try to raise a foreign loan of 50 million to 100 million taels until provincial revenues could support the government.[33]

Dr. Sun and Huang Hsing arranged several quick loans from Japanese companies, one for ¥150,000 for the purchase of arms, and another for ¥300,000 in a private transaction with the Mitsui Bank in Shanghai, with Chang Chien serving as guarantor.[34] They negotiated for another loan on the security of the Han-Yeh-P'ing Company, which was to be reorganized under joint Chinese and Japanese direction, but the effort came to nought at this time, though some Japanese money may have been advanced.[35] The revolutionary leadership also tried to mortgage the Kiangsu-Chekiang railways, the property of the China Merchants' Steam Navigation Company, and other public properties, but quickly ran into opposition from officials and the public.[36] Though apparently these deals could not be consummated, the fact that they were tried provides some perspective on Dr. Sun's later efforts to raise foreign loans for causes he deemed just.

One source paid off as never before—the overseas Chinese. According to the researches of Dr. Shelley Hsien Cheng, in the period from October 1911 to July 1912, the T'ung Meng Hui was able to raise some HK$2.38 million overseas in relief funds and donations, the sale of bonds, and loans.[37] However, much of this money went directly to Kwangtung and Fukien rather than into a headquarters account. Chinese in America contributed funds for six airplanes, which actually arrived in Nanking but were not used before the provisional government was transferred to Peking.[38]

After the "Second Revolution," when Sun was an exile in Japan and many comrades turned to him for support, he sent emissaries to the United States and Southeast Asia to raise funds for the struggle against Yuan Shih-k'ai. There was bitter competition for the dollars of Chinese in Southeast Asia between Sun's agents, especially Teng Tse-ju, and the rival revolutionaries such as Ch'en Chiung-ming, Po Wen-wei, and Li Lieh-chün. Sun insisted that whatever was collected should be sent directly to headquarters in Tokyo—that is, to himself for allocation.[39] How much was raised is unclear, but in January 1917 a Chung-hua Ko-ming Tang newsletter stated that Sun Yat-sen had borrowed more than Ch$1.7 million from Chinese abroad and another million from Japanese.[40] Liao Chung-k'ai has left some information on the uses of the funds raised to overthrow Yuan.[41] The fund raisers in the United States cooperated better than those in Southeast Asia, probably because of Huang Hsing's prestige and magnanimity. Before Yuan Shih-k'ai's death in June 1916, the Republican Preservation Society in the United States had raised about ¥1.2 million which was sent to Dr. Sun in Tokyo or taken to Sun personally by Lin Sen after the Leader had returned to China.[42]

After Yuan's passing, when Li Yuan-hung became president and the old Parliament was restored, Sun Yat-sen tried to get the government to pay his obligations. He asked Liao Chung-k'ai, his representative in Peking, to request this of President Li; or, according to a different account, he telegraphed the president directly, requesting that the government give him $2 million so he could repay those who financed the revolutionary movement. This request aroused some public controversy, and how the matter was settled is in dispute.[43]

In 1917 and thereafter, as the Leader created governments in the South and tried to mount military campaigns, there were more solicitations among overseas Chinese. According to an American working in the Shanghai Post Office, Dr. Sun received no less than 25,000 registered letters from all over the world, but the dates during which he received these letters are unspecified.[44] During his first military government in Canton in 1917–18, the grand marshal solicited gifts and launched a bond-selling campaign. A detailed report of the government's income, aside from tax revenue, during the eight-month period that Dr. Sun headed the "Constitution Protection Movement," shows a precise total of $494,212.35. Much of this money came from Chinese communities all over the world, duly noted.[45] Dr. Sun's government issued bonds and treasury notes, and there are records of those given out for sale in the provinces of China and abroad, and of the agents who took them. The bonds issued came to a total face value of about $15 million, but how much money was actually raised by the sale of the two sorts of instruments is a puzzle.[46] I suspect that nothing near $15 million could have been sold on a voluntary basis. However, it seems that Dr. Sun, personally, raised a great deal to get that government established in September 1917.

In April 1919, Liao Chung-k'ai wrote to T'ang Shao-i, who was then the South's chief delegate to a North-South peace conference in Shanghai, asking him to bring up the matter of funds which Dr. Sun had raised for the movement to protect the constitution, a sum of $1,392,700. This sum, together with expenses for the army in the 1913 revolution and the 1916 uprising, comprised a total of $4,192,700, all borrowed from merchants in China or abroad, according to Mr. Liao. He hoped that the conference would arrange for this sum to be paid to Dr. Sun so he could recompense the various lenders. Mr. Liao's figures might seem to be a rough statement of Sun's debts outstanding, but since the conference failed to reach a settlement, we doubt that Sun's creditors were paid through Liao's effort.[47]

In January 1920, the Kuomintang leader asked the overseas comrades to raise $500,000 to finance the publication of an English language journal and also the operations of a printing press in Shanghai.[48] Yet Dr. Sun had a much bigger ambition: to return to Canton after the province had been cleared of the Kwangsi clique. Later came the need for money to finance the northern campaign which Dr. Sun planned to undertake in the spring of 1922. A fundraising bureau was set up in August 1921 and staffed by many notables. It sent appeals to Chinese communities abroad and, judging by the available correspondence, a great deal of money was remitted for the cause.[49]

During the entire year 1922, the Shanghai headquarters of the Chung-kuo Kuomintang received Mex$1,187,687.73, according to

[51]

Tsou Lu, who was much involved in party affairs at the time and who later devoted his talents to writing a history of the party based upon documents. He records the accounts for December, showing sources of income and four categories of expenditures.[50] The most numerous items of income were dues or contributions from overseas Chinese, aggregating Mex$11,962, at least. The total for the month of December was Mex$117,956.57, and of this more than half came through six unattributed donations turned over by "The Leader"; two for Mex$25,000, one for Mex$4,100 and three for Mex$4,000 each, in addition to $20,000 contributed by Nanyang Brothers Tobacco Company.[51] Of the month's total income, Mex$105,439.29 was spent and listed under the category "special expenditures"; it is not difficult to guess that this meant the money was spent for military purposes.

The ground is fairly firm with respect to another revenue-gathering operation set up in Hong Kong in October 1922; its efforts were reported in meticulous detail by Teng Tse-ju, who was in charge of finances in Dr. Sun's Hong Kong office.[52] The list of contributions and loans reveals a great deal about the basis of Dr. Sun's support. The total received was HK$406,270.79 (equivalent to about US$231,300 at the exchange rates of late 1922). The eighty-six entries for income—probably covering about four months—range from a gift of HK$10 to a loan of more than HK$70,000. Branch offices of the Kuomintang sent about HK$27,000, more than half coming from the Kwangtung Provincial Branch, and the rest from such places as Batavia, Haiphong, and San Francisco. But in addition there were large donations credited to individual Chinese living abroad, such as Huang Ta-yuan from Rangoon (HK$16,000, figures rounded), Hsiao Fu-ch'eng from Bangkok (HK$9,400), and four individuals from Singapore (total, HK$6,600). Gifts from overseas Chinese not channeled through Kuomintang branches totaled about HK$40,000. Not listed in Teng Tse-ju's figures were the 60,000 guilders (approximately US$22,650), raised by Huang Fu-sheng in the Dutch East Indies.[53] A third of the income of Sun's Hong Kong office was borrowed in forty-one different loans (HK$151,831), though what rates of interest were offered and what liens against future revenues were promised, is not stated. We are also informed in detail about how the money was spent. Most of it went to finance the military campaign which drove Ch'en Chiung-ming from Canton in January 1923.

Some of it went to pay creditors. Several items among the out-payments in Teng Tse-ju's meticulous accounting are revealing. For example, Wu T'ieh-ch'eng was given HK$5,000 to redeem bonds, and there was another payment of HK$10,000 for provincial bonds. The large loan of HK$70,080, arranged by Hu Ching-jui, was partly repaid (HK$22,500 and interest at HK$780); and Tsou Lu, as commissioner of finance for Kwangtung, later repaid $47,580 in silver. A man who had borrowed for the cause in Siam was given two payments, totaling HK$3,200, to repay the loans, while four other persons were given HK$4,515 toward similar repayments. Dr. Sun reviewed the accounts after his return to Canton in February 1923, declared them accurate and clear, and ordered the commissioner of finance to manage the matter, which meant repayment of the outstanding loans of HK$55,885. If they were paid, we assume the money came from Cantonese tax-payers.[54]

These scattered figures in varying currencies over a lifetime of solicitation are far from being the total that Dr. Sun and his closest colleagues raised. They do not include money he received from his Chinese military allies and from foreign patrons and governments. However, they are enough to show what a strong appeal he could make, even after the fall of the Manchus, for the causes he thought just. In raising money he had staunchly faithful collaborators. He made great efforts, obviously, to keep account of where his funds had come from. It was wise, however, to keep the sources secret. Also, he seems to have been prone to large promises of advantage to those who contributed to his work. He did try to acquire government money to repay the loans that he and his collaborators had negotiated and to redeem bonds. But redemption was impossible to carry out completely. Many Chinese creditors probably never expected to be repaid: their motives were patriotic, and they seem to have supported Sun Yat-sen through admiration for his audacity and his principles.

CHAPTER THREE
The Search for Foreign Aid against the Manchus

During the sixteen years that Dr. Sun worked to overthrow the imperial system his most effective foreign supporters were Japanese, but at various times he also interested a few British, French, and Americans in his cause. In this chapter I shall try to show the consistant elements in his ceaseless efforts to secure foreign support.

Early Western Helpers

Most of the leaders of the first Canton revolt in October 1895 were men who had "mixed with Europeans and imbibed a taste for change and progress," in the words of the British consul in Canton.[1] Some were, like Dr. Sun, Christians. These conspirators had useful foreign contacts. Thomas A. Reid, the British editor of the *China Mail* in Hong Kong, attended some of their planning meetings and tried to create a favorable foreign opinion for the movement by publicizing its aim to open China to civilizing Western influences. He dwelt on the advantages of greater foreign trade and the opportunities for investment in railways and mines that would follow upon its success. The new regime would have foreign advisers, would honor China's treaty obligations, and would use Maritime Customs revenues as security for loans. Editor Reid urged the Western powers not to repeat the mistake of aiding the Manchus, which they had made at the time of the Taiping Rebellion. While Dr. Sun may not have been the direct source of the allurements Editor Reid proffered, they are themes that appear repeatedly thereafter in his writings and negotiations. Another of Dr. Sun's techniques was a pragmatic, try-all-angles approach, seen in the effort to secure both German and Japanese support through their respective consuls in Hong Kong.

Dr. Sun had certain characteristic problems. He found a few loyal foreign friends and attracted not a few short-term adventurers, but he found it difficult to interest foreign governments in Chinese revolution. After the 1895 revolt was crushed, his friends came immediately to his aid: a Portuguese friend aided Dr. Sun's escape in Macao; an American missionary in Canton helped to get the release of another leader, a Christian; and the American consul in Canton tried, unsuccessfully, to prevent the execution of Sun's Christian companion, Lu Hao-tung, who he asserted had not participated in the revolt. Yet it was British police intelligence in Hong Kong, passed on to Canton, which exposed the revolutionary plot in the nick of time, and the Christian connection of several of the revolutionary leaders embarrassed the missionary community in Kwangtung. Furthermore, the Hong Kong government banished Dr. Sun and several other conspirators from the colony and tried to prevent its becoming the base for further attacks on the adjacent province.

Loyal foreign friends demonstrated their value a year later when Sun Wen was a captive of the Chinese legation in London. Without the determined efforts of two eminent British physicians, James Cantlie and Patrick Manson, to alert Scotland Yard and arouse a sluggish Foreign Office, Sun's revolutionary career probably would have been chopped off near its very beginning. Some months after his dramatic release, Dr. Sun wrote an article for the *Fortnightly Review*, subtitled "The Reform Party's Plea for British Benevolent Neutrality," which contained a number of pledges that had already appeared in Mr. Reid's publicity in the *China Mail*. The Reform Party, said Dr. Sun, would establish good government with pure administration by Chinese, but this would require "at first, Euro-

pean advice, and, for some years European administrative assistance." He promised that the new government would provide Britain with large commercial and investment opportunities in China,
which the incumbent regime had not granted.[2]

In 1900, when plotting to detach Kwangtung and Kwangsi from
Manchu control, Dr. Sun and his allies in Hong Kong tried to enlist
the governor, Sir Henry Blake, as an intermediary with the viceroy,
Li Hung-chang. At this time the Boxer disturbances in the North
had reached their peak. British documents show that Governor
Blake did in fact try to effect a junction between Sun and Li.
Though in the end the effort was fruitless, Professor Schiffrin con-
cludes that Sun Yat-sen came closer then to receiving British governmental approval than at any other point in his career.[3]

Japanese Helpers

During his pursuit of revolution Dr. Sun spent more time in
Japan than in any other country, some six years scattered in six or
seven periods. There he made some of his closest foreign friends
and adopted a new name—Nakayama, which in Chinese became
his most elevated *hao*, Chung-shan. He changed to modern Japanese dress and learned the language fairly well. In Japan he received extensive financial assistance, which came from the government—circuitously—and from businesses and private supporters.
During his period of longest residency, 1897–1902, he developed,
under Japanese leadership, sentiments of Pan-Asianism and antiimperialism—seeing Japan as China's "natural ally," sharing a common East Asian cultural heritage and similar victimization by the
West. Toward the end of his Japanese period, however, he probably
became disillusioned as Japan, by then an imperialist power, grew
more conservative. He was expelled in 1907 and most sources of
Japanese assistance dried up. The story of Sun's early Japanese experience has been brilliantly reconstructed by Professor Marius Jansen and recapitulated with additional detail by Professor Harold
Schiffrin,[4] and we need mention only a few points.

Sun's staunchest Japanese friend was Miyazaki Torazō, an ex-samurai, onetime Christian, and student of Chinese, who was dedicated to the idea of Japan leading the yellow race to freedom from Western domination.[5] In the autumn of 1897 when the two men first met—Sun Yat-sen not yet thirty-one and Miyazaki twenty-seven—the former had gained world notoriety from the London kidnapping episode and the latter had but recently come under the patronage of Inukai Ki, a prominent liberal politician in the camp of Ōkuma Shigenobu. Miyazaki led Dr. Sun to Inukai, who arranged for a wealthy nationalist, Hiraoka Kōtarō, to provide Sun with a house and allowance. The young Chinese revolutionary soon met many prominent Japanese, including Tōyama Mitsuru, a noted proponent of Japanese expansionism. These contacts opened undreamed channels of money and assistance.

One of the first cooperative enterprises was a phase of Japanese assistance to the Philippine independence movement against the United States in 1898–99. Dr. Sun acted as financial agent and intermediary in the shipment of Japanese arms—providing a Chinese cover; his *shishi* friends, Miyazaki and Hirayama Shū, were more direct participants in the insurrection; and behind the scenes were Japanese expansionists, a general, and Inukai. The enterprise floundered when the first arms shipment sank in a storm; a second, purchased by Sun, was off-loaded on orders of the Japanese government because of American protest. Still, Sun may have made a commissioner's profit from the deal.[6] The episode was an example of the Pan-Asianism which Sun Yat-sen shared with his closer Japanese friends, and it was, in a way, a dress rehearsal for Japanese involvement in the Huichow (Waichow) revolt of 1900.

In this endeavor, Sun's adventurer friends channeled funds, assisted in his contacts with Chinese secret-society leaders, and served as intermediaries in negotiations with important officials in Canton, including Li Hung-chang. Dr. Sun acknowledged Japanese gifts of HK$5,000 (though there may have been more), and one Japanese lost his life carrying a message to the field commander, "the first foreigner who laid down his life for the Chinese Republic," in Sun's words.[7] Despite such help the revolutionary leader had reason to be disappointed: his efforts were nullified, in part, when the

Japanese governor-general of Taiwan withdrew his support and when Sun discovered that he had been swindled by a Japanese in the arms he planned to ship to the leader of the revolt, his valiant Triad friend, Cheng Shih-liang.

Another aborted effort was the military school which Dr. Sun and his Japanese friends set up in Aoyama, near Tokyo, to train Chinese students as revolutionary military leaders. This miniscule academy only existed for a few months in 1903 and, strange to say, Dr. Sun left for a world tour only a month after its establishment.[8]

One of the greatest services Japan performed for the revolution was the hospitality the nation provided for thousands of Chinese students during the first decade of this century. Coming to Japan from all parts of China, these students saw the material progress of an Asian nation that had set out on the course of modernization. Russia's occupation of Manchuria and then Japan's victory over the tsarist armies and navy provided a tremendous stimulus to Chinese nationalism. The years from 1903 to 1907 were a period of radical ferment among the young Chinese in Japan, Shanghai, and other Chinese cities. Dr. Sun's Japanese friends polished the image of this lower-class fugitive and put him in contact with revolutionary student leaders in Tokyo.

In 1902 Miyazaki published an autobiography in which he presented a glowing picture of Sun Yat-sen; the book caught the attention of Chang Shih-chao, who published an abridged translation in Chinese, and a more complete translation appeared in 1903. The Chinese student-revolutionary world began to take an interest in this furtive figure.[9] Soon, he had attracted a small coterie among Cantonese students in Japan. By July 1905, upon his return to Tokyo from a world tour during which he had added a student following in Europe, Dr. Sun's name was favorably known to many students in Japan, though he still had few contacts with them. It was Miyazaki who brought the most eminent revolutionary leaders to him. Dr. Sun acted forcefully to broaden his base. With the active assistance of Miyazaki, Uchida Ryōhei, and Suenaga Setsu, and his new friends, Huang Hsing, Sung Chiao-jen, and other activists, he formed the Chung-kuo T'ung Meng Hui to unite the scattered revolutionary efforts. Dr. Sun was elected its leader. Akiyama Teisuke became one of the main fund raisers for the new organization. Dr. Sun dunned him almost daily, and Akiyama-san went deeply into debt for the cause.[10]

Finally, Dr. Sun's revolutionary speeches and other activities became so blatant that the Manchu government protested, and the Japanese government concluded that it should expel him. The Foreign Office did so with chivalry, allocating a large sum for his traveling expenses.[11] However, Sun's acceptance of Japanese funds without consultation with other leaders, and his departure from Japan with most of the money, caused an uproar within the T'ung Meng Hui command, and Sun almost lost his position of leadership. Chang Ping-lin, the editor of *Min Pao*, was particularly outraged that Dr. Sun had left so little money for the paper's expenses.[12]

After March 1907, Dr. Sun was persona non grata in Japan, and the government's agents abroad kept an eye on his movements. Yet he must have had hopes for more Japanese help, for in October he gave Miyazaki Torazō, a commission or, in Western parlance, his "power of attorney." This power gave Mr. Miyazaki "full authority" in Japan to raise funds, purchase equipment, and obtain supplies for the revolutionary army. "All terms negotiated with capitalists shall be arranged at his discretion." [13] We do not know what "terms" the revolutionary leader had in mind. Later he gave his power of attorney to several other foreign acquaintances.

Despite the Japanese government's abrupt termination of hospitality, Dr. Sun had derived great benefits from the country during the years between his chance arrival in 1895 as a fugitive from Manchu wrath and his kindly expulsion early in 1907. Japan had been his most stable sanctuary and had provided him with large sums of money.[14] There he had furthered the revolutionary cause, matured intellectually, and grown greatly in prestige. Though not so trustful by 1907 as he once had been, he tried again and again thereafter to use Japan to forward his causes. Of course, individual Japanese and some groups in the government had used Sun Yat-sen for their own ends, as well.

A French Interlude

Recent explorations in French archives are beginning to shed interesting new light on Sun Yat-sen's relations with various Frenchmen. While still based in Japan he probed the possibilities for help in his revolutionary schemes from French military officers and investors, and after Japan expelled him he immediately moved to Hanoi, which was to be the new base for uprisings in South China. "The French Connection that Failed" is the appropriate title of an article by Professor J. Kim Munholland which explores Sun's efforts and frustrations on the French front between 1900 and 1908, as revealed in Parisian archives.[15] Supplemented by records on the Chinese side, this obscure relationship can be slightly illuminated.

The first important contact with a French official seems to have been in Tokyo when, at his own request, Dr. Sun met the French minister, Jules Harmond, probably early in June 1900. It was Boxer time in Peking, and Dr. Sun was about to sail for Hong Kong in connection with his plan to detach Kwangtung and Kwangsi from imperial control. He outlined for the minister his hopes to overthrow the Manchu regime and expressed his wish for arms and perhaps French military advisers. In exchange, according to M. Harmond's report, he proposed to give France generous concessions in southern China; but M. Harmond did not specify exactly what these generous concessions would be.[16] The French minister gave Sun no encouragement, but he did agree to write Paul Doumer, the governor-general of Indochina, and suggest that he meet Sun when he came to Saigon. In Paris, however, the foreign minister and the Colonial Ministry both opposed any French support for the revolutionary plotter, and M. Doumer was warned against encouraging him. When Dr. Sun arrived in Saigon early in October,[17] he was permitted an interview with a member of the governor-general's staff but received no encouragement; nor did his plans impress M. Doumer when the latter learned about them. Cheng Shih-liang's Huichow revolt was about to collapse; it was all over by the end of October 1900.

Nevertheless, about a year later, according to Sun's account,

M. Doumer invited Sun to Hanoi to see a trade exhibit, at which time, he proposed, they could meet.[18] By the time Sun arrived in Hanoi, late in December 1902 or in January 1903, the governor-general had been recalled.[19] His successor, Paul Beau, had his private secretary see Dr. Sun, who, as customary, gave an optimistic estimate of the chances for success of a new revolt then being planned, if he could use Tonkin for smuggling arms into China. According to the French account of this interview, Dr. Sun promised that after his federal republic was established in South China it would turn to France for assistance and would make broad concessions to obtain her support. The new governor-general was not impressed. He set a watch on the plotter and prohibited shipment of arms for the rebels through the colony. This interview, too, corresponded with an abortive effort to stage a revolt in Canton. The governor-general's decision was entirely in accord with official French policy.[20] Nevertheless, Dr. Sun was allowed to stay on in Indochina, where he found a few recruits among Chinese residents and set up a tiny branch of the Hsing Chung Hui in Hanoi.[21] Obviously this was not all he did during a nearly six-month stay. By about the end of July he was back in Yokohama after a quick trip to Saigon and Siam.[22]

In February 1905 Dr. Sun was in Paris after his discouraging effort to recruit new supporters and raise funds among the Chinese in Hawaii and the United States. He had appealed for American sympathy and support in the little pamphlet, *The True Solution of the Chinese Question,* issued in New York in December 1904. In Paris he met at least two members of the Foreign Office and probably also Paul Doumer, whom he had missed twice before. Raphael Réau, a French consular official who had first met Dr. Sun in 1903, described for the Foreign Ministry the conversation the two men had early in February 1905. Dr. Sun suggested that France become the principal backer of his movement, replacing Japan; he had in mind subsidies and military aid.[23] Apparently this suggestion led to nothing immediately so far as the French government was concerned, though M. Réau was soon posted to the consulship in Meng-tzu, a "treaty port" in Yunnan near the border with Indochina. He remained in contact with the revolutionaries during a period when France was considering supporting Sun's revolutionary attempts.[24]

A by-product of the Paris visit was a curious episode in which the revolutionary leader reached an understanding with a French military intelligence officer in China concerning collaboration.

By prearrangement Sun Yat-sen met Major Boucabeille on October 11, 1905 aboard a French passenger ship in Shanghai harbor, while en route from Yokohama to Saigon. It was only two months after the establishment of the T'ung Meng Hui, and Dr. Sun was off for a fund-raising tour among the Chinese in Southeast Asia. The result of the eight-hour shipboard conference has been well described by Professor Munholland from the French viewpoint.[25] Dr. Sun apparently was led to believe that the major was offering to support his movement with the blessing of the French government, which was far from being the case. For his part, Major Boucabeille was setting up an intelligence network in South China and wished assistance. Dr. Sun arranged for Liao Chung-k'ai to go to Tientsin to serve as liaison with the major, who then assigned three officers to South China. Hu I-sheng and Li Chung-shih had participated in the shipboard conference, and they now accompanied the French officers on tours of Central and South China.[26] Major Boucabeille was pleased with the results of these tours and seems to have become partial to the revolutionary cause on which he was supposedly gathering intelligence. In the spring of 1906 he assigned one of the officers, Captain Ozil, for a second tour of Hupeh and Hunan, while Tokyo headquarters deputed Kao I-sheng to escort him.[27] The captain, too, seems to have become a partisan, for, at a welcoming meeting at Wuchang sponsored by an association of comrades, he made a speech on the French Revolution, which he thought exemplary for China. Of course he was overheard by imperial agents, who were already reading Major Boucabeille's letters to Sun Yat-sen. The Chinese Foreign Office protested to the French minister in Peking, who had no part in the intelligence operation, and as a result the French government closed it out in October 1906.[28]

Not much is known about Dr. Sun's stay in Saigon and Hanoi between October 1905, after his shipboard conference with Major Boucabeille, and February 1906, when he departed for Singapore. He may have been prospecting chances for using Tonkin as a base of operations in China. In addition to the thousand-dollar bonds he tried to place with wealthy Chinese, he got a French friend, Z. Leoni of Saigon, to print "four boxes" of hundred-dollar bonds for sale to foreigners. They were printed in French on one side and in English on the other and bore the name of "The Chinese Revolutionary Government." Dated "1st January 1906," and signed by "The President Sun Wen," they promised to pay the bearer $100 one year after establishment of the government in China on demand at the treasury in Canton or by its agents abroad.[29] How many of these bonds were sold is not known.

Here the trail becomes confused. One account has Dr. Sun making a quick trip to France, but this seems implausible considering his appearances in several other places.[30] The French consul in Shanghai had him interviewed in April, probably while he was en route to Japan.[31] In Canton the French consul turned down the request of the governor of Kwangtung that Sun be extradited from Tonkin, replying that he was a political agitator, not a common criminal; however, he recommended to the governor-general of Indochina that Sun be denied access to the colony.[32] Yet after Sun's expulsion from Japan in March 1907, he headed straight for Hanoi, using it as his base for revolutionary activity in China's neighboring provinces.

The governor-general of Indochina, Paul Beau, was surprisingly tolerant toward the revolutionary leader's doings in the colony. The French resident in Tonkin reported that Sun's revolutionary speeches in Hanoi and Haiphong were known, but since he caused no trouble and was law-abiding there were no grounds for expelling him.[33]

In fact, however, during his ten-month stay in Hanoi he directed five uprisings in South China, and some of his comrades crossed and recrossed the border to fight in these always unsuccessful battles. Dr. Sun dispatched commanders, sent money, and he or his agents purchased arms in the colony.[34] It seems improbable that he could have done these things without the help and protection of some Frenchmen. Coincidentally, just as Dr. Sun was directing these attacks from Hanoi, French scholars at the École Française d'Extrême-Orient in the same city were preparing for publication probably the earliest extended Western account of Sun's revolutionary fulminations, including the speech in January 1907 at Waseda University that led to his banishment from Japan, but there is no sign that these scholars knew Sun was actually in Hanoi trying to put his threats into action.[35] Despite protests by the Ch'ing government against Sun's criminal acts and its demand for his extradition, the governor-general declined to deport him because he considered him, under international conventions, to be a political refugee. Yet the French Colonial Ministry and the Foreign Ministry found his presence in Indochina a great embarrassment in France's relations with China. Also, the colonial government saw the dangerous possibility that revolutionary agitation might spread to its own subjects.[36]

Finally, Huang Ming-tang's brief capture of a Chinese fortress at Chen-nan-kuan in southwestern Kwangsi near the border brought about Dr. Sun's expulsion from Indochina. The fortress was taken on December 2, 1907. On learning of this Sun, Huang Hsing, Hu Han-min, Hu I-sheng and several others, including a Japanese newspaper correspondent and a French artillery officer on leave (and perhaps some other Frenchmen), boldly took a train to a point near the border, hiked across, and briefly entered the fray; they then hurried back to Hanoi to purchase rifles and ammunition. Dr. Sun had the arms that he succeeded in purchasing sent forward by train, but they were discovered and detained by French customs at the border. Then, upon orders of higher French authority, they were allowed to be sent across.

Too late! Huang's small force had been defeated; it found safety by crossing into Indochina.[37] When the colonial government put the facts of this campaign together and knew clearly of direct French military involvement, it put the clamps on. The matter was seriously compromising French relations with China. Sun Yat-sen could not be found immediately, but on January 15, 1908 he was arrested in Hanoi, ordered banished, and on January 25 he was put on a boat bound for Singapore.[38]

There was another significant incident in December 1907, before Dr. Sun's enforced departure from Indochina, which leads to speculation about his French "connections." When he returned to Hanoi from Chen-nan-kuan, a French banker allegedly offered to float a revolutionary bond issue of Fr20 million in France, but he would not make an advance until Sun's force had captured Lung-chow, a prefectural capital and "treaty port" in southern Kwangsi. The negotiations continued until December 9, when news came of the revolt's failure.[39] It was probably during this time that Sun ordered Feng Tzu-yu to send him the remaining bond certificates (presumably those printed in French and English), but they were seized by Haiphong customs.[40] A large bond issue is unlikely to be floated unless there is a prospect of tangible advantage, but the revolutionary leader had little to offer save promises for the future. When we consider his propensity to promise concessions, such as mining rights, to prospective large donors, it seems not improbable that French businessmen were toying with the prospects of future gains in Kwangsi and Yunnan, which French imperialists regarded as their sphere of interest. However, we do not know any details, nor that any bonds actually were sold in France.

Sometime in the spring of 1908 while Dr. Sun was raising funds in Singapore, a French businessman is said to have invited him to Paris to negotiate a loan of Fr10 million (about $2 million). It took much effort before Dr. Sun could raise the money needed for his traveling expenses. As usual he was optimistic; if such a loan could be raised he believed the major problems of the revolution would be solved.[41] On May 19, 1909 he sailed for Europe and arrived in France on June 20.[42] Once again, he was disappointed. While his activities in France are clouded in obscurity, it appears that the man who had invited him was only a broker and was unable to deliver. Dr. Sun then appealed to Paul Doumer, the former governor-general of Indochina, to work for the loan. Apparently M. Doumer was having some success, but in July the cabinet of Georges Clemenceau fell; the new premier, Aristide Briand, opposed giving permission to French financiers to raise funds for Chinese revolutionaries. Dr. Sun received the bad news late in October while in London trying to work out another loan, one which perhaps would be less compromising. The British loan, he informed his comrades, would not require "special profit rights" but merely ordinary interest. But this dream also ended in disillusion.[43]

Dr. Sun visited France twice more. En route to America, he spent a week in Paris at the turn of the year 1911, probably hoping to see officials,[44] but the New Year's season must have been a poor time for his sort of business. Again in November 1911, on his way back to a China in revolt, he spent three days in Paris during which he saw Georges Clemenceau and a few French friends in public life.[45] He tried unsuccessfully to arrange a republican loan with La Banque d'Indochine. Its director, Stanislas Simon, told him that the bank intended to remain neutral and would support neither side.[46] The French government had already adopted this position, and the banking consortium had decided at a conference in Paris on November 10 not to advance money until a responsible Chinese government had emerged from the confusion.[47] Probably Dr. Sun had no direct influence on this decision, which was a matter of high politics among the major European powers, the United States, and Japan; but no doubt it gave him satisfaction to hear—as he had already been told in London—that the consortium would not grant a loan to his enemies.

In his memoirs, Dr. Sun asserted that his old friend, the French consul at Hankow, persuaded his colleagues that the uprising of October 10 had occurred on Sun's instructions and was nothing like the Boxer Uprising but was rather a political revolution; hence, the French adopted a policy of nonintervention and neutrality, which had a favorable effect upon the outcome. The unnamed consul was Raphael Reau, but his report to the French Foreign Ministry does not indicate from whom the initiative for this decision came. He did, however, as a practical matter, establish regular contacts with the revolutionary government at Wuchang.[48]

We may conclude, then, that after Dr. Sun lost his base in Japan, and before 1912, France was important in his hopes for foreign financial assistance. What aid he may have received and for what promises of future concessions, remains uncertain. During 1907 he used northern Indochina as a base for several abortive uprisings across the border, until he became an embarrassment and the colonial government deported him.

He then continued his wanderings, first trying to use Singapore as a base. Frustrated, and ultimately asked by the government of the Straits Settlements to leave, he departed for the United States, his new hope, in December 1910.

American Adventurers in Sun's Life

North America lured Dr. Sun with prospects of support from the many Chinese communities in the United States and Canada, but also with the possibility of a big deal with a group of American promoters. This was high finance, with a target of $10 million and possibly military aid as well. In March 1910, on his previous visit, Dr. Sun had worked out plans with the American promoters. By early 1911, Dr. Sun's hopes were fading but the project was not yet dead.

Professor Key Ray Chong has described this adventure in revolutionary financing in an article based on the unpublished correspondence of Charles Beach Boothe,[49] one the American principals in the enterprise. Dr. Sun did not initiate the scheme, but he was readily drawn into the plans of Homer Lea and Charles Boothe to engineer the overthrow of the Manchu government in order to gain profitable business rights in China.

Homer Lea was an amateur military strategist and romantic adventurer,[50] who had collaborated intermittently from 1900 to 1908 with K'ang Yu-wei and Liang Ch'i-ch'ao. He had also tried unsuccessfully to gain support from the American government and from businessmen for a joint Chinese-American military expedition against the Manchu regime. In 1908 Lea interested Mr. Boothe, a retired New York banker living in California. Boothe made a trip east to find support for the project and also enlisted his boyhood friend, W. W. Allen, as a promoter. Mr. Allen had connections with large American financial houses. At about this time Lea and Boothe ditched K'ang Yu-wei as the object of their support and shifted attention to Yung Wing.[51] Once a prominent reformer, Mr. Yung was now eighty years old and living in retirement in Hartford, Conn. He enthusiastically joined the plan but hardly was the man to lead a revolt or head a new government in China. Consequently, early in 1909, the promoters began to turn their thoughts to a real revolutionary, Sun Yat-sen, who was then on the other side of the world.[52]

Boothe and Lea were hoping to raise $5 million for the military campaign and were ready to promise prompt repayment after its success; they also planned to offer mining and railway concessions to the fortunate backers thereafter. Mr. Allen raised the sights to $9 million and took the proposal to J. P. Morgan and Company in February 1909, but he was summarily turned down. Then the promoters drew up new plans offering larger concessions of Chinese business rights to American bankers, and Mr. Allen called on Mr. Morgan personally in September. Again he failed.[53] By chance, Dr. Sun was just then on his way to the United States, his hopes for a French loan dashed.

Sun Yat-sen had met Homer Lea previously, probably in San Francisco in the spring of 1904, but Sun had been away from America for nearly five years and apparently the acquaintance had lapsed. In 1909 he read Lea's sensational book, *The Valor of Ignorance*, an analysis of the Japanese military threat to the United States. Probably while in London, Sun wrote the author requesting a meeting in New York, where Sun was due in November.[54] Though Mr. Lea was too ill to come to New York, Dr. Sun met Mr. Allen through the good offices of Yung Wing. Allen, however, formed an unfavorable impression of the revolutionary leader, whose thinking he found incoherent and illogical.[55] When Sun Yat-sen reached San Francisco in early February 1910, he received a letter from Homer Lea inviting him to come to Los Angeles for a discussion, and Sun replied on February 24 that he would come as quickly as possible.[56] Through Yung Wing he asked Lea and Boothe to make $1.5 million available to him immediately with another $2 million later.[57] Probably on March 14, Sun, Lea, and Boothe met in

Long Beach and got down to serious planning.[58] At that time Dr. Sun was forty-three, Homer Lea, thirty-three, and Charles Boothe, fifty-nine.

They made several decisions.[59] To begin with, plans for uprisings in the Yangtze valley and in South China should be stopped until a large-scale uprising could be mounted after careful preparation and the recruitment of troops and officers. Mr. Boothe would borrow funds for the uprising from New York financial agencies, and Dr. Sun, in his capacity as president of the T'ung Meng Hui, appointed Boothe "Foreign Financial Agent." To fill the revolutionary ranks a certain number of officers trained in America would be sent to China.[60] The three men drew up a budget amounting to $3.5 million, under four categories, for the preparations and actual cost of the uprising. This budget is preserved in the Boothe papers and reveals some interesting information.[61]

Somewhere on the coast of the Gulf of Tonkin an army training base and ammunition dump would be located. Camps would be established for 1,000 men each in certain special concession areas.[62] Funds were earmarked for down payments on rifles, cannon, and ammunition, for suborning divisions near Peking and units of the Chinese navy, and there was a large contingency fund. The budget category for preparations amounted to only $650,000. Larger sums were allocated to recruit and pay 5,000 troops; to hire American officers, engineers, medical men, and interpreters; to uniform the force; to complete the payment for arms; and to ship all off to China. This category came to $1.1 million. There was another category that designated a million-odd for an additional force, apparently to take the field after the initial assault; and a fourth category of $795,000 allocated as a battle fund. The budget specified who had the right to spend or to authorize expenditures under the various headings. The *Hui-chang*—that is, Dr. Sun—had most control but the financial manager—Boothe—and the commander—Lea—had powers of expenditure also. For example, Lea was to control the battle fund.

The Americans agreed to raise the $3.5 million within seventeen months and to pay Dr. Sun in four installments, presumably corresponding to the four main categories of the budget.[63] To coordinate efforts the three men created a "Syndicate" to be run jointly by Sun and Lea. As president, Sun appointed Lea "Commanding General" to lead the revolutionary army drawn from the Heaven and Earth Society (estimated by Sun to have 10 million members in China) and the Revolutionary Party (supported, he alleged, by 30,000 students and intellectuals at home and abroad). Dr. Sun appointed Boothe as "sole foreign agent" for both the syndicate and the T'ung Meng Hui and gave him power of attorney to handle loans and purchase all military and naval supplies. The syndicate reserved the right to authorize loans for the construction of railways, to grant concessions for Manchurian mining lands to American backers, and to transfer loans for the economic reconstruction of China after the formation of a provisional government.[64]

Dr. Sun then returned to San Francisco where he assembled a batch of loyalty oaths from his followers, dated March 20, 1910 and sealed with the great seal of the T'ung Meng Hui; he sent these to Mr. Boothe as evidence backing his claim to control the revolutionary forces of South China.[65] Through Yung Wing he asked Boothe to raise $10 million rather than $3.5 million, and he pledged to repay in ten annual installments of $2 million each—that is, to repay double—with an annual interest of 15 percent. He also promised that members of the syndicate—presumably meaning investors—would be named commissioners of customs in Kwangtung for a period of fifteen years, or be given management of the tele-postal service and certain specified trade monopolies.[66] He wrote Homer Lea offering to try to get the Japanese secret mobilization plans against the United States, and he asked Lea to find out whether the War Department would be interested. In a second letter written March 24, 1910, from shipboard en route to Hawaii, he sent Lea a list of twelve "documents of a certain military Power," which he had received just before sailing.[67] We do not know whether Homer Lea followed up Sun's offer of espionage. Sun also wrote or cabled Huang Hsing about the military planning, and this communication later generated a strong reaction from General Huang.[68] In a letter to Teng Tse-ju, Sun confided that he had hopes for either a British or an American loan; if he secured the latter, there would be little difficulty in working out a method for revolt.[69]

From Honolulu he wrote Boothe to ask about Mr. Allen's fundraising efforts in New York, unaware that Allen was not keen about the matter.[70] Mr. Boothe replied on May 12 that he was steadily working on the project but could not report final results, though "so far," he said, he had received "very satisfying encouragement." [71] Sun then wrote separately to Boothe and to Lea, explaining the need for an agreement with France that would permit the assemblage of troops on territories under its control—probably referring to the Kwangchow Bay area—and the shipment of arms there from Hong Kong. If American funds were forthcoming, Sun hoped Lea would go quickly to Hong Kong.[72]

Dr. Sun then sailed for Japan where he arrived on June 10 under an assumed name. Due to his indiscretion in sending a wireless message announcing his coming to a colleague, the Japanese authorities easily apprehended him and told him to move on. He sailed for Singapore on June 25, informing Lea that he had told his comrades about the plans. They were ready but would delay the uprising until winter.[73] Meanwhile, early in June, Mr. Allen again tried to interest J. P. Morgan and Company in the required loans. For the third time he failed.

With Dr. Sun so much of the time at sea, it must have been difficult to maintain contact. He wrote Boothe on July 15 from Singapore but then moved to Penang. His money-raising endeavors were going poorly. On September 4 and 5 he wrote separately to Boothe and Lea. He asked Mr. Boothe for a personal loan of $50,000, which he promised to repay double, and he reported optimistically on the chances for a coming uprising. To Lea he promised great results along the lines of their planning at Long Beach if only Boothe would send him $50,000. If financial hopes in New York failed, he begged Lea to find some other means to send the money quickly. "All our hopes are pinned on the American plan." If the money were forthcoming, he wanted Lea to meet him in London so they could win British approval for the planned uprising. He asked to be told frankly if the Americans' financial efforts had failed completely.[74]

Boothe and Lea called a meeting of the syndicate on September 10, 1910 but were unable to raise any money from prospective members. Sadly, Boothe wrote to Dr. Sun on September 21, admitting his inability to raise the required funds, though he claimed to be "sparing no efforts or expense to bring about the desired results." Dr. Sun may not have received this discouraging letter for he had moved on to Penang; from there he wrote to Lea on November 7 complaining that he had not heard from Boothe about the result of the syndicate's meeting, and "so I do not expect much from his side." Sun now thought he could succeed in the planned revolt with far less money than they had originally proposed: ". . . even a tenth of our original sum would be enough. Can you get that anyway quick?" [75] Then, banished from Malaya, he sailed for Europe on December 6. En route he wrote Boothe once more, announcing that now he would have to take independent measures to raise funds, but still begging for a few thousand dollars to help with the Canton uprising. [76]

Such was the glimmering ember of the once multimillion dollar scheme to overthrow the Manchu government, when Dr. Sun arrived in New York on January 19, 1911. Mr. Boothe made one more try to help him, appealing in February to a personal friend to invest in Sun, "the real ruler of China," as he described him. When this effort failed, Boothe resignedly confessed to Sun on April 13 that the obstacles to their plans had been insurmountable. [77]

So ended the syndicate. Perhaps the news was not so bad because Dr. Sun had anticipated it, and it was tempered by his successful fund-raising tour among Chinese communities in Canada. But, only a few days later, he learned the disheartening news of Huang Hsing's failure in the Canton uprising of April 27, in which many colleagues were killed.

We are fortunate to know so much in detail about this American scheme because Mr. Boothe preserved his papers, which are now housed in the Hoover Library at Stanford University. Dr. Sun doubtless had other American friends besides Boothe and Lea to whom he looked for encouragement and financial help, but the trail is obscure. During the last two years before the revolution, he spent fifteen months in the United States, the Territory of Hawaii, and Canada. Unwelcome in virtually all of eastern and southern Asia, the revolutionary leader found a last useful refuge in North America. Of all Western countries, he came to know the United States best.

Angling for Support from Western Governments

After the Wuchang revolt, the prospective president stopped in Washington, London, and Paris, hoping to influence the American, British, and French governments to favor the revolutionary side in the Chinese conflict. In Washington he was rather furtive, registering in a hotel under the name of Chungsan and sending a note on October 18 to Philander Chase Knox, the secretary of state, asking for a secret meeting.[78] It seems there was no meeting, but whether Dr. Sun was able to see other influential persons in the American capital is uncertain. He probably spent no more than four days in Washington, for he arrived in New York on October 20 and soon thereafter sailed for London.[79]

Homer Lea joined him in London and acted on his behalf in discussions with bankers, hoping to persuade the Four Power Banking Consortium not to go through with loans already negotiated with the Ch'ing Government. Lea also tried, without success, to secure loans for Dr. Sun.[80] He accompanied Sun back to China, stayed with him during his provisional presidency and then, his own health wrecked, was sent back to California in a helpless state. Homer Lea died on November 1, 1912. Perhaps he was, in a way, Sun Yat-sen's Lafayette.[81]

The revolutionary leader had some staunch friends in England, such as Dr. and Mrs. James Cantlie, with whom he sometimes stayed on his brief visits to London, but his relations with the British government and its agencies were scarcely satisfactory for his cause. After 1895 he was excluded from Hong Kong, his natural base for operations against Canton. This exclusion proved a serious obstacle; after 1895 others always had to act for him in the colony. The colonial government of Singapore certainly did not welcome

Dr. Sun, though it tolerated him when he behaved as the police thought he should. They sometimes made things inconvenient, as in the case of the foreign bonds he wanted to sell, and he had to watch his step when propagandizing overtly for revolution. Yet Sun visited Singapore seven times before he was banned, and he lived there and in Penang for months on end.[82] In fact, after his expulsion from Indochina early in 1908, the Straits Settlements were the only places with large Chinese populations that afforded Sun near access to China. Only late in 1910 was he banished from this British colonial area, and when he departed he left his wife and daughters in Penang.

The question of Sun's attempts to influence the British government, and its attitude toward him before the establishment of the Nanking provisional government, will doubtless be exposed in another volume of Professor Schiffrin's biography of Sun Yat-sen. A foretaste of this discussion is found in his account of Sun's proposal in November 1911 for an alliance.[83] Sir Trevor Dawson of Vickers Sons and Maxim, who apparently hoped to sell arms and munitions to Sun's prospective government, submitted to the British Foreign Office a memorandum signed by Sun and Lea.[84] Its substance was that Sun's party wanted to make an alliance with Britain and the United States, and that Philander Knox and Elihu Root—the present and the previous secretaries of state—were interested and prepared to lend £1 million if Britain agreed. Sun and Lea even proposed that the Foreign Office check this assertion with Knox and Root!

Dr. Sun promised to act under the advice of the British government, and if his government came to power—as of course he was confident it would—he promised Britain and the United States preferential treatment over all other nations. He would place the Chinese navy under command of British officers subject to his own orders, and his attitude toward Japan would be determined by British advice. He claimed the sworn support of 30,000 to 40,000 of the best-educated young Chinese, and he stated that secret societies having 35 million members backed him for the presidency.

Truly, this was a "desperate bluff," as Professor Schiffrin terms it, and the Foreign Office was not taken in. Two days after receiving

Sun's memorandum, the British foreign secretary, Sir Edward Grey, telegraphed the British minister in Peking: "We have conceived very friendly feelings and respect for Yuan Shih-k'ai." Grey went on to describe the sort of government in China which the Foreign Office hoped would emerge under Yuan's leadership.[85] The most which Dr. Sun got from the foreign office was permission to stop over briefly in British colonies on his way back to China.

So far as is known, before 1912 no government supported Dr. Sun, and he was sadly disillusioned in his schemes for foreign loans. Looking back from a present-day perspective, some of Dr. Sun's promises to prospective lenders seem audacious and even compromising. Perhaps he had no qualms in offering privileges, positions, and concessions since his mind was focused upon one great goal, the overthrow of the hated Manchus and the establishment of a progressive regime to benefit the Chinese nation. The first decade of this century was an age of loans to China and competition among foreign countries to gain railway and mining concessions. Furthermore, because of his own experience, Sun Yat-sen believed in foreign tutelage in the realms of education and administration. He also considered foreign investment to be the way to modernize the Chinese economy.

By the age of forty-five, after sixteen years of exile, Dr. Sun had become a worldly gentleman, but he was experienced in almost nothing but fomenting revolution. His general lack of knowledge helps to explain the impracticality of the schemes in which he tried to interest foreigners. On his way back to join the revolutionaries late in 1911, he probably knew more about conditions in Japan and America than he did about those in his native land. He had straddled several cultures and all of them had profoundly influenced him.

CHAPTER FOUR

Attempts to Harness Foreign Power

Upon taking up life in China, Dr. Sun continued his Japanese and Western contacts, although he no longer pretended to birth in Hawaii and hence to being an American subject.[1] His second wife was an Americanized young Chinese woman of a Christian family, and she provided him with a home life in Western style, both in Shanghai and Canton.[2] Dr. Sun read, spoke, and wrote English easily, though his written English has some basic flaws. During his second exile in Japan, from 1913 to 1916, he began to build an extensive library of Japanese and English books; those in English, at least, he read attentively.[3] He read the English language newspapers in Shanghai, and for a time he directed the editorial line of one of them.[4] Being a professing Christian, he had many friends among missionaries and Chinese Christians, and he maintained a correspondence with his early foreign mentors.[5] He enjoyed meeting foreign dignitaries and giving interviews to newsmen, but he was also eager to keep abreast of world developments by quizzing visiting foreigners and Chinese who had returned from abroad. Besides his several foreign advisers, he attracted many Western and Japanese-educated Chinese to his service, and toward the end of his career "returned students" flocked to Canton to join his movement.[6] Thus, Dr. Sun had a broader knowledge of the world outside China than almost any of his colleagues in the revolutionary movements he headed, though many of them also had had extensive experience abroad.

Dr. Sun's cosmopolitanism made him a man for his times in China—a period of exceptionally pervasive foreign influences and pressures. During his later political years, from 1912 to 1925, the erosion of Chinese sovereignty by Japan and the West became the overriding national problem for most concerned Chinese. Governmental revenue, armaments, factory industry, transportation and communications, mining, marketing, banking and finance, education—these and many more aspects of the complex national society were under Japanese and Western influence and partial control. All major Chinese political leaders had to deal with this foreign presence: to try to restrict and contain it, or to roll it back, and usually to exploit it for personal or factional ends. There was no way to escape from this intertwining of the outer world with Chinese political and economic life. Sun Yat-sen was not in the least hesitant about trying to harness foreigners or their governments to his own ends.

Because of his broad exposure to the Western world he wanted China to be modernized, not only economically but politically and socially. He had absorbed a common Western belief that once artificial obstacles to trade had been removed China would be a vast market for foreign goods. The record leaves the impression that Sun was confident he could conduct business with foreign companies and governments effectively,[7] and that they would accept his right to grant concessions, contract loans, issue bonds, and even—it sadly appears—to alienate Chinese territory, on behalf of his cause. The record also shows him both imaginative and persistent in his search for foreign support, but not notably successful except on a few occasions.

Early Foreign Involvements after the Revolution

Upon his return to China in December 1911, Dr. Sun's international standing changed. No longer a somewhat shadowy conspirator, he became an important political personality, first as provisional president of the new Chinese Republic, and then, on several occasions, as head of a southern opposition regime. Foreign governments paid some attention to his political initiatives; foreign dignitaries sought him out for interviews; and he had ready access to the international press. He attempted to open correspondence with prominent foreign officials and with heads of state. He tried to block his Chinese rivals by appeals to foreign governments and attempts to manipulate opinion abroad.

Illustrative of the difference from his earlier status was the financial assistance he was able to secure for the provisional government at Nanking from a leading Japanese business firm. The revolutionaries, still bargaining with Yuan Shih-k'ai to oust the Manchus, desperately needed funds for arms and for payment of troop commanders. Through the help of Yamada Junsaburo, a Japanese friend who had joined his entourage in Hong Kong near the end of December 1911, Dr. Sun was able to arrange with the Shanghai manager of Mitsui Company a loan of ¥150,000 for the purchase of arms. This was far less than the huge sum he had hoped for.[8] Then he and Huang Hsing secured a second loan for twice the amount from the Mitsui head office, with Chang Chien serving as guarantor. Again Sun's Japanese friends assisted.[9] His government also received an advance—or at least the promise of an advance—of ¥3 million on loans previously negotiated.[10] Then there was the surreptitious—and now confusing—negotiation conducted by Sheng Hsuan-huai for joint Sino-Japanese control of the important Han-Yeh-P'ing Company, with the Nanking government to receive as a loan some of the Japanese capital invested in the company. When this deal became known there was much Chinese opposition to it, but by then Yuan Shih-k'ai was about to replace Sun Yat-sen as provisional president of China, and the loan to Nanking, naturally, did not go through.[11] There were also abortive attempts to mortgage the ships and facilities of the China Merchants' Steam Navigation Company, the Kiangsu Railway, and apparently other public properties. These attempts were not just Dr. Sun's doing. He headed a government struggling to survive, and some of his revolutionary colleagues were as involved as was he in the desperate efforts to find money by issuing bonds, securing loans from Chinese chambers of commerce, and borrowing abroad. In fact, all sides in the political contest, provincial regimes as well as central ones, competed for foreign funds, often at risk to China's future interests.[12]

The well-informed British journalists, Bland and Backhouse, reported the "Four Nation Banks" made a loan to the revolutionary government of 2 million taels in order to head off a Mitsui loan against mortgages of China Merchants' S.S. Company vessels, which would have given Japan great advantage in the Yangtze River and coasting trade. The money was paid through the Hong Kong & Shanghai Bank at Shanghai on February 28, they asserted, "and once more the Chinese had successfully played off the barbarians against each other." [13]

The leaders of the young republic naturally strove for foreign recognition of their new government. To play one power off against another was an old Chinese game, which the revolutionary leader tried frequently when seeking recognition of the various governments he headed. We have already mentioned his offer in November 1911 through Homer Lea to ally his coming republic with Great Britain and the United States. With Japanese advisers soon joining his entourage and assisting him with loans, it seems likely he made the same sort of offer to Japan. In any case, he tried to prod the United States by warnings of Japanese offers to him. Using the occasion of a confidential interview with Frederick McCormick and with Dr. C. D. Tenney, the Chinese secretary of the American legation, Sun sent a confidential message to Secretary Knox, stating that the Japanese were pressing the Chinese Republic to form an offensive and defensive alliance, promising recognition and Japanese assistance in organizing the army and navy; and further, that Japanese influence was delaying the Manchu abdication in order to force the republic to accede to Japanese terms. This offer, Sun said, had come through a Japanese elder statesman, who controlled the government, and that the negotiations were with him.[14] Apparently this warning, or threat, did not move Secretary Knox, who had received contradictory assurances from the Japanese government.

We have already described Dr. Sun's efforts to negotiate contracts for railway building in China after Yuan Shih-k'ai appointed him director of national railway planning, his visit to Japan in February 1913 to study railways and, more importantly, to set up a Sino-Japanese corporation with Japanese capital for industrial enterprises in China. He returned from that visit euphoric. He telegraphed the Peking government and various provincial governors to assure them of Japan's good will and to urge cooperation. In a press interview he said that his visit had satisfied him of Japanese friendship for China. He assured the public that Japan only wanted increased trade, not Chinese territory, and was following a peaceful policy. The *China Republican,* edited by Ma Soo in Shanghai "but Sun Yat-sen's paper," was full of praise for Japan after Sun's return. [15]

The test of Japanese friendship came when Sun parted ways with Yuan Shih-k'ai. Would Japan support Yuan or himself? Japan, of course, was not the single entity he had been generalizing about in his praise. Japanese relations with China involved many different economic interests, a variety of political groupings and ideological proclivities, and rival theories concerning Japan's national strategy. In the matter of financing Yuan's government through the twenty-five-million-pound "Reorganization Loan," which Sun came to oppose, would Japanese bankers in the consortium heed his pleas or would they proceed with business? They proceeded with business.

The situation described above provides an example of Dr. Sun's attempts to shape public opinion abroad. The long-negotiated loan agreement, dated April 26, 1913, was signed in Peking in the early hours of April 27 despite the obstructive efforts of some members of Parliament, which had recently convened but had not approved the loan. [16] A group of them passed a resolution declaring the loan unconstitutional, and on May 1, Hu Han-min, the military governor of Kwangtung and a close associate of Dr. Sun, issued a circular telegram denouncing Yuan's illegal method of securing it. Similar telegrams were issued on May 5 by military governors of four other provinces and in the names of some 300 members of Parliament. [17]

Dr. Sun made his objections known to the consular body at Shanghai. He warned that completion of the loan without reference to Parliament would cause a breach between North and South

China.[18] He also tried to stir up opposition abroad. On May 2 he sent a telegram to his friend Sir James Cantlie in London, and at about the same time he sent another for publication in Paris. He asked Sir James to submit his appeal to the British government, Parliament, and the governments of Europe and to give it the widest publicity. Ironically, the day Sun launched this campaign against Yuan Shih-k'ai abroad was the day on which the United States, whose bankers had withdrawn from the loan at the behest of President Wilson, recognized Yuan's government, the first of the powers to do so. Dr. Sun accused the Peking government of implication in the murder of Sung Chiao-jen and warned that implementation of the loan would provide the government with the sinews for civil war at the cost of great suffering to the Chinese people. He argued that if the funds were withheld Yuan would be forced to compromise. "I appeal to all who have lasting welfare of mankind at heart," he closed, "to extend to me in this hour of need their moral assistance in averting unnecessary bloodshed and in shielding my countrymen from hard fate which they have done absolutely nothing to deserve." [19] The telegram to Paris was published there on about May 9 and republished in the United States.[20] Dr. Sun also appealed to his Japanese friends, who mounted a public campaign against Yuan, while the more influential ones worked upon the Japanese government.[21] Yet these efforts did not divert the Japanese bankers. The same was true of the efforts of Sun's advocates in England. An advance of some £2 million was made to Yuan on about May 10.[22]

Revolt was in the air as a result of revelations in the Sung Chiao-Jen case and Yuan's bypassing of Parliament in procuring his loan. The American consul general in Shanghai received details of an interview with Dr. Sun on May 1. The doctor was sure that Yuan had been responsible for the murder, and he seemed to be contemplating war against Yuan. He said 300,000 men could be put in the field at once, and the war would be over in six weeks! When the interviewer said that in the event of civil war, Japan would promptly take Manchuria, Dr. Sun replied that Manchuria was not all China; when warned that Russia would then complete the takeover of

Mongolia, Sun indicated that what remained was the true China; when told that France might seize Yunnan and Germany, Shantung, Dr. Sun replied that then the Chinese people would fight. Consul General Wilder thought "the deluded man has thrown himself absolutely into the hands" of Japan. He wondered whether Dr. Sun believed that by giving Japan its will in the matter of territory, it would aid him in another revolution. He also wondered whether a revolution in China was just what Japan would like to see.[23]

All this leads to the delicate question of whether in planning the "Second Revolution," Dr. Sun and Huang Hsing accepted a proposal from Mori Kaku, a Mitsui executive and an official in Sun's newly organized China Industrial Company. According to a Japanese biography of Mori, the three men agreed in principle to the cession of Manchuria to Japan in exchange for ¥20 million and equipment for two divisions. A warship was to be sent for Sun to bring him to Japan to work out details, but somewhat later he pleaded inability to leave China and designated Huang as his alternate. According to Huang's biographer, Professor Hsüeh, the story cannot be confirmed from Chinese sources.[24] Yet Dr. Sun did look to Japan for support against Yuan and apparently contemplated going there to work out an alliance. He confirmed this by implication in *The Memoirs of a Chinese Revolutionary* by including a letter from Ch'en Ch'i-mei to Huang Hsing, the burden of which is how right Dr. Sun had been during the period of 1912 and 1913, and how wrong his comrades had been. Ch'en recalled that when the war against Yuan was being planned, Sun Yat-sen had intended to go to Japan to work out an alliance in person, and Ch'en confessed that he and other comrades had opposed him and tried by all means to prevent his going.[25] In any case, the proposed deal turned out to be merely talk.

Shortly after this obscure incident, Dr. Sun was again in exile in Japan, and he tried repeatedly to persuade high Japanese officials to provide him with direct support against Yuan Shih-k'ai. His eagerness verged upon recklessness.

Searching for Aid against Yuan Shih-k'ai

Dr. Sun's old patron, Inukai Ki, introduced him to Prime Minister Ōkuma Shigenobu, who had been brought out of retirement in the spring of 1914. Dr. Sun seized this opportunity. He wrote the prime minister on May 11, proposing a close alliance between China and Japan which, he argued, would be of enormous benefit to both countries. He offered unrestricted residence for the Japanese in China, a customs union, and Japanese commercial dominance. To gain these benefits, Japan should arm and assist the Kuomintang forces against Yuan Shih-k'ai, thereby earning the undying gratitude of the Chinese people. Sun portrayed Japan as playing the role in China that France had played in assisting revolution in the American colonies or that the English had played in helping Spain to overthrow Napoleon.

> Though it may be an extraordinary matter for a Government to support the people's party of another country to overthrow their government, yet only extraordinary men can accomplish extraordinary deeds in order to attain extraordinary results. You are the extraordinary man and this is the extraordinary opportunity which awaits you to exhibit your extraordinary ability and talent.[26]

In a second letter, dated March 14, 1915, and found in the files of the Japanese Foreign Office after World War II, the revolutionary leader addressed Koike Chōzō, who then headed the Political Affairs Section of the Foreign Office. The date is significant: Japan was just then pressing its "Twenty-One Demands" upon Yuan Shih-k'ai, and the Chinese public was aroused to resistance. Determined to return to China and overthrow President Yuan, Dr. Sun submitted the text of a proposed treaty of alliance between Japan and China—that is, a China represented by himself. In return for help in "removing the evil government of China," Japan would receive benefits which, we may only conclude, equaled those she was attempting to wrest from Yuan's government. China would give priority to Japanese officers when employing military advisers and would use Japanese arms, ammunition, and equipment for both its army and navy. When employing foreign specialists in its central

[83]

and local governments, China would give priority to Japanese. A Sino-Japanese bank would be established with branches in all important cities in the two countries, and China would ask Japan first for foreign capital needed for mining, railroads, and coastal trade. Japan was to help China in reforming her government and military system, and to support her in changing the treaties that regulated customs, extraterritoriality, etc. "The contents of the foregoing articles having been agreed to by the proper authorities of China and Japan and by those initialling the treaty of alliance, neither party to form an alliance with any other powers." The letter containing this sample treaty was written in Japanese and, according to Professor Marius Jansen, "the signature is Sun's." [27]

The Japanese government opposed Yuan's monarchical plan and decided toward the end of 1915 to assist the various Chinese groups attempting to overthrow him. The General Staff of the Japanese Army worked on this project in collaboration with the Foreign Office. Gen. Tanaka Gi'ichi, deputy chief of staff, was in charge, and other high-ranking officers were sent to China to assist Yuan's opponents. A Japanese businessman, Kuhara Fusanosuke, was selected to be the intermediary with Sun Yat-sen. On February 20, 1916, Kuhara made a loan of ¥700,000 to Sun Wen, who signed a receipt, pledged his dedication to the cause of "peace in the Orient and amity between China and Japan," and promised that the loan would be paid either by the republican government or by himself. He also promised to assist Kuhara's business interests in China. Wang T'ung-i, a follower of Dr. Sun, received ¥200,000 from Kuhara on March 8, signing a receipt on the letterhead of the Chinese Republican Navy; Sun and Wang jointly acknowledged another loan of ¥300,000 on March 16; and Sun received two additional ¥100,000 loans on April 8 and 27. In all, Japan loaned Sun and Wang ¥1.4 million through Kuhara, who kept the receipts till the end of his life in 1965. Thus Dr. Sun had a Japanese war chest of around $700,000 from this contact in 1916, in addition to the money his followers had raised among the Chinese overseas. [28]

The Japanese officers sent to China assisted Dr. Sun's lieutenants,

[*84*]

particularly Chü Cheng and Ch'en Ch'i-mei. The revolutionary leader transmitted funds to China through two Japanese banks; and he sent shipments of discarded Japanese arms to units attempting to stage uprisings.[29] Back in Shanghai by the end of April, Dr. Sun telegraphed to Huang Hsing in Japan on May 21, 1916, asking him to negotiate with the Japanese General Staff for a shipment of arms, which Dr. Sun had previously tried to obtain, and General Huang agreed to try.[30] All these military efforts failed to topple Yuan Shih-k'ai, and his sudden death on June 6, 1916 ended the campaign.

Thus did the Japanese government attempt to use Dr. Sun and a number of other Chinese leaders to overthrow Yuan Shih-k'ai. Sun Wen's efforts to enlist Japanese aid are understood best in the light of past Japanese assistance to his revolutionary cause, his Pan-Asiatic sentiments, his bitter hatred for Yuan, and his tendency to identify the interests of the Chinese people with his own leadership.

In his desperate hope to drive out his enemy, Dr. Sun turned in the same years to the United States also, where he had an acquaintance with Mr. James Deitrick. A poignant series, *10 Letters of Sun Yat-sen, 1914–1916,* was published in 1942 by Stanford University Libraries in facsimile, but there are more items among the Deitrick papers which clarify the facts of the relationship and reveal more of Dr. Sun's hope for aid from America during the period of World War I.[31]

James Deitrick was a self-made American businessman who began his career as a telegraph operator at the age of twelve, was a train dispatcher at sixteen, a superintendent at twenty, and president of a railway company at thirty-five. With this background he became a promoter of railway construction in the Americas and Siberia and of mining and land development in Mongolia and Nicaragua. In 1912, the date of the first extant letters to Dr. Sun, he was registered as vice-president of the Atlantic-Pacific Railway, which engaged in railway, river, and ocean transportation. The two men had met in London, perhaps late in 1911, for the early letters indicate an established personal relationship, and in one of them Mr. Deitrick reminded Dr. Sun that he had met the son of former President U. S. Grant "in my rooms here." Born on August 14, 1864, Mr. Deitrick was then forty-eight years old, two years Dr. Sun's senior.[32]

Mr. Deitrick had two major purposes in the 1912 correspondence with Sun Yat-sen: to secure contracts for financing and building railways in China—a passion the two men held in common; and to persuade Dr. Sun of the importance of developing a nationwide Boy Scout and Girl Scout movement to train Chinese youth in patriotism and in technical skills for service to their country. Mr. Deitrick said he could raise large amounts of money for both enterprises. Nothing came of these proposals, so far as the correspondence reveals, except that the American promoter apparently implanted in Dr. Sun's mind the idea that he had extensive business connections and was an able financier. Probably for this reason, the revolutionary leader turned to his friend for help in August 1914, when he so badly needed money to finance his movement to overthrow President Yuan.

Even before involving Mr. Deitrick, Dr. Sun wrote to Mrs. Homer Lea on June 17, explaining a plan to solve his financial difficulties "by means of Department Stores." His explanation was that when such stores had been set up in each Chinese city they would help to stabilize the prices of goods and the value of China's paper currency. He asked if Mrs. Lea could find organizers versed in such matters. "If such could be found would they come and help us, thus doing away with our chief difficulty?" [33] Two months later he elaborated the plan in a letter to Mr. Deitrick.

Dr. Sun first asked Mr. Deitrick to try to prevent loans which Yuan might attempt to raise in America, and to try to raise at least $10 million for Sun's cause. He asked Mr. Deitrick to approach various capitalists with the promise of franchises to operate department stores in China after Dr. Sun had driven out Yuan Shih-k'ai and established a new government. His friend should also recruit experts to assist in various fields, particularly in the management of department stores. On October 12, 1914, he gave Mr. Deitrick power of attorney to contract for the establishment and operation of department stores and industrial enterprises in China upon the advance of $10 million "to me and my party," though he could negotiate for smaller amounts in exchange for the right to operate stores in specific districts. If there were no takers, the revolutionary leader authorized his friend to "close up a deal" with prospective contributors "to undertake work in such industrial lines as Mining, Iron and Steel Works, Transportation, Grain Elevators, Manufactures, and Arsenal for the Navy and Army of China, etc . . . with the understanding that half its shares must be owned by the Government." If a cash transaction resulted from Mr. Deitrick's efforts, "You will have the money deposited in a bank in my name and to my credit and have the bank send me certificates of deposit of said monies." On October 19, he explained why he needed money urgently: it was to buy out the enemy's troops with their arms. "Thus our success will be assured." [34]

This was not a giveaway offer. Capitalists willing to aid Dr. Sun in his return to power in China would, in exchange, receive franchises to conduct businesses which would aid China's economic development, but the enterprises were to be joint companies with half the stock owned by the government which Dr. Sun expected to establish. He saw this as a means to stimulate production in China and, through department stores, to control distribution. Such an arrangement would provide the government with its finances and eliminate the financial control of foreign banks. The companies would not be permitted to issue paper currency as foreign banks operating in China did. "Thus China can be independent both politically and economically." [35] Dr. Sun had already been impressed by the advice on the issuance of paper currency sent him by Henry Clifford Stuart, a Washington lawyer, and he asked Mr. Deitrick to find out what sort of a person Stuart was and, if he thought advisable, to bring him into the department store scheme. In later letters he asked his American friend to locate experts on the engraving and printing of currency, which Mr. Deitrick did.[36]

In an unpublished letter of November 30, 1914, Dr. Sun informed Mr. Deitrick that he had learned by cablegram from "Young China San Francisco" that the Morgan Company was contracting a hundred-million-dollar gold loan for Yuan Shih-k'ai. He gave the texts of cablegrams he had sent to President Wilson begging him to prevent the loan, and a warning to J. P. Morgan and Company that "we will repudiate all new loans" after the struggle against Yuan had succeeded. He asked his friend to publicize the cables and, in cooperation with the San Francisco organization, to get Chinese all over the United States to demonstrate in order to scare off subscribers. In a letter which crossed Dr. Sun's, Mr. Deitrick told of his efforts to create a press campaign against the loan, outlined plans for establishing a pro-Sun press bureau in Washington, and warned Sun against W. W. Rockhill, former U.S. minister to China, who was in the employ of Yuan and "the money interests," in Mr. Deitrick's opinion. He also informed Dr. Sun confidentially of a conversation with His Excellency, Liang Tun-yen, minister of communications and commerce, from whom he had learned that the effort in New York was to raise a forty-million-dollar short-term loan.[37]

On November 20, 1914 Dr. Sun reduced his request to "half a million or more cash immediately." He added a plea for ten airplanes of the latest type, or at least ten motors and necessary equipment, to be sent to Manila. On January 1, 1915 he cabled Deitrick asking if he could send the money, but his friend was forced to reply on January 9, "Have tried every possible means/Impossible at present." In a follow-up letter of the same date, he described his solicitation of business acquaintances and why they had found it impossible to subscribe to so speculative a loan: ". . . they finally decided that to lose largely upon their present holdings to simply go in upon an investment entirely problematical as they viewed it, it was not good business." He assured Dr. Sun that "They are warm admirers of you and of your people and hope to be able to join in financing later on . . ." The war in Europe was making severe financial difficulties, Deitrick admitted, but he had another plan for financing which would take about six weeks to develop and would require his "going across to the other side." If he did go, he would pay a visit to Dr. Sun. He reassured him that no loans to Yuan Shih-k'ai would come from American bankers. He also proposed that Dr. Sun consider coming to America for a six- or eight-week speaking tour on the Chautauqua circuit, and stated that both Secretary of State Bryan and former President Taft lectured on the series.[38]

A letter from Deitrick written from Washington on December 30, 1914, alarmed Dr. Sun for he shot back a telegram in their secret code. Mr. Deitrick had told of meeting Gen. Huang Hsing and of arranging for an extended discussion with him in New York. He planned to introduce General Huang to "my friends in New York concerning the loan of a million dollars. The details of the loan, if we are able to close the transaction, are extremely important and of course the General can be useful in the negotiations." He inclosed a copy of a cordial letter to General Huang of the same date, mostly concerning the general's attempts to influence American public opinion, but also urging that they confer soon. Dr. Sun's secret cable, which arrived in New York on January 27, 1915 said: "Must not use/Huang/To negotiate/Loans/Afterward." In a letter he then explained why. Deitrick should not "mix with Huang and his men too much, for they did not join me yet in the new organization which I formed since the failure of the second revolution. Until he swear his loyalty to me and obey my order implicitly, I would have nothing to do with him and his men." (Dr. Sun was referring to the Chung-hua Ko-ming Tang, formed in Tokyo in 1914, which had split the ranks of the Chinese revolutionaries.) Lin Sen, the president of the organization in the United States, could be consulted on all matters, Dr. Sun wrote, and Mr. Dang Ja Yen—i.e., Teng Chia-yen—a student in Columbia University, was also "one of my loyal followers," so Mr. Deitrick could rely on him.[39]

In reply to the Chautauqua proposal, Sun cabled his friend not to make any agreement, and followed with a letter of explanation on February 5. He could not come to America till May, "for up to that time I am going to do some wonderful work." If the project failed he would come to give a course of lectures which would "surprise the American public with something quite new to them." So he asked Mr. Deitrick not to schedule any alternate Chinese speaker "for I fear it might spoil the matter, for no others can give a satisfactory view of China as I wish." Better to leave the matter undone, he advised, "than to give a superficial view, and disappoint American public." [40]

In March, Mr. Deitrick wrote to Dr. Sun from Petrograd. He confessed that the English bank had not resumed payments and that he had been unable to discount the account. Unable to make collections, he could not personally send anything. "I am very sorry for I would love to help out." (He had written letters from Copenhagen and Stockholm, which presumably had explained his efforts with an English bank, but copies seem not to be preserved.) The European war, Deitrick explained, had so disturbed matters in the United States that "it appears impossible for my friends to get together any large sums for your affairs." Hence he was suspending further work on the subject for the present. However, he planned to go on to Irkutsk, then to Peking on other business, and he hoped to see Dr. Sun in Tokyo. He also told him that "The trouble with Hwang [Huang Hsing] is that he wants to be President." Because Huang spoke no English, Deitrick at first had not been able to fathom his intentions, but Huang's interpreter, S. K. Tong, "soon made the story very plain." Mr. Deitrick confided that he must keep on friendly terms with Huang and clearly understand his plans, and added: "But you can rest assured that they are doing your cause no good in America, except in so far as to show up Yuan and of their own fitness for the position." [41]

Here the correspondence lapsed, and Mr. Deitrick did not come to Tokyo. But Dr. Sun was not to be diverted. In November 1915 he wrote to Mr. Deitrick in New York asking what results he was having in negotiating a loan. In May 1916, after he had returned to Shanghai with Japanese help, he asked most urgently for $5 million in gold. "With this sum I can accomplish the chief desire and object of my life—to restore my country into peace, *within a short time*. For I have determined upon the shortest cut to the goal, and that is to strike at the most vital point—Peking." He explained the chaotic political situation in China and begged his friend to "do *your best* to help me in obtaining this fund, without which all will be lost. You can arrange the terms at your own discretion, for I have full confidence in your ability and honour." Apparently, Mr. Deitrick had been at work on a scheme for he cabled Dr. Sun on June 30: "Underwriting can be done on following terms/ 50,000,000/Government securities/ If you can combine/ Provinces/ There is every prospect of/ 10,000,000/ By offering at public sale/ Must prepare everything/ After arrival/ According to report." It seems Mr. Deitrick did not comprehend the changed situation in China after Yuan Shih-k'ai's death. His cable drew a quick response, "Situation changed await letter Waicy." [42] (Waicy was Dr. Sun's Shanghai letter drop.)

In a letter of July 5, the revolutionary leader explained the new situation. If only he had had the necessary funds he could have established a provisional government long before Yuan's death and there would have been no need for a compromise between north and south. But Li Yuan-hung had filled the presidential vacancy according to the constitution and, for the sake of peace and order, Dr. Sun had successfully effected an understanding between the two sides. He was now being consulted on all national and international affairs, "and though I am not taking any position, yet my influence is as strongly felt as ever, and I possess the great confidence of the people." Under the changed conditions, he asked Mr. Deitrick to cancel whatever political loans he had under negotiation and to return the papers granting him power of attorney. He repeated the request on November 24, but Mr. Deitrick did not return the document, which remains in the Stanford libraries. [43]

Although the correspondence between Sun and Deitrick seems far from complete, and has been treated only in summary fashion here, it reveals Dr. Sun's vision of himself, his hopes for China, and his endless frustrations. The strongest theme of his letters is the desperate need for cash, which he clearly saw as the key to all his plans.

Opposition to China's Participation in World War I

Early in 1917, Dr. Sun began a strenuous involvement in China's foreign relations in a campaign against the breaking of diplomatic relations with Germany, which was a step toward entering the war on the side of the Allies. He tried to influence opinion both at home and abroad, and became absorbed in partisan politics.

On January 31, 1917 the German government announced its policy of unrestricted submarine warfare, and on February 3 the United States broke relations with Germany and sent a circular note to neutral states inviting them to take similar action. The American minister in Peking, Dr. Paul S. Reinsch, pressed the Chinese government to follow the American lead and gave assurances of American support beyond his authorization. After consulting with the British and Japanese governments, China sent a note of protest to the German government on February 10.[44] Very quickly the question of continued neutrality or participation in the war became a highly contentious one in Chinese governmental and public opinion circles. The political issue underlying the conflict concerned which among the contending groups in China would reap the benefits of either course of action. Premier Tuan Ch'i-jui strongly advocated China's entry into the war, and his faction stood to gain enormously from such participation, whereas the largest party in Parliament, the old Kuomintang, as well as President Li Yuan-hung and his followers, could only lose.

On grounds of principle Dr. Sun opposed China's giving up its neutral position. He believed this action could do China little good and was very risky. In February he is said to have formulated his arguments orally to Chu Chih-hsin and had him draft a long essay, *Chung-kuo Ts'un-wang Wen-ti* [The Question of China's Survival]. This work is known in its much later translation as *The Vital Problem of China*, the authorship of which seems to be erroneously attributed to Dr. Sun.[45] Without access to the original manuscript, it is probably impossible to know what part Dr. Sun may have had in his colleague's final product, though he apparently approved its reasoning.

On March 7, 1917 Sun sent an open telegram to Lloyd George, Britain's wartime prime minister, protesting in friendly terms British pressure for China to join the Allies, arguing the results could only be harmful to China and to British prestige in the Far East. Dr. Sun also warned of the danger of antiforeignism in China in case she were dragged into the war; he implied a threat of revived boxerism.[46] Yet this message did not reveal the bitterness toward England that was soon poured out in *Chung-kuo Ts'un-wang Wen-t'i*.

Sun also sent an open telegram to both houses of Parliament in Peking, just after they had voted to break relations with Germany, opposing the move. Tuan Ch'i-jui had mustered such coercive force that President Li was compelled to acquiesce, and on March 14, 1917 he declared the severance of diplomatic relations with the Central Powers. German diplomats in China used all their influence and resources, naturally, to induce China to stay out of the war; hence their interest in Sun Yat-sen, who was already laying his prestige behind continued neutrality.

A secret report kept in the German central archives in Potsdam, signed by the former German consul general in Shanghai and dated December 20, 1917, asserts that after the break in diplomatic relations between China and Germany, the German minister, Adm. P. von Hintze, ordered the consul general in Shanghai, Herr Knipping, and an interpreter named Schirmer, to contact Sun Yat-sen and induce him to overthrow Tuan Ch'i-jui and his cabinet, using German funds to the extent of $2 million. The German legation's contact man with the Kuomintang, Abel Tsao—Sun's friend Ts'ao Ya-po—was to go quickly to Shanghai to assist. Mr. Schirmer and Sun Yat-sen conducted secret negotiations, probably early in April. According to the German consul's report, Dr. Sun declared himself ready to overthrow Tuan Ch'i-jui and "demanded two million dollars for the purpose of influencing the Army and Navy." The report claims great results from Dr. Sun's efforts and also credits the pressure of the German officials for his departure in July for Canton, where he soon set up a rival government.[47]

This is evidence from only one side and does not prove that Dr. Sun accepted a large sum of money from the German consulate in Shanghai. In fact, in a letter to the American consul general in Canton, he denied categorically that he had ever received German funds.[48] Yet the Germans' proposition would have fitted his personal inclinations, and it is true that in May and June he and his colleagues worked hard to prevent a Chinese declaration of war on Germany and for the dismissal of Tuan Ch'i-jui. When General Chang Hsün coerced President Li to dissolve Parliament on June 13, and particularly when he attempted to restore the Manchu dynasty,

Dr. Sun and his supporters began organizing an opposition government. They induced some hundred parliamentarians and part of the Chinese navy to depart for Canton. This action must have been costly, particularly in the case of the seven naval vessels which left for the South. In August 1917, after Dr. Sun had arrived in Canton, the military governor of Kwangtung, Ch'en Ping-k'un, told Mr. P. S. Heintzleman, the American consul general there, that he had positive knowledge that the Germans in Shanghai had supplied Sun Yat-sen with Mex.$1.5 million of which $500,000 was given to the navy and $300,000 to members of Parliament; the remainder was transferred to Canton through the Holland Bank and the Bank of Taiwan, and General Ch'en claimed to know where the money was deposited.[49] This intelligence was quite separate from the secret German report.

Earlier, on June 8, Dr. Sun telegraphed to President Woodrow Wilson begging him to use his influence among the Allied powers to prevent China from being dragged into the European war, promising that if he did "this friendly act we can easily destroy militarism and anarchism in China." President Wilson had apprehensions. "These and earlier telegrams about the possible action of China make my conscience uneasy," he wrote to Secretary of State Robert Lansing. "We may be leading China to risk her doom." On June 4, when the political situation in Peking was in turmoil, Mr. Lansing had sent a message to Minister Reinsch for the Foreign Office saying that China's unity was more important than her participation in the war, and he also sent a circular telegram to the same effect to American ambassadors in France, Great Britain, and Japan, inviting those countries to make similar representations to China. Perhaps this was the reason that, in response to Dr. Sun's telegram, Mr. Lansing recommended that President Wilson not comply with his request.[50]

In the light of Dr. Sun's opposition to China's entry into the war, it seems ironic that in August and early September, he and his prospective civil governor of Kwangtung, Hu Han-min, approached the American consul in Canton, Mr. Heintzleman, to inform the American government of their government's intention, under

American leadership, to declare war on Germany. Both men pled for American financial assistance. Dr. Sun also reported that Chang Chi, former speaker of the Senate, had been sent to Japan to urge the Japanese not to make a loan to the northern government; Chang was to attempt to conclude a Japanese loan to purchase munitions for the southern fleet. Dr. Sun stated frankly that financial aid, munitions, and recognition by foreign governments were the paramount needs of his party, which was very short of funds. Friends in New York were willing to finance the movement, he averred, but due to British censorship in Hong Kong he could not get in touch with them. Dr. Sun proposed that Americans build arsenals and assist in all kinds of internal improvements, and assured Mr. Heintzleman that Americans would be given preference by the new government in the way of grants of an industrial nature. A few weeks later, the newly elected governor, Hu Han-min, called on Mr. Heintzleman at Dr. Sun's request and told him that the Japanese were pressing loans upon the new government, but that so far these were being resisted out of suspicions regarding Japanese motives.[51]

On August 14, 1917 the Peking government declared war on Germany and Austria-Hungary. On September 26, the Military Government at Canton, headed by Generalissimo Sun, issued a proclamation "recognizing" a state of war with Germany and Austria and promising to abide by the international rules of warfare.[52] The "Extraordinary Parliament," which passed the resolution behind this proclamation, also authorized the Military Government to raise a loan of $50 million for military purposes through the sale of bonds.[53]

No foreign government recognized the southern regime, nor did the United States grant it a war loan. In fact, the Division of Far Eastern Affairs of the State Department went out of its way to try to prevent the bonds from being sold in the United States and the Philippines.[54] How successful the Military Government was in selling its bonds in China and abroad is impossible to say, but there was a steady flow of contributions to the generalissimo's headquarters from overseas Chinese, including many groups in the United States and the Philippines.[55]

In the closing months of the war, Dr. Sun made another try for German aid, arguing that Germany and China should cooperate to free China from the dominance of England, Japan, and their allies. He sent Abel Tsao to Berlin with a proposal that Germany and Russia should jointly organize and equip an army of Chinese living along the borders of Russia and use this force, together with about a division of German troops, to capture Peking and overthrow the government there. Germany could then procure food and raw materials in China and transport them home by Russian railways. Thereafter—presumably after victory—Germany could assist China's finances, help it regain control of the Maritime Customs, and construct railways. Germany should also help modernize its educational system and develop technical skills so that Chinese products could be transported across Russia to Germany.

It is unclear exactly when Abel Tsao left China on this mission and by what route he reached Germany, but we can deduce that he left before Dr. Sun quit Canton in disgust toward the end of May 1918. He arrived in Berlin near the end of November, after the armistice, and presented the proposal in a letter of his own writing to a Lieutenant Phanberg and Admiral von Hintze, who called on him on December 1. By then, of course, it was impossible for defeated Germany to be of any assistance.[56]

It may be difficult to credit this unrealistic scheme to Sun Yat-sen, and it might be argued that its author was Ts'ao Ya-po, himself, were it not for the fact that the proposals contained several ideas which Dr. Sun continued to pursue. One was a Russo-German alliance with Dr. Sun's China; another was the plan to create a military force of Chinese residing in Russia to capture Peking on Sun's behalf; and the third was the concept of German economic and technical assistance to China for the benefit of both countries.

Dreams of Foreign Aid for China's Modernization

Dr. Sun left Canton in May 1918 after a reorganization of the government there reduced his position to that of one out of seven directors. He settled down at his home in the French Concession in

Shanghai, and during much of the next two and a half years he was absorbed in study and writing. From this period came his seminal work, *The International Development of China*. Starting the work shortly after the armistice of November 11, 1918, he dreamed enormous dreams for international investment in the economic development of his country. His plans took shape during a period when the American government was promoting an international consortium of bankers as a means to channel investment funds to China and elsewhere without producing international competition which would lead inevitably to special concessionary rights and spheres of influence. Dr. Sun reasoned that with the end of the world war there would be a vast war industry needing to be converted to peaceful purposes and that China was an inexhaustible field for industrial enterprise. He proposed that the recent belligerents spend a quarter of their final war year budgets upon China—$60 million in gold a day! The book as it finally evolved was a broad-gauge scheme to reshape China into an industrial society.

To carry out his projects, Dr. Sun proposed that the governments of capital-supplying powers agree to form an international organization, using their wartime administrators and experts to formulate plans and standards. He cautioned, however, that the confidence of the Chinese people must be gained to assure their cooperation and support. The next step would be formal negotiations for a contract with the Chinese government, but only with a government supported by the people.[57]

By February 1919, Dr. Sun had formulated the broad outlines of his plan for the economic development of China. These called for 100,000 miles of new railways and 1 million miles of macadam roads; improvement of existing canals and construction of extensive new ones; river conservancy on a large scale; creation of "world ports" from which railway networks could fan out to the farthest reaches of Tibet, Sinkiang, Mongolia, and Manchuria; the development of modern cities equipped with public utilities; waterpower development; new iron and steel plants and cement works; mining in all aspects; agricultural improvement; large-scale irrigation projects for Mongolia and Sinkiang; reforestation of Central and North

China; and the Chinese colonization of Manchuria, Sinkiang, and Tibet.[58]

He sent this sketch to the American minister in Peking, Dr. Reinsch, and received an encouraging reply, although the minister cautioned him gently against the fiscal unreality of his plans.[59] Also in February Sun sent a copy to Hendrick Christian Andersen, himself an international planner, who in turn sent a copy to President Wilson in Paris, "urging him to give the matter his full and deep consideration." Thus began an extended correspondence between Dr. Sun and Mr. Andersen, each urging his own scheme upon the other.[60] In March, Dr. Sun sent copies of his preliminary plans to the U.S. Department of Commerce, to members of the British Cabinet, and probably to leaders among the other Allied powers.[61] In the same month the *Far Eastern Review,* published by Sun's friend, George Bronson Rea, printed the introductory sketch under the title, "The International Development of China. A Project Designed to Assist the Readjustment of Post-Bellum Industries. By Sun Yat-sen, ex-President of the Republic of China." Other parts appeared in this journal from time to time until November 1920; these articles essentially constituted the work as it finally emerged in book form, with some illustrations appropriated from other works.[62] Dr. Sun was helped by some of his Chinese Christian friends in Shanghai, and a Chinese version of the early plan appeared in August 1919 in the new party magazine, *Chien-she Tsa-chih.*[63]

Three separate "Programs" elaborated Dr. Sun's ideas for the development of three great Chinese ports, one in the North near Tientsin, a rebuilt Shanghai, and a rebuilt Canton, each nourished by improved waterways and trunk railways. By March 1920 he had completed his third program,[64] dealing with Canton, and later, when back in that city heading a government, he attempted to put the plan into effect with the help of foreign businessmen.

Dr. Sun had an opportunity to lay his scheme directly before Thomas W. Lamont of J. P. Morgan & Company early in April 1920. Mr. Lamont was on a mission to the Far East for the American Banking Consortium, and indirectly for President Wilson, to explore Japanese governmental attitudes towards the consortium and to consider investment possibilities in China. The revolutionary leader invited Mr. Lamont to his home and there, according to George Sokolsky who served as an escort for the Lamonts in Shanghai, he showed the American banker a series of maps of projected railways. Mr. Lamont was curious as to how Dr. Sun thought the railways would be financed, Mr. Sokolsky recalled. "I ask you to pay for them now," Sun replied, "China will ultimately pay." Mr. Lamont had a very different memory of the interview; he recalled only a discussion of Chinese politics. He explained to Dr. Sun that President Wilson had asked him to find out whether there was any way to bring peace between the South and the North in China. " 'Peace between South and North?' repeated Dr. Sun crisply. 'Why yes. Just you give me $25,000,000, Mr. Lamont, and I'll equip a couple of army corps. Then we'll have peace in short order.' " This reply, Mr. Lamont decided, would "be a bit disappointing to President Wilson." [65] The two versions of this incident—perhaps cases of selective memory—are not inconsistent with an ambivalence within the revolutionary leader himself: on the one hand planning for his country's welfare through economic and political reform and, on the other, searching for short-cut methods to overthrow those rulers who stood in his way.

In writing up this vast foreign aid program, Dr. Sun was thinking as a reforming socialist. In his conclusion he offered it as a practical solution to the three great world problems—international war, commercial war, and class war. He wrote,

> The goal of material civilization is not private profit but public profit. And the shortest route to it is not competition but co-operation. In my International Development Scheme, I propose that the profits of this industrial development go first to pay the interest and principal of foreign capital invested in it; second to give high wages to labor; and third to improve and extend the machinery of production. Besides these provisions the rest of the profit should go to the public in the form of reduced prices in all commodities and public services. Thus, all will enjoy, in the same degree, the fruits of modern civilization. . . . In a nutshell, it is my idea to make capitalism create socialism in China so that these two economic forces of human evolution will work side by side in future civilization.[66]

Although Dr. Sun's prodigious plans, taken as a whole, were highly impractical, there is a far-sighted and modern quality to the thought which underlay them: the modernization of an underdeveloped country through cooperative foreign efforts.

Disappointments with America

There is no evidence so far as I have learned that the American Banking Consortium considered financing any part of Dr. Sun's scheme. When he first proposed it he was a retired politician; then by late 1920 he was back in Canton heading a government that attempted to rival the Peking government, which had international recognition.

Sun Yat-sen probably laid his main hope for foreign support on the United States during the years from 1919 until mid-1922. Japan had taken advantage of the war to make great gains at China's expense, and Dr. Sun was disillusioned with the Japanese government. His attitude is expressed in several letters. Sometime after the May Fourth Incident of 1919 he wrote to a correspondent of *Asahi* in response to a query as to how Japan could remove China's antagonism. Sun berated Japan's militarists for becoming imperialistic and forgetting the idealism of the earlier generation of reformers. Japan's seizure of Tsingtao was like that of a younger brother joining a band of robbers—i.e., other imperialist powers—to rob the house of his elder brother. "The Japanese people used to advocate friendship on the grounds of a common racial stock and culture, but their way of treating China is more reprehensible than that of other foreign Powers. No wonder the Chinese hate the Japanese and befriend the Europeans and Americans." He urged Japan to change its policy, for only thus could East Asia enjoy peace, reconstruction, and prosperity.[67]

In July 1920, Dr. Sun wrote a scorching letter to General Tanaka, who was then minister of war in the Japanese government. A draft of the letter found its way to the U.S. State Department from a "fairly reliable source"—that is, young George Sokolsky, who was then on Dr. Sun's staff. Dr. Sun's ostensible purpose in writing to "one of my intimate friends" was to induce Tanaka Gi'ichi to reverse Japanese policy toward China, which Dr. Sun described as military and financial imperialism. Japanese policy, he charged, is "always [to] support the conservative and reactionary elements among the Chinese people, and to discredit all movements of social reformation and political reconstruction along lines of democracy and republicanism." He then detailed Japan's support of various reactionary generals and officials—Yuan Shih-k'ai, Ts'en Ch'un-hsüan, Chang Hsün, Tuan Ch'i-jui, and currently, Chang Tso-lin. Dr. Sun regarded the former bandit, Chang Tso-lin, as Japan's tool to disrupt peace talks between the North and South. He put it to General Tanaka bluntly: "The whole people regard Japan as China's national enemy," and this unfriendliness was caused only by Japan itself. "If the Japanese Government continues to intrigue here, the result will be something more than a boycott." [68]

Great Britain, it appears, had also become a bête noire for Dr. Sun. It was a great colonial power and controlled the lives of millions of Chinese in Hong Kong and southern Asia. He had objected to Britain's efforts to bring China into the world war. In 1921 he had a particular grievance against the government of Hong Kong, and on three occasions spoke to the American consul in Canton in very bitter terms about British policy. Particularly rankling was an order prohibiting the Chinese in Hong Kong from publicly celebrating his inauguration as president in May 1921. Later an official proclamation forbade Chinese in the colony to contribute funds for his military campaign. [69]

Revolutionary Russia also excited Dr. Sun's interest, but the country was passing through a devastating civil war and famine. Victorious France and defeated Germany were both virtually prostrated, although by 1921 Dr. Sun had conceived a scheme to harness German industrial ability to his cause. The United States, on the other hand, had emerged from the war as a very powerful country, and Dr. Sun had long admired American democracy and economic strength. He also had several American advisers and many of his friends in Shanghai and Canton were American-educated, as was his second wife.

The United States disappointed him. There were two main reasons for this. Key American officials concerned with China problems did not take him seriously when he was in retirement. When he headed a government in Canton they regarded him as a threat to China's unity. The American government tried to uphold that unity by recognizing only one Chinese government, the one in Peking, and by refusing to deal with any other Chinese authority except on the consular level. There follow a few examples of Dr. Sun's efforts to use the American government against his rivals, and of his frustrations.

On November 18, 1918, shortly after the signing of the armistice, Sun telegraphed President Wilson to congratulate him and to explain why he, himself, had so strongly opposed China's entry into the war—his belief that such action would only aid militarism in China. He maintained that the results had vindicated his position and that the contest between the North and the South had been "a war between militarism and democracy pure and simple." He appealed to the American president to save democracy in China as he had saved it in Europe, by telling the Peking militarists that China's originally elected Parliament must be respected and restored. On the advice of Secretary of State Lansing, who had an unfavorable opinion of the southern leader, Sun received only an indirect reply.[70]

Dr. Sun also wrote the American minister in Peking, still Dr. Reinsch, on November 19,

> Through you alone will the President and the people of the United States see the true state of affairs in China. Your responsibility is indeed great. Whether Democracy or Militarism triumphs in China largely depends upon Your Excellency's moral support of our helpless people at this stage.[71]

After forming his second government in Canton and being inaugurated as its president on May 5, 1921, Dr. Sun wrote to President Warren G. Harding appealing for immediate recognition of the new government,

> . . . for the reason that we regard America as the Mother of Democracy and champion of liberalism and righteousness, whose disinterested

friendship and support of China in her hour of distress has been demonstrated to us more than once. . . . Whether democracy in China triumphs or fails much depends on the decision of America.

This letter was handed in to the State Department on June 16 by Ma Soo, who served as Dr. Sun's agent in Washington, but another letter to President Harding, sealed, was forwarded to the State Department by a young American vice-consul in Canton, Ernest B. Price. That letter was returned by the department unopened, to be delivered to the sender, and Mr. Price was given a reprimand for "permitting the Consulate General to make itself the vehicle of official communication for an organization in revolt against a Government with which the United States has friendly relations." Leo Bergholz, the consul general at Canton, found himself unable to return the letter, for somehow it had been opened. He recommended that since three months had transpired, the department "let the incident pass into oblivion to spare Dr. Sun, the one honest and patriotic administrator in China, the mortification of having his letter returned to him." The State Department did not consent! [72]

Once more Dr. Sun appealed to President Harding. [73] His private foreign secretary, Mr. Eugene Chen, wrote to the secretary of state, Charles E. Hughes, on September 20, 1921, requesting that an enclosed letter be handed to President Harding personally, and he added, "The contents of this communication are considered of so vital an importance to the American people that President Sun reserves the right of bringing the same, if necessary, to their notice."

In the signed, ten-page missive, written as plans for the Washington Conference were maturing, Sun Yat-sen argued vigorously for recognition of his government as a key to peace in the Orient. He warned that Japan planned to take over Manchuria, the historic route for the conquest of China, and predicted that the seizure of Manchuria would be completed by 1925, giving Japan control of China and rendering her invulnerable in a war with the United States. But America could prevent this by withdrawing recognition of the Peking government, "the tool of Japan," and by recognizing the legal Chinese government, his own. "The immediate recognition of my Government means (I) a *Chinese* China for which my

Government stands as a against a *Japanese* China for which Peking stands by virtue of its acts and deeds, and (II) a measure of high policy costing not one cent while calculated to save America billions of treasure and the lives of millions of her youth and manhood."

The government in Canton was now very strong, Dr. Sun stated, and was committed to democratic rule and extensive economic development; but without recognition it could not negotiate international loans even for purely industrial and public utility purposes. He asserted that the foreign powers could not base their policies toward China safely if they failed "to recognize the permanent character of this Administration . . . at Canton today or at Peking tomorrow." "As Peking has admittedly ceased to bear even the semblance of a national government, being illegal in its origin, pro-Japanese in policy and wholly incompetent and disintegrating in administration, I claim that the sole internal stabilizing force in China today is the Government whereof I am the Chief Executive." He urged the United States to make a broad act of statesmanship in its own interest by recognizing the government that would be China's stabilizing force. He warned President Harding against presumptuous advisers and recited a version of his own role in modern history to prove how correct he had been in the past. He begged the president to choose rightly.

It is not clear how this carefully prepared document was transmitted to the State Department, but it reached the office of the secretary of state on November 3 and the Division of Far Eastern Affairs the same day. There, according to the initialing, it was seen by E. T. Williams. Apparently it never went to President Harding but only to the files! This kind of treatment was part of a pattern.

In fact, files of the State Department covering the period of Dr. Sun's second administration in Canton show that those American officials concerned with China opposed him and frustrated his efforts to gain influence and support in the United States. We will cite here only a few examples.

The American minister in Peking, Dr. Charles R. Crane, sent a dispatch unflattering to Dr. Sun in February 1921, only part of which was seen fit to reprint in *Foreign Relations of the United*

States.[74] When, on Sun's instructions, Ma Soo telegraphed to congratulate Warren Harding on his inauguration as president and to express Sun's hope that "henceforth Republican America and Republican China may be drawn still more closely to each other," Dr. J. V. A. MacMurray, head of the Division of Far Eastern Affairs, instructed that the telegram not be acknowledged.[75] When Mr. Ma sought an interview with the president's secretary, Mr. Christian was advised in a letter drafted by Dr. MacMurray to "decline to receive this gentleman" since he professed to represent Dr. Sun Yat-sen, who claimed to be the president of China in opposition to the government in Peking which, alone, had received international recognition.[76] When Mr. Ma approached the State Department on behalf of the southern government, arguing that it should be represented at the forthcoming Washington Conference, memoranda by Nelson T. Johnson and E. T. Williams countered the argument that Sun's regime had a proper constitutional basis.[77]

Given this fixed position in the State Department—that Sun Yat-sen was a rebel against a friendly government—it is not surprising that he got little assistance in his efforts to carry out plans for the improvement of Canton with American business help. In fact, the State Department obstructed him.

On January 17, 1921, Sun Yat-sen signed a "Preliminary Agreement Between the Government of the Republic of China and George H. Shank of Chicago" for the financing of industrial enterprises in Kwangtung, which Mr. Shank agreed to try to undertake. There is an extensive file on this matter in the State Department archives.[78] By the terms of the agreement, the Republic of China was prepared to issue bonds to the amount of $100 million in gold in denominations of $1,000, bearing interest at 8 percent, the proceeds of which would be applied to industrial development "within the provinces of the Republic of China." George H. Shank undertook to have the bonds sold in the United States to underwriters at 95. As soon as he had sold enough to finance a definite enterprise, a permanent contract of operation would be executed. In consideration of his services, the government of the Republic of China agreed to pay him one-third of the net profits on all such industries for twenty years. Operational expenses would be paid out of the bond loan and from the proceeds of the enterprise, which Mr. Shank should operate for the full period of the contract. This preliminary agreement having been signed, Mr. Shank was to return to the United States immediately and, after consultations, cable his willingness to take up all or any part of the bond issue, upon which the government of the Republic of China would cause the bonds to be printed and executed in the required amount. If any of the bonds were used in payment for materials from the U.S. government, Mr. Shank would receive 25 percent of the purchase price. He agreed to provide expert engineers and a technical staff and to begin work within four months of the time the bonds were delivered to him, or the contract would expire.[79]

We cannot go into Mr. Shank's frustrated efforts to win the State Department's "permissive consent" and the U.S. Shipping Board's agreement to sell him excess wartime engineering and construction equipment with the Chinese bonds as collateral, nor his failure to interest the American group of the consortium in floating the bonds. From the record, however, it is clear that Dr. J. V. A. Mac-Murray and Mr. Frank P. Lockhart in the Far Eastern Division of the State Department discreetly but officially obstructed Mr. Shank's efforts. To them, the southern Chinese government was not recognized by the United States and had no authority to issue bonds, which in any case would be of very little value; and the State Department could give no support or protection to American projects carried out in the territory of a regime in rebellion against the Peking government, which the United States recognized.

General Yeh Chü's coup on June 16, 1922 brought the Shank venture to an end. So far as the record shows, during the seventeen months that Dr. Sun pursued this will-o'-the-wisp he did not receive any funds from the sale of bonds to the American public, nor was any constructive work carried out in Kwangtung by the Shank enterprise.[80]

Similar frustration befell a project to improve the Canton waterfront and to construct a bridge joining that city with Honam. The James A. Rabbitt Engineering Corporation of New York undertook to do this work and received a charter or franchise dated September 15, 1921, granted by the Canton Municipal Council. The charter was signed by Ku Ying-fen, on behalf of Governor Ch'en Chiung-ming, and by the mayor of Canton, Sun Fo. Again the work was to be financed by the sale of bonds—a mere 10 million—issued by the Canton municipality, and backed by a first mortgage on all the properties covered by the projects and the entire revenue from all municipal bunds, wharves, and warehouses on the city's waterfront. Mr. Rabbitt informed Consul General Bergholz that a New York financial house was prepared to float the bonds provided the State Department approved the charter and agreed to protect the interests of the corporation against any foreign government that might endeavor to have the charter annulled. He argued that because it had been granted by a city it did not need the approval of Peking, and explained that the local government would not receive or handle any part of the money, nor would the joint commission representing the municipality and the financiers be authorized to use any part of it for purposes not mentioned in the franchise.

Apparently the central flaw was the ratification of the franchise by the "Government of the Republic of China" and its president, Sun Yat-sen, signed and attested by his seals. Mr. Bergholz, in forwarding this information, quoted a passage of a letter from the secretary of state to the secretary of commerce of March 31, 1921, in connection with the Shank case, which stated, "This Government is therefore not in a position to approve or further any transactions of its citizens with the Canton Government as a political entity acting independently of the Central Government." [81]

The Department of State maintained this policy when a representative of an American financial firm called in November to inquire whether there was any official objection to financing the contract of the Rabbitt Engineering Company, involving an expenditure of $10 million. The assistant secretary, F. M. Dearing, replied (in a letter written by Frank P. Lockhart in the Far Eastern Division) that "The Department of State cannot concern itself in any way with a contract which does not have the approval of the recognized Government of China." [82] There followed much correspondence between the department, the American legation in Peking, and the Canton consulate, from which it is evident that the State Department would not support the project without the Peking government's approval, but that the Canton government would withdraw from the project if Peking became involved. It was one of those Chinese diplomatic impasses! After Dr. Sun was driven from Canton, Mr. Rabbitt journeyed to Peking, allegedly with the idea of bribing an official there to approve his project, but the legation told him it would not recognize the signature unless properly informed by the Ministry of Foreign Affairs that the act was official and according to Chinese law. Thus the matter lapsed and the contract expired.[83]

Dr. Sun kept hoping that the American government would recognize his southern regime. In an interview with Isaac F. Marcosson, a writer for the *Saturday Evening Post*, which he gave at Shao-kuan in mid-May 1922, while launching his ill-fated northern campaign into Kiangsi, the southern president denounced the Washington Conference, "which gave Japan freedom of action instead of limitation of power"; defended his alliance with Chang Tso-lin as a matter of expediency; argued that the government of Peking was kept alive only by recognition of the foreign powers; and asserted that his was the only legal government of China. After an enthusiastic discussion of his plan for the international development of China, he asserted, "If the United States would recognize me the stumbling bloc to unification would vanish." His parting words to Mr. Marcosson were, "Help us get recognition by the United States, for that will mean victory." [84] Within a month, however, the southern president had been driven into refuge by the coup d'etat of June 16.

Hopes for German Recognition and Aid

While trying to enlist American diplomatic and financial support, Dr. Sun was also exploring possibilities with Germany. The Peking government concluded a treaty of peace with Germany on May 20, 1921, and the two countries resumed diplomatic relations. Germany had lost its extraterritorial rights and other special privileges in China during the war, and it now recognized China's full sovereignty and equality. In September a German vice-consul, Herr Wagner, arrived in Canton to reopen the consulate. When he paid his courtesy call upon Sun Yat-sen, the southern president broached the subject of cooperation between his government and Germany. He told Mr. Wagner that he had already sent a representative to Germany, Gen. Chu Ho-chung, to study the situation and, he hoped, to work out plans for mutual cooperation. During September and October, the southern foreign minister and his deputies tried, through obstructive tactics with Wagner, to pressure Germany into recognizing their government. Since the southern republic had not ended its state of war with Germany, and professed not to recognize the Sino-German treaty concluded with Peking, Dr. Sun demanded that Germany start treaty negotiations. He held out the prospect that by becoming the first country to recognize his government, Germany would receive preferential treatment in China. He was disappointed, however, for the German government would not be drawn onto that path.[85]

The Chu Ho-chung mission to Germany was secret, but some details were disclosed with the discovery of correspondence in Liao Chung-k'ai's safe after the coup d'etat of June 16, 1922. On September 22, the *Hong Kong Telegraph* printed photographic reproductions of two communications to Sun Yat-sen from Chu Ho-chung in Berlin, dated January 1, 1922, and a secret letter from Sun to Liao Chung-k'ai in Canton, dated Kweilin, March 8.[86] The letters revealed that Dr. Sun had sent Mr. Chu to Berlin in July 1921, where he had negotiated with Admiral von Hintze, the former German minister to China. Mr. Chu reported that the admiral had already thought of concluding a "triplace" between China, Germany, and Russia, "a plan which would conform to your secret objects." The admiral, Mr. Chu said, was now giving all his time to the matter and in two months when all arrangements were made he would ask the German prime minister for authorization to leave for China. Mr. Chu then went into detail concerning the bureau "which we intend to establish"—presumably in Canton—of which he thought von Hintze would be director-general. This involved hiring experts and providing materials, but Mr. Chu did not mention what sorts of enterprises were to be undertaken. "Above all," he cautioned, "because of his great notoriety, Hintze must assume a false name, and his participation must be kept in the dark from the German public."

Apparently Dr. Sun expected results from the negotiations, for he instructed Liao Chung-k'ai to send $3,000 to Mr. Chu, and requested that "Brother Ya-po" stand by in Canton on a salary of $300 a month; when Admiral von Hintze reached Hong Kong, Ya-po was to meet and escort him to headquarters, that is, to Kweilin. Ts'ao Ya-po was Admiral von Hintze's contact man with the Kuomintang in 1917 when, allegedly, a large sum of German money was passed to Dr. Sun, and then when he visited Germany late in 1918 to discuss further help. Mr. Liao was instructed to burn the correspondence, but he put it in his safe where it was found after Dr. Sun was driven from Canton.

German records amplify this account. According to Chu Ho-chung's statement to the German Foreign Office, he had submitted proposals for an economic agreement to several German industrial concerns, such as Hugo Stinnes in Hamburg, and had also recruited some Germans to serve as advisers to the Canton government. He had also invited Adm. P. von Hintze, to visit Canton to discuss with Sun Yat-sen the principles of possible Sino-German-Russian cooperation. At the same time Canton was trying to persuade Germany to extend formal recognition to the government in South China.[87]

After the letters were published, the German government stated officially that it knew nothing of the negotiations or of the alleged mission of Admiral von Hintze to Russia, and the admiral declared he had not conducted any negotiations for such an alliance.[88] Dr. Sun issued a statement, published September 30, in which he did not repudiate the letters though he considered them poorly translated, but he denied the implication that the correspondence proved he had "been conspiring for an alliance between China, Germany and Russia, *based on Bolshevist ideals.*" As proof, he referred to his book, *The International Development of China,* and his repeated offers to American, British, and other quarters to supply foreign capital and technical assistance for China's industrial development. He stated that Germany, no longer enjoying extraterritorial rights, was not aggressive towards China, and expressed the belief that Germany and Russia would deal with China *"as an equal and full sovereign state."* Therefore, he favored a policy looking towards a closer rapprochement with these two powers.[89]

This can scarcely be the entire record of Dr. Sun's efforts to gain foreign support in these years. It does not adequately tap British, French, Japanese, and other foreign records. If read with sympathy these incidents reveal Dr. Sun's vision of himself—the true president of the real Republic of China, working for the cause of the Chinese nation. On each of the occasions when he established a government in Canton he sought for diplomatic recognition from the foreign powers, but none ever granted it. Seen in this perspective, Dr. Sun's eagerness for Russian assistance and his acceptance of Soviet aid in 1923 comes into clearer focus.

CHAPTER FIVE
Groping toward
Soviet Russia

It seems natural that, as a revolutionary and a socialist, Dr. Sun Yat-sen should interest himself in Soviet Russia. He had a lively interest in political developments in all major countries, and the Russian Revolution was an important foreign development of its day. Furthermore, in the years from 1920 to 1922 several emissaries from Russia courted him, implanting in his mind various possibilities for help. The available record of Sun's contacts with the center of revolution is, however, quite sporadic—a few telegrams or letters exchanged, a few conversations with persons who could describe conditions in Russia, and, shortly before he was driven from Canton in August 1922, a couple of more protracted talks with Comintern representatives. These scattered contacts, furthermore, were strands in the broader fabric of Sun's relations with the foreign world. They were not signal efforts by Dr. Sun to court the socialist motherland as some recent Russian writers have attempted to show, for he searched for support, as we have seen, in Japan, Germany, Great Britain, and the United States at the same time as he probed Soviet Russia.

Certain themes appear in the record of Dr. Sun's Russian contacts. He showed much sympathy for the Russian Revolution, and his words suggest that he made a psychological identification between the Russian Revolution and his own efforts, and between himself and Lenin. Indeed, he was encouraged in these sentiments by communications from Soviet officials. Another theme is his eagerness to be informed on the latest developments in the USSR. Sun came to believe there was much to be learned from its revolutionary experience, and he expressed frustration at the geographical isolation of his Canton regime from Soviet Russia and sought ways to improve communications. A third theme is the hope for direct military assistance. Despite the vast distances that separated Sun's base from Siberia and Soviet Central Asia, he sensed the possibility of capturing Peking by a joint effort of military forces supporting him and Chinese units in the Red Army. As the Soviet government sought official relations with the Chinese government in Peking another theme developed. Dr. Sun opposed the establishment of official relations until after he had succeeded in taking the northern capital and establishing a government there under himself. Twice while attempting to organize military campaigns northward towards the Yangtse, he expressed a realistic caution about an open relationship with Soviet Russia for fear of British obstruction of his rear or support for his enemies. Nevertheless, shortly before his downfall in Canton in June 1922, Dr. Sun's hopes for direct Soviet assistance quickened, and he began to understand the terms under which aid might be given.

These themes are derived from the following chronological account of Sun Yat-sen's Soviet contacts during the four years from mid-1918 to mid-1922, but the account is doubtless far from complete because much information which might be supplied from Soviet Russian and Chinese Nationalist archives has either been withheld or issued on a selective basis, apparently for political purposes. Yet there are younger scholars both in the Soviet Union and in Taiwan who are delving into the archives and bringing forth interesting and revealing materials.[1]

Early Feelers from Each Side

The first known initiative came from Dr. Sun. In the summer of 1918, after he left Canton in disillusionment with his own effort to set up a government, he telegraphed Lenin in the name of the South China Parliament and the Chinese Revolutionary Party, congratulating him on the relentless struggle of the revolutionary party in Russia and expressing the hope that the Soviet and Chinese parties might join forces in a common struggle. The fact that a socialist republic had existed in Russia for eight months gave hopes to the peoples of the East, he said, that a similar new system might be set up there.[2] Considering the chaotic state of Soviet Russia and his own powerlessness, Dr. Sun's expression of hope for a common struggle of the two revolutionary parties was premature but prescient.

Georgii Chicherin, the people's commissar for foreign affairs, sent a letter of reply on August 1, in which he quoted Dr. Sun as saying, in effect, that the Russian and Chinese revolutions had the same aims, to liberate the peoples and establish lasting peace, based upon the community of interests of the Russian and Chinese proletariats.[3] However, the Chinese revolutionary leader later asserted that he never received this letter.

Probably Sun Yat-sen was as indignant as most patriotic Chinese with the decision taken at Versailles late in April 1919 to award German rights in Shantung to Japan rather than return them to China, and presumably he shared the general excitement when news of the first Karakhan Manifesto of July 25, 1919 reached China in March of the following year. The deputy commissar for foreign affairs announced to the Chinese nation that his government was renouncing all special privileges acquired from China by the tsarist government. In the text which was publicized in China, the Manifesto stated that,

> The Soviet Government returns to the Chinese people without any kind of compensation the Chinese Eastern Railway, and all mining, gold, and forestry concessions which were seized from them by the government of the Tsars, that of Kerensky, and the outlaws Horvat, Semenov, Kolchak, the Russian generals, merchants, and capitalists.[4]

This evidence of Soviet revolutionary foreign policy—contrasting so markedly with the decisions of the Paris Peace Conference—induced a flood of laudatory editorials and pronouncements by Chinese organizations. The Shanghai *Min-kuo Jih-pao*, the news-paper of the Nationalist Party, carried two editorials contrasting the unequal treaties with this generous offer. Although the Soviet gov-ernment later denied it ever had made such a blanket promise, and in fact attempted vigorously to regain control of the Chinese Eastern Railway for Russia, the impression of this first statement and the generosity still offered in the more diplomatic second Karakhan Manifesto of September 1920, left a favorable image of Soviet inten-tions toward China among the patriots. Unfortunately, Dr. Sun's personal reaction is not documented.

After spending nearly a year in revolutionary Russia, a young American journalist named George Sokolsky became a member of Dr. Sun's entourage in Shanghai, probably early in 1919. He must have been a prime source of information for he had witnessed the Bolshevist seizure of power in November 1917 and, as editor of the English language *Russian Daily News* of Petrograd, had become ac-quainted with Lenin, Trotsky, and Bukharin. In March 1918, Mr. Sokolsky was evicted, put on a train for Harbin, and after a difficult six-week journey across war torn Russia, arrived in Tientsin. After a brief tour as a reporter on the *North China Star*, the twenty-five-year-old Sokolsky came to Shanghai and got a job on the English language *Shanghai Gazette*. He later recalled that he came every af-ternoon to discuss editorial policy with Dr. Sun and became quite close to him.[5] He also reported on his boss's Russian contacts to the American consulate.

Early in 1920, Mr. Sokolsky informed the American consul gen-eral, Edwin S. Cunningham, about Dr. Sun's meetings with two Russians, a General Potapoff, "who had been posing as a Bolshe-vik, but who had no credentials," and a Colonel Popoff, "who came with credentials from the Commander of Bolshevik troops of the Amur district." Dr. Sun discussed plans for cooperation between the Kuomintang and the Bolshevists with each of these officers, ac-cording to Mr. Sokolsky, who added that Colonel Popoff thought Dr. Sun's plans impossible of fulfillment since the Russians were tired of fighting and wanted peace. The colonel characterized Dr. Sun as "an old fashioned militarist who saw no way of saving his country except through arms." [6] Later it became a fixed Soviet Russian aim to convert Sun from his reliance on armies to achieve political goals.

The direction of Dr. Sun's thinking about Soviet aid early in 1920 is suggested by the report of one Liu Chang, known to the Russians as Federov, who called on him in Shanghai. Liu was a member of the Organization Bureau of Chinese Communists in Russia, apparently an émigré group, and he brought a plan the group had formulated for a march on Peking in conjunction with a drive from the South. Federov submitted a report on his trip which is preserved in the Russian archives. He described a plan for "an immediate unification of the revolutionary movement of Chinese forces who are situated in the territory of South China, Central Russia and the Far East." From the Russian side the drive would proceed through Sinkiang and Manchuria, and the leading center of the revolutionary march was to be in Blagoveshchensk on the Amur. It is not clear whether Dr. Sun learned of this plan before or after he talked with Colonel Popoff. Though nothing came of it, and two years later General V. K. Blücher put his veto on a similar scheme, the idea apparently was implanted in Dr. Sun's mind.[7] As late as the summer of 1923 when he sent Chiang Kai-shek to Russia, he apparently hoped for aid to "my forces in and about the regions lying to the Northwest of Peking and beyond." This plan is discussed below.

In June 1920 Dr. Sun was invited to visit Soviet Russia. Liu Tse-jung, the chairman of a Union of Chinese Workers there, sent him a telegram stating that Sun and Lenin had been chosen honorary chairmen of a congress of Chinese workers which was about to meet in Moscow. Liu invited him, on Lenin's behalf, to visit the USSR. A second telegram embodying a resolution passed by the congress, went to Dr. Sun on July 5, with the request that it be widely publicized. It combined revolutionary propaganda with an appeal for speedy Chinese recognition of Soviet Russia. Dr. Sun had it printed in the Shanghai *Min-kuo Jih-pao* and replied, with a bit of propaganda of his own, to the effect that China must first go through another revolution to sweep away the monarchist and military groups in power.[8] Perhaps it was about this time that Lenin sent a telegram in French via London inviting Dr. Sun to Russia "to see how they'd done," an offer which Sun had to turn down.[9]

Gregory Voitinsky, the twenty-seven-year-old agent of the Communist International, called upon Sun Yat-sen in Shanghai, probably during November 1920. Voitinsky had arrived there in May and encouraged the formation of a Communist group among Chinese intellectuals and a Socialist Youth Corps. The only available details on their meeting come from the account which Voitinsky wrote five years later, just after Dr. Sun's death. Mr. Voitinsky was taken to see Dr. Sun by "Comrade Ch.," probably Ch'en Tu-hsiu. He recalled that Dr. Sun received him in his book-lined study and immediately began to question him intensively about Soviet Russia and the revolution there. Both men were competent in English. Toward the end of the interview it became evident that the Chinese leader was greatly interested in how the struggle in South China, only recently freed of enemy troops in Canton, "could be joined with the struggle in faraway Russia." He complained that "the geographic position of Canton does not permit us to establish contact with Russia," but asked repeatedly whether Russia might establish a powerful radio station in Vladivostok or Manchuria for communications with Canton. The purpose, as Mr. Voitinsky recalled, was "so that the Canton government could keep informed about what the Russians were doing and draw on their experience." [10] Shortly after the meeting, Dr. Sun left for Canton, where he set up his second southern government.

During his twenty months in the South he had several scattered contacts with persons from Soviet Russia which began to open a vista of possible Soviet support for his revolutionary cause. Early in 1921, one Alexieff opened a branch of the Soviet news agency, "Rosta," in Canton. Here was a channel through which Dr. Sun could learn more about developments in Russia. He also met a member of the Yurin mission from the Far Eastern Republic, and there is a suggestion that he received material support from the republic.[11]

In June 1921, soon after becoming president of the South Chinese

Republic, Dr. Sun received a letter from the Soviet foreign minister, Georgii V. Chicherin, written the previous October. In the fragment of the letter available, three points stand out.[12] Mr. Chicherin complimented China for consciously beginning to struggle against "the world-suppressing yoke of Imperialism"; proposed that trade relations between China and Russia begin at once; and urged that China "enter resolutely the path of good friendship with us." Dr. Sun's reply, dated August 28, 1921 and transmitted via London, insisted that this was the first and only letter he had received from anyone in Soviet Russia and denied rumors in the capitalist press that he had received official offers from Moscow. After admitting his own blunder of 1912 in giving up the presidency to Yuan Shih-k'ai, and denouncing Chang Tso-lin as "the head of a gang of murderers" and a tool of Japan, Dr. Sun cautioned Moscow against attempting to open relations with Peking. (The southern president was soon to ally himself with Chang Tso-lin!) Dr. Sun argued that his was both the de jure and the de facto government of China, and lamented that because of Canton's geographical position it "is impossible for me at present to enter into effective trade relations with you." He told Moscow it "must wait until I put an end to the reactionaries who always appear in every country on the very next day after a successful revolution." In short, Soviet Russia should wait until Dr. Sun had taken Peking. In the meantime, however, he hoped for personal contact with his friends in Moscow, and expressed particular interest in "the organization of your soviets, your army, and educational system." Dr. Sun closed his letter to Mr. Chicherin with "best wishes to you, to my friend Lenin, and to all who have done so much for the cause of human freedom." [13]

Each side was feeling out the other.

Comintern Delegates Contact the Southern Revolutionary

Dr. Sun's meeting with the Comintern agent, J. F. M. Sneevliet, in Kweilin late in December 1921 was among the most significant of all his foreign contacts before the summer of 1922. Mr. Sneevliet, who used his Comintern name "Maring" as one of his aliases in

China, was a Dutch socialist with long experience in Indonesia guiding the forerunner of the Indonesian Communist Party. After his expulsion from the Dutch colony in December 1919, he returned to Holland and then went to Moscow where he attended the Second Congress of the Communist International in July and August 1920. He was secretary of the Commission on National and Colonial Questions in which Lenin set forth his famous theses that laid the theoretical basis for the cooperation by communist parties in colonial and semicolonial countries with bourgeois national liberation movements. Maring supported Lenin against M. N. Roy and other opponents of this strategy. He then became head of a new bureau of the Comintern in China, arriving in Shanghai in early June 1921.[14] He was about thirty-seven years old. After participating in the founding congress of the Chinese Communist Party in July, he remained in Shanghai until December, when he left for Hankow and Changsha, accompanied by Chang T'ai-lei, one of the earliest young Chinese Communists, who had just returned from Irkutsk and planning sessions for the Congress of the Toilers of the Far East. Chang served as Maring's interpreter. In Changsha they interviewed Governor Chao Heng-t'i, who gave them a small escort for the dangerous overland journey through southwestern Hunan to Kweilin, where they arrived on December 23.[15]

During Maring's stay at the military headquarters for the northward campaign which President Sun was hoping to launch into Hunan, the two men had several long talks. From Maring's report to the Comintern and his later reminiscences, it appears that Sun inquired extensively about the Russian Revolution, the development of Soviet republics, the New Economic Policy (inaugurated in about March 1921), the type of propaganda used in Soviet Russia, and the political training of the Red Army. Maring urged upon Dr. Sun the importance of winning the support of Chinese workers and peasants, which might be done with the aid of revolutionary students.[16] He may also have suggested some sort of alliance between Soviet Russia or the Comintern and the Kuomintang. This is a theme of some Chinese accounts of the meeting.[17] Summarizing these, Professor George Yu states that Maring made three basic proposals:

that the Kuomintang be reorganized to include peasants and workers; that a military academy be established to create an armed foundation for the revolution; and that the Kuomintang cooperate with the Chinese Communist Party.[18] Sun is said to have rejected the idea of an alliance with Soviet Russia for the present because his troops were soon to launch a campaign into the Yangtse valley. This was the British sphere of influence, and should the British learn of an alliance between Sun and Soviet Russia they would create dangerous obstacles to his campaign, Dr. Sun reportedly told Maring. Later, after he had taken Peking, they could plan for complete cooperation.[19]

After the meeting, Dr. Sun communicated to Liao Chung-k'ai his great satisfaction in hearing of the New Economic Policy in Russia, which he considered similar to his Plan for the Industrial Development of China.[20]

In a speech delivered shortly after Maring's departure, Dr. Sun described France and the United States as old-fashioned republics and Soviet Russia as the only republic of the new type. The Chinese, he said, should build the newest type of republic, one in which the nation is converted into a single family. (It was characteristic of Dr. Sun to hanker after the latest Western model in government or material things.) To build a new country required putting into effect his Three Principles of the People, said Dr. Sun, who gave a very simplified version of them: the first, *min-tsu*, meant equality among the races, none dominating over others; the second, *min-ch'uan*, meant equality among the people of a nation, with no minority oppressing the majority and everyone enjoying his natural rights; and the third, *min-sheng*, referred to economic equality and the absence of exploitation of the poor by the rich. Dr. Sun illustrated *min-sheng* by describing Hung Hsiu-ch'uan's effort at economic egalitarianism in the T'ai-p'ing Heavenly Kingdom and present-day communism in Soviet Russia. He urged his compatriots to carry out the Three Principles.[21]

Because the record is so scanty we do not know whether anything concrete emerged from these Sun-Maring talks. It seems very likely, however, that ideas for cooperation between the Kuomintang, the

Chinese Communist Party, and Soviet Russia, were explored and that each side emerged with a clearer understanding than before of the other's requirements.

On February 7, 1922 Mr. Chicherin replied to Dr. Sun's letter of the previous August. The Soviet foreign minister expressed his pleasure in becoming acquainted with the Kuomintang representative at the Congress of the Toilers of the Far East, which had just closed. He said the Kuomintang representative and he were in accord on all points concerning "the question of our future relations," but that these would be clarified by further talks and by "our friend who will visit you." (Possibly Chicherin was referring here to Maring, unaware that Maring and Sun had already met.) In answer to Dr. Sun's plea that Soviet Russia not enter diplomatic relations with the government in Peking until he himself had succeeded in capturing the city, Chicherin was frank. No matter what one thought of it, the Peking government was the official government of the Chinese state "and we are striving to establish normal relations with it." [22]

The Kuomintang representative at the Congress of the Toilers of the Far East to whom Mr. Chicherin referred was doubtless Chang Ch'iu-pai. Mr Chang was one of four delegates chosen for a call upon Lenin. He was either the only Kuomintang delegate or the chief one, but it is uncertain how he was appointed. [23] He returned from Moscow and went to Canton, where he saw Dr. Sun, providing Sun with yet another window on Soviet Russia. It seems unlikely, however, that he would have described conditions in the USSR favorably, for the Congress of the Toilers was held in the dead of winter, when the country was barely recovering from famine. Furthermore, the Kuomintang had been sternly criticized in the congress by Zinoviev and Safarov, and there also had been unpleasantnesses between young Chinese Communists and the Kuomintang representative. [24]

Dr. Sun had another opportunity to learn about Soviet Russia and to bid for Soviet assistance during a series of talks he had with Serge Dalin in Canton from late April to mid-June 1922. Dalin, then in his early twenties, had come to Canton to participate in the First Congress of the Chinese Socialist Youth Corps. According to his reminiscent account based, he says, upon his original notes, Dalin saw the southern president a number of times for talks of at least two hours each. Sun Wen asked about everything concerning Soviet Russia and told the young man about his own party, its program, and his future plans. The conflict between Ch'en Chiung-ming and Sun Yat-sen was growing tense, yet at the same time President Sun was preparing to launch his military campaign into Kiangsi from the northern borders of Kwangtung.[25]

When they discussed Sun's Three Principles of the People, Dalin pressed Dr. Sun to know why he did not carry through his agrarian program—mainly conceived as tax reforms—in the parts of Kwangtung already under his authority. Sun's answer was that his prime task was military: he first had to liberate the whole of China from the militarists; only then would it be possible to realize the agrarian program. According to Dalin, Dr. Sun well understood that the origins of the modern class struggle were in capitalism. He meant to prevent the emergence of capitalism in China by forbidding private ownership of large industrial enterprises, railways, and mines. This was why, he told young Dalin, he agitated for the socialization of land and capital. Dr. Sun asked many times whether it would be possible for Soviet Russia to help him realize his plan of railway building, especially to help build the line connecting Moscow with Canton via Soviet Central Asia! [26]

Dalin's relations with Dr. Sun were complicated by the fact that the young Russian was meeting regularly with the Canton Communists, who supported General Ch'en Chiung-ming in his controversy with Sun. Dr. Sun was aware of this and, naturally, suspicious of Dalin. In one conversation he twitted Dalin with the proposal that he try to organize a soviet government among the Miao people who, Sun said, were "more capable of grasping communism than the residents of our cities, where modern civilization made them opponents of communism." Sensing the meaning behind this probe, Dalin presented the Russian view that at the present stage of the Chinese revolution it was necessary to organize a united national-revolutionary front. He set forth the possible program for such a front. "These problems came to dominate our conversations." [27]

Dr. Sun broke the discussions to go to Shao-kuan on May 6 to launch his northern campaign into Kiangsi. This campaign was initially quite successful. He returned to Canton on June 1, and in his next talk with Dalin assured the young man that his forces would take Hankow within a month. When they did, he said, he would officially recognize Soviet Russia. He explained that he could not do so immediately because if he did the British, nearby in Hong Kong, would begin action against him. Furthermore, there were enemies of Soviet Russia even in his own government and Parliament, and Dr. Sun hinted that Wu T'ing-fang was one of them.[28] At their last meeting Dr. Sun repeated to Dalin his regret that Kwangtung was so far from Soviet Russia. He complained about the shortage of workers fully devoted to the revolution and his lack of administrators and technical specialists. He exclaimed how good it would be if he could have some cadres from Soviet Russia.[29]

The meetings were ended by General Yeh Chü's coup d'etat on the night of June 15–16, 1922, but Dalin received successive messages from Dr. Sun, transmitted through Eugene Chen, who secretly visited his leader at night on his gunboat refuge. The first message assured Dalin that Sun had taken all the documents pertaining to their negotiations with him. This seems a significant statement: it elevates the discussions to the level of written communications, possibly even draft agreements. Considering the haste of Dr. Sun's escape from the presidential residence, we infer that he took the documents because he regarded them as important or compromising, or perhaps both. In another message, Dr. Sun expressed his disillusion with nearly everything in which he had previously believed. He was now convinced, Eugene Chen told Dalin, that the only real and sincere friend of the Chinese Revolution was Soviet Russia. In his last message Sun said that because of his conviction of Soviet friendship he had decided to go to Shanghai to continue the struggle. If he failed, he would go to the USSR. Mr. Chen also handed Dalin a note scribbled by Dr. Sun upon a page torn from a copy book. This asked Dalin to tell Chicherin about the situation and to assure him that Sun would continue his struggle. He also conveyed his friendly feelings for Lenin.[30]

This account of Dr. Sun's negotiations comes exclusively from the

Russian side, from Serge Dalin's notes and memory, and without Chinese confirmation. However, many details of Dalin's account of other happenings in Canton are confirmable.

Dr. Sun held a discussion on foreign policy with some of his followers on his last day in Canton waters before boarding a British gunboat for Hong Kong and his voyage back to Shanghai. In this intimate talk he stressed the importance of good relations between China and Soviet Russia. He expressed his conviction that the USSR was not without a government—i.e., was not anarchistic—and that the government had given up communism and adopted state capitalism. Under the New Economic Policy it no longer prohibited private ownership. He argued that Chinese were fearful of Soviet Russia because there had been much false propaganda directed against its bolshevism by a country in mortal and unsettled conflict with the Soviet Union. He also singled out Germany as a power which could do much to help China's economic development and from which she need have no fear of incursion. He deplored the fact that China permitted itself to be led by other powers in its foreign relations. China should calculate for itself where the benefits lay, said Dr. Sun, who clearly conveyed his conviction that they lay in close relations with Germany and Soviet Russia.[31]

When Sun Yat-sen left Canton in defeat he certainly realized that Soviet Russia was moving towards a deeper involvement in China, seeking diplomatic relations with Peking, expanded trade, and a strong hand in the Chinese revolution. There was little he could do to forestall relations between Moscow and Peking but, on the basis of his talks with H. Maring (Sneevliet) in Kweilin and S. A. Dalin in Canton, he could still hope for Russian assistance to his revolutionary cause.

CHAPTER SIX
The Dynamic Setting for Alliance with Russia

Dr. Sun was not one to admit defeat readily. His return to Shanghai in August 1922 opened for him the vista of the presidency in Peking. This had been his aspiration even while president of the republic in the South. Could foreign influence be used to help him achieve this goal?

His hope to become president of a reunited nation is revealed in a number of incidents. When war between the Chihli and Fengtien cliques was imminent early in 1922, and while he was preparing for his northern campaign, the southern president negotiated with each side to form an alliance against the other.[1] His terms were that he should be given the presidency in a newly formed Peking government. The leader of the Fengtien clique, Chang Tso-lin, was agreeable, but Wu P'ei-fu, the main power in the Chihli organization, apparently was not. Dr. Sun then allied himself with General Chang and with a former enemy, Tuan Ch'i-jui.[2]

Wu P'ei-fu won that war in the North even before Sun Yat-sen could get his northern campaign into action. The leaders of the Chihli clique then called for the resignation of both presidents—Hsü Shih-ch'ang in Peking and Sun Yat-sen in Canton—the reconvention of the original Parliament which President Li Yuan-hung had been coerced to dissolve in 1917, and the reinstatement of President Li. In short, it was a call to recreate the constitutional situation of five years earlier, before Chang Hsün's attempt to restore the Manchu dynasty and before the creation of a separatist Canton regime. Hsü Shih-ch'ang did resign on June 2 but Sun Yat-sen did not.[3] Instead, on June 6 he issued two proclamations. One called for the disbandment of half the nation's troops, who should then be converted into laborers on public works; the Chihli clique must lead the way, upon which "this President" would order all sides to stop the war, restore peace, and jointly plan for reconstruction. The other proclamation called upon the foreign powers not to recognize Peking's new bogus president—that is, Li Yuan-hung—as previously they had interfered in Chinese domestic matters by recognizing the illegal president, Hsü Shih-ch'ang.[4]

After Yeh Chü's coup d'etat of June 16, the American consul in Canton, J. C. Huston, interviewed Dr. Sun in his refuge on a gunboat. Sun denied any agreement to resign if President Hsü retired, and asked, "Why should I resign when I am the constitutional President of China?" [5] Yet he was rather quick to seek a graceful way of leaving Canton. On June 23, Mr. Huston reported Dr. Sun's willingness to leave if granted a dignified exit; for this he sought the good offices of the Canton consular body. The American government would have no part in helping Dr. Sun to withdraw.[6]

On June 25, Dr. Sun sent Mr. Robert Norman, his American legal adviser, to call on Mr. Huston to discuss a guarantee of safe passage to Shanghai. The consular body thereupon drafted a letter to Yeh Chü asking him to guarantee Dr. Sun's safety, but Mr. Norman made it clear that Dr. Sun really wanted the consular body *to request his departure* in the interests of trade which, of course, was considerably disrupted by the fighting in and around Canton.[7] Thus, Dr. Sun wished to involve the foreign powers in his politics, for he hoped to campaign for the presidency in Peking. The British consul general learned through a Chinese source that Mr. Norman had carried to Yeh Chü the proposed terms of a settlement. As these directly concerned Dr. Sun, the city was to bid him farewell "in a manner consonant with the dignity of his high office" and when Parliament in Peking held its presidential elections, the Kwangtung government "agrees to pay Dr. Sun $1,000,000 (one million dollars) as 'expenses fee'." [8] General Yeh did not accept these terms, and the departure was finally arranged only after Dr. Sun had been deserted by the larger vessels of the fleet and had given up all hope of being rescued by his expeditionary forces. A British river gunboat took him to Hong Kong on August 9, after the American consulate had declined to grant him similar facilities. [9]

To Turn Defeat into Victory

Arriving in Shanghai on August 14, 1922, Dr. Sun burst into sustained political activity. It was one of the busiest periods of his life. At first his eyes were fixed on Peking and the presidency, though he was arranging at the same time for the recapture of Canton. Later, as his hopes for Peking dimmed, he devoted most of his efforts toward a triumphal return to the South. Against his broader pattern of negotiating, alliance building, fund raising, and army buying, we search out those elements that reveal his efforts to draw upon foreign help.

First, to restore his shattered prestige, he issued two manifestoes upon his arrival, one directed to the Chinese public and a somewhat different version addressed to the foreign powers. These explained and justified his efforts to uphold constitutionalism by creating a southern regime, blamed northern militarists for China's disunity, excoriated Ch'en Chiung-ming, and set forth ideas for national reunification, to which, fortunately, Sun Wen could now devote full attention. Parliament must reconvene and be supreme: he pledged to abide by its decisions concerning his own constitutional status. Militarism must be eliminated by the disbandment of armies and the conversion of troops into labor corps. The country's resources should be developed for the benefit of the entire people, as outlined in his *International Development of China*. And the political system should be reorganized to encourage self-government. He was ready to devote all his effort to complete the construction of the Chinese Republic. [10]

The American consul in Shanghai was amazed to find Dr. Sun the center of a web of negotiations. "Rejected in the South, he has become an even greater national character than when head of the Southern Republic. His support is sought by a large number of prominent and well known military and civil officials in the North."[11] Acting President Li had sent a delegate to invite Sun to Peking, and representatives of Ts'ao K'un and Wu P'ei-fu also called upon him. An Associated Press dispatch in the *New York Times* reported that "Sun has become the center and keystone of a series of factional conferences in Shanghai. His home has become a mecca for political leaders of all shades of opinion and the scene of numerous dinners at which politics is the main dish."[12] A few days later, Dr. Sun had become "a pivotal figure" in the reorganization of the Chinese government with the receipt of a telegram from Wu P'ei-fu endorsing his recent maifesto and pledging his support for Sun's peace plans. Li Yuan-hung's delegates had returned to Peking with a cordial letter from Sun expressing his willingness to advise and aid in the reconstruction and reunification of China. The *Chicago Tribune* service carried news that a hundred southern members of Parliament were departing for the capital where they might provide a quorum for the election of a president, and the *Times* (London) learned that Dr. Sun had advised its members to proceed to Peking to take up their parliamentary duties, since the war that had been dividing the North and the South for six years had now ended.[13] However, the financial situation in Peking was growing ever more critical.[14] These reports were basically correct,[15] and much of the information in them probably came from Dr. Sun, himself, or from his supporters, since he was using the press to advance his cause.

Dr. Sun hoped to be in Peking soon. Dr. Paul S. Reinsch, the former American minister to China who had recently returned in an advisory capacity, wrote to Sun on August 21, and Dr. Sun replied on August 26 reciprocating the hope that they might meet in Peking "at an early date. This is quite possible if success attends certain efforts which are about to be made to secure the 'financing' of the Government."[16] Dr. Sun sent along some notes he had used in outlining for the press his ideas for financing; these notes, unfortunately, seem not to have been preserved, but the essential scheme was probably the one he had just presented in interviews. He told J. B. Powell of the *Chicago Tribune* that political reunification of China would be impossible without a settlement of the financial crisis which faced the government in Peking. Though he urged all factional leaders to proceed there, he made his own departure contingent upon some reasonable expectation of solving the financial question. America and the other powers to whom China was indebted should extend the period for repayment, and he hoped that a consortium would make the necessary advances during a period of financial reorganization so that the government could carry on the ordinary work of administration. Dr. Sun advanced another idea for the longer future. The essential scheme was for the United States to take over that part of China's foreign debt owed to European creditors as part payment for European war debts to America. The United States then might give China easier terms for repayment, or it might partially remit the debt as it had done with its share of the Boxer indemnity.[17] Thus, Dr. Sun was trying to link China's financial problems to the European reparations question, which was then under discussion. Unfortunately, I have not been able to discover whether serious consideration was given to his plan. However, in calling for a consortium loan to solve China's immediate financial problem, he was in step with Wu P'ei-fu, the power behind the Peking government, who was trying to arrange such a loan.

Apparently Wu P'ei-fu seriously considered bringing Sun Yat-sen to Peking to help in national reunification. General Wu was an admired figure, who maintained a strongly nationalistic position. Cooperation between the two men might have served national unity well. Negotiations through intermediaries went on for several months.[18] General Wu may also have assisted Dr. Sun financially as, reputedly, did Chang Tso-lin.[19]

While feeling out the leaders of the Chihli clique and trying to muster support in the reconvened Parliament, Dr. Sun sent emissaries to negotiate with leaders of the Anhui clique, Generals Wang Yung-ch'uan in Fukien and Lu Yung-hsiang in Chekiang, and, of course, with the Fengtien military leaders.[20] He also began an extensive correspondence with commanders in the Southwest, trying to enlist them for a drive on Canton down the West River route.[21] Ultimately these negotiations resulted in his return to the South rather than in the overthrow of the Chihli clique in the North.

Russian Aid Becomes a Possibility

This was the bustling atmosphere in Dr. Sun's home and headquarters in the French Concession of Shanghai, when Maring saw him again, probably during the last week of August, 1922. The Comintern representative had returned to Holland and gone to Moscow, where he made his recommendations concerning policy in China to the Executive Committee of the Communist International.[22] He then traveled to China with Dr. Adolph Joffe, who was sent to negotiate a treaty with the Peking government. Dr. Joffe arrived in Peking on August 12, while Mr. Maring went on to Shanghai with the Executive Committee's instructions,[23] and possibly with a letter from Joffe to Sun Yat-sen.[24]

Several immediate developments forwarded Sun Yat-sen's Soviet orientation. He began to correspond with Dr. Joffe, admitted leaders of the Chinese Communist Party into the Kuomintang, and began a reorganization of his party in order to revitalize it. These are complex matters about which there is a large literature, and I shall simply summarize the development of a tripartite understanding. The Communist Party advocated a revolutionary alliance with the Kuomintang but Dr. Sun rejected that approach; he insisted that all Chinese revolutionaries join his organization. Maring, after his talks with Dr. Sun in Kweilin and the good impression he gained in Canton of the Kuomintang's revolutionary potential and influence with labor, had recommended to the leaders of the Chinese Communist Party and the Comintern that the Chinese Communists join and work within the Kuomintang. Now he served as broker, gaining the agreement of some leaders of both parties in Shanghai, though this may overstate the importance of a foreigner's role in a situation where virtually no contemporary evidence—as opposed to later reconstructions—is available.[25] Whatever the inner details of this arrangement may have been,[26] Dr. Sun inducted a few leaders of the Communist Party into the Kuomintang early in September, and he appointed the chief of them, Ch'en Tu-hsiu, as a member of a nine-man committee to plan for the reorganization of his party.[27]

During the period from August to December 1922, Joffe and Sun exchanged letters: four from Joffe and three from Sun are preserved in Soviet archives but have not been published so far as I can discover. Professor S. L. Tikhvinsky has summarized their contents, at least partially.[28] He reports that the Soviet diplomat informed Dr. Sun about the domestic and international situation of the Soviet Republic and of his difficulties in negotiations with the Peking authorities. Dr. Sun's letters, according to Professor Tikhvinsky, show that he did not clearly understand the aims of Soviet foreign policy, nor did he always comprehend how it differed from the policies of other foreign states. He expressed concern about rumors of alleged preparations to send Soviet troops into northern Manchuria, and about the intention of the Soviet government to enter into an alliance with the militarist group of Wu P'ei-fu in order to drive Chang Tso-lin from the northeastern provinces. Nor did he understand why the Soviet government did not wait to hold negotiations normalizing Soviet-Chinese relations until after he had resumed power in the South and organized a new campaign to take Peking. Professor Tikhvinsky, in a different summation, says that Dr. Sun described the current political situation in China, shared his political and military plans, and denounced the Peking government as "the agent of a certain foreign power." He quotes further:

> It is quite obvious that some powers do not want China to reach agreement with Russia before they have compelled Moscow to accept terms of economic capitulation. At the same time, they do not relish the prospect of an agreement of any kind between us which would free China from their clutches politically and economically.[29]

Unfortunately, the dates and full contents of these letters are not revealed, hence they cannot be placed exactly in historical context.

In sharing his political and military plans with Adolph Joffe, Dr. Sun may have been reaching for an alliance against Peking, though this can only be deduced. In his letter of August 30 to Chiang Kai-shek, after mentioning his exchange of letters with "their representative"—i.e., Joffe—he said he had asked him to send his military aide to Shanghai for detailed discussions of military matters. He thought the aide would arrive soon and so requested Chiang to come to Shanghai to make complete preparations.[30] Joffe's military aide was Col. A. I. Gekker,[31] but it is uncertain that he came at that time for discussions with Dr. Sun. Presumably the preparations that Chiang was instructed to make were for a mission to Moscow. This is deduced from the fact that another letter to Chiang,[32] dated November 21, says that Sun Wen believed his relations with Russia were developing favorably and that he had virtually succeeded in arranging for Chiang's plans regarding the West. This enigmatic statement seems, in the context, to refer to Chiang's hopes of going to Moscow; and indeed Dr. Sun did have in mind to send an emissary there, as he stated in a letter to Lenin dated December 6. He proposed "that in the near future a plenipotentiary representative be sent to Moscow for the purpose of a joint discussion with you and other comrades of a joint action in the legal interests of Russia and China." He also warned Lenin of the futility and danger of negotiating with the present government in Peking.[33]

One of Dr. Sun's letters to Joffe was brought to him by Chang Chi early in December. The purpose of the mission, according to recent Russian scholarship, was to arrange a meeting between Joffe and Sun in Shanghai.[34] Many years later Chang recalled that Dr. Joffe, who was ill with a nervous complaint, received him at his sickbed. After reading the letter, he asked Mr. Chang to explain to Dr. Sun that Soviet Russia's situation was very dangerous and it was essential to make connections. From this statement he deduced that Dr. Sun had protested about the Soviet effort to enter treaty relations with the Peking government.[35]

From this inadequate record of Dr. Sun's approaches to Soviet Russia we may at least conclude that he was irked at the Soviet decision to negotiate with Peking; what he longed for was Russian assistance so he might replace the Peking government with his own.

For his part, Dr. Joffe became disillusioned about his mission to Peking, and, through correspondence and discussions with emissaries, he had learned something about Sun Yat-sen and the Kuomintang. He sent an article to Moscow entitled "Chinese Puzzle" which was dated December 12 and appeared in *Izvestiia* on January 5, 1923. In it he praised the Kuomintang as the only Chinese party with a truly revolutionary platform, a party which served as the meeting point of nationalism and revolution. He expressed the hope that "Wu P'ei-fu, who is politically isolated, in spite of his dictatorial instincts, will perhaps extend his hand to Sun Yat-sen, who is no less isolated, and both of them would then march in the vanguard of the Chinese revolution." [36] This was not an isolated statement. A number of Russian, Comintern, and Chinese Communist leaders had been advocating a coalition between Sun and Wu.

The Presidium of the Communist International's Executive Committee, meeting in Moscow on January 10 to 12, 1923, heard a report by Maring, fresh back from China, and then adopted an important resolution "On the Expected Attitude of the Chinese Communist Party toward the Kuomintang." This resolution described Sun's party as the only serious national-revolutionary group in China, and instructed the members of the young Chinese Communist Party to remain and work within it. Yet the Chinese Communist Party, itself, was to be autonomous, with its own centralized apparatus, and should act independently in organizing the masses and creating trade unions. (The execution of this policy during the next several years caused endless friction within the Nationalist Party.) The resolution also instructed the Chinese Communist Party to influence the Kuomintang to unite its efforts with those of Soviet Russia in a struggle against European, American, and Japanese imperialism. [37] Thus, the Russian leadership began to edge closer to collaboration with Sun Yat-sen and the Kuomintang.

Dr. Sun's public views on foreign relations during this period in Shanghai were expressed on several occasions. When his correspondence from Chu Ho-chung and to Liao Chung-k'ai concerning negotiations with Admiral von Hintze was published in the *Hong Kong Telegraph,* as described above, he issued a statement on September 30, 1922. This made clear that China would welcome capital and technical assistance from America, Britain, and "other quarters," but emphasized that he favored closer relations with Germany and Russia, which no longer had special rights in China and would, he believed, deal with China as an equal and fully sovereign state. He tried to set at rest the accusation that he favored bolshevism by stating that China was unsuited for it; and he added that there was nothing to fear from Soviet Russia so long as it "continues true and loyal to its non-imperialistic policy." [38] On the same occasion his friend, George Bronson Rea, publisher of the *Far Eastern Review*, wrote an impassioned editorial, which must have reflected their personal discussions in Shanghai. Entitled "Sun Yat-sen. Will China Come under the Influence of Germany and Russia, or Drift into an Alliance with Japan?", the editorial argued that Sun had all along been a liberal democrat who had struggled to establish democratic government in China. Yet he had been consistently neglected and scorned by the Western powers and vilified by Western journalists in China. Mr. Rea pled for America, Great Britain, and Japan to support Sun Yat-sen so he would not be driven into the arms of Soviet Russia and Germany.[39]

The *Japan Advertiser* translated and published a sensational interview which Dr. Sun had with a Japanese reporter from the *Jiji* press in about mid-November. He stated that Japan should have joined Germany in the world war, as he said he had urged various Japanese statesmen to do. Had Japan declared war on the Allies, Dr. Sun believed that Annam and Singapore would have risen in arms against France and England; the Indians would have revolted against Great Britain; and the Turks and Chinese would have supported Japan in its efforts to unite Asia. Because Japan joined the Allies, the Pan-Asiatic plan had been delayed indefinitely. Because Japan had failed, China would be called upon to make Asia a place for Asiatics. But it was not too late, according to the Japanese newsman's account of the interview. Sun Wen is reported to have said, through the veil of double translation:

> If Japan really wishes to see Asia controlled by Asiatics she must promote relations with Russians. Russians are Asiatics. There runs in their veins

Asian blood. Japan must make common cause with the Russians in opposing the aggression of the Anglo-Saxons. In shaking hands with Russia
in the work of asserting the rights of the Asiatic alone lies the hope of
salvation from the catastrophe to which Japan and the other Oriental
countries are being forced by the insatiable ambition of Anglo-Saxons.[40]

The pro-Russian sentiment in this statement may have reflected
Dr. Sun's rising hopes for Soviet assistance. His urging that Japan
grasp the hand of the USSR came at a time when Dr. Joffe hoped to
reach a Russo-Japanese settlement.

As matters turned out, Dr. Sun was unable to effect arrangements
that would take him to power in Peking, but by mid-January his
vigorous efforts had achieved success in two other directions:
troops in his pay drove Ch'en Chiung-ming from Canton, opening
the way for his return to a regional base; and Soviet Russia's chief
emissary to China came to Shanghai to consult with him.

Sun and Joffe Talk Shop

On the evening of January 17, 1923, two days after Ch'en Chiung-
ming had withdrawn from Canton, Adolph Joffe arrived in Shanghai. He was not in good health, and his diplomatic mission in Peking had been a failure. Dr. Sun had just reorganized the Kuomintang and was in the process of selecting new department heads
and councilors. He planned to return to Canton very soon, and
must have been in a triumphant mood, but he still hoped for Soviet
aid.

The southern leader wasted no time. He entertained Dr. Joffe at a
dinner on January 18 and thereafter they conferred repeatedly at Dr.
Sun's residence in the French Concession. On January 23 Dr. Joffe
gave a dinner for the Kuomintang leader and a number of his closest associates at the Great Eastern Hotel.[41] Remarkably little is
known about the discussions between these two lifetime revolutionaries, one fifty-six and the other about forty, and both at ease
when speaking English. Nationalist Chinese sources are particularly
reticent concerning these meetings, but recent Soviet publications
have provided some information based upon archives.

One Soviet account says that Dr. Sun informed the emissary that he planned to reform his army and the Kuomintang and also intended to organize an expedition to take Peking. He explained that since his resources were insufficient, and because he lacked specialists capable of organizing an army that could accomplish this plan, he would like to receive financial and advisory aid from the USSR.[42] Another account published recently has Dr. Sun stating his intention to send a military mission to Soviet Russia to study the organization and functioning of party and government agencies, and to negotiate for assistance to the Chinese revolution; he also expressed the thought that it would be very useful if Moscow assigned him advisers on military and political problems. Dr. Joffe is said to have advised him on the reformation of his party and on the reorientation of the Three Principles of the People in order to make them specifically antiimperialist. Joffe promised to inform Moscow in detail about their negotiations, and they agreed to make public a joint declaration.[43]

British Intelligence was curious, naturally, about what was going on. A report on the meetings from information supplied by "two well placed agents in Shanghai," says that some military questions arose and as a result "Gen. Gecker," the military attache of Joffe's mission, was hastily called to Shanghai, arriving on January 25. His appointment as a military adviser to Dr. Sun may have been discussed, but apparently no decision was reached. He left for Peking on January 28.[44] The agents also reported that Joffe had offered Soviet moral and financial support to Sun and the Kuomintang on condition that they agree: (a) immediately and openly to recognise the Soviet as the legitimate government of Russia; (b) to conclude an open alliance with the Soviet government; and (c) to place no restrictions on Bolshevist propaganda in China. "As far as could be ascertained," the report hedged, Dr. Sun was agreeable to the first two conditions but not to the third, probably because of friction between the capitalist supporters of the Kuomintang and those members who advocated communism; he could do nothing without the support of the rich members of the party. The final agreement, "according to the information received," was that Sun and the Kuomintang would recognize the Soviet government once they had achieved supremacy in China; in return, the Soviet government would give moral and financial support to Sun Yat-sen.[45]

Until the minutes of the conversation or the agreement have been published from the archives of one or both parties, the real substance of bargaining cannot be much further ascertained. The Joint Statement issued in English on January 26, the day before each of the men was scheduled to sail, Joffe for Japan and Sun for Hong Kong, reveals only a bit more.[46]

Joint Statement

Dr. Sun Yat-sen and Mr. A. A. Joffe, Russian Envoy Extraordinary and Plenipotentiary to China, have authorized the publication of the following statement:

During his stay in Shanghai, Mr. Joffe has had several conversations with Dr. Sun Yat-sen, which have revealed the identity of their views on matters relating to Chinese-Russian relations, more especially on the following points:

(1) Dr. Sun Yat-sen holds that the Communistic order or even the Soviet system cannot actually be introduced into China, because there do not exist here the conditions for the successful establishment of either Communism or Sovietism. This view is entirely shared by Mr. Joffe, who is further of [the] opinion that China's paramount and most pressing problem is to achieve national unification and attain full national independence, and regarding this great task, he has assured Dr. Sun Yat-sen that China has the warmest sympathy of the Russian people and can count on the support of Russia.

(2) In order to clarify the situation, Dr. Sun Yat-sen has requested Mr. Joffe for a reaffirmation of the principles defined in the Russian Note to the Chinese Government, dated September 27, 1920. Mr. Joffe has accordingly re-affirmed these principles and categorically declared to Dr. Sun Yat-sen that the Russian Government is ready and willing to enter into negotiations with China on the basis of the renunciation by Russia of all the treaties and exactions which the Tsardom imposed on China, including the treaty or treaties and agreements relating to the Chinese Eastern Railway (the management of which being the subject of a specific reference in Article VII of the said Note).

(3) Recognizing that the Chinese Eastern Railway question in its entirety can be satisfactorily settled only at a competent Russo-Chinese Conference, Dr. Sun Yat-sen is of the opinion that the realities of the sit-

uation point to the desirability of a *modus vivendi* in the matter of the present management of the Railway. And he agrees with Mr. Joffe that the existing Railway management should be temporarily reorganized by agreement between the Chinese and the Russian Governments without prejudice, however, to the true rights and special interests of either party. At the same time Dr. Sun Yat-sen considers that General Chang Tso-lin should be consulted on the point.

(4) Mr. Joffe has categorically declared to Dr. Sun Yat-sen (who has fully satisfied himself as to this point) that it is not and has never been the intention or purpose of the present Russian Government to pursue an Imperialistic policy in Outer Mongolia or to cause it to secede from China. Dr. Sun Yat-sen, therefore, does not view an immediate evacuation of Russian troops from Outer Mongolia as either imperative or in the real interest of China, the more so on account of the inability of the present Government at Peking to prevent such an evacuation being followed by a recrudescence of intrigues and hostile activities by White Guardists against Russia and the creation of a graver situation than that which now exists.

Mr. Joffe has parted from Dr. Sun Yat-sen on the most cordial and friendly terms. On leaving Japan, to which he is now proceeding, he will again visit the South of China before finally returning to Peking.

Shanghai, January 26, 1923.

This document reveals nothing about agreements on Russian help for Dr. Sun, if such were reached, but it suggests some things about Sun Wen, himself. The Joint Statement is written to appear as though it were a state paper, a formal agreement between a Chinese official responsible for foreign policy and a foreign envoy. Articles two to four concerned issues of prime contention between China and Soviet Russia, the very ones which had prevented even the commencement of formal negotiations in Peking between Mr. Joffe and Dr. Wellington Koo. The southern leader is pictured as pressing the envoy for reassurances of Soviet Russia's intention to give up, as promised by Karakhan, the special privileges in China won by tsarist Russia. He is also depicted as being fully assured by Joffe's statements and as supporting the reasonableness of the Soviet position with regard to the Chinese Eastern Railway and Outer Mongolia. Thus, the joint statement was useful propaganda for both parties.

Why should Dr. Sun wish to record publicly in the first article his belief that communism and the Soviet system could not be introduced into China? Perhaps he took this opportunity to express his convictions: he had, indeed, made similar statements before. Perhaps he felt it prudent to make a disclaimer on the occasion of the first public hint of an understanding between himself and Soviet Russia. There were influential members of his party who opposed radical tendencies, and furthermore, the USSR's foreign revolutionary activities were regarded by all the great powers with deep suspicion. It is also possible that this article reflected bargaining in which Dr. Sun demanded that Russia support the Kuomintang and not the Chinese Communist Party, but this is speculation.

Mr. Joffe's position was quite flexible: he merely agreed with Dr. Sun's opinion,[47] capped it with a plug for the national liberation goals of unity and independence, and promised Russian support to the vague entity, "China." His position was consistent with Comintern policy toward national revolution in colonial and semicolonial countries and it echoed the "General Theses on the Oriental Question" of the recent Fourth Congress of the Comintern.[48] Any discerning reader would guess that the China to receive Russian support would not be the China of the government in Peking!

The document had domestic political ramifications. Dr. Sun inserted into the text his opinion that Chang Tso-lin should be consulted on any new arrangement for operation of the Chinese Eastern Railway. General Chang and Dr. Sun were quasi-allies against the Peking government, and the railway ran through Chang's sphere. The insertion signaled that Dr. Sun had not forgotten his ally's interests. Shortly after the statement appeared, Sun wrote a private letter to Chang Tso-lin giving an account of his discussions with Joffe. This letter has not been published, but General Chang's reply, dated February 7, 1923, is preserved in the Kuomintang archives. The general expressed deep admiration for Sun Wen's foresight and calculation; the fundamental issues had been covered and the situation was under control. Sun had taken steps to guard against Wu P'ei-fu's scheme to drag Soviet Russia into aggression against the eastern provinces, thus relieving them of future worry and securing the nation's boundaries.[49]

Eugene Chen, who participated in the discussions, published an editorial on January 27 in a Shanghai newspaper in which he asserted that the outcome of the Sun-Joffe conversations would depend upon the attitude of the great powers. "Continued hostility to Russia, and what appears like hostility to Sun Yat-sen on the part of certain great powers might force an alliance between Russia and China. . . . It is clear that the conversations necessarily alter the international rating of Sun Yat-sen, and he emerges as a world force. The support of Russia seems pledged to him." [50]

Apparently Dr. Sun had some reason for optimism as a result of the talks, for he sent one of his closest associates, the American-born and Japanese-educated Liao Chung-k'ai, to Japan to confer further with Dr. Joffe. Chinese sources are most unrevealing about the supposedly month-long talks between the two. If Liao wrote to Sun, the letters remain unpublished, and it is unknown whether any further agreements were reached. Nevertheless, Liao did become a bulwark of Dr. Sun's later orientation toward Soviet Russia.[51] Shortly after the talks in Japan, possibly influenced by Mr. Joffe's advice, the leading organs of the Russian Communist Party and the Soviet government decided to render assistance to Sun Yat-sen and send him advisers. Even more specifically, we are told by A. I. Kartunova that in March 1923, the Soviet government decided to render financial aid amounting to about Mex $2 million to the revolutionary government of Sun Yat-sen.[52] It took some time, however, before the aid could become effective.

Exploring Other Options

While the talks between Dr. Sun and Mr. Joffe were under way in January, the southern revolutionary leader had his eyes fixed on Canton. He was booked to sail for the South on January 27, and he planned to reestablish a government there. He had appointed officials who took up their posts after Ch'en Chiung-ming had been driven from Canton. His larger hopes were revealed in a circular telegram dated January 26 (the same day as he issued the Joint Statement with Mr. Joffe) and addressed to President Li Yuan-hung and the most important regional military leaders. There he declared that with the removal of Ch'en Chiung-ming the way was open for the reunification of China by peaceful means; reunification was now up to the four great parties, Chihli, Fengtien, Anhui, and the southwest provinces—that is, his own claimed sphere. His intention was to work for peaceful reunification, and he proposed that all parties involved agree to disband half their troops. If this plan were accepted, he suggested that the leaders then join in inviting a friendly foreign power to assist in effecting troop disbandment and in raising a reconstruction loan to be used under the supervision of a foreign expert and five Chinese delegates representing the interests of agriculture, labor, commerce, education, and the press.[53] It was an eloquent plea, expressing Dr. Sun's deep concern for the state of his country, torn by civil wars and dominated by militarists. Several more times he was to propose this idea of voluntary troop disbandment and the assistance of foreign powers to set China's house in order.

Whatever understandings Dr. Sun may have reached with Soviet Russia's envoy, he attempted simultaneously to improve relations with Great Britain and more especially with Hong Kong. As the following narrative indicates, he was continually eager for foreign assistance from any and all quarters.

He sent Eugene Chen to call upon Sir Sidney Barton, the British consul general in Shanghai, first on January 11 and again on January 19. Mr. Chen told Sir Sidney that his chief was anxious to adopt a course that would win British sympathy, and that he would give proof of his appreciation of improvement in relations; but Chen coupled this plea with intimations that lack of sympathy from Great Britain and other powers "with whom Dr. Sun had really more in common," might lead to a rapprochement with Japan, Russia, and Germany. In his second call Mr. Chen urged Sir Sidney to make Dr. Sun's present attitude known to the proper British authorities, and hinted that an interview between Sun and the governor of Hong Kong would be desirable. The British minister, Sir Ronald Macleay, was then in Hong Kong and was sent a copy of the dispatch on this matter; this probably laid the basis for the surprisingly friendly reception the Chinese revolutionary leader received when he stopped in Hong Kong in February.

When the British minister reached Shanghai on February 1 on his way to Peking, Dr. Sun sent Eugene Chen and C. C. Wu to call upon him. The southern revolutionary had been forced to remain in Shanghai because of Gen. Shen Hung-ying's coup against his Cantonese military supporters and civil appointees, but Sun still expected to return to Canton. Minister Macleay assured Dr. Sun's emissaries that Great Britain had no personal animosity toward Sun whatsoever. From his discussion with Messrs. Chen and Wu, Macleay gained the impression that Dr. Sun did not plan to set up another independent republic in the South, but Macleay still sent along a message to Sun that he could scarcely expect British sympathy and support if he did so, since it was the fixed policy of the British government to promote the cause of a stable and unified China. In his confidential report to the Foreign Office Macleay advised that the government be friendly toward Dr. Sun so long as he refrained from stirring up trouble among laborers in Hong Kong, because "there is no doubt about his remarkable influence in South China and amongst Chinese residents in the Straits and Malay Islands and in America, which must always be a factor to be reckoned with." [54]

On February 15, 1923 Dr. Sun and a party of six sailed for Hong Kong on the S.S. *President Jefferson,* and by coincidence Mr. Nelson T. Johnson of the Far Eastern Division of the State Department was a fellow passenger. Eugene Chen had a long talk with Mr. Johnson on the first morning out, presenting Dr. Sun's scheme for foreign intervention to help China put its house in order. "He now argues (with much apology for his apparent unfaithfulness to the cause of the Chinese people) that the only way in which reunification can be brought about is for the foreign powers to intervene effectually and force the suspicious and contending leaders to unite," Mr. Johnson wrote to his colleague in Washington, Dr. John Van Antwerp Mac-Murray, chief of the Far Eastern Division. According to Dr. Sun the powers exercised control over the revenues of the country and thus had already intervened in China's internal affairs by payments of surplus revenues to Peking. They should now intervene in a still more effective manner by cutting off those payments until a government that enjoyed the confidence of the whole country had been organized. If this were the announced policy of the powers, the effect would be immediate and reunification an accomplished fact. "It was Dr. Sun's plan," according to Eugene Chen, "to ask America to step in and send to China a strong man, Mr. Hughes for example." Dr. Sun believed that as a neutral person Hughes could bring together the mutually suspicious Chinese leaders and make it possible for them to unite in carrying out some scheme of government.[55] (In January 1924 this plan for American intervention to help China solve its internal problems was proposed again, by Dr. Sun himself, to the American minister, Dr. Jacob Gould Schurman.)

Dr. Sun received a handsome reception in Hong Kong. He was a guest in the home of a wealthy Chinese businessman, and many notables called upon him. The governor, Sir Edward Reginald Stubbs, entertained him at lunch the day after his arrival, and he had tea in the afternoon with Sir Robert and Lady Hotung. Sir Robert was a British subject of Chinese nationality, a noted civic leader and one of the colony's wealthiest citizens, and Dr. Sun outlined to him his plans for reorganizing the Canton government and told of his need for funds to disband half the soldiers in the province.[56]

Governor Stubbs reported to his superiors that Dr. Sun "seems to have undergone a very great change. He appears to be anxious to be on good terms with us." Actually, the governor himself had undergone a great change since early January when he had proposed to advance government funds to Ch'en Chiung-ming in order to prevent Dr. Sun's return to Canton. Then Sir Edward had regarded him as "a danger to civilization." Now, in February, he said, "I am satisfied that things will go more smoothly than in the past if we endeavour to work with him in a friendly spirit."[57] Dr. Sun concurred in the governor's view that Hong Kong and Canton should cooperate, and there were similar exchanges between members of Dr. Sun's entourage and the governor's staff. In a private talk with G. R. Hallifax, secretary for Chinese affairs, Eugene Chen revealed that Dr. Sun did not plan to resume his presidency and was eager to arrange foreign loans and wanted foreign assistance and advice in the army, in finance, "in fact, everywhere."[58]

On February 20, the day before his departure for Canton, Dr. Sun visited the University of Hong Kong, had tea with the manager of the Hong Kong & Shanghai Banking Corporation, and in the evening addressed a group of Chinese labor and commercial leaders, appealing for support. At the university, enthusiastic students carried him on their shoulders to the lecture hall where he gave a much publicized address on the virtues of Hong Kong's orderly and efficient administration. The theme of his talk was that as a student in Hong Kong he had developed his revolutionary ideas upon noting the difference between its good government and the corrupt administration of his native Hsiang-shan county only fifty miles away. "Student friends!" he concluded, "You who are receiving your education in this British colony as I did at the same school, we must take England as our model and must extend England's example of good government to the whole of China." [59]

The Hong Kong interlude must have seemed a great success. The cordial reception afforded by the government and the city's civic leaders appeared to open the way for the material support and political accommodations that Dr. Sun would need in trying to reestablish his authority in Kwangtung. Clearly Sun was attempting to keep his British options open, even as the colonial government was seeking a fresh start with him. He displayed his usual buoyant self-confidence and was as replete with plans as ever. Now in his fifty-seventh year, the optimistic, idealistic, and resourceful leaders sailed on the morning boat of February 21 for Canton, a city he had left as a fugitive on a British river gunboat on the previous August 9. He had just probed for Russian, American, and British support.

Back in Canton, and probably unsure whether Soviet Russia would really assist him, Dr. Sun faced his familiar problem of trying to organize a government without adequate money and with no real command over military forces. His image of the foreign powers and of his own position is conveyed in an interview with an old American acquaintance, Fletcher S. Brockman, sometime in March.[60] The following passages give Dr. Sun's main themes:

> The real trouble is that China is not an independent country. . . . She is really in a worse condition than Korea or Formosa. They have one master: we have many. . . .
> If the foreign countries will let us alone, China will have her affairs in

shape within six months. The foreign powers have pursued the disastrous policy of endowing a corrupt and inefficient clique in Peking and insisting upon the fiction of calling it a Government. . . . America in particular must accept responsibility for our present debacle.

It was America that led us into the European war. Up to that time we had one responsible Government. It was the act of the Tuan Chi-jui Government in getting us into the war that created the first division between North and South.

The Peking Government could not stand for twenty-four hours without the backing it receives from foreign Governments. . . . Its only revenue comes from the maritime customs and the salt gabelle. . . . The people could easily overthrow the whole military system if not for this backing of foreign countries. . . .

The foreign countries have blindly and persistently declined to recognize the Southern Government, which is really the *de jure* Government, although Peking is the *de facto* Government. Six provinces are already loyal to the South. The revenues from the maritime customs and part of that from the salt gabelle, all of which is collected by the power of foreign countries, is not used for the good of the people from whom it is collected. It goes to Peking, and a considerable proportion of it is used to fight us. The foreign powers are helping the autocratic and bureaucratic Peking Government by taking these taxes out of South China and turning them over to Peking.

Dr. Sun then made a startling proposal in the light of his later anti-imperialistic utterances, but one not out of keeping with his hopes in 1923 that the Western powers would rescue China. Mr. Brockman reported him as saying,

. . . We do not ask these nations to collect the taxes from our people and turn them back to us. We ask that they shall collect the taxes, North and South, and hold them until we Chinese ourselves can straighten out our internal affairs and establish one government that will truly represent the Chinese people.

Mr. Brockman queried Dr. Sun about his combining forces with Chang Tso-lin, "a known autocrat," and Sun defended the action as being similar to America's combining with Japan in war against Germany.

We have lost hope of help from America, England, France or any other of the great powers. . . . The only country that shows any signs of helping us in the South is the Soviet Government of Russia.

[145]

Asked, "Do you call the Soviets democratic?", Sun replied without hesitation, "I do not care what they are if they are willing to back me against Peking."

Despite his profession of having given up hope of help from the powers, Dr. Sun was looking toward England and probably toward Japan for aid at this very time. On March 7, in the company of his American legal adviser, Mr. Robert Norman, he called upon the British consul general. The ensuing conversation concerned such practical projects as improving Whampoa port, extending the Canton-Hankow Railway and linking it up with the Kowloon-Canton line, and also the possibility of British officials assisting in the financial reorganization of the Canton government.[61] Mr. Liang Shih-yi, the very influential Cantonese financier and former Peking official under Chang Tso-lin's patronage, had an interview in Hong Kong with Mr. S. F. Mayers of the British and Chinese Corporation, a few days after Mayers had talked railways with Dr. Sun. Liang proposed a consortium loan to Sun's government, guaranteed by the salt revenues which Canton had retained and which brought in $5 million to $6 million annually. Mr. Liang thought a loan of $100 million was about right! Three-quarters of this money would be for constructive purposes, specified and supervised by the powers, but the rest must be "free money," which was absolutely essential for any Chinese government, Liang said.[62] Dr. Sun followed this proposal by a speech on March 18 in which he waved an olive branch toward Hong Kong, talking about railway building and opportunities for foreign capital. He let it be known that he was negotiating for a loan between Canton and the government of Hong Kong, in which Peking was not to interfere.[63] On April 1, Eugene Chen, who often served as Dr. Sun's spokesman to the Western press, issued a "Declaration of Future Foreign Policy." It was a request for Western aid, outlining plans for fiscal reforms and for construction. Foreign experts would be engaged for the modernization of Canton. All nations were to be welcomed in financing, but America and Great Britain were preferred.[64].

In May 1923, George Bronson Rea published "Dr. Sun's Message to the World" in the *Far Eastern Review*. This brief statement laid the blame for the lawless and chaotic condition of China to the support and encouragement which "the liberal powers" had extended to "the hirelings of the military oligarchy posing as the government at Peking." The statement was another plea to the powers to withhold payment of revenues collected by the Maritime Customs Service and Salt Gabelle; Sun stated that the funds should be held in trust for a future unified government. If the great powers which had fought to make the West safe for democracy could not openly support the liberal movement in China—by which Sun meant his government in the South—they should at least "stand aside in strict neutrality by withholding financial support to Peking while the Chinese settle their own problems in their own way." [65] Nothing came of this plea, and the new foreign minister in the southern government, Dr. C. C. Wu, soon demanded a share of the customs revenue for its treasury.

Such bids for foreign financing for the modernization of Canton got nowhere. However, the idea of British officers assisting Dr. Sun in reorganizing his government's finances was kept alive briefly. The governor of Hong Kong reported that Dr. Sun wished to enlist the services of British experts, and wondered if the British government would approve "any of my officers being lent to him." Foreign Office officials were opposed, but wired to the British minister in Peking for his opinion. Sir Ronald Macleay replied near the end of May that the consul general in Canton was well disposed to the idea, should fighting cease and conditions return to normal, but Macleay argued that Britain should not assist Sun in that way because such action would be regarded both in China and in the United States as intervention on Sun's side. "He has probably reached some understanding with Bolsheviks and has coquetted with communism and Indian sedition. In spite of friendly remonstrances he has infringed reorganization loan agreement by tampering with British salt administration." The Foreign Office then informed the Colonial Office that they concurred: it was best to continue an attitude of friendly neutrality, but not to comply with Sun's request.[66]

The Alliance Draws Closer

While Britain was maintaining "friendly neutrality," Soviet Russia was moving toward active assistance after the decision in March 1923 to devote some $2 million to the revolutionary government. On May 1, the Soviet government sent a telegram to Sun Yat-sen expressing "readiness to render necessary assistance to China." [67] If Sun received the telegram, he must have been encouraged. Toward the end of May, Col. A. I. Gekker was back in Moscow selecting the first team of military officers to go to China. Five of them arrived in Peking on June 21.[68]

In Canton, Sun Yat-sen faced great difficulties. Gen. Shen Hung-ying, with the backing of Wu P'ei-fu, had tried to seize control of the city in April. Sun's battle against Shen and his Kwangsi mercenaries lasted a month. By mid-May the Kwangsi forces had been driven back up the North River and West River routes, but immediately thereafter Canton was threatened by Ch'en Chiung-ming's armies in the East. During June, Dr. Sun repeatedly went to key points on the eastern front to direct the fighting.

During this critical period Maring, the Comintern representative, was in Canton after his winter visit to Moscow.[69] As he saw it, his mission was to guide the reorganization of the Kuomintang, and he later reminisced that he saw Dr. Sun three or four times a week.[70] In his reports to his superiors in the Comintern, Maring stated that he and Ch'en Tu-hsiu had worked out plans for the Kuomintang reorganization, had discussed them with Dr. Sun, and that the latter had accepted them.[71] Kuomintang historians are silent on this point. In Maring's scheme, propaganda was to occupy the central place in the reorganized Kuomintang, though he wrote of his pessimism about the plan's realization so long as Sun Yat-sen concentrated all his strength on the conquest of Kwangtung.[72] In view of Sun's military difficulties, it seems likely the generalissimo would have been eager to know when the Soviet aid would be forthcoming.

The Comintern representative also attended the Third Congress of the Chinese Communist Party, convened in Canton during mid-

June.[73] Communist influence in the North, especially with labor, had been shattered by Wu P'ei-fu's suppression of the railway unions in February 1923, and the party was in considerable disarray. By now a good many Communists had joined the Kuomintang, as the new strategy prescribed. After bitter debate and under pressure from Maring, the Third Congress adopted resolutions which became part of the iron framework for the party's operations. The congress resolved that the Chinese Communist Party should center its activities on the development of the national revolutionary movement; recognize the Kuomintang as the leader and nucleus around which this movement was to be organized; have its members join the Kuomintang; positively help in the Kuomintang's formal organization as the political party of the masses; help strengthen its influence among the workers and especially among the peasants; and take the initiative to transform the Kuomintang into a genuine political party.[74]

Crucial issues for the Communists, however, concerned the true nature of the cooperation between the two parties: which one actually would direct the national revolution—a revitalized Kuomintang or the Communist Party working within it? A more specific issue was how diligently the Communists should assist the Kuomintang in expanding its base of support. And a third issue was the extent to which Communists should subordinate themselves to the Nationalist Party and concentrate their efforts on its work.[75]

A resolution devoted specifically to "The National Movement and the Kuomintang Problem" illustrates some of the objectives of the infiltration strategy.[76] "We join the Kuomintang but preserve our own organization, and we should especially endeavor to attract genuinely class-conscious revolutionaries from among all labor organizations and from the left wing of the Kuomintang, gradually enlarge our organization and tighten our discipline, in order to lay the foundation of a powerful mass Communist Party." Communists within the Kuomintang were to steer it away from compromise with any imperialist or militarist, strive to bring it together with Soviet Russia, and "regularly admonish the Kuomintang not to be duped by the avaricious and crafty Powers." In addition, the Communists should prevent the Kuomintang from concentrating all its strength on military activity to the neglect of propaganda aimed toward the masses, and should prevent any compromising tendency in the political movement or reformist tendency in the labor movement. Within the Kuomintang "all speech and action of members of the Communist Party and of the Youth Corps should be in unison."

Clearly the leaders of the Chinese Communist Party, tutored by the Comintern and urged on by Maring, hoped to refashion the Kuomintang and reorient its strategy. They also intended to keep their own organizations under separate control. And they expected to enlarge these organizations by recruiting from the Kuomintang and from the labor unions under its influence.

The question we cannot answer is how well Sun Yat-sen and his close advisers understood these purposes in mid-1923. Long afterwards, Ch'en Tu-hsiu, in describing this period and the resistance of the Nationalist Party to reformation by the "International's delegate," wrote to his former colleagues,

> Many times Sun Yat-sen said to the delegates of the International: "Since the Chinese Communists have joined the Kuomintang, they should obey the discipline of the Kuomintang and should not openly criticize it. If the Communists do not obey the Kuomintang, I shall expel them from it. If Soviet Russia stands on the side of the Chinese Communists, I shall oppose Soviet Russia." Consequently, Maring, the Comintern's delegate, returned to Moscow despondently. Because Borodin, who came after Maring, carried in his briefcase a large sum of material aid for the Kuomintang, only then, in 1924, did the Kuomintang launch the policy of reorganization and of an alliance with Soviet Russia.[77]

During the summer of 1923 the Soviet leadership selected two new representatives to guide the double-barreled effort to strengthen Soviet Russia's position in China—Lev M. Karakhan, deputy people's commissar for foreign affairs, to conduct diplomacy in the North, and Michael M. Borodin (original surname Gruzenberg) to guide the national revolution in the South.[78] At about the same time, Sun Yat-sen was at last able to send a delegation, headed by Chiang Kai-shek, to Soviet Russia to negotiate for military aid.

[150]

Chiang Kai-shek, then thirty-five years old, of abrasive personality, ambitious, and fitting very uneasily into the southern leader's entourage, had been briefly the chief of staff of the generalissimo's field headquarters. On July 14 he departed Canton in disgust for his home in Chekiang, leaving behind a critical letter in which he intimated his desire to be assigned to a mission of investigation to Soviet Russia.[79] Thereupon Dr. Sun directed him to meet with Maring, by then in Shanghai, and several of the most important Nationalist leaders, "to plan for and to organize 'The Delegation Representing Dr. Sun Yat-sen to Visit Russia, Reciprocating an Ambassadorial Visit' and to investigate government and party affairs".[80] The instruction to see Maring suggests that Dr. Sun had discussed the matter with the Comintern delegate in Canton, and we speculate that Maring had indicated that a delegation would be welcome. The mission left for Russia on August 16; besides its leader the mission included Shen T'ing-i and Chang T'ai-lei, two young Communists who were also members of the Kuomintang, as well as Wang Teng-yün, about whom little is recorded.[81]

The mission arrived in Moscow on September 2, the very day that Ambassador Karakhan arrived in Peking. Dr. Sun was soon in correspondence with Mr. Karakhan, and in a letter of September 17, he told him the purpose of the mission:

> What follows is rigidly *confidential*. Some weeks ago I sent identical letters to Comrade Lenin, Tchitcherin, and Trotsky introducing General Chiang Kai-shek, who is my chief of staff and confidential agent. I have dispatched him to Moscow to discuss ways and means whereby our friends there can assist me in my work in this country. In particular, General Chiang is to take up with your government and military experts a proposal for military action by my forces in and about the regions lying to the Northwest of Peking and beyond. General Chiang is fully empowered to act in my behalf.[82]

What was this enigmatic, not to say quixotic, proposal for military action by Sun's forces *northwest of Peking and beyond?* And how did Soviet Russia fit in? The generalissimo was simply reviving a long-cherished dream that he could take Peking with the help of Soviet arms and men—what we may call "The Northwest Plan".

As described earlier, in 1918 Dr. Sun had dreamed of Germany equipping and leading Chinese troops on the Sino-Russian borderlands in an invasion of Peking. In 1920 Sun had discussed with Liu Chang ("Federov") the idea of a joint drive on Peking by revolutionary forces in the South coordinated with Chinese units in the Red Army marching via Manchuria and Sinkiang. At the end of December 1922, Sun wrote to Adolf Joffe in Peking about a scheme to lead an army of 100,000 troops from Szechwan to Outer Mongolia for a drive on the Chinese capital. Sun wanted Soviet Russian arms, equipment, and instructors. In reporting this plan, Joffe called it Sun's "old dream".[83] Now in Moscow, General Chiang and the other members of the delegation described the current strategic plan in a meeting with E. M. Skliansky, deputy chief of the Revolutionary Military Council, and General S. S. Kamenev, commander in chief of the Red Army. As revealed by recent Russian research, the Soviet archives contain the following account of the plan set forth in that first meeting on September 9.

The delegates reported on the unreliability of the southern army, the inadequacy of its arms supply, and its precarious strategic position, with hostile Hong Kong at its rear and the Yangtse River patrolled by British and American gunboats before it. The imperialist foreigners would never permit the southern army to defeat Wu P'ei-fu decisively, the delegation stated. Given this situation, the general staff of the southern army had resolved to transfer the center of military operations to northwestern China, and the delegation had been sent to Moscow to present this plan. General Chiang then elaborated. Although Sun Yat-sen possessed only the province of Kwangtung, his influence extended throughout the provinces of the southwest. There were 80,000 troops in Sun's army, the same number as in the army controlled by Wu P'ei-fu and his ally, Ts'ao K'un, and approximately the same as in the army of Chang Tso-lin. Hence, the proposal was to organize Shensi guerrillas and reinforce them with units from the South to create an anti-Wu concentration in Shensi. A new army for Sun Yat-sen composed of Chinese living along the borderlands and in western Manchuria was being created on the Chinese-Mongolian border not far south of Urga. This army which was being organized on the pattern of the Red Army, formed the second column, and its offensive had already begun. Furthermore, the so-called bandits of Central China were being used for guerrilla actions against Wu P'ei-fu and Ts'ao K'un; the delegates alleged that the recent attack on the Tientsin-Pukow Railway—they were referring to the "Lin-ch'eng Bandit Incident"—was an example of such activity.[84] The Russians listened, then asked for a written plan and time to learn more about actual conditions in China.

Their reply was given on November 11 and was completely unfavorable. Skliansky lectured the Chinese delegation on the necessity of prolonged and painstaking organizational and political work among the masses. In Skliansky's opinion, to begin the military operations outlined in the submitted project would be an adventure doomed to failure.[85]

Soviet sources reveal that the Chinese delegation had another objective: to develop closer relations between the Kuomintang and the leadership of the Russian Communist Party. To discuss details, a commission was set up with representatives from the delegation and from the Comintern. We know nothing more of the commission's work, but General Chiang consulted several times with Maring (now back in Moscow) and with Voitinsky, and was invited to attend a session of the Comintern's Executive Committee on November 25, on which occasion he made a speech.[86] The executive's Presidium then passed a resolution "On the National Liberation Movement in China and the Kuomintang Party", which so angered General Chiang that—so he later recorded—he could barely force himself to say his farewells before departing for China.[87] One cheerful note: at Chiang's last call on Trotsky on November 27, Trotsky asked him to inform Dr. Sun: "Except direct participation by Soviet troops, Soviet Russia will do her best to help China in her National Revolution by giving her positive assistance in the form of weapons and economic aid."[88] Actually, it was nearly a year before the first Russian shipment of arms reached Canton.

Other Explorations and Continuing Difficulties

While Chiang Kai-shek was in Moscow, Dr. Sun was sending appeals for foreign support in other directions. Pressed by Ch'en

Chiung-ming and in dire need of funds, he began negotiations through his foreign minister to get a share of the most stable and constant revenue available to any Chinese government—monies collected by the foreign-controlled Maritime Customs Service. On September 5, Wu Ch'ao-shu sent two memoranda to the Peking diplomatic corps through the British consul general in Canton stating the reasons why the Canton government should receive a share of the "Customs surplus." It was a lucid and persuasive argument based on legal and moral grounds.[89] Had the diplomatic corps accepted the argument and ordered the payments it would merely have reinstated a procedure practiced during 1919 and part of 1920—a time, incidentally, when Sun Yat-sen was not participating in the southern government. In March 1920, payments to Canton had stopped, though for a number of months its share had been accumulated in foreign banks. The Canton government now calculated that the amount due it was $12.6 million, and in one of the memoranda, Minister Wu stated the constructive purposes for which his government contemplated using these funds. There the matter rested while the diplomatic corps in Peking considered the problem. Having received no definite reply, Minister Wu addressed another memorandum on October 23, when the war with Ch'en Chiung-ming was growing ever more critical. Near the end of the year the issue became explosive and led to a military confrontation between the generalissimo's government and a number of powers, which we discuss briefly below.

Dr. Sun also tried to revive the project for German assistance. On August 18, just after sending Chiang Kai-shek to Moscow, he wrote to Teng Chia-yen in Germany asking him to consult the government and German capitalists about a scheme for cooperation in the economic, administrative, and military reconstruction of China.[90] He complained about the financial stringency which made it impossible to buy arms. He hoped that some major German enterprise and the German government would work out a large reconstruction program through which the two countries would cooperate in the development of China. After China had become rich and powerful its entire strength would be available to help Germany free itself from the shackles of the Versailles Treaty. Such an alliance would also benefit Germany economically, Dr. Sun wrote, and he urged Mr. Teng to explore the possibilities.

Teng Chia-yen called on the Foreign Office in Berlin, and handed over a letter sent to him by Sun Yat-sen, which inquired whether the German government might still be interested in the proposal that Chu Ho-chung had raised in 1921. If so, Dr. Sun wished to be informed immediately. The Foreign Office was cautious but did not discourage Mr. Teng from carrying on private negotiations with German industrialists. The German government was not to be involved, yet the Foreign Office requested a more concrete proposal from Sun Yat-sen. While Teng Chia-yen was exploring in Berlin, the German consul general was negotiating with the Canton government for expanded commercial relations; this brought a protest from the Peking foreign ministry to the German legation, charging that the consul general was violating the new Sino-German treaty. It seems that little resulted from these efforts of Dr. Sun, but he kept trying to draw Germany into closer relations in the hopes of military and economic aid.[91]

Shortly after arriving in Peking on September 2, Ambassador Karakhan began an exchange with Sun Yat-sen. He telegraphed thanking him for his "friendship with Russia at the difficult time of her struggle for independence and freedom", informing him of the purpose of his mission, and expressing the hope that the two governments—that is, in Moscow and in Peking—would do their utmost "to fulfill the great task of achieving genuine friendship between the two peoples".[92] Dr. Sun replied by telegraph a few days later in a style that is unmistakably Eugene Chen:

> I am deeply moved by your generous appreciation of my friendship for New Russia; and I affirm that no criticism of the order of ideas for which you stand, can or will prevent me from holding with you that the real interests of our respective countries demand the formulation of a common policy which will enable us to live on terms of equality with other Powers and free from the political and economic servitudes imposed under an international system resting on force and working through methods of economic imperialism. . . . My fellow countrymen, I am sincerely persuaded, wish for the success of your mission, particularily on the matter

of formal recognition of the Soviet Government. But your most formidable difficulty lies in negotiating with a political group which, being wholly unrepresentatitve of the Chinese people, has ceased to bear even the simulacrum of a national government, and whose diplomacy is in reality guided more by the wishes and desires of certain foreign powers than by the vital interests of China as an independent and sovereign state . . .[93]

Dr. Sun praised Mr. Karakhan for a rebuff he had given Dr. C. T. Wang, who was to conduct negotiations, by saying that Soviet Russia would never follow the example of the United States in its policy toward China.

On September 17, Dr. Sun wrote to Mr. Karakhan telling him of Chiang Kai-shek's mission to Moscow, as already quoted. His main purpose, however, was to entice the Soviet ambassador to Canton. He again warned that Peking would make formal recognition of the Soviet government dependent upon stipulations set by America and the other capitalist powers. He then made an offer:

If you see no prospect of successful negotiations with Peking on terms which would give New Russia international equality with other foreign powers without infringing the sovereign rights of the Chinese people, you may have to consider that advisability of coming to Canton to negotiate with my new government now being formed, instead of returning to Moscow empty-handed. The capitalist powers will try, through Peking, and by Peking, to inflict another diplomatic defeat on Soviet Russia. But please bear it always in mind that I am prepared and am now in a position to crush any such attempt to humiliate you and your government.[94]

In September, while Dr. Sun was corresponding with Mr. Karakhan in Peking, Robert S. Norman, his American legal adviser, sent at least two appeals to the United States for support of Dr. Sun's plan for a national unity conference under American sponsorship. Mr. Norman asserted that his initiative was "not inspired by the Canton Government or anyone connected with it".[95] This seems doubtful, for the idea of a disbandment conference was much on Dr. Sun's mind, and there is his letter to Sir Robert Hotung of nearly the same date regarding a proposed conference of China's military-political leaders and members of the diplomatic corps to try to bring about Chinese unity. Dr. Sun promised to attend the conference "if other principal leaders will meet me" to devise means to settle the grave state of the nation.[96] Mr. Norman argued that establishment of a stable government in China would benefit the world, since China's need for railways, highways, factories, and goods could be realized and be paid for by coal, iron, and other raw materials.[97] These ideas were, of course, among Dr. Sun's themes in the *International Development of China*. In the State Department, it appears, Mr. Norman's appeals were merely noted and filed.

The generalissimo's military campaigns seemed to go on and on. After Gen. Shen Hung-ying was driven from Kwangtung, Dr. Sun supported an attempt by T'an Yen-k'ai to invade Hunan and overthrow Governor Chao Heng-t'i. T'an was an eminent Hunanese scholar, revolutionary, and former provincial governor, and he was now part of the southern rival government. Near the end of July he left Canton for the southern border of Hunan with a bodyguard of Yunnanese troops and apparently a good deal of money. He was able to bring several Hunanese divisional and brigade commanders over to his side. When T'an reached Hengchow, Generalissimo Sun appointed him "Commander of the Northern Expeditionary Rebel Punishing Army". The forces cooperating with General T'an drove Chao Heng-t'i out of Changsha briefly in September, but Wu P'ei-fu lent enough support to Governor Chao to tip the scales the other way. By early October, representatives of the Hunanese rivals were discussing peace terms.[98]

The military situation for Canton itself was quite serious. From late August to late September Generalissimo Sun spent much of his time at Sheklung directing the war against Ch'en Chiung-ming. He was always in need of funds. He tried to raise them abroad, by dunning his distant ally, Chang Tso-lin, by the sale of public lands in Canton, and by a variety of new taxes. These actions began to stir up strong opposition to his regime.[99]

The Peking government, too, was very unstable. During the previous five years presidents, premiers, and cabinets had been turned over in rapid succession. In June 1923 President Li Yuan-hung had been driven from office by the ambitious Ts'ao K'un. Then, on October 5, General Ts'ao was elected president through bribery of Parliament. As would be expected, Sun Yat-sen reacted sharply. He issued orders for the punishment of Ts'ao and the members of Parliament who had voted for him; telegraphed Tuan Ch'i-jui, Chang Tso-lin, and Lu Yung-hsiang calling for united action against Peking; told reporters that another northern expedition would be undertaken; and issued an appeal to the powers not to recognize "the new Peking usurpers".[100] All in vain! Ts'ao K'un was inaugurated on October 10 and five days later the doyen of the diplomatic corps congratulated him on behalf of his colleagues.

Such was the situation when Michael M. Borodin arrived in Canton on October 6, accompanied by two young Russian officers recruited by Colonel Gekker, and bearing a letter of introduction from Ambassador Karakhan. With his arrival began a new phase of Dr. Sun's political career. At the moment the southern leader was ill and probably rather downhearted. But now he had in his city a representative of the Russian government which had promised him aid. Ambassador Karakhan's letter clearly informed him of the significance of the new Russian move.

Dear Dr. Sun:

The absence in Canton of a permanent and responsible representative of our government has long been keenly felt in Moscow. With the appointment of M. M. Borodin, an important step has been taken in this direction. Comrade B. is one of the oldest members of our party, having worked for a great many years in the revolutionary movement of Russia. Please regard Comrade B. not only as a representative of the Government but likewise my personal representative with whom you may talk as frankly as you would with me. Anything he says, you may rely upon as if I had said it to you personally. He is familiar with the whole situation and besides, before leaving for the South, we had a long talk. He will convey to you my thoughts, wishes and feelings.

Hoping that with the arrival of Comrade B. in Canton things will be pushed ahead much more speedily than, to my sincere regret, it was possible till now, and heartily wishing you success in your work, I remain with friendly regards.

Yours,
(signed) L. Karakhan

P.S. I thank you very much for your telegram. It has inspired me with great faith in our common cause in China.[101]

Sun Yat-sen and the Powers—A Summary

This survey of Dr. Sun's foreign activities when considered together with the domestic political scene reveals something of his goals and methods. He wanted a reunited China, a country at peace, and a government operating according to a constitutional order. He opposed the reunification efforts of the Chihli clique but took a pragmatic view of other military factions. Could he use them against his enemies, those who had overturned the constitutional order or stood in the way of his own efforts to reunify China? During most of the time after 1920, he had his eyes fixed upon Peking and the presidency of the Chinese Republic. The drive to achieve this goal was fueled, we assume, by personal ambition as well as by confidence that he had the solution to China's problems. When confined to his Canton base he presented himself as head of a legitimate government and, at times, as head of the de jure government of China. But this was natural: the stance of "legitimacy" was essential for any Chinese ruler. He did all the symbolic things which the head of a Chinese republican government should do.

Sun Yat-sen yearned for foreign aid to achieve his domestic goals. There was nothing unusual about that; most modern Chinese governments tried to manipulate foreign wealth and power to achieve their ends. He apparently believed his prestige as a revolutionary and his influence with overseas Chinese, together with the use of foreign power, would redress his weak domestic position.

In trying to recruit and use foreign power, Dr. Sun responded to immediate situations but also pursued long-range plans. On immediate matters he issued proclamations either requesting recognition of his government or opposing the recognition of some new Peking regime. He wrote to foreign heads of state or influential persons arguing against loans to his rivals, and he had his friends and followers abroad mount opposition campaigns too. Such tactics were his coin from 1912 onward. Yet it would be difficult to show that Dr. Sun ever diverted a foreign government from a course it intended to pursue.

For the longer pull he used military, diplomatic, and economic strategies to achieve his principal goals, and he tried to involve foreign governments or business concerns in all of them.

Militarily, he conspired repeatedly with local Chinese regimes to mount campaigns against Peking. Yesterday's enemy might become today's ally—in short, he played Chinese military politics. In 1921 he tried personally to lead a northward march, and he would try this strategy once again. To oppose the North he needed a base; this need accounted for two campaigns to capture Canton, in late 1920 and late 1922. The Kwangtung base had to be defended—hence more fighting. All this activity took a great deal of money and munitions. While lodged in the Kwangtung base, Dr. Sun tried to raise money abroad by bond sales and grants of contracts. He also tried to arrange for military advisers and arsenal experts from Germany and Russia, and doubtless from other countries as well. Beside the alliance strategy and the northern campaign strategy, Dr. Sun developed his "Northwest Plan" by which he hoped to draw Soviet Russia into a drive on Peking.

On the diplomatic front, Dr. Sun tried to negotiate his way to Peking without war, as he did upon his return to Shanghai in August 1922. Another scheme was to convene a unity conference among the principal military factions, of which he counted the South as one. The southern generalissimo wanted the foreign powers, particularly the Allies of World War I, to sponsor such a conference, and he hoped the United States would take the lead. Sure that a peaceful China would be a great field for foreign investment—and he regarded that as good for his country—he thought there was a chance to persuade the powers to supervise a peace. Also, he hoped to cause the collapse of the Peking government, by persuading the powers to withhold the "surplus" revenues collected by the foreign-controlled Maritime Customs and Salt Gabelle. The powers, however, were committed to support the Peking government, which they all recognized. To them, Dr. Sun was an obstacle to national unity, at least from late 1920 onward.[102] (We avoid the complicated question whether some of the powers—Japan, say—preferred a divided China.)

In the economic realm, Dr. Sun had a broad-ranging plan for China's development through international cooperation and investment. The plan was not divorced from his own aspirations,[103] but he conceived it and toiled over it for his country's benefit. When administering Canton he tried to carry out parts of his plan. One or two projects that we know of might have brought "free money" which his government badly needed. Yet he seems to have gotten very little, if any, foreign financial help in the modernization of Canton.

Dr. Sun's problem in enlisting the foreign element was credibility. What validity was there to his boast of heading the legitimate government of China or of governing six southern provinces? How long could his government last, surrounded as it was by rival military factions and supported by unstable military coalitions? Taken as a whole, his later efforts to enlist foreign support proved abortive until Soviet Russia came to his aid.

To explain this failure without careful study in the archives of the governments concerned is an exercise in speculation. Few scholars have concerned themselves with this obverse side of Dr. Sun's career—the foreign forces and policies working against him—and I can only give impressions.[104]

A foreign government's policy toward Dr. Sun's regime would be conditioned, naturally, by its more general goals and policies toward China. By early 1922, the major powers, except for Soviet Russia and Germany, had enunciated a common policy toward China at the Washington Conference. The signatories to the Nine Power Treaty formally condemned spheres of influence, upheld the principle of equal opportunity, and confirmed the "sovereignty, the independence, and the territorial and administrative integrity of China". They agreed to provide China with the fullest opportunity to develop and maintain an effective and stable government. While by no means satisfying Chinese aspirations for abolition of the "unequal treaties," the conferees did agree, in principle, to allow an increase in China's tariff rates and to examine later the question of abrogation of extraterritoriality. The government with which the powers were concerned was that in Peking.

The government of the United States had taken the lead in calling the Washington Conference; it was also a strong supporter of the international arms embargo which aimed to curtail civil war in China. Favoring a unified, orderly, and peaceful China, the U.S. government recognized the regime in Peking as the sole government of the Chinese Republic. By late 1920, when Dr. Sun set up his second administration in Canton, the American government was not sympathetic to him as a political leader, if it ever had been. Effectively this meant that the head of the State Department's Division of Far Eastern Affairs, Dr. J. V. A. MacMurray, and a few associates in the division, and the ministers to Peking, Mr. Charles R. Crane and Dr. Jacob Gould Schurman were unsympathetic to Sun. Was this because of their personal conservatism? Or because America by then had become antirevolutionary? Or was it because of the long-sanctioned policy to recognize only one government of a country? Whatever the psychological, historical, or legalistic reasons, the State Department took the view by 1921 that Dr. Sun was in rebellion against the Chinese government which the United States recognized. It so advised other departments of the federal government as well as potential American investors when they sought advice. Yet surely the American ministers to China and responsible State Department officials, had they been more imaginative and less rigid in their attitudes, could have devised a more affirmative policy towards this frustrated idealist and his aspiration to create a democratic and progressive republic. He yearned for American help; but apparently no responsible official put his mind to the problem of aiding him toward his constructive goals.

Britain, too, was committed to the principle of the unity of China under a single government. As the leading "Treaty Power", with large economic and financial stakes in China, Great Britain certainly did not favor Dr. Sun's attempts to make Kwangtung a separate state or the base for more civil war. Great Britain had a vested interest in the Maritime Customs Service, since the inspector general was to be British so long as Britain had the largest share of foreign trade with China; and it was strongly committed to the unity of that service as one of the few administrative agencies which supported centralized government. In the interest of trade and the stability of Hong Kong, it was British policy to maintain good working relations with all successive Canton regimes: policy toward Dr. Sun's regimes derived from this framework. Britain dealt with them through the consulate general at Canton but discouraged pretentions to their being national regimes. (An example was an ordinance in Hong Kong forbidding Chinese to celebrate publicly Dr. Sun's inauguration as president on May 5, 1921). It seems that the British consuls general in Canton and Shanghai, Sir James Jamieson and Sir Sidney Barton, as well as the governor of Hong Kong, Sir Edward R. Stubbs, regarded Sun Yat-sen with disdain, though they were pleased, briefly, when he began his third administration with a bid for improved relations with Great Britain.

Japan's interests were concentrated in China's northeast, especially in southern Manchuria, both for strategic and economic reasons. But, like Great Britain, Japan had trade and business enterprises widely scattered in China. It possessed Formosa as a colony and hence had a particular concern with Fukien province, and during World War I it had torn from Germany its special privileges in Shantung. Apparently the formulation and execution of Japan's policies in eastern Asia were not under the control of a single authoritative body during the wartime and early postwar years, so one may speculate that some elements of the Japanese power structure encouraged the southern government against Peking. But in early 1922, Japan committed itself with the other powers at the Washington Conference to a cooperative approach that would restrain them from interfering in China's domestic affairs. During the early postwar years Dr. Sun was outspokenly critical of Japan's activities in China. His statements sound as though he was much disappointed with Japan for assisting his enemies.

France, like Britain, had a colony with an important Chinese population in which Sun Yat-sen had a following; and France also had a leased territory, Kwang-chow Wan, on the coast of Kwangtung.

There were French railway and mining interests in the three southern provinces, and thus a continuing French concern with the politics of the South. When Dr. Sun was not heading a regime in Canton, he lived in the French Concession in Shanghai; this gave the consul general there a particular responsibility to protect, and also to observe, him. How these elements translated themselves into relations with Sun Yat-sen's regimes, I do not know, but France does not seem to have figured much in his later foreign calculations.

Germany's situation with respect to China was quite different from that of the victorious Allies. It was no longer an imperialist power enjoying rights under the "unequal treaties". The Chinese government had abrogated all treaties and agreements between China and the Central Powers upon joining the war. Until May 1921, China and Germany were still technically belligerents, and after diplomatic relations were restored, the German government was quite cautious in its relations with China. Its main purpose was to reestablish and develop trade relations, which once had been quite important. Because of the terms of the Versailles Treaty, Germany was in no position to provide China or local regimes with arms and munitions. Heavily burdened by reparations and struggling to recover from the drain of a long war, Germany was unlikely to invest in Sun Yat-sen's scheme to build a southern base. He persisted in his hopes but they were ill founded.

The Soviet Union's principal national interests in China were in the North, and its primary concern was the security of the Pacific maritime provinces and Siberia against Japan. Security required that Russia control the Chinese Eastern Railway and that the Soviet Union maintain the dominant position in northern Manchuria and Outer Mongolia: in these security goals the Soviet government was not greatly different from the tsarist. As Russia emerged from the devastations of revolution and civil war, it became important, also, to establish intergovernmental relations with its great eastern neighbor. The establishment of relations required negotiations with the government which all the powers recognized, the government in Peking; to this end revolutionary Russia sent four successive missions, under Yurin, Paikes, Joffe, and finally Karakhan. Locked in his southern base or a fugitive to Shanghai, Sun Yat-sen could contribute little to the achievement of these major Soviet objectives, except perhaps to serve as a burr under the saddle of a recalcitrant Peking regime. The Soviet leaders began to see him in the light of another, broader, strategy—the promotion of revolutionary movements in colonies that might undermine the strength of capitalist states and ultimately, at a second stage, usher in socialism. "World revolution" was a goal of Communists everywhere, an ideal which commanded great dedication. After several years of exploration, the Comintern leadership had, by early 1923, fixed upon the the Kuomintang and Sun Yat-sen as the outstanding candidates in China to lead a national liberation movement, and they were ready to back Sun—conditionally. He must reform his party, clarify its goals and make them antiimperialist, and permit the Communist Party to work within it to create a mass proletarian movement.

It was impossible to know how long it would take for this strategy to succeed in liberating China from its dependent status and in making her a firm ally of Soviet Russia, but the experienced revolutionaries in Russia saw a process lasting many years. Dr. Sun was always impatient for quick results. Although he had long favored socialism, admired the achievements of the Russian Revolution and hoped to emulate them, and had eagerly sought for Soviet support, his objectives were quite different from those of the Russian and Comintern leaders. Each side hoped to use the other for its own ends.

CHAPTER SEVEN

Working with Russian Aid

With the arrival of Michael Borodin in Canton on October 6, 1923, Sun Yat-sen's long-frustrated hope for foreign aid began to be fulfilled. This chapter will describe the advice and material assistance which Soviet Russia rendered to the Chinese revolutionary movement through its agent in Canton during Dr. Sun's last year there. This aid began a process both of revitalizing the Kuomintang and of strengthening the Chinese Communist Party, which had great significance for subsequent Chinese life. As an early example of Soviet Russian revolutionary work and foreign aid the topic has a further interest. Dr. Sun's selective implementation of Borodin's advice created some serious problems for him and his party, which we will bring out, but it is not our intention to present a detailed account of the workings of the Soviet alliance. Out interest is in those matters of major historical significance and those which affected Dr. Sun most closely.

There are serious historiographical problems in writing of these events. Half a century later the record of Soviet aid and of Chinese acceptance is still shrouded in secrecy. Neither side has published its archives nor opened sensitive parts to foreign scholars. Scattered archival material has found light in secondary publications, and a raid on the Soviet military attaché's office in Peking in April 1927, disclosed some revealing documents. For the most part, however, an account must be pieced together from old and new fragments. Another serious problem is that of ideological bias. Because of the

intense conflict between China's two main branches of the revolutionary movement, Nationalist and Communist, it is nearly impossible for Chinese writers to view the period of Soviet aid with de-
tachment. For most Nationalist writers Dr. Sun's close involvement
with Soviet Russia is an embarrassment and Russian motives very
suspect. Westerners reporting at the time tended to view Soviet involvement with deep suspicion; the belief that Soviet Russia was
stimulating Chinese hostility toward the West and fomenting revolution—and that was considered bad—has colored much scholarly
writing. Recent Soviet publications on the subject have a tenden-
tious character; they glorify motives and generosity, both to recapture for a new Russian generation the youthful spirit of revolution
and to score points in the post-1960 polemics with the Chinese
Communist Party. These are some of the pitfalls. Of course every
writer has his biases, and mine will undoubtedly be evident in the
following account.

Challenging Problems

What was Dr. Sun's situation when Borodin arrived? Since his return to Canton in February, he and his supporters had succeeded in
creating a base of operations in the wealthy and populous Canton
delta region, and they had established a partially functioning governmental organization. This organization was most effective in
Canton where Sun Fo (Dr. Sun's son) was mayor. Yet within the
generalissimo's territory the military situation was in great disorder. In addition to various brigades and divisions of the much
divided Kwangtung Army theoretically commanded by Hsü
Ch'ung-chih, there was a provincial peace preservation force under
Wu T'ieh-ch'eng, Li Fu-lin's private army on Honam Island across
from Canton, and many local people's corps and bandit gangs for
hire. In addition, there were "guest armies": four autonomous Yunnan corps under separate commands, a Kwangsi army, an army
under T'an Yen-k'ai (then campaigning in Hunan), and smaller
units from Kiangsi, Hupeh, and Honan. The total force guarding
Canton may have numbered between 30,000 and 40,000 men,

[167]

though some claims were much higher.[1] Looking outward, Dr. Sun and his colleagues saw eastern and southern Kwangtung held by hostile armies and the neighboring provinces of Kwangsi, Hunan, Kiangsi, and Fukien at least partly controlled by generals allied to the Chihli clique, which schemed to suppress the Canton government.

The coordination of the military forces supporting the generalissimo's regime was a difficult political operation. Dr. Sun had to assign or confirm their garrison areas and adjudicate their conflicts. But the deeper issue was, who controlled whom? Could the generalissimo direct the "guest armies" and the heterogenous Cantonese forces against his enemies, or was he merely a figurehead? Virtually the only lever he had was a financial one, and here lay another problem.

Generalissimo Sun's financial difficulties were similar to those of any militarist in China—how to extract enough revenue from the local base to provide the sinews of war, and how to keep enough of the collecting under his own control as to make commanders dependent upon him. Every commander wanted his own source of income both to enrich himself and to pay his troops, the ultimate basis of his power. The "guest armies" which Dr. Sun had lured to drive out Ch'en Chiung-ming had quickly fastened upon lucrative taxing stations which most of them would not give up. To send troops into battle cost extra. While fighting Ch'en Chiung-ming, the Generalissimo's Headquarters required no less than $10,000 in emergency funds each day.[2] Dr. Sun became very dependent upon the municipal taxing administration of Canton, which had to squeeze the inhabitants hard and also invent many extra levies. During 1923 municipal income increased from a 1922 level of about $3 million annually to $9 million, but the books showed $6.2 million in "loans out"—almost certainly for the war chest, and most of it from the sale of confiscated and public lands. The government was also collecting about $400,000 a month in salt revenues, appropriated in defiance of the foreign-managed Salt Gabelle, but provincial revenues seen in Canton were about half the annual average.[3]

It is difficult to draw a balanced picture of conditions in Canton since the press was filled with grim reports. An eyewitness account written in October by a foreigner may serve as an example.[4] In it business is described as coming to a standstill; long lines of launches were tied up at the bund for fear of piracy on the rivers; and the merchants of the city had formed a 7,000-man Volunteer Corps "to oppose the government and all buccaneers." Conscription of labor, imprisonment and extortion of citizens, and arbitrary assessments had become commonplace. Taxation, piracy, robbery, and government seizures had destroyed the foundation of credit. In the writer's opinion, conditions were much worse in Canton than in the North. However, Mr. O. M. Green, the editor of the *North China Daily News,* visited Canton early in December and interviewed Dr. Sun; he found the business situation not abnormal.[5]

The Kuomintang was a weak organization. There were only two centers in China where significant work could be carried out on a regular basis. Party headquarters were in Shanghai, and Canton had a branch office. There were, of course, groups of individuals in other cities who had historic party connections, and there were many lodges in Chinese communities overseas. The party was skilled in propaganda work and published several newspapers, and, as we have seen, it could raise considerable sums of money if the cause had strong appeal. But Dr. Sun was not a particularly effective organizer and tended to neglect the Kuomintang when busy with administration in Canton. Despite his claims that the party had several hundred thousand members, this was a fiction created by the alleged en masse enrollments of armies or labor unions. If we conceive of Kuomintang membership as consisting of those who personally joined as individuals and paid dues, it may have been quite small in October 1923. For example, in November, Canton had about 3,000 registered members, and in December, after intensive recruitment, Shanghai had only 1,203 members. By mid-January 1924, after several months of effort, the total membership in China was reported as "more than 23,360," and there were about 4,600 members overseas.[6]

However, it was not so much numbers of members which counted, as leadership and tradition. Because of its consistent espousal of nationalism and social reform, the Kuomintang had a political influence and a potential ideological attraction. Its leadership, a few score people, came from various professions and strata of society; there were politicians, educators, journalists, generals, labor leaders, and secret-society bigwigs. The party had considerable potential to lead a nationalist movement but needed better organization to make it an effective instrument.

In early October 1923, Sun Yat-sen was hoping to revitalize his movement and was considering ways to reform the Kuomintang. He called a week-long conference in Canton, to begin on October 10, to discuss means to strengthen the party. About eighty veteran members attended this "Fraternal Conference," though Dr. Sun was ill on the opening day and could not attend. He appointed a committee of eleven to discuss a real reconstruction and called on all members to sacrifice individual liberty for the cause, contrasting the success of the Russian revolutionary party with the weaknesses and failures of the Kuomintang. In a speech to the entire conference on October 15, Dr. Sun emphasized the importance of propaganda. Party membership must be purified of opportunists, and the rest must devote themselves to winning the hearts of the people. If this were not done, he warned, the party could not even hold the small base it now had in Kwangtung. He advocated starting a school for propagandists, but his basic formula was for each member to convert ten others, these then to convert ten more, and so on until the entire population was won over. He reminded his listeners that revolution had two aspects—the military aspect which involved a struggle to overthrow evil government and drive out warlords and bureaucrats, and the propagandistict aspect which involved the reformation of society and the conversion of the masses.[7] This was scarcely a concrete plan for revitalizing the Kuomintang.

As Borodin recalled the situation five and a half years after his arrival in Canton, Sun was on the Honam Island sick and broken, preoccupied with the idea of carrying out a northern expedition to "punish Wu P'ei-fu." In Canton there was an army of 200,000 troops attached to a large number of militarists not in sympathy with the Kuomintang; the workers were divided; the peasants were asleep; and the Kuomintang office was seldom frequented. The revenue of the government was no more than Mex $300,000 a month.[8] Though it appears that Borodin was inaccurate in the figures, his perception of the general situation seems near the mark.

Borodin's Revolutionary Experience

When he arrived in Canton at the age of thirty-nine, Michael Borodin was an experienced revolutionary who had spent most of his adult years in the United States.[9] Born into a "Hebrew priestly family" in the Vitebsk region of Bielorussia on July 9, 1884, Michael Gruzenberg grew up in Latvia, was educated in a Russian school, and at about the age of sixteen began to participate in the work of the Latvian Social Democratic Party. When not quite twenty, and probably as a university student, he joined the Bolshevist wing of the Russian Social Democratic Labor Party. He won his spurs in the revolution of 1905 under the name "Kirill," which was his party name until he chose Borodin. The next year he was arrested in Petrograd, where he worked as a party organizer, and was permitted to leave Russia. He settled in the United States early in 1907 when he was twenty-three years old. There he shortened his name to Berg, attended Valparaiso University, married another Russian student, Fanny Arluk, and settled in Chicago, where he and his wife ran a school for immigrant children. He seems to have acquired American citizenship, joined the Socialist Party in America, and constantly extended his education.

In July 1918, Borodin returned to Russia and plunged into revolutionary work. He became fairly close to Lenin and knew many of the governmental leaders well. After the founding of the Communist International in March 1919, he became active in its work, visiting Spain, Mexico, and the United States performing organizational tasks. His last foreign assignment before China was to Great Britain, which he entered in 1922 under the name of George Brown with the mission of helping reorganize the British Communist Party. However, he was arrested in Glasgow, Scotland in August and sentenced to six months in prison and deportation. Shortly after his return to Moscow, probably in the spring of 1923, he was selected to work in China. He prepared himself by reading all he could find on that country, and also no doubt was well instructed in Comintern and Foreign Office policy. Sometime in September he arrived in Peking, where he and Ambassador Karakhan had long talks in order to coordinate their work. Toward the end of the month he left for Shanghai and Canton. Borodin's intelligence and magnetic personality are attested to in many of the Western and Chinese accounts of the period.

Sun, Borodin, and the Chinese Communists

The first meeting of the two lifetime revolutionaries, both fluent in English, was a moment full of portent. We have no record from the Chinese side, but Borodin reported on the meeting to his superiors shortly thereafter:

> Sun Yat-sen welcomed me very warmly, made me sit with him and looked at me fixedly for several seconds. I conveyed to him the greetings of Moscow, and of the Political Representative, Comrade Karakhan, adding that the latter looks forward to an interview with him on the first favorable occasion. Then I shortly explained to him the aim of my coming to Canton and asked him several questions about the situation in the country and particularly in Kwangtung. . . . He expressed the opinion that if he could stay in central China and Mongolia he would be able to act quite freely with respect to imperialism. As regards Central China everything depends on the success of the northward movement of his troops. He is also waiting for the result of the negotiations of his representatives in Moscow. Evidently he expects great things from these negotiations. The Mongolian base is very attractive to him. Mongolia, he said, offered great possibilities, first of all because in the north, he had more followers than in the south. In Mongolia, with friendly Russia at his rear, he would be able to carry on a more open and effectual policy. For the present he finds it necessary to hold Kuang-tung and therefore his army must be increased and strengthened. To do this he needs help, which, as he thinks, may be extended to him through Vladivostok. The direct steamer route from Vladivostok to Canton, not calling at Hong Kong, may be used to this effect. But the establishment of such a direct communication between Vladivostok and Canton must be in some way explained and this could be easily done, because Canton needs timber,

fish, beans, etc., which could be imported in exchange for local products. This line would at once create what he most needs, viz. a direct connection with Russia (the U.S.S.R.). Military supplies which are indispensable and which, owing to the blockade, cannot be received, could be brought from Vladivostok.[10]

This account reflects very closely Sun Yat-sen's hopes for Soviet Russian aid as we have come to know them. But Mr. Borodin had a different plan.

In early meetings with leaders of the Communist movement in Canton, he outlined his plan to reorganize the Kuomintang by creating a provisional national committee of twenty-one under the chairmanship of Sun Yat-sen, and consisting of the most prominent members of the Kuomintang, the Communist Party, the Socialist Youth Corps, and workers' unions. An executive committee of nine would organize Kuomintang provincial committees and subcommittees. On October 13 Borodin informed a meeting "that most probably Dr. Sun Yat-sen and other prominent members of the Kuomintang would consent to the reorganization of the party approximately as outlined in his plan." He reported at a meeting on October 17 that, having become acquainted with conditions in China and particularly in Canton, he concluded that with firm and assiduous effort something might be accomplished, a view which, he said, was shared by the important Chinese Communist leaders, Li Ta-chao, Ch'en Tu-hsiu, and T'an P'ing-shan.[11]

Michael Borodin also reassured his Communist listeners. Shortly after his arrival in Canton as head of a Russian "trade delegation," he had given a press interview in which he praised the potential of the Kuomintang, though it "has not as yet organized itself sufficiently to undertake the accomplishment of its historical mission. But this will come and come soon." Because the party has Sun Yat-sen at its head, "his experience will enable him to give his party what it lacks, a spirit of militancy and national organization, thus enabling it to draw added strength from the mighty spirits of nationalism to which China is rapidly awakening." The most important condition for the development of the labor movement in China, Borodin said, lay in "its alliance with the national struggle for the unification, freedom and independence of China. . . . This can be attained only upon the success of the struggle led by the Kuomintang party. So long as China remain in her present state of semi-colony labour has no hope of ever achieving its aims." [12]

To set things straight at the meeting of October 17, which was composed of the most prominent Communists, leaders of the Socialist Youth Corps and of workers' unions, he stated, "In the press I spoke of the Kuomintang, but to us it means I was speaking of the increase, in the end, of the influence of the Communist Party." While working for the stabilization of the Kuomintang, "it must never be forgotten that in reality the work is done for the stabilization of the Communist Party, which aim should be always kept in mind." [13]

What Borodin was advocating openly—revitalization of the Kuomintang by making it more militantly nationalistic, and cooperation of the labor movement in this nationalistic struggle under Kuomintang leadership—as well as what he was saying more confidentially—that the ultimate purpose was to strengthen the Communist Party—were by now standard elements of Comintern strategy. But did Borodin understand the Chinese proclivity for political gossip?

Dr. Sun promptly set about to reorganize the Kuomintang once more. On October 19, he telegraphed the Shanghai office informing the comrades there that he had appointed Liao Chung-k'ai, Wang Ching-wei, Chang Chi, Tai Chi-t'ao, and Li Ta-chao as commissioners for the Kuomintang reorganization, and he requested Sun Hung-i to telegraph secretly to Peking urging Mr. Li to come to Shanghai for the discussions. [14] These men constituted a leftist group among party leaders, and Li Ta-chao was the Communist elder whose admittance in September the year before had signaled the beginning of the policy of admitting Communists into the Nationalist Party. On October 25, Dr. Sun appointed a nine-man Provisional Central Executive Committee, with five alternates, to draft a new party platform and constitution, to supervise the registration of members in local branches, and to prepare for the party's first national congress. He appointed Borodin adviser to this committee. The fourteen persons constituting this committee were more representative of the various factions and tendencies within the party than was the first five-man group.[15]

On the same day, Dr. Sun telegraphed to Chiang Kai-shek in Moscow, and Chiang transmitted the message to Chicherin: "It has now become entirely clear who are our friends and who are our enemies." Dr. Sun conveyed his thanks "To the friendly government and party which sent their representative, Borodin, to Canton to aid warm-heartedly and sincerely," and "we deliberate with the various comrades on the best course." [16] But Dr. Sun also had some confidential advice for his followers. He explained the need for reorganizing the Kuomintang to Tsou Lu, one of his most trusted aides, as follows. The spirit of the party members was best during the T'ung Meng Hui period when there was a very close relationship among them. Now, because the large membership was scattered throughout China and abroad, it was difficult to direct the entire vital spirit of the party towards the revolution. "The present reorganization should preserve our party's original elan but adopt the Soviet Russian organization, thus acquiring its benefits while rejecting its evils. We may merely yoke up Soviet Russia and mount it." [17]

A Military Crisis Surmounted

Within the month of Michael Borodin's arrival in Canton, Generalissimo Sun's hold on the city was in grave danger. For three months his forces had besieged Ch'en Chiung-ming's base at Huichow (Waichow), ninety miles east of Canton, without success. By the third week in October the tide of battle had begun to turn against Dr. Sun.[18] Because the Yunnan and Kwangsi armies in the East River region had lost their fight—having been bought out?— Sun made an inspection tour on October 21 to the Tiger Gate forts and the gunboats protecting Canton, taking along his wife, Soong Ch'ing-ling, and his new Russian adviser. The next day Liao Chung-k'ai telegraphed Sun to warn of the great danger from Lin Hu's attacking troops. As a precaution Dr. Sun brought all gunboats back to Canton, but on October 30 four vessels deserted, probably bought out by the enemy. On November 5, Lin Hu's army was moving on Canton, and by November 8 the Yunnan, Kwangsi, and Kwangtung forces were in a general retreat. Next day the generalissimo placed Canton under martial law, because enemy troops had reached Shihlung (Sheklung) on the railway only forty miles away. Ch'en Chiung-ming's forces took Shihlung on November 12, and Dr. Sun's troops began retreating into Canton, establishing their defence lines in the eastern suburbs.

During the next several days the crisis mounted. There were desperate efforts to raise money and to create a volunteer force of Kuomintang members. Some officials sent their families to Hong Kong for safety. It was even reported that most leading members of the Canton government, such as Liao Chung-k'ai, Yang Shu-k'an, and Yeh Kung-cho, had taken refuge in the foreign concession of Shameen on the night of November 13.[19] By November 18, enemy forces were reported to be within three miles of Canton, and Yang Hsi-min, the Yunnanese general whom Dr. Sun had appointed supreme commander, was demanding a big price to drive them off. Money was found, and then the Hunan force, which T'an Yen-k'ai had assembled in his abortive northern campaign, arrived in Canton in the nick of time to join in a general counterattack, which succeeded in preserving Canton as the base for the Kuomintang's future revolution.[20]

Had Ch'en Chiung-ming succeeded, Borodin's mission presumably would have been aborted. During the critical days, he was advocating a radical policy to win the support of Kwangtung peasants and Canton labor. On November 13 he met with a group of Chinese leaders and urged the issuance of two decrees and a manifesto. One decree should promise land to the peasants through the confiscation and distribution of landlord holdings, while the other should promise labor an eight-hour day, a minimum wage, and other rights. The manifesto would explain to the city's petty bourgeoisie how they would benefit from the higher living standard of the masses. Borodin argued that if these promises were directly publicized to the peasants and workers, they would rally to the support of the troops fighting Ch'en Chiung-ming. Liao Chung-k'ai translated the

1. *Sun Yat-sen and Japanese sympathizers in Tokyo about 1905. From left: Suenaga Setsu, Uchida Ryōhei, Miyazaki Torazō, Oyama Yūtarō, Kiyofuji Kōshichirō, and Sun Yat-sen. People in the picture were identified with the assistance of Professors Marius Jansen and Eto Shinkichi, and Ms. Miwa Kai.*

2. *Sun Yat-sen in Singapore with a group of Chinese supporters in 1906. Front from left: unidentified, Chang Yung-fu, Ch'en Ch'u-nan, Sun Yat-sen, Yu Lieh, Liu Chin-sheng, Lin I-shun; rear from left: Wu Wu-sou, Chang Hua-tan, Chang Chi, Ch'en Ho, Teng Tzu-yü, Huang Yao-t'ing, Chang Ping-keng.*

3. *Dr. Sun in about 1913, after his retirement from the provisional presidency.*

4. Dr. Sun, the essayist, in Shanghai in July 1918, after retiring from the Canton military government.

5. Sun Yat-sen with Mme Sun aboard the cruiser Yung Feng on August 14, 1923, commemorating the escape from the coup d'etat of the previous year.

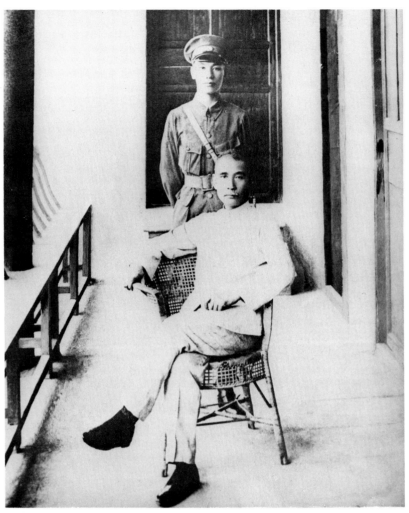

6. *Sun Yat-sen and Chiang Kai-shek during the formal opening of the Wampoa Military Academy on June 16, 1924.*

7. *A meeting of Kuomintang leaders in Canton, probably the Second Plenum of the Central Executive Committee held in August 1924. The background is Sun Yat-sen's head-quarters in the cement works on Honam Island. Front from left: Lin Tsu-han (?), Chang Chi, En-k'e-pa-t'u, Liao Chung-k'ai, Po Wen-wei, Sun Yat-sen, T'an Yen-k'ai, uniden-tified, Li Lieh-chün, Buyantai (Pai Yun-t'i), and Ting Wei-fen; rear from left: Tsou Lu, T'an Chen, Ch'ü Ch'iu-pai, Fu Ju-lin, Shen T'ing-i, next four unidentified, and Wang Fa-ch'in. According to the records of the Kuomintang Archives, the picture was taken on January 19, 1924, on the occasion of the preparatory meeting for the Kuomintang First National Congress. However, five of the identified persons did not attend the congress, namely, Chang Chi, Li Lieh-chün, Tsou Lu, T'an Chen, and Ch'ü Ch'iu-pai, whereas all the identified persons attended the Second Plenum. Professor Chiang Yung-ching, Dr. Bernadette Li Gentzler, Mr. Li Lu-chao, and Professor Tang Tsou helped to identify the people in the picture.*

8. Sun Yat-sen and Michael Borodin reviewing cadets at the Wampoa Military Academy on November 3, 1924. On the right is Wu Ch'ao-shu.

speech phrase by phrase and, according to Borodin's report to his superiors, "it was, generally speaking, well received, especially by the ranks of the 'extreme left,' i.e., by Communists and the socialistic youth. . . . My proposals were accepted unanimously and the meeting distributed the work among the regions. The members of the government went to the house of Sun to draw up the decrees." [21]

In his reminiscences, Mr. Borodin stated that the Executive Committee of the Kuomintang, "somewhat in a panic" adopted all his suggestions; a "tremendous propaganda apparatus was set in motion to explain to workers and peasants"; and there was an immediately favorable effect at the front. Then, as he remembered the circumstances, Kuomintang leaders began to waver, and some went to Dr. Sun "to sabotage enactment of the decrees into law." On November 16 Borodin went to see Sun at his home in Honam. The revolutionary leader did not object to the labor reforms, but there was strong Kuomintang opposition to the land measures. After considerable bargaining, Dr. Sun agreed—as Borodin recalled the incident—to a decree reducing land rent by 25 percent, and to another decree providing for the establishment of peasant unions, to which Mr. Borodin attached great importance. [22]

The radical program which Borodin advocated was in line with the Comintern directive of May 1923 to the Chinese Communist Party, particularly in its emphasis upon the expropriation of landlords' land and its distribution to poor peasants to win their support for the Nationalists' armies. [23] During his subsequent work with the southern revolutionaries, Borodin laid great stress upon organizing a radical peasant movement. It was not till three years later, however, that the Kuomintang resolved to reduce rents by 25 percent.

After the crisis had passed, Dr. Sun made a speech to the comrades on the reasons for the party's past failures and the path to pursue in the future. [24] This was on November 25, shortly before Borodin was to depart for Shanghai on revolutionary business. The main purpose of the present reorganization, said Dr. Sun, was to expand the party's influence to all parts of China and free it from exclusive dependence on military force. Its foundation must now be the support of the people. The aim was to build a centralized mechanism and stimulate all comrades to apply themselves single-mindedly to actualizing the Three Principles of the People and the Five Power Constitution. Previously the party had lacked a model and a precedent; now it had them in the Russian Revolution. "Now a good friend, Mr. Borodin, has come from Russia. . . . If we hope for victory in revolution we should study the Russian methods of organization and training."

To those who objected to learning from a country dominated by a radical party, Dr. Sun responded that the Communist Party was chosen by the Russian people from among many contending parties because its ideology suited their desires, but that in practical matters it was not extreme. Mr. Borodin had told him how important a force nationalism had been in winning support for the revolution in Russia. Popular support had made it possible to defeat internal enemies and the attacking powers; their troops had been driven off and foreign economic aggression eliminated. The Russian people were no longer the slaves of the powers. China's struggle had not succeeded because the party had not made good use of nationalism.

> What our party and they advocate are the Three Principles of the People: the ideologies are similar. But our party still lacks effective methods and should study theirs. . . . Henceforth we must fight as an organized group and engage in disciplined struggle. Since we wish to learn their methods, I have asked Mr. Borodin to be our party's director of training; he is to train our comrades. Mr. Borodin has much experience in party management and I hope all comrades will give up prejudices and earnestly study his methods.

Dr. Sun told the audience that Mr. Borodin had said that, given six months, Canton could be transformed into the party's firm base, while in a year or two the revolutionary spirit would spread to the entire nation and the revolution be victorious. From this day forward, Dr. Sun exhorted, let us all unite and struggle as a single body, relying on the party and not on the army alone for victory.[25]

Two other glimpses of Dr. Sun's foreign policy sentiments are available for this time. On November 16 he wrote to Inukai Ki, his old Japanese friend and patron, pleading for assistance and trying to convince him that a Russo-Japanese rapprochment against the imperialist powers—Great Britain, France, and their potential ally, the United States—was desirable. Japan need not fear bolshevism, which was essentially no different from the Confucian concept of *ta-t'ung* (universal harmony). Japan should be the first, he urged, to recognize Soviet Russia.[26] A few days later in an interview which he and his wife gave to Dame Adelaide M. Anderson, a British humanitarian and expert on labor conditions in factories, he turned the conversation into an attack on England for supporting the conservative side in China rather than him. "I stand for progressive and good government, not Bolshevik nor extreme in any way." He defended his demand for surplus customs revenue—an issue that was soon to become explosive—and seemed to hope to change British governmental policy, which he felt did not reflect the sentiment of the British people. "Chinese and English are alike, peace-loving, noble, fine." Dame Anderson concluded that Dr. Sun greatly desired British understanding.[27]

The Provisional Central Executive Committee, appointed by Dr. Sun to plan for the revitalization of the Kuomintang, met twenty-eight times between its formal inauguration on October 28, 1923 and January 19, 1924, the day before the commencement of the First Kuomintang Congress. It made formal decisions on some 400 matters.[28] In preparation for the congress, it drafted a proclamation, party program, and constitution, and also prepared an agenda. In addition it was responsible for certifying the election or selection of delegates. The committee also reregistered the local membership and organized the Canton municipal headquarters and district and subdistrict offices in the city. It established a weekly journal, *Kuomintang Chou-k'an*, to crystalize opinion in the party, explain revolutionary ideology, and publicize the true intent of the planned reorganization. It unified two propaganda organizations within the Generalissimo's Headquarters, set up a school to train members of executive committees at the district and subdistrict level, and drafted plans for an expanded party press and a propaganda school. The committee instructed Kuomintang members not to disclose their opinions on party affairs to outsiders. It also undertook an investigation of conditions among farmers, workers, and the middle class. In much of these initiatives one detects the advice of Mr. Borodin, but only through a careful reading of the committee minutes would it be possible to observe, in part, his manner of steering the reorganization.[29] He was away from Canton from November 28, 1923 until about January 10, 1924.

Protests Against the Kuomintang's New Orientation

Some Kuomintang leaders began to oppose the trend of these changes. After Borodin and Liao Chung-k'ai left for Shanghai, eleven leaders of the party's Kwangtung branch, led by the influential Teng Tse-ju, sent Dr. Sun a petition. His handling of this opposition permits a glimpse of his strategy and his understanding of relations between the Kuomintang, Soviet Russia, and the Chinese Communists. His answer, written in early December, is preserved in photographic reprint.[30]

The petitioners complained that the system of organization together with the drafts of the party's constitution and program had emerged under the direction of Borodin, but that the policies had been decided upon previously by Ch'en Tu-hsiu's Communist Party. They accused Ch'en of pulling the strings through his disciple, T'an P'ing-shan. The motivator of the present cooperation with the Communist Party was, they charged, the Communist International in Moscow, whose policy was to stir up class struggle in capitalist countries in order to hasten a social revolution, while uniting labor, peasants, and the middle-propertied class in nascent capitalist countries to produce a national revolution. They attacked Ch'en Tu-hsiu for his previous disparagement of Sun Yat-sen and his theories, yet for now bringing his adherents into the Kuomintang. This was a plot to borrow the body of the Kuomintang but infuse it with the soul of the Communist Party. The slogans "Down with Imperialism" and "Down with Militarism" were devices to create trouble for the Kuomintang at home and abroad. Ch'en hoped to use the Russians to influence the Leader in order to bring the Kuomintang secretly under the Communist Party's direction. They warned Dr. Sun against the proposed new election system in the Nationalist Party, and predicted that within five years Ch'en might be elected party leader.

This was to be the first of several serious challenges to the policy of admitting Communists and allying with Soviet Russia. Indeed, after Dr. Sun's death the party's leadership split over the issue. Sun was much beholden to some of the protesters, and most were long time comrades. Teng Tse-ju, among the most faithful attenders of Provisional Central Executive Committee meetings, had been a party leader since 1907 and was one of the most effective fund raisers among overseas Chinese. When Dr. Sun was driven from Canton in mid-1922, Mr. Teng's money-raising efforts at the special office in Hong Kong made his return possible. Another stalwart, and the second to sign the petition, was Lin Chih-mien, who had led Dr. Sun to safety in his escape from Yeh Chü's soldiers on the night of June 16, 1922. When Dr. Sun left Canton he had deputized Mr. Lin to act for him, and like Teng Tse-ju, Lin had worked hard in the Hong Kong office to bring Sun Wen back. Huang Lung-sheng, Teng Mu-han, and Chao Shih-chin, all old members, were section heads of the Kuomintang's Kwangtung branch office, and Mr. Chao was Dr. Sun's appointee as head of the southern government's highest court. Three others had been overseas Chinese supporters of the revolution as early as 1906.[31]

Dr. Sun met the impeachment head on, denying allegations and offering assurances.[32] The draft of the new party constitution, he wrote, "was prepared by Borodin at my request and checked by myself. The original was in English and was translated by Liao Chung-k'ai. Ch'en Tu-hsiu had no part in this and no suspicion should be cast on him." He then stated that the reason the Russian Revolution had succeeded but the Chinese Revolution had failed was because Kuomintang members still did not understand the Three Principles of the People. "Essentially there is really no difference," he wrote, "between the Principle of People's Livelihood and communism." (This point became one of his constant themes.)

The young Communists who sneered at the Three Principles were bigots who adored the Russian Revolution; they attacked and criticized the Kuomintang because they wanted to monopolize Russian friendship and prevent Russia from dealing with our party, Dr. Sun wrote. But, he reassured the protesters, the Russian leaders were experienced people and not to be fooled by these youngsters. "Consequently they disagreed with them, corrected them on our behalf, and ordered them to join the Kuomintang and act in unison with us. In case of non-compliance they would be disavowed." The Russians also explained to them the importance of the Principle of Nationalism. "Thus many of them were enlightened and joined our party." Dr. Sun's most revealing lines are the following:

> If Russia wants to cooperate with China, she must cooperate with our party and not with Ch'en Tu-hsiu. If Ch'en Tu-hsiu disobeys our party, he will be ousted.
>
> The Chinese revolution has never been welcomed by the foreign powers, who have often helped our opponents in attempts to destroy our party. The capitalist countries will never be sympathetic to our party. Sympathy can only be expected from Russia, the oppressed nations, and the oppressed peoples. It was not Ch'en Tu-hsiu's but Russia's idea to befriend us. If we suspect Russia because of our suspicions of Ch'en Tu-hsiu, we shall fall into Ch'en's trap and help him to realize his plan. . . .

There can be many interpretations of this remarkable message. Dr. Sun knew that it was on Russian insistence that members of the Chinese Communist Party had joined the Kuomintang, but apparently he did not regard this as a strategem to strengthen that party or to remake the Kuomintang. One wonders whether he believed that Russia *had to* cooperate with the Kuomintang and not with Ch'en Tu-hsiu, or whether he was expressing his fundamental anxiety that Russia might bypass himself in lending aid for the Chinese revolution. One interpretation of Sun's remark that Ch'en Tu-hsiu would be ousted if he disobeyed is that Sun expected to "Kuomintangize" the Communists, not to communize the Kuomintang. That the Kuomintang could expect sympathy only from Soviet Russia and not from the capitalist countries was an opinion which Dr. Sun often gave out at this time. On the record, he was correct.

The Customs Crisis

Dr. Sun got quick confirmation of the opposition of the capitalist powers in the "Customs Crisis" of December. We can only sketch this complex issue.[33] The southern government was desperately in need of funds. On October 23, Mr. C. C. Wu addressed a second communication to the diplomatic body in Peking prompting it to act on the request for Canton's share of the "Customs Surplus." The claim had been argued on both legal and moral grounds: legally, that the southern government had received a share of the surplus customs revenue in 1919-20 and was entitled to it including arrears, now; and morally, because it was wrong to turn over to the faction in Peking moneys collected in the South, thus freeing funds for the northern militarists to use for war against the South, which then had to tax its population more heavily in order to defend itself. "Since the scheme of distributing the surplus as now carried on is illegal, unfair and unjust," Mr. Wu's memorandum of October 23 concluded, ". . . It is therefore submitted that the question . . . be reopened in its entirety and be settled and adjusted by all parties interested in it, including this Government." [34] Still, Mr. Wu received no answer.

Apparently the diplomatic body thought that the collapse of the Canton government was imminent and that another flight by Sun Yat-sen "would provide a solution of this embarrassing question." However, warnings sent on November 20 by Sir James Jamieson in Canton to the British minister, Sir Ronald Macleay, convinced him that further procrastination was impossible. Dr. Sun had expressed the view that if the controversy led to war, he would be only too glad to be defeated by Great Britain, which then would be responsible for the death of democracy in China. Heretofore he had turned a deaf ear to overtures by Bolshevists and Indian agitators who had sought his cooperation in an endeavour to overthrow British power in the East. It would be better, Dr. Sun warned, to have him as a friend than as an enemy. He made it clear that he was considering the seizure of the Canton customshouse and the installation of his own appointees.[35]

The diplomatic body sent a telegram to the senior consul in Canton on December 1, warning the local authorities that the diplomatic body were not prepared to admit any interference with the Chinese Maritime Customs and would, if necessary, take forcible measures to meet the situation. On December 3 this message was conveyed informally to the southern government.[36] Sir Ronald also wrote privately to Mr. Wu arguing that the diplomatic body did not have the right to allocate the customs revenue, which was the prerogative of the Peking government, and trying to impress Wu with the fact that the powers would not permit Dr. Sun to interfere with the customs service.

While these private communications were passing back and forth, France, Great Britain, Italy, Japan, Portugal, and the United States prepared to resist, with naval forces if necessary. The American minister, Dr. Schurman, advised his government to take any measures short of actual warfare to prevent the Canton government from seizing the customs. Secretary of State Hughes recommended to President Coolidge that naval vessels of the U.S. South China fleet join in a show of force at Canton, and the president gave his approval.[37] Decisions of the same sort probably were being reached in other capitals for there were nine gunboats at Canton on December 5 when Sun Yat-sen stated his government's intention to order the commissioner of customs to cease remitting funds to Peking and retain them for local use, though he would wait two weeks before taking definite action. Dr. Sun's case was well argued and widely publicized to the world. His interview on December 4 with O. M. Green, editor of the *North China Daily News,* made the *Times* (London), the *New York Times* and Mr. Green's influential Shanghai daily.[38] When asked whether he would fight if the powers prevented seizure of the customs revenue, Sun said he could not overcome such force, but then would have the glory of being defeated by all the powers, which he would regard as an honor. Then, he said, he would enter the second phase. This, he hinted, meant an active alliance with Soviet Russia, "whose agent, M. Borodin is now in Canton." (If Mr. Green added this, he was mistaken. Mr. Borodin was then in Shanghai.) Dr. Sun seemed sincerely desirous of maintaining friendly relations with the powers, especially with Great Britain, Mr. Green reported. It is doubtful that Dr. Sun still planned to use force after the gunboats appeared in numbers, but he seemed to welcome the confrontation.[39]

On December 14 the consular corps in Canton transmitted the formal reply of the diplomatic body in Peking that it was not within its province to grant or refuse the claim of the southern government to a share of the customs surplus, and that the previous arrangement by which the first government at Canton had received a percentage in 1919 and 1920 had been an arrangement between that government and the one at Peking, in which the diplomatic body neither took the initiative nor acted as an intermediary. Nor could it do so now.[40] The consular corps decided, in addition, to address an informal communication to the chief of the Chinese military forces to warn that, if Dr. Sun attempted to seize the customs, the powers would place marine guards in the customshouse.[41]

Clearly, the powers would not permit Dr. Sun to shatter the unity of the Maritime Customs Service and appropriate its locally collected revenues; this, they foresaw, could lead only to further fragmentation of government in China.

Dr. Sun and his associates saw things entirely differently. They asserted the legitimacy of the southern government and demanded the revenues collected within its domain—a matter in which foreign governments had no right to interfere. They countered the response of the diplomatic body with a campaign in the Chinese press and with mass rallies and parades. The United States and the American minister in Peking were particular objects of attack—or so it seemed to Consul General Jenkins. He was told by Mr. Norman that Dr. Sun flew into a rage upon hearing that the United States would join in protecting the customs and that American destroyers had been ordered to Canton.[42] The southern revolutionary cabled a protest "To My Friends, the American People," in which he compared his contemplated action to the Boston Tea Party.

> The revenues belong to us by every right known to God and man. We must stop the money from going to Peking to buy arms to kill us, just as your forefathers stopped taxation going to the English by throwing En-

glish Teas into Boston harbor. Has the country of Washington and Lincoln foreswarn its faith in freedom and turned from liberator to oppressor? [43]

This appeal was echoed by scores of telegrams from Chinese groups in the United States and Canada addressed to the president and the secretary of state protesting the American naval presence in Canton.[44] It was clearly an orchestrated campaign.

By December 19, the day Dr. Sun had set for taking action, there were sixteen foreign warships at Canton—six American, five British, two each from France and Japan, and one Portuguese. The southern government issued its order to the local commissioner of customs to hold in custody all revenues collected within its jurisdiction after deduction of sums due in respect of foreign obligations. It also issued a twelve-point statement of its case; announced to the inspector general its orders to pay over the retained revenues and to make good all arrears of the customs surplus due the government since March 1920; and stated that if the order were not obeyed it would appoint new customs officials who would recognize its authority.[45] The moves and countermoves were widely reported in the native press. Dr. Sun also cabled Ramsay MacDonald, leader of the British Labour Party, asking him to publicize "the grave situation which British representatives in China mainly have been instrumental in creating. . . ." He pointed to the British minister in Peking, the consul general in Canton, and the British inspector general of customs as the ones primarily responsible, and argued that British trade with China could not be made secure by gunboat diplomacy.[46] The southern leaders also attempted to create suspicion between the Americans and British in Canton, to subvert sailors by propaganda, and to use the governor of Hong Kong as a way around the British minister and consul general.[47]

All these efforts were of no avail. The crisis passed; the gunboats began to depart; and the antiforeign demonstrations subsided.

Frustrated in his hope to secure the large and steady income of the Canton customs, Dr. Sun nevertheless gained great sympathy among patriotic Chinese for standing up to the powers in a completely unequal struggle. The crisis intensified his belief that the

Western governments were against him and that Soviet Russia was his only hope. Apparently the conflict put him under immense emotional strain. Two incidents illustrate this: his visit to Canton Christian College on December 22, 1923 and his interview with Dr. Schurman on January 6, 1924.

At their invitation Dr. Sun addressed the students of the college (known in Chinese as Lingnan) during the height of the customs crisis, going by launch to the beautiful campus on Honam Island. He clearly hoped to inspire them. After praising the wonderful American college and congratulating the students on their unique opportunity, Sun spoke glowingly of American accomplishments and urged the students to adopt high ambitions of service to their own country. In the more nationalistic part of his speech he warned his Chinese listeners not to become denationalized, pointed to the disgrace of many foreign gunboats in Canton waters, and talked of the shame of China's semi-colonial status, a condition worse than the slavery of Koreans and Annamese. He directed the students' attention to the American Revolution in which only a small number of people had overthrown English rule. Yet, because there was so much praise for Western civilization, the talk did not seem antiforeign in tone. China needed hundreds of Lingnans, said Dr. Sun, so that the country could become rich and strong like the West. If all strove unitedly, such a state could be achieved in about ten years.[48]

In a smaller meeting with a group of faculty members and representative students, however, Sun impressed some of his Western listeners as emotionally unbalanced. To a British teacher he said that Britain was consistently hostile to China. Whatever friendly advances the Hong Kong government might make, Downing Street was anti-Chinese. He predicted a world war within ten years in which India would be united with China, Russia, Germany, Afghanistan, Persia, and the Negroes of America and Africa in a great struggle for freedom. Today, he said, the Chinese and Russians were very close, giving each other mutual assistance, and Russia was the greatest power in Europe with the strongest army in the world. China would draw the technical help it needed from Germany and then, in turn, would help India. In this war between the underdogs and their persecutors, Britain and her self-governing dominions together with America, "always subservient to the British in foreign policy," would be greatly outnumbered, though Sun was uncertain which side Japan would join. He asked the Americans in the circle how they would feel if sixteen or eighteen foreign warships steamed into New York harbor to overawe the city and interfere in its internal affairs. "The Chinese have long memories, and you will not soon live it down," he warned. Asked how representatives of foreign governments were to know what China really wanted, he replied, "Ask me. What I think China thinks. Look at the reception the people give me. They know I am their true leader. That is why the British government is so determined to crush me." According to this account of the meeting, no one else was allowed to state his views or distract Dr. Sun from "his tirade." The Chinese and foreigners in the room were all deeply depressed.[49] The writer of another account thought that "the extremity of his utterance would seem to indicate almost an unbalanced state of mind; . . . at least an extremely dangerous, neurotic state." [50]

The American minister, Jacob Gould Schurman, came to the same conclusion when he met with Dr. Sun on January 6, 1924. "For the first fifteen minutes of the conversation lasting two hours," Dr. Schurman wrote to President Coolidge, Sun Yat-sen "talked to me like a man really insane about the coming conflict between the world-oppressors and the oppressed—China, Russia, Germany, India, etc. being in the latter group and the 'capitalist nations,' including America, in the former." [51] Dr. Schurman also reported that while talking on this subject, "his speech and manner were so incoherent and excited as to lend color to the local report that his mind has become affected." [52]

It is not wise, however, to be categorical about Dr. Sun's ideas at any particular moment. In the same interview he appealed for American aid in solving China's internal political problems. According to Dr. Schurman, he outlined "with much enthusiasm" a plan for a conference of Chinese leaders concerning unification and the disbandment of troops, which he desired the American government, after consulting with other powers, to call.[53] A few days later the details of this scheme appeared in the *New York Times* as related to its correspondent in Shanghai by Minister Schurman. Dr. Sun had told Schurman that America was the only nation which the Chinese regarded without suspicion and hence the only nation which could mediate as suggested.[54] Apparently, however, the American minister thought so little of the idea that he never bothered to report the details to the State Department.[55] As Consul General Douglas Jenkins recalled the incident a few years later, on their return by launch from their call on Dr. Sun, he and Schurman referred to the proposal but dismissed it "as entirely impractical at the time because Dr. Sun controlled only an infinitesimal part of the country and had no means of inducing powerful military leaders of the north to accept any measure fathered by him." [56] Dr. Sun repeated the bid in an interview with an American correspondent on January 13, just a week before the opening of the Kuomintang First Congress. Since the Chinese people trusted America, all Chinese would welcome an American call for a peace conference at Shanghai or some other central place, he asserted, adding that the various powers would be sure to join.[57] Mr. Borodin, after his return to Canton, tried hard to persuade Dr. Sun to give up this illusion.

Thus, at around the turn of the year, the southern leader seemed to be hesitating at a forking in the ways. One way, though probably a mirage, led toward assistance from the Western powers, whom he hoped would recognize his government to the extent of granting it a share of customs revenue. He also hoped, perhaps more remotely, that such Western assistance would lead to intervention that would stop internal wars and assist in China's reconstruction. The road toward Soviet Russia possibly led to a "world revolution" in which China would line up with Russia, Germany, India, colonial Africa, and other oppressed nations and peoples, including, he hoped, Japan, against the major Western powers. At the end of December, in a talk before the Canton YMCA he confessed, "we no longer look to the Western Powers. Our faces are turned toward Russia." [58] But his talk with Minister Schurman a week later shows he had not given up hope. There seemed to be an ambivalence between his desire for Western help and his growing determination to free China from Western domination.

The Kuomintang Holds a Congress

The First National Congress of the Kuomintang met in Canton from January 20 to January 30, 1924, and must have been a great satisfaction to its leader. The congress confirmed a plan of genuine reorganization which had been worked out by the Provisional Central Executive Committee with Borodin's advice, and it approved a fairly radical reorientation of party objectives. Upon its adjournment, a newly chosen leadership set about vigorously to create a mass party, extend its influence throughout China, and make of the Canton region a real base for a national revolution. Dr. Sun addressed the congress eight times, made the final selections for new central committees of the party, and saw his name written into the constitution as "The Leader," with veto authority.

Delegates attended from every province and the four major cities of China and also from many Chinese communities overseas; some were even said to represent Mongolia, Sinkiang, and Tibet; and there were three specially appointed women delegates. Among the 196 delegates listed, about half were appointed by the party's head, the rest being chosen by their respective party organizations. Most were veterans of revolutionary organizations headed by Dr. Sun, but there was also a sprinkling of Communists. The delegates met morning and afternoon in commissions or in formal sessions under a presiding committee appointed by Dr. Sun and made up of Hu Han-min, Wang Ching-wei, Lin Sen, Hsieh Ch'ih, and Li Ta-chao, four veterans and the distinguished cofounder of the Chinese Communist Party. The delegates heard speeches by Dr. Sun and reports on the state of the party in various places, and they formed commissions to study and debate the drafts of the new constitution and party program. On the last day they elected the slates proposed by Dr. Sun for two important committees that would be in charge of affairs until the next congress: the twenty-four-man Central Executive Committee with seventeen persons in reserve, and the five-man Central Supervisory Committee with five alternates.[59]

The members of the Canton consular body received invitations to attend the opening meeting but did not accept. By contrast, Lev Karakhan, the Russian envoy in Peking, sent a telegram of congratulations and stressed Soviet Russia's friendly sympathy for the Chinese people's struggle for national liberation and independence. "All those who are oppressed by world imperialism are our brothers," he wrote; "all those who strive for the people's freedom are our comrades, and we are all in a common struggle." [60] Lenin died on January 22. When this news reached Canton, the congress sent a telegram of condolence and adjourned for three days of mourning. Borodin made an address. Foreign Minister Chicherin and Ambassador Karakhan sent telegrams of thanks for the condolences. On the other side, a telegram to Ramsay MacDonald and the new Labour Cabinet in England apparently went unanswered.[61] These contrasts suggest the aloofness of the Western powers toward Dr. Sun and the eagerness of Soviet Russia to draw the Nationalist movement to its side: they also reveal Dr. Sun's increasing inclination towards the Russian utopia.

Yet this is an exterior view. Behind the scenes there were doubts and controversy over the direction in which the party was being led, a situation illustrated by several incidents.

In a speech on the opening day of the conference, Dr. Sun seemed to be persuading. He stated that the Russian system of placing party above government was the most modern in the world, and China should emulate it. In its revolution, Russia had emphasized the Principle of Nationalism, and it now encouraged other countries such as Persia, Afghanistan, and Turkey to do so also. As to communism, after six years of experience, it was gradually becoming similar to the Principle of the People's Livelihood. The Russian method of revolution should be a model.[62] Next day, Sun spoke directly to the suspicions of the old comrades, which arose, he averred, because of their misunderstanding of the livelihood principle. He recalled that some students in Peking had become enamored of the idea of communism and had gone to Russia to study, but the Russians had advised them to join the Kuomintang and study its ideology in order to save the country. Older members became suspicious that they merely intended to use the Kuomintang name. Sun Wen had received numerous telegrams from overseas members asking if the party were to be changed into a Communist Party, in which case they would withdraw. Hence he must explain to them. First, their suspicions of Russia were due to their living in imperialist countries where they were drenched with anti-Russian propaganda. They did not realize that hostile public opinion was altering; foreign scholars now believed that Russia was changing and progressing and the parliaments of England, France, America, and Japan were considering recognition of Soviet Russia. He then explained that the Principle of the People's Livelihood actually encompassed the doctrine of socialism, which in turn encompassed two lesser doctrines, communism and collectivism. (Sun provided a diagram to illustrate the circles within circles.) There was no great difference between the Kuomintang's principles and communism. Furthermore, the application of communism did not originate in Russia but in Hung Hsiu-ch'uan's Taiping Heavenly Kingdom. Nor did Russia practice pure communism; what it had put into effect really was a policy of the people's livelihood. If the old comrades understood all this there should be no misunderstanding between old and new members.[63]

Yet Dr. Sun had his own doubts over the direction the party was moving. Was the declaration which the congress was debating before issuance too radical? Borodin has left a record of his efforts to get a radical declaration drafted and then to persuade Dr. Sun to support its passage.[64] In early January, as the date for the congress drew near, there was intense debate within the inner circle over drafts of the declaration, party program, and new constitution. A committee of four—Liao Chung-k'ai, Hu Han-min, Wang Ching-wei, and Borodin—spent many hours debating the phraseology of the program. Borodin tried hard to get included a specific statement on the expropriation of lands held by large and absentee landlords and the distribution of such lands to tenants, as well as a clear statement of the Chinese Nationalist movement's united front with revolutionary Russia. On neither point could he persuade Dr. Sun, who even rejected a passage in which the Kuomintang would state the necessity of establishing a united front with the national-revolutionary movements against imperialism in other oppressed countries and with "that revolutionary movement which has a common goal with our party, that is, to fight for the liberation of colonial and semi-colonial countries." According to Borodin's account, Dr. Sun feared to arouse the antagonism of England and France by such a forthright statement.

On January 23, just before the drafts of the declaration and its attached program were to be voted upon by the congress, Dr. Sun hesitated. He suggested to Borodin that it might be better to withdraw them and to use instead a program that he had drawn up for a national government. The rightists at the congress would find nothing objectionable to this one, he believed. According to Borodin, representatives from the overseas branches of the party, officials, merchants, and landowners—whom he regarded as scoundrels—did everything possible to persuade Dr. Sun to give up the originally prepared declaration. Borodin used all his powers of persuasion to get Dr. Sun to support the statement which spelled out clearly the new direction the Kuomintang was to take. He was aided by Dr. Sun's fears concerning the impression that would be made on the Chinese public by Minister Schurman's revelation of part of their talk on January 6, in which Dr. Sun had sought American assistance in solving China's internal problems. Borodin urged him to deny the revelation and make a forthright antiimperialist speech. "In a word, you must decide whether you will join the national revolutionary movement of the whole world, or will, as before, seek to persuade Schurman of his injustice towards China and even expect intervention from him or any other big power to help in settling China's internal affairs." Thereupon Sun was persuaded, according to his Russian adviser's account. He shook Borodin's hand and went down to the congress, presided during the report of the commission on the declaration and the subsequent debate, and was the first to cast a favorable vote. The declaration was then passed. Thus was the party's official statement of policy in both foreign and domestic matters but narrowly placed on record.[65]

The Persistent Issue: Communism within the Kuomintang

Another incident which reveals the ambiguities of the First Kuomintang Congress was the debate over permitting Communists to be Kuomintang members. Their entrance into the larger party was a central point in Comintern strategy; Maring, particularly, had overridden all objections, and, at its Third Congress the previous June, the Chinese Communist Party had adopted that strategy officially by a narrow margin. About 10 percent of the listed delegates to the First Kuomintang Congress were members of the Communist Party, including the two founders, Ch'en Tu-hsiu and Li Ta-chao.[66] Yet there were many veteran Kuomintang members who were suspicious. On January 24, Ho Shih-chen, a delegate from Shanghai, proposed to the committee studying the draft of the new constitution that a rule be added to forbid any Kuomintang member from belonging simultaneously to another party. The Communist members then held a caucus to decide how to meet this challenge. They chose Li Ta-chao and two others to prepare a statement.[67] At a session of the congress on January 28, when the constitution was to be voted upon, Fang Jui-lin of the Canton delegation proposed an amendment to prohibit dual party membership. In response, Li Ta-chao presented his famous statement explaining and defending the policy of Communists in the Kuomintang.[68]

Couched in words of great sincerity, humility, and courtesy towards the "Senior Comrades" of the Kuomintang, Li's statement explained that the Communists wished the entire strength of the nation to be united in a single comprehensive movement against imperialism and militarism, and since only the Kuomintang could perform this role, the Communists had decided to join it to struggle for national revolution under its leadership. They joined in order to contribute to the Kuomintang and not to use its name to promote communism. They joined as individuals and not as a party. The Communist Party was a branch of the worldwide Third International and, since the present revolution was both national and worldwide, the Communist members served as a link between the Kuomintang and the Third International. Dr. Sun had permitted them to retain membership in the Third International.

Theirs was an open and upright action and not a secret plot, Mr. Li assured the delegates. "So long as we are in the Kuomintang, we shall carry out its program and observe its regulations; if we fail to do so, we are ready to be corrected. We hope our Senior Comrades will not suspect us nor set up precautions against us. . . . Suspicions and restrictions can only obstruct the Kuomintang's advancement and should be recognized and swept away now at this time of reorganization. Our future actions and attitude as we serve in the Kuomintang should prove whether or not we are completely loyal to the national revolution and to this party, and we hope our Senior Comrades will help and guide us."

The debate on Fang Jui-lin's motion to prohibit dual party membership was conducted in Dr. Sun's presence. Liao Chung-k'ai spoke strongly against it, and Wang Ching-wei made a telling point: Anarchists had been taken into the Kuomintang so why should not Communists be admitted also? He mentioned three distinguished delegates all of whom had been Anarchists—Wu Chih-hui, Li Shih-tseng, and Chang Chi. Some delegates said that so long as Dr. Sun was satisfied that the Communists recognized his Three Principles and obeyed the Kuomintang constitution and the party's discipline, there was no reason to fear their presence. The proposed amendment had its supporters also. Finally there was a vote, and though we do not know the tally, the result was the defeat of the amendment, which might have prevented known Communists from being registered in the Kuomintang.[69]

Despite this vote there was an anomoly. The Kuomintang constitution described a system of secret "Party Fractions" (*Tang T'uan*)—groups of Kuomintang members in other organizations that should act in unison to try to steer such organizations, under guidance of the Kuomintang Central Executive Committee.[70] This was modeled on Bolshevist practice. The Chinese Communist Party had a closely similar plan to capture control of labor unions under Kuomintang leadership.[71] Its own members, and those of the Socialist Youth Corps were to be under strict and unified discipline while serving within the Nationalist Party. Thus, at the very time the Kuomintang planned to penetrate other bodies in tightly disciplined fractions, the Chinese Communist Party was using the same technique to penetrate the Kuomintang! Li Ta-chao might state officially for his party that its members joined as individuals, not as a party within the party, yet even the decision for him to make this statement was reached in a separate Communist caucus.

It is unfair to leave it at that. From the viewpoint of ardent young Communists, no doubt, their purpose was to give life to the Kuomintang and to steer it in the true and destined direction of revolution, for the benefit of their country.

Dr. Sun may not have known of Communist intentions in detail, but he surely understood the basis for objection to dual party membership. He reaffirmed his policy by the slate of twenty-four persons he proposed for the Central Executive Committee, which was elected by show of hands on the last day of the congress. Scattered among the prestigious veterans of the Kuomintang were three Communists, T'an P'ing-shan, Li Ta-chao, and Yü Shu-te; and there were seven among the seventeen Sun proposed as reserve members, Shen T'ing-i, Lin Tsu-han, Mao Tse-tung, Yü Fang-chou, Ch'ü Ch'iu-pai, Han Lin-fu, and Chang Kuo-t'ao.[72] There were none among the five members and five alternates in the Central Supervisory Committee, a sort of censorate. Appointment of ten Communists to the Kuomintang's highest executive organ shows the Leader's broad-minded approach and his self-confidence as he granted the lesser party a minority voice in his party's affairs.

After the congress, the process of national party building gained momentum as a central apparatus was created at Canton and most members of the new central committees returned to their homes to set up regional offices that would supervise the development of provincial and metropolitan branches. Before departing, the Central Executive Committee members met in plenary session and appointed a three-man standing group to manage daily business, Liao Chung-k'ai, Tai Chi-t'ao, and T'an P'ing-shan—all leftists. They also decided upon a central apparatus and appointed bureau chiefs. Central party headquarters, located at Canton was to consist of a secretariat and eight functional bureaus, with the following heads appointed: Organization (T'an P'ing-shan), Propaganda (Tai Chi-t'ao), Youth (Tsou Lu), Labor (Liao Chung-k'ai), Farmers (Lin Tsu-han), Women (Tseng Hsing), Overseas Chinese (Lin Sen), Military Affairs (Hsü Ch'ung-chih), and Investigation (name withheld).[73] It took time, of course, to get the organization staffed and in operation.

A remarkable feature of this early Kuomintang central apparatus is the key role played by leftists and, among them, Communists. T'an P'ing-shan, a thirty-six-year-old Communist, headed the bureau which supervised Kuomintang membership and the certification of party branches; another Communist, Lin Tsu-han, headed the Farmers' Bureau; and Liao Chung-k'ai (not a Communist) was to guide the Labor Bureau, not a field in which he had been prominent, but one in which the Kuomintang had considerable experience. The secretary of each of these bureaus was a Communist, respectively Yang P'ao-an, P'eng Pai, and Feng Chü-po. We may note, however, that T'an was a Kuomintang member before he joined the Communist Party, and had also served in Dr. Sun's staff the previous year, as had Feng; Liao was one of Dr. Sun's closest associates and a "wheel horse" in both governmental and party affairs; and Lin was a T'ung Meng Hui veteran, who had become a member of the Kuomintang reorganization group in November 1922, and the next year was deputy chief of the party's General Affairs Bureau in Shanghai headquarters. In short, they were among the party's more radical group who could be expected to guide it leftward and to the masses, which was what Borodin had been trying to persuade Dr. Sun to do with the Kuomintang for the previous four months.

Intensified Nationalism

There being no official and up-to-date version of Dr. Sun's basic political philosophy, he undertook to fill the gap by delivering a series of lectures on the Three Principles of the People at the Kwangtung Higher Normal School. The first of six talks on the Principle of Nationalism began on January 27 and ran through March 2. As generalissimo and party leader, Dr. Sun was a very busy person. He had little time to prepare his lectures, but he corrected the transcripts and this first series was rushed into print as propaganda material. He then proceeded with six lectures on democracy, between March 9 and April 26, after which there was a gap, probably due to his illness in May and an intraparty conflict in June. On August 3 he began the third series on the People's Livelihood; he got through lecture four on August 24, but thereafter he was absorbed by a crisis with the Canton Merchants' Corps and with plans for a northward military campaign, so he never completed this series nor had a chance to revise all the transcripts.[74] In printed form the 16 lectures run to about 150,000 characters, and more than 500 pages in translation. Though little read now in the West, the *San Min Chu-i* is a gold-mine for those interested in the convictions and sentiments, breadth of knowledge as well as the fleeting ideas, of this ambitious and frustrated patriot during the last year of his life. After his death, the work became virtually a Kuomintang bible; later it became compulsory study material for students in China under the Nationalists.

The lectures on nationalism aimed to create a sense of national pride and to stimulate the Chinese public to commence a giant struggle against the political and economic privileges of foreigners in China. It is not possible to present here a condensed version of these lectures, and there is sure to be bias in a selection of highlights. Yet, since it was in these lectures that Dr. Sun expressed most vigorously his beliefs about China and the outer world, let us point to some of them.[75]

Dr. Sun began his lectures with the straightforward assertion that the Three Principles of the People were, most simply, the way to save the country; they were the principles which would lead China to a position of equality with other nations and secure her permanent existence. After a general discussion of what constitutes "race" and "nation," he presented what might be called his race peril theme. The Chinese race of 400 million people (including a few million Mongols, Manchus, Tibetans, Mohammedans, and Turks), the largest in the world, the greatest, and with a civilization dating back more than 4,000 years, had become the poorest and weakest nation in the world, in danger of being destroyed as a nation and extinct as a race. Promotion of nationalism was the way to escape this danger. One source of danger lay in China's stagnant population: it had failed to grow since the eighteenth century, Dr. Sun asserted, while such countries as England, Japan, Germany, Russia, and the United States had increased from three to tenfold in the past century. He was horror-struck at the thought of China standing still and being swallowed up by other peoples increasing so rapidly!

Touching on the Slavic population reminded Dr. Sun of the Russian Revolution and how the new socialist state had adopted a policy of overthrowing imperialism and capitalism. This policy aroused the fears of the capitalist class and, "because the government of every country is controlled by capitalists," the various countries of Europe opposed Russia and refused to recognize it as a nation state. Russia's policy was to "check the strong, assist the weak, oppress the rich, help the poor, and throughout the world to spread justice and overthrow inequality." This policy had brought on a great change in the trend of the world, and Sun foresaw inevitable new international wars, but not between different races. "They will start between members of the same race, White against White, Yellow against Yellow. They will be wars of social classes, of oppressed against oppressor, of right against might." [76]

The second lecture resumed the theme of population danger but emphasized foreign political and economic oppression, which could mean the extinction of the race in scarcely ten more years unless the tide were rolled back. Dr. Sun listed China's territorial losses, beginning with the scramble for concessions and working back through Japan's seizure of Korea and Formosa, the losses of Burma and Annam, and finally back to Russia's appropriation of trans-Amur, trans-Ussuri, the Ili valley, and Khokand. He also named former tribute-paying countries such as Loochoo, Siam, Borneo,

Sulu, Java, Ceylon, Nepal, and Bhutan, and implied that they all were part of China's great domain. But since the Chinese Revolution the powers realized they could not divide up China and so had turned to economic exploitation, which was even more dangerous because it was so difficult for most people to perceive. Economic oppression rendered China a colony of all the powers, a condition much worse than the fate of Korea and Annam. Dr. Sun then listed ways in which China was being exploited. The customs crisis evidently was still much on his mind. Because China did not control its tariffs, it could not use protective rates to save its handicraft industries and encourage native factories. The unfavorable trade balance was growing larger by the decade; and, by using straight-line projection, Sun predicted that in ten years China would be paying a tribute of $1.25 billion annually through trade deficit alone. Another drain was caused by the foreign banks in China, which printed paper money to exchange for Chinese goods and profited from currency transactions between ports; in addition they held vast deposits of wealth belonging to the former imperial family and various warlords which they lent out at high interest. The transportation of Chinese goods on foreign ships—inland, coastwise, and abroad—cost at least $100 million, while China lost $400 or $500 million annually in taxes and land rents on such "concessions and leased territories" as Hong Kong, Formosa, Shanghai, Tientsin, Dairen, and Hankow. Then there were the profits of foreign business in China and the enormous indemnities for the Sino-Japanese War and the Boxer Uprising. In all, Dr. Sun estimated the total probable annual losses at $1.2 billion, and this huge leakage would increase each year. The Chinese, already weak and impoverished, must be rescued quickly or face extinction as a race, like the American Indians. If China did not have to pay this awful tribute to foreigners, what could not be accomplished with the money!

Why had China lost her nationalism? In his next lecture, Dr. Sun laid the blame upon history and Manchu policy. After China had subjugated the smaller nations of Asia by its "imperialism of the kingly way," its educated class espoused cosmopolitanism, that is, no distinction between Chinese and barbarians. Cosmopolitanism was fatal to nationalism. The Manchus tried by every means to encourage cosmopolitanism among the educated, but nationalism was preserved among the lower classes in the secret societies, upon whose histories Dr. Sun reminisced. He opposed those who esteemed cosmopolitanism and thought nationalism not in accord with world opinion. He then quoted what a Russian had told him the day before.[77]

> Why did the world's Great Powers attack Lenin? Because he dared to make this statement: 'There are two categories of people in the world; of one there are 1,250,000,000, and of the other, 250,000,000. The former are oppressed by the latter.'

The oppressors, said Dr. Sun, act against nature; we who oppose might are in accord with nature. China must join its 400 million to the 1.25 billion oppressed peoples of the world. But first the Chinese must unite, and nationalism was the means to achieve unity. "Together we shall use right to fight might. When might is overthrown there will be no more madly ambitious people in the world, and then we may talk of cosmopolitanism." [78]

In the next lecture devoted to modern world history, Dr. Sun attacked the Anglo-Saxons who, as part of the white race, occupied more of the world than any other race and were the strongest and wealthiest. With Europe and America as its base, the white race went forth to swallow up the races of other color, exterminating the American Indians, with the blacks of Africa soon to be wiped out and the browns of India in the process of being wiped out. The yellow race was in danger. Europeans were imbued with the poison of imperialism; it was one of the prime causes of the Great War. Then Woodrow Wilson had enunciated the doctrine of national self-determination, which had great attraction to the colonial peoples, inducing them to aid the Allies. Yet at the peace conference, the victorious Allies reneged; they produced a very unjust peace treaty, to the bitter disappointment of the colonial peoples and the weaker nations of Europe. However, an unexpected result of the war was the Russian Revolution, and now the Russians advocated exactly the Wilsonian doctrine. The 150 million Russians were thinking of allying with the weaker and smaller Asiatic nations to resist the tyrannical races. This left only 250 million whites, yet these still tried to conquer the other 1.25 billion. Hence all mankind would soon be divided into two warring camps.

Anticipating another theme, Dr. Sun spoke of the high development of Chinese civilization. China had experienced the much talked about anarchism and communism several thousand years ago, as seen in the anarchistic theories of the Yellow Emperor, Lao-tzu, and Lieh-tzu; and in the recent communism actually practiced by Hung Hsiu-ch'uan. Europe's superiority lay purely in material culture and not in political philosophy; in fact, Europeans still sought enlightenment on the true principles of government from China.

How to revive nationalism? The fifth lecture again emphasized China's peril. The first danger was military. China was so weak that Japan could conquer her in two weeks, the United States in a month, Britain or France in two months. The country had been preserved thus far only because of mutual suspicion among the powers, none being willing to permit another to grab China. The Washington Conference had done no more than decide how to divide up rights and privileges in China without conflict among the powers. This pointed to the second danger: the powers could wipe out China simply by agreement among their diplomats. "One morning will suffice to do away with China by common accord." The third danger lay in economic oppression, and here Dr. Sun repeated the economic peril theme: every year foreigners robbed China of $1.2 billion, and in ten years the figure would be $3 billion. China must awake, revive its spirit of nationalism, and all must cooperate. The best means to cooperate was to unite by family, by clan, and then under the state. Here there followed an extended description of the Chinese lineage system which, when all clans were united and linked together, would serve as the basis for a unified state.

On the basis of India's example of noncooperation with England, Dr. Sun then advocated that the Chinese refuse to work for foreigners or to buy imported goods. They should promote the use of native goods, refuse foreign banknotes, and accept only the Chinese government's currency. In short, they should break economic relations with foreigners. Thus, there were two methods to fight foreign oppression—positively, by promoting the national spirit, the people's power, and the people's livelihood; and negatively, by noncooperation and boycott.

The final lecture on nationalism, delivered March 2, concerned the restoration of China's standing as a nation. Dr. Sun expanded upon the theme of Chinese superiority in morality and ability. China must revive its ancient morality embodied in the terms *chung* (loyalty) and *hsiao* (filiality), *jen* (humanity) and *ai* (charity), *hsin* (trustworthiness) and *i* (justice), and finally *ho-p'ing* (peace). After some discussion of these Confucian concepts, Dr. Sun declared, "In all these virtues China formerly was superior to foreigners and is still so in the love of peace. We must cause this virtue to shine with an even greater splendor. Then we shall recapture our standing as a nation." [79] The second prescription was to revive China's superior wisdom and ability, especially shown in its political philosophy regarding relations between the people and the state. Here Sun quoted a passage from the *Great Learning:* "Investigate into things, attain the utmost knowledge, make the thoughts sincere, rectify the heart, cultivate the person, regulate the family, govern the country rightly, bring peace to the world." This doctrine, beginning with the individual's inner life and extending to the pacification of the world, surpassed any developed abroad. Yet, Dr. Sun lamented, recently the Chinese had lost the art of personal cultivation. He gave examples of crudity in manners and urged his countrymen to comport themselves properly, especially when in the company of foreigners. First practice personal culture, he exhorted them, and then you may talk about "regulating the family and governing the country rightly."

In the past, he argued, China had surpassed foreigners in ability, as shown by the fact that all the objects which foreigners prized most highly were Chinese inventions or discoveries—the mariner's compass, printing, porcelain, gunpowder, tea and silk, the arch and the suspension bridge. But now the Chinese must study those things in which Europeans and Americans excelled. He assured his listeners that this would not be difficult. A few years would suffice to catch up, just as Japan had done. The next ten years spelled life or death for China. If she awoke like Japan, then in ten years she should be able to rid herself of all foreign oppression—political, economic and racial—and solve all misfortunes. With a population ten times that of Japan and with thirty times the territory, China could become as strong as ten powers. Thus would she recover her former standing.

Dr. Sun concluded his series on nationalism with a ringing summation:

> We shall 'govern the country rightly and bring peace to the world.' To do this we must first restore our nationalism and our national standing, and then unify the world on the basis of our distinctive morality and peace, and create a government of Great Harmony. This is the duty of our four hundred million. You, sirs, are part of these four hundred million, and should all shoulder this responsibility: such is the true spirit of our nation.[80]

The talks on nationalism expressed much greater hostility toward the Western powers and far more anxiety about China's condition than any previous speeches by Dr. Sun that I have read. They clearly mark a shift in his beliefs and mood from the time of his Hong Kong speech a year before, with its praise for British colonial rule, or even from the speech at Lingnan the previous December, when he was very complimentary to America. He now seemed intensely anti-Western, pro-Russian, and nearly hysterical about China's peril. Clearly, the speeches were intended to rouse nationalistic passions, and they did. We can deduce that the shift in Dr. Sun's beliefs and mood was primarily the result of two factors—his growing frustration at being rejected by Western governments (and this was intensified by the customs crisis) and the coaching of Michael Borodin. The Russian adviser had been with Dr. Sun a little more than three months in two periods, and was about to leave for the North again on March 8, shortly after Sun's delivery of his sixth lecture on nationalism.

During March and April Dr. Sun kept up his busy speaking schedule, delivering six more lectures on the Three Principles, and giving several orations to officers and men in his armies, to Ling-nan students, and to prospective teachers at the Girls Normal School. The lectures on democracy, or better, on the people's power, displayed his considerable knowledge of the development of Western political institutions, but far from extolling Western democracy they dwelt upon its defects and retardation. Westerners had fought for liberty because they had so little of it, but the Chinese, having too much liberty, were like a tray of loose sand; what they needed was unity in order to achieve national liberation. The same was true of another Western battle cry, equality. The Chinese, having passed beyond feudalism 2,000 years ago, had experienced very little inequality of class; all that was now needed was to assure the people their political equality. Bismarkian Germany, with its state ownership of railways, heavy industry, and banks, and its extensive social legislation, seemed the best of the older Western systems, while the "dictatorship of the people" in Soviet Russia was a great improvement over representative government. In order to advance beyond Europe and America, the Chinese revolutionaries intended to remake their government into a republic of all the people, he said. This new government would be distinguished by two separate powers; the power of the people over government and the power of the governmental machine itself. The first would be brought about by the rights of suffrage, recall, initiative, and referendum; these would assure "government by all the people." Administrative power would be lodged in five functional organs—judicial, legislative, executive, examinational, and censorial. This was the "Five Power" constitutional system, which Dr. Sun had proposed as early as 1906. It added two traditional Chinese functions—selection of officials by examination and the system of supervision over officials—to the three functions held carefully separate in Western democracies.[81]

On April 12, Dr. Sun issued his "Fundamentals of National Reconstruction for the National Government of China." This summarized his political philosophy and his dream for the country's future, but its twenty-five articles are so condensed that further reduction is difficult. The first four articles announced that the national government should reconstruct China on the basis of the Three Principles of the People and the Five Power Constitution; and among the principles, the first necessity was to improve the people's livelihood, the next to train the people to exercise their sovereignty, and the third to assist the country's racial minorities to self-government and to restore China's equality and independence among the nations. Dr. Sun then described a familiar concept, the stages through which national reconstruction was destined to move: that of military rule first, followed by political tutelage province by province, and finally the achievement of constitutional government. The national government was to conduct the tutelage—there is no mention of party—beginning at the county level; there an infrastructure for administration should be developed, and the people trained to exercise their four powers. Counties would carry out Dr. Sun's favorite land tax scheme, and the local government would retain the revenues to use for the people's needs, but large-scale enterprises beyond the locality's financial capacities would receive central government assistance, and the profits would be divided equally between the two administrations. Counties had the obligation, however, to forward between 10 and 50 percent of their revenues to the central government, as the people's representatives should determine. Each county, after achieving self-government, would elect one delegate to a national assembly. Only officials who had been examined and certified by the central government might serve in local government or at the center.

When all counties of a province were self-governing the stage of constitutional government would begin in that province, where an assembly of people's representatives would elect a governor to supervise provincial affairs and to act under the direction of the central government in national affairs. The last few articles described the process by which an elected central government was to be created for the constitutional period. The process would begin by the drafting of a constitution when more than half the provinces had become self-governing; and the constitution would be promulgated by a people's congress. Then a national election would be held, and three months after its completion the national government that had guided this development would turn its functions over to the elected government, "whereupon the great task of national reconstruction will have been accomplished." [82] This document was considered by his followers as one of Dr. Sun's most important statements. It tended to bind them—somewhat—in their own political efforts after his death.

The Russian Impact

Michael Borodin's influence on Dr. Sun and the Kuomintang is evident through much that has been narrated above, though he built on groundwork laid by Maring and Joffe. So far as we know, he had only a small staff, Stoianovich as head of the local Rosta agency, and two young officers, Iakov Guerman and Vladimir Poliak, who were joined on January 25 by two other officers, Alexander Cherepanov and Nikolai Tereshatov. Their job was to help with a Kuomintang military academy being planned with Russian advice and funds. How much monetary assistance Mr. Borodin brought to Dr. Sun is still a secret.

Clearly, Borodin was a shrewd judge of character and a skillful persuader. In addition he was an experienced revolutionary and an alert student of his environment. He was tireless in his efforts to guide Dr. Sun and played upon the Leader's ego,[83] but he also worked industriously with other Kuomintang leaders and with important Communists.

Dr. Sun was not a pliant individual. Although he may have accepted much of the proffered advice, he still was the final judge of what was safe and wise to do. Thus the reshaping of the Kuomintang and the establishment of its new revolutionary direction were in some degree the result of the interaction of two men upon each other, each experienced, each a forceful personality, and each with a vision of the China to be. They were aided and constrained by other men, and all were operating within an intractable environment.

Borodin overreached himself at times. Tsou Lu gives two examples. After 50,000 copies of the declaration of the First Congress had been printed, it was discovered that part of the section dealing with the people's livelihood differed from the version passed by the congress. Wu Chih-hui and other members of the Central Supervisory Committee in Shanghai sent a letter of inquiry to central party headquarters. The passage at issue pertained to China's farmers, but Mr. Tsou does not specify the alterations that had been made. Upon inquiry, Liao Chung-k'ai stated, "Adviser Borodin found that this passage did not conform to his ideas, so it was revised. Since there has been an official inquiry, it may be revised back to the original text. But that will not be to Borodin's liking." As a result, the first printing was recalled and a correct version issued.[84]

The second example of Borodin's overreaching had to do with finances. According to Tsou Lu, Soviet Russia had agreed to help with Kuomintang expenses. After the party's budget had been passed by the Central Executive Committee, Liao Chung-k'ai, as financial commissioner, made a report at the next Central Executive Committee meeting which did not accord with the budget passed at the previous one. Everyone was surprised, and the matter was inquired into. Liao said, "This was revised by the Russian adviser, Borodin." Everyone criticized Mr. Liao, so Mr. Tsou tells it, and it was decided to find a way for the party to provide for its own expenses. When the Shanghai members of the committee learned of the matter, they were angry and sent Wang Ching-wei back to Canton to settle the affair. It was therefore decided that the salt commissioner and the mayor of Canton should make monthly allotments to cover party expenses, which were running at about $30,000 per month.[85]

During Dr. Sun's lifetime the major Russian financial contribution and investment of personnel probably was for the party's new military academy, popularly known as the Whampoa Military Academy, derived from the name of its site on an island about ten miles south of Canton, where earlier provincial military and naval schools had been located. The purpose of the academy was to produce a reliable and politically indoctrinated corps of junior officers as an essential element in a new and loyal party army. The idea probably had been pressed on Dr. Sun by Maring in December 1921 and discussed by Joffe and Sun in Shanghai, and by Joffe and Liao in Japan. It was pressed upon Chiang Kai-shek on his trip to Moscow, and Borodin discussed the matter with Dr. Sun and other Kuomintang leaders as early as November 1923. Much has been written about Whampoa,[86] but most of its success came after Dr. Sun's departure for the North, so we shall merely touch upon the benefits he derived in the military field from his Russian orientation.

After his return from Soviet Russia, Chiang Kai-shek was appointed head of the preparatory committee for the academy by Dr. Sun on January 24. Yet after attending only one meeting Chiang left Canton in disgust on February 21; the disgust may have been due to a disagreement with Borodin.[87] From then on the overworked Liao Chung-k'ai and a committee of seven carried the burden of planning for the academy, establishing it physically, selecting most of the staff, examining a large number of applicants and admitting some 500 for the first class. Financing was a problem, and is still something of a riddle. In trying to persuade Chiang to return, Sun Yat-sen telegraphed him on February 29 stating that the problem of finances for the academy had been settled. Mr. Liao, after repeatedly urging Chiang to take up his duties, telegraphed him on April 3, "As to funds for the military academy, I will not ask about disbursements and you will not ask about sources. There is no lack of funds, and you can proceed to administer with peace of mind." [88] But where did the funds come from? Probably both from Kwangtung taxpayers and from Soviet Russia.

The Provincial Finance Office paid $186,000 in silver for preparatory expenses, and on May 22, weeks after the academy had started operations, the financial commission decided upon its initial monthly expenses—$30,000 to be derived from four governmental agencies.[89] However, a Russian report from Canton, dating about April 1926, states that "This school was organized by us in 1924 and at first was maintained at our expense." And several years later, Borodin told Louis Fischer that the Soviet government made a grant of Rub 3 million for the organization of the school and its initial running expenses. This would be about Ch$2.7 million.[90]

The Russian contribution to Whampoa was much more than financial. The Soviet concept of equal emphasis on political indoctrination and military training and the idea of party representatives ("Commissars") at each level of the military structure were adapted at Whampoa and later in the party army. And from the beginning Russian officers served as military instructors at the academy, trying to bring the cadets up to Russian tactical standards. Small groups of new Russian instructors came in July and October 1924.[91]

On June 16, the generalissimo had the satisfaction of presiding at a daylong ceremony formally inaugurating the Army Officers Academy (*Lu-chün Chün-kuan Hsüeh-hsiao*). Accompanied by Mme Sun, party leaders, commanders of various armies, and officials of his government, Sun reviewed the cadets, presented the academy flag, and heard the swearing of the academy oath. He delivered a long inspirational speech in which, though he did not mention the Soviet Russian contribution to the founding of the academy, he praised the great success of the Russian Revolution and asked why it had succeeded while in China the results had been so meager. The secret and the lesson were Russia's creation of a revolutionary army to consolidate the victory. Now China was soon to have its revolutionary army, and the Whampoa cadets were to be its foundation. He then discoursed upon the glories of the death-defying spirit of the martyrs of the 1911 revolution. This spirit must be captured by the cadets. With it the victory of the revolutionary army over the unspeakably evil militarists was assured.[92] It was one of Sun's most emotional speeches, with surprisingly little mention of party ideology.

There was one Russian military officer who actually lost his life in Dr. Sun's cause: Gen. P. A. Pavlov, a well-educated, thirty-two-year-old commander who had distinguished himself as a leader in the Red Army during the Russian civil war.[93] He came to Canton on about June 20 under the name Govoroff, accompanying Borodin on his return from the North with his wife and one son.[94] Although General Pavlov made suggestions for improving the military instruction at Whampoa, his main efforts were directed toward the unification of the heterogenous armies clustering around Sun Yat-sen, and toward the creation of a more adequate defense of Canton. He proposed the creation of a Military Council, which was decided upon July 11 at the first meeting of the Kuomintang Political Council—itself a new body suggested by Borodin to Dr. Sun. General Pavlov also undertook to estimate the potentialities for success of a northern campaign, which Generalissimo Sun was even then contemplating; Pavlov's preliminary view was negative. He then went off to inspect the eastern front and was tragically drowned in the East River near Shihlung on July 19, after only a month as Dr. Sun's chief foreign military adviser.[95] His replacement, Gen. Vasily Konstantinovich Blücher, arrived in Canton in October, under the pseudonym Zoi Vsevolodovich Galin; [96] by then, however, Dr. Sun had only a few weeks remaining in Canton.

On October 7, the first shipment of Russian arms for Dr. Sun's cause arrived in Canton, aboard the *Vorovsky*, which had come from Odessa via the Indian Ocean and was enroute to Vladivostok. The ship brought several thousand rifles and ammunition, some machine guns and field pieces, as well as nine Russian officers for the Whampoa Military Academy.[97] The arms arrived just about a year after Dr. Sun had first asked Borodin for such concrete help. On October 7 Sun was off at Shao-kuan organizing another northward military campaign, and when he heard of the arrival of the arms he ordered Chiang Kai-shek to have them offloaded directly at Whampoa, in defiance of customs.[98] They were much needed to equip the First Training Regiment, which was being formed as the initial unit of the future party army. The arms came at a very tense moment, when the conflict between Dr. Sun's government and the Canton merchants was approaching its climax.

Soviet Russia assisted the Canton government in yet another important way—the establishment of the Central Bank. In May 1923, Dr. Sun had tried to set up such a bank but did not have the resources to do so. Then, on August 2, 1924, after considerable preparation, he appointed his Harvard and Columbia-trained brother-in-law, T. V. Soong, to be manager of the Central Bank of China. The bank was to be the government's financial agent with the exclusive right to float foreign and domestic bonds, issue banknotes, and serve as the government's treasury for all receipts and disbursements. At the formal opening of the bank Dr. Sun made a speech in which he announced that the capital of $10 million had been provided by a foreign loan. Some, if not all, of the financing came from the sole friendly foreign government, Soviet Russia, but whether as an actual transfer of funds or merely as a promise of support is not clear.[99]

In his speech at the opening, Dr. Sun urged military officers and officials present, some of whom apparently had other ideas as to how the money should be used, to regard the capital as seed grain or as a laying hen, which could produce wealth in abundance. He promised that all notes issued by the bank would be backed 100 percent by cash reserves. He begged the public to trust and support the bank; if they did so, the bank could prevent foreigners from controlling the money market, assist the revolution, and change China into a rich and strong country. But by then Dr. Sun had expropriated a shipment of arms belonging to the Merchants' Corps, and no appeals from him could persuade the merchant community to accept the notes. They believed the bank had no reserves at all, though Dr. Sun's friends let out the news that it actually had nearly $60,000 on hand. The merchants threatened a strike, and the notes were not forced upon the public.[100] After suppression of the Merchants' Corps two months later, resistance ceased. After Dr. Sun had left Canton, The Central Bank gradually became a pillar of the regime.

Drawing the Masses into the Revolution

Another important way in which Soviet Russia assisted Dr. Sun's nationalist enterprise was by energizing mass movements, particularly among the farmers in Kwangtung. Borodin was keen on this aspect of revolutionary work, not only because he was a Marxist-Leninist, but also because of a specific decision of the Comintern's Executive Committee that was based on considerable recent theorizing about revolution in colonial and semicolonial countries. In May 1923 the Executive Committee of the Communist International issued a directive on policy for the Third Congress of the Chinese Communist Party.[101] A central feature of this directive was a statement of the need for an agrarian revolution. The national revolution in China could be successful, the directive argued, only if the basic masses of the Chinese population, that is "peasants and small landowners," were drawn into the movement.

2. Thus the *peasant problem* becomes the central point of the entire policy. To ignore this basic point . . . is to fail to understand the full significance of the social and economic foundation upon which alone can be based the victorious struggle against foreign imperialism and the complete destruction of the feudal regime in China.

3. Therefore, the Communist Party, which is the party of the working class, must aim at an alliance between the workers and the peasants. . . .

This task could be carried out, the directive stated, only through continuous propaganda and through the actual implementation of the slogans of agrarian revolution, which included confiscation of the land of landlords, monasteries, and churches, and "passing it" to the peasants without compensation. Rack rent, existing systems of taxation, tax-farming, internal tariff boundaries, and the mandarinate all must go. Organs of peasant self-government must be created to take charge of land confiscation.

8. The Communist Party must continuously influence the Kuomintang in favor of the agrarian revolution. In the places occupied by the troops of Sun Yat-sen, it is imperative to insist that confiscation of the land be carried out in favor of the poorest peasantry, and that a number of other revolutionary measures be taken. Only thus can we ensure the success of Sun's revolutionary army and its popularity with the peasantry; and only thus can we widen the basis of the anti-imperialist revolution.

This was a formidable assignment, for Sun Yat-sen and most of the senior Kuomintang members opposed so radical a land policy. Dr. Sun favored interclass unity around his movement, and many Kuomintang leaders, particularly wealthy overseas supporters, probably were themselves large landowners in Kwangtung. Furthermore, a program of land confiscation could arouse instant and strong opposition among men with real power in the province.

As we have shown, Borodin tried at least three times to induce the reluctant Kuomintang to accept his radical land program: in November 1923, during the critical days of Ch'en Chiung-ming's drive on Canton; early in January 1924, while working out the party program for the First Kuomintang Congress; and then in February, when he rewrote the less radical plank adopted by the congress so as to incorporate his own ideas. Doubtless he lectured Dr. Sun on the need for a drastic agrarian program, but on the question of land expropriation and redistribution, Dr. Sun was unyielding.[102]

The political program adopted by the Kuomintang at its First Congress showed a sentiment for rural reform: the government should regulate size of land holdings, limit land taxes, find useful employment for bandits and vagrants, and assure a sufficiency of food for all. The party leadership did intend to draw China's vast farming population into the national revolution, and immediately after the congress the newly elected Central Executive Committee established a Farmers Bureau and appointed Lin Tsu-han as its head. Lin was about forty years old, a Hunanese revolutionary who had joined the T'ung Meng Hui in 1905 and the Kuomintang in 1912, and who had worked with Sun Yat-sen during his second exile in Japan after the abortive revolt against Yuan Shih-k'ai.[103] He was also an early member of the Chinese Communist Party. However, in April 1924 Lin left Canton for organizational work in Hankow and was replaced by P'eng Su-min, a leftist among the non-Communist members of the Kuomintang.[104] Before he departed, Lin recommended P'eng Pai as secretary of the Farmers Bureau, and from then till about mid-1925, P'eng, a Communist with two years' experience in organizing a radical movement among poor farmers in his native Hai-feng County, was the driving spirit of the Kuomintang Farmers Bureau. This remarkable young activist came from a very rich landlord lineage, had been given a traditional education and then gone to Waseda University where he was radicalized; he had been further stimulated by the May Fourth Movement and been drawn into the Socialist Youth Corps, and had returned in 1921 to his native county to spread the "new culture" under the patronage of none other than Ch'en Chiung-ming. The farmers' associations in Hai-feng that P'eng organized—or, they may be called peasant unions, for those who prefer—grew to many thousands of members and became militant in their demands for rent reductions—so militant that large landowners begged Gen. Ch'en Chiung-ming to suppress the movement, to which he consented early in 1924. P'eng Pai fled to Canton where he soon became a leader in the Kuomintang's effort to mobilize farmers for its nationalistic goals.[105]

Work started very slowly, with a three-man bureau that was somehow supposed to reach and move the millions of farm families in Kwangtung. The first proposed step was an investigation of farmers' economic conditions and of existing farmers' organizations, as well as planning for a new organization and movement. After several false starts, on June 30 the bureau got a plan accepted by the Kuomintang Central Executive Committee, which called for the establishment of a farmers' movement headquarters somewhere near Canton, the appointment of twenty special deputies to go into the field as organizers, the creation of a Farmers' Movement Training Institute to prepare field organizers, and a farmers' congress in September to establish a provincial farmers' association.[106] Thus, the movement was in the planning stage up until July.

The Farmers' Movement Training Institute admitted its first class of thirty-eight on July 3, and the course lasted seven weeks. The recruits were mostly young persons influenced by the May Fourth Movement ideal of "going among the people," although there were a few farmers and workers who had experience in unionization work. In addition there were two female students.[107] Two anti-Communist writers who could have known the facts, assert that only Communists were admitted to this first class.[108] P'eng Pai was in charge of training; he emphasized theory and much practical field work as well. Twenty-four of the thirty-three graduates were selected as special deputies to organize farmers' associations in Canton suburbs and in nearby counties. The organizers decided to enroll a much larger class for the second term, realizing that the few graduates of the first "were only a trifle in relation to Kwangtung's 94 counties and twenty-four million farmers." They recruited 225 students and gave them a two and a half months course under the direction of Lo Ch'i-yüan. This group received military training, and about halfway through their term the students were organized into a "farmers' corps" and sent up to Sun Yat-sen's expeditionary headquarters at Shaokuan for some field training. About 140 of this class completed the training and graduated on October 30, and at least 14 became special deputies. [109] Thus, by the time Sun Yat-sen left for the North, the institute had given short courses to 175 specialists for the farmers' movement, and there was a field staff of some 40 or more.

Dr. Sun visited the training institute on August 21 or 23, and lectured the first group of graduates on the proper approach to their work. He stressed the importance of bringing farmers into the national revolution; this largest of China's classes must be roused to an understanding of the Three Principles of the People, and be told how the principles would benefit them and how the government planned to assist them. China's landlords squeeze their tenants to the last drop, Sun said; in this respect the Chinese farmer is worse off than were the Russian serfs before their emancipation. Russia has abolished landlords and divided the land among the peasants so the tiller has his land and pays only a tax to the government, Dr. Sun averred. This should be emulated for a fundamental revolution in China, but it could not be carried out quickly. China should not follow the aggressive methods the Soviet government had used in trying to destroy the bourgeois class because China's social conditions were very different. Essentially, Dr. Sun argued that the farming class must be drawn to support the national revolution, but he cautioned against class struggle. The farmers should be organized into unions but urged to cooperate with other classes. The rural problems of China would be solved through peaceful cooperation between the government and farmers and between farmers and landowners, rather than through force, conflict, and destruction. "For the present," Dr. Sun admonished the graduates,

> you must be very cautious in your propaganda, speak only of the farmers' suffering, and teach them how to unite—beginning with *hsiang* and county, then by prefecture and province, and finally throughout the country. You should especially persuade all farmers to cooperate with the

government, and deliberate carefully on the method to solve the relation of farmers to landlords so that the farmer will benefit and the landlord not suffer loss. . . . The objective is that the tiller shall have his land, receive the results of his labor, and not have it seized by another.[110]

This conservative approach was very far from Borodin's ideas of forced land redistribution and from the concept of interclass struggle which the young activists were absorbing in their reading and training. In Hai-feng, P'eng Pai had just recently led a poor farmers' movement characterized by class warfare, and he knew the difficulty, or perhaps the impossibility, of persuading tenants to accept a peaceful solution of their conflict with landlords.

Farmers' associations were to be organized according to a simple plan which was issued in June 1924, but it reveals a notable concept. Farmers' associations (Nung-min hsieh-hui) were to be completely autonomous bodies not under outside restraint. They were to organize guards for the coming period of struggle and to protect themselves against bandits and soldiers, and these guards were to be the only armed unit in a village. The government would supervise the guards but could not use them for activities not connected with the defense of their own villages. Farmers' associations had certain specific rights: to accuse judicially, to serve in the collection of land taxes, and to "solve land-tax questions," but they did not have executive authority, which was reserved for governmental agencies. The basic level of organization was at the hsiang (or sub-sub county), and an association could be established if there were twenty-five or more members age sixteen sui and above. Excluded from membership were persons owning 100 or more mou (sixteen acres or more), those practicing usury, teachers of religion such as spiritualists, pastors, Buddhist, Taoist, and Confucian priests, mediums, etc., "those who were manipulated by imperialism," and opium smokers and gamblers. There was to be a five-tiered structure—hsiang, ch'ü, county, province, and national level—parallel to the structure of the Kuomintang itself, but the associations were not to be under that party's control in view of their mandated autonomy.[111] Activists in the associations, might, however, be recruited into the Kuomintang.

Another organizational matter deserves attention. A frank bit of history by an unnamed Communist author, probably Lo Ch'i-yüan, relates how the Communist Party organized itself to direct the farmers' movement in Kwangtung. At the third Chinese Communist Party congress held in Canton in June 1923, the task of directing policy for the farmers' movement was taken away from the Socialist Youth Corps and given to the Communist Party. After the Kuomintang reorganization in January 1924, when it had recognized the farmers' movement as a form of revolutionary work, the writer says, "we used the name of the Kuomintang Central Farmers Bureau" to organize the Farmers' Movement Training Institute. At this time (referring to the summer of 1924), a farmers committee (*nung hui*) was organized in the party—that is, the Chinese Communist Party—"to direct the work of the Kuomintang Central Farmers Bureau." It then states that the farmers committee directed not only that bureau but other parts of the farmers' movement apparatus as they were established.[112] Thus the system of farmers' associations was to be entirely autonomous; the leaders of the movement vehemently insisted upon this. Yet the Communist Party itself intended to control the development and orientation of the system. It seems likely that Mr. Borodin, with his strong interest in bringing the rural population into the revolution, acted as an adviser to the "Farmers Committee" of the Communist Party in Kwangtung when he was there; and we know that in July 1924 he was appointed adviser to a three-man committee within the central apparatus of the Kuomintang that was to study farmers' conditions.[113]

During the period when Dr. Sun was still in the south, the main locale for developing farmers' associations was the suburbs of Canton and in the nearby counties where Sun's government had some influence. Two aspects are most interesting. One is the slowness of the start in the area around Canton. An official report says that by September 1924 some 47 associations had been created, including 5 county associations.[114] Yet as late as the next April there were only 1,500 members reported in the Canton suburbs, while the 5 adjacent counties had 91 associations with a stated total of 10,890 members. The memberships are all given in round numbers; in one case 4,000, which must be an estimate only. In Hsiang-shan, Dr. Sun's home county on the southern coast, there were 58 associations with a reported total of 8,000 members.[115] This is a small showing for eight months' effort, although in two more distant areas, under quite special circumstances, associations had been created in large numbers.[116]

The second notable point is the violent conflicts that erupted as soon as associations were formed. In October and November 1924, conflicts emerged as graduates of the first two classes of the Farmers' Movement Training Institute began organizing in their native counties. Typically, men of power and property set people's corps (*min t'uan*), or simply hired toughs, against the new associations that were mobilizing farmers to resist some customary tax or uniting tenants to demand rent reduction. A few association headquarters were wrecked, a village or two burned down, and some militants were killed. Not many such cases are known before Dr. Sun's departure, so he may not have been aware of anything unusual in the normally violent Kwangtung countryside; but the conflicts increased as the number of associations grew. They began to introduce the raw stuff of class struggle into the national revolution.

One well-reported case occurred in Kwang-ning County, a poor and backward region on the northwest of Kwangtung.[117] There the farmers' movement got an early start when unionized oil workers from Canton returned to Kwang-ning and set up farmers' associations. In May 1924 these were crushed by "landlords and evil gentry," who also succeeded in blackening the names of the organizers among the conservative farm folk. In August, a group of young Communists led by Chou Ch'i-chien arrived in Kwang-ning to reenergize the movement, and they were immediately confronted by a landlord organization, the "Society to Protect Property." This organization began to mobilize *min t'uan*, recruit bandits, and purchase arms. P'eng Pai arrived, probably in September, and by early November he was joined by some twenty graduates of the second class of the institute who were natives of the county and had had military training. Both sides mobilized their respective strengths: on the one side, wealth, prestige, the appeal to customary morality, and control of the local militia stiffened by mercenaries; on the other side, determined leadership, tight organization, a large number of tenant farmers with accumulated grievances, and, in the background, the latent power of the government at Canton. Battles erupted late in November, and it was not till February 1925, after a complicated political struggle, that the outside organizers won the fight against powerful gentry lineages, and then only with the help of troops sent from Canton. (Borodin allegedly gave distant assistance in this, as in some of the other, farmers' struggles.[118]) After the victory, farmers' associations flourished in Kwang-ning. By April there were said to be nearly 55,000 members in 294 local units.

Thus was the farmers' movement launched with Russian encouragement as an element in Dr. Sun's "Soviet alliance"—a heritage for the future.

The Kuomintang needed no Russian encouragement to involve itself in the labor movement. In the south it had a long history of organizing unions and being supported by them. Unionization was more advanced in Canton and Hong Kong than elsewhere in China: in 1922 Canton had some 200 registered guilds and unions. Characteristically there were both socialist and anarchist strains among the leadership, but Communists had very little influence in the southern labor movement before 1924. The attempt in May 1922 to unite all unions under the leadership of the Communist Labor Secretariat at the "All China Congress of Workers" had failed, and it left a legacy of suspicion among southern non-Communist labor leaders.[119]

Canton labor organizations were a melange of the traditional and the modern.[120] There was the labor boss recruitment system; traditional monopolistic craft guilds, which included both employers and workers; benevolent societies to aid workers and associations to encourage modern industry; and the more recently organized unions in the modern sector such as those of seamen, railway workers, mechanics, and factory workers. There were also federations of several sorts. Probably the strongest was the Kwangtung Mechanics Union (*Kwangtung Chi-ch'i Kung-hui*), a province-wide federation of unions among engineers, electricians, mechanics, and foundrymen. Among its leaders were Huang Huan-t'ing and Ma Chao-chün, and the union generally supported Sun Yat-sen. The Seamen's Union, which early in 1922 had won a spectacular strike against British shipping and set off a wave of unionization throughout China, had its headquarters in Canton and branches in Hong Kong and other southern ports. Its leader, Ch'en Ping-sheng, had a long association with the T'ung Meng Hui and other predecessors of the Chung-kuo Kuomintang. There was also a Mutual Aid Society (*Hu Chu She*), founded by the Columbia-educated Socialist, Hsieh Ying-pai, a close associate of Dr. Sun's. [121] This society tried to bring together unions and intellectuals that worked with labor, and its members were supposed to be members of the Kuomintang also. In 1922 Mr. Hsieh and Mr. Huang were among the main organizers of the Kwangtung General Labor Union (*Kwangtung Tsung Kung Hui*), which supposedly embraced sixty-eight unions in Canton. The complexity of the situation is revealed by the fact that Mr. Hsieh also had a part, in March 1922, in the reorganization of the Young Men's Socialist Society, which became the Canton branch of the Socialist Youth Corps. The corps was the principal subsidiary of the Chinese Communist Party. Among the society members were such Cantonese radicals as T'an P'ing-shan, Ch'en Kung-po, T'an Chiht'ang, Feng Chü-p'o and Yang P'ao-an, all of whom were, or became, Communists and were active in the southern labor movement. [122] Except for Ch'en Kung-po, who was in New York studying at Columbia, these were among the people that Borodin reassured on October 17, 1923, shortly after his arrival in Canton, that he would be working to increase the influence of the Communist Party even though in his press interview he had spoken of the Kuomintang. [123]

In June 1922 the Canton labor movement was badly shattered when Gen. Yeh Chü's troops drove Sun Yat-sen to refuge on a gunboat in Canton waters. Some unions and their leaders supported Dr. Sun but others supported Ch'en Chiung-ming. Several of Dr. Sun's followers among the labor leadership had to flee. [124] Thus the Canton labor movement was fractured in its structure and divided by the dissension among its would-be leaders. Organized labor in Hong Kong was not so seriously affected by the split between Dr. Sun and General Ch'en, but beside the persistence of guilds along with more modern unions, there were two rival federations there. While passing through Hong Kong in February 1923, Dr. Sun tried, unsuccessfully, to persuade the federations to unite. He also sought their financial support.

Dr. Sun was well known to be prolabor though moderate in his social views. After his return to Canton it was easy to mobilize unions in his support.[125] But factional rivalry persisted. After the First Kuomintang Congress a new Labor Bureau was established with Liao Chung-k'ai in charge. Personally loyal to Dr. Sun and favoring the Russian orientation and admission of the Communists into the Kuomintang, Mr. Liao was overburdened with many posts. He had to leave much of the responsibility for the Labor Bureau to its secretary, the Communist, Feng Chü-p'o. But Feng had the ill-will of conservative labor leaders, who were on guard against any attempt to undermine their authority or spread Communist influence in their unions. For their part, the Canton members of the "party of the proletariat" were intent on using the Kuomintang to gain control of organized labor in the South. This was one of the principal reasons why they had joined the other party. An instruction to the Socialist Youth Corps in the Canton region as late as April, 1924, states: "The comrades should beg admittance to the Kuomintang labor unification movement and, under the Kuomintang banner, guide labor into the struggle for the national revolution as well as economic struggles." [126] This instruction stemmed from basic Communist policy—capture control of the labor movement.

In an effort to unite the labor movement, Liao Chung-k'ai planned a Labor Day parade and rally for May 1, 1924. All unions were to be included, in the hopes of bringing them into the national revolutionary forces. Thousands of workers marched and Dr. Sun addressed them at noon. The thrust of his argument was to direct Chinese labor away from a domestic class struggle and into a struggle against foreign economic privilege in China. Since China was a colonial country subject to all the powers, he stated, the position of labor naturally was low. Chinese workers should create one great organization just as in advanced countries. Chinese labor was oppressed only by foreign capitalists not by Chinese, and the heart of the oppression lay in foreign control of the Maritime Customs which prevented a protective tariff and permitted the influx of foreign goods which ruined Chinese industry and depressed wages.

In Soviet Russia there was a labor dictatorship and in England a labour government, the result of workers' organization and struggle. Chinese workers should organize also and oppose foreign economic oppression by abolishing all unequal treaties. Though British and Russian labor were China's models, the fundamental method should be the Three Principles of the People and the Five Power Constitution. "If you laborers can follow my principles and advance my method," Dr. Sun exhorted, "you can capture the same high social position held by British and Russian labor. The great issue is not struggle between Chinese labor and capital but the political question, which will be solved by upholding the Three Principles of the People and joining my revolution." [127]

Shortly after May Day, Dr. Sun became seriously ill, apparently exhausted by a sixteen-hour schedule during which he made several long speeches to labor groups. On May 14 he was reported dead, and some foreign newspapers published obituaries.[128] Was this an early symptom of the cancer which took his life ten months later?

During the first week of May, as part of his scheme to unify labor in Canton, Mr. Liao convened a conference of "Canton Workers' Delegates," but most of the union leaders preferred to stick to the provincial federation while the Mechanics Union clung to its autonomy. The conference passed a series of resolutions, which reveal the difficulties the Kuomintang had in persuading existing unions and labor clubs to amalgamate and federate; they also reveal how elementary were the reforms in employment practices the leaders hoped to win. The resolutions were unpolitical and undoctrinaire: they seem purely reformist.[129] The most important problems seemed to be organizational: how to bring workers into larger unions, how to amalgamate existing unions, and how unions and confederations were to be governed—problems of centralization as against autonomy. The conference leaders hoped to create industry-wide unions, breaking away from specialized craft guilds; they also hoped to federate unions covering all branches of transportation and communications, so as to embrace workers on the three railway lines leading from Canton and workers in all branches of shipping. The complicated procedures laid out for organizing executive committees in unions and federations suggest the strong rivalries which had to be accommodated.

Concerning labor benefits, the organizers wanted the union shop, no contracting by foremen, grievance committees, limitation of work by apprentices to nine hours daily without reduction of pay, equal pay for equal work, and schools for workers to be set up by the government but managed by the executive committee of the Conference of Workers' Delegates (*Kung-jen Tai-piao Ta-hui*), as the new body was named. The head of the Executive Committee was to be the head of the Kuomintang Central Labor Bureau, currently Mr. Liao.

The most obviously political resolution was one on "The Merchants' Corps Problem." This demanded that the government forbid the Merchants' Corps from mixing in union business and forbid workers from serving the Merchants' Corps, which were partly manned by clerks. Most importantly, the government should permit workers to organize their own self-defense corps. Soon after the conference, an armed workers' corps was established with Dr. Sun's approval. T'an P'ing-shan became its chief. A sanguinary clash between this group and the Canton Merchants' Corps erupted on October 10.

In June the first conference of the Transport Workers of the Pacific, organized by the Red Trade Union International, met in Canton with representatives from the suppressed railway unions of North China and delegates from the Philippines and Indonesia, as well as leaders of some Canton unions. Gregory Voitinsky, the Comintern representative who had replaced Maring in China, and

Leo Heller, a Profintern official, attended and presumably steered things. The twenty-five delegates had no common language. Liao Chung-k'ai substituted for Dr. Sun as a main speaker. Judging from the resolutions that concerned China,[130] the conference was to aid Communist Party efforts to bring Chinese railway workers, seamen, postal employees, telegraph and telephone operators, and electrical workers into a single federation under its control—i.e., the most politically strategic sector of the working force. It is difficult, however, to estimate the utility or success of this secret conference.[131]

The strike of Shameen workers, which lasted from July 15 to August 20 was a strike with strongly antiimperialist resonance, pitting Chinese workers under Kuomintang leadership against foreigners. This strike gave the Labor Bureau an opportunity to rally unions and radical patriots in a common effort and to work out methods of mobilizing public support. It turned out to be a dress rehearsal for the great Canton-Hong Kong strike and boycott of the next year.

The issue which precipitated the strike concerned new security measures on Shameen island, the small concession held by Britain and France just off the Canton bund. British and French authorities imposed these measures after an Annamite revolutionary attempted to assassinate the visiting governor-general of French Indochina, M. Merlin, on June 19. The leaders of the French community were at a dinner in Governor Merlin's honor at the Victoria Hotel on Shameen. The soup had just been served, when Pham Hong Thai threw a handbag containing a bomb through a window. The bomb landed on the dinner table and exploded, killing five people and wounding twenty-eight. The governor-general escaped injury, while his assailant fled, dived into the river, and drowned.[132]

The consular body addressed a note to Liao Chung-k'ai, who was then civil governor, requesting the Canton authorities to suppress plots and movements against foreign governments in areas within its jurisdiction. Not satisfied with the reply, the Shameen ratepayers decided to institute a system of passes with photographs which would be required of all Chinese entering the island after 9:00 P.M., to begin August 1. This was taken as an affront to Chinese dignity, and the strike was incited to protest the regulations. Liu Erh-sung, a Communist labor leader, is credited with being the main organizer.

Many of the Chinese who worked on Shameen left on July 15, and gradually all the Chinese employees of consulates, banks, and stores, house servants, and Cantonese members of the police force walked off their jobs—some 2,000 men and 300 women. The strike quickly took on its antiimperialist character with slogans against the unequal treaties, foreign control of the customs, and other grievances. Strike pickets guarded the bridges leading to the island in order to prevent Chinese from entering, and a "People's Association Against the Shameen Regulations" gathered funds. At least twenty-six unions allied themselves with the strike; cargo boatmen and stevedores serving British ships were brought into the movement; and threats to Chinese sailors on vessels under foreign register induced many to quit their ships. The organizers hoped to cut off all supplies of food to the island, but this proved impossible. The British and French brought gunboats to Canton, which prevented that form of pressure from being effective.

The Shameen strike lasted thirty-six days, though it was difficult to hold it together. Chinese depositors in foreign banks could not get at their money and so were eager that the strike be settled. Many workers could not afford the loss of pay, although various groups raised money to support them. The sticking point in the negotiations was whether or not Chinese constables who had quit Shameen should be rehired. After two abortive settlements, a compromise saved the face of the constables but left the Shameen authorities the final decision on their permanent reinstatement. Sun Yat-sen promised to put any displaced constables in the Canton police force; and the British and French authorities agreed to rescind the regulations and take back the Chinese police temporarily. This was a psychological victory for the revolutionists in Canton and for Dr. Sun's government, which had been supporting the strike.[133]

Michael Borodin was back in Canton at the time of the strike and served again as Dr. Sun's main foreign political adviser. There were ten or more Russian military men serving at Whampoa, and two labor experts, Voitinsky and Heller, had been in Canton in late June and might still have been there in mid-July. However, the sources I have seen do not reveal whether or not there was any Russian advice or assistance in this antiimperialist strike.

Certain features of the Shameen strike foreshadowed the great strike and boycott of the following year. On the organizational side was a strike committee directly under the Kuomintang Labor Bureau. Its functions were to coordinate the strike effort, solicit funds and distribute relief to the strikers, and elicit sympathy strikes from unions not directly involved. The committee organized the pickets who guarded the bridges to prevent Chinese from entering the island without passes issued by the committee itself. In addition, the committee used the pickets to prevent a return to work until negotiations settling all the issues were completed. "The People's Association" gathered funds, and theatrical folk and schoolgirls assisted in the campaign.

Another presaging feature of the Shameen strike was the position taken by the generalissimo's government—that of mediator between the strike committee and the British and French authorities. Sun's government pretended not to be directly involved, which was only technically the case. It seems that Sun Yat-sen and his close associates, had to mediate among the Kuomintang moderates, the more radical leaders who wished to prolong the strike for ideological benefits, and the strikers themselves, eager to resume work but prevented by the strike committee.[134]

The antiimperialist slogans and patriotic fervor produced by the strike were most congenial to the nationalist movement. They drew support to the Kuomintang just as it began to face the armed opposition of the Chinese merchant community in Canton and surrounding towns. In addition they won the support of the overseas Chinese and the sympathy of patriotic Chinese in places reached by the modern press.

By August 1924 the Kuomintang had begun to bring the fragmented labor movement in South China under its leadership and into the movement against imperialism. But it was only a start.

Below the surface were rivalries between various labor affiliations, conflict between radical and conservative leaders of the party, and Communists' ambition to radicalize and dominate the labor movement, that doctrine prescribed to be the Communist Party's primary sphere as leader of the proletariat.

CHAPTER EIGHT

Frustrations and the New Hope

All did not run smoothly in Dr. Sun's newfound relationship with Soviet Russia, although the veil which has been drawn around the facts makes it difficult to judge how rough or smooth the relationship truly was. At the personal level there are few clues as to how Dr. Sun and Mr. Borodin got on with each other.

Problems with the Sino-Soviet Treaty

One divisive issue probably was the Sino-Soviet negotiations being conducted between Ambassador Karakhan and the Peking government. As we know, Dr. Sun strongly opposed the Peking regime; he often begged the powers not to recognize successive northern presidents, and he had particularly urged Moscow not to negotiate with Peking but either to wait until he himself had captured the capital or negotiate with his government in Canton. The purpose of the Karakhan mission, however, was to negotiate a treaty of mutual recognition with the Chinese government that was recognized by all the powers and thereby to gain large benefits for Russia.

Without going into details of the negotiations or of the treaty itself,[1] it is enough to say that on March 14, 1924, Dr. C. T. Wang, representing the Chinese government, and Mr. Karakan, representing the government of the USSR initialed (or signed?) an agreement on general principles for the settlement of questions at a forthcoming conference. In this agreement, Soviet Russia recognized, and was recognized by, the government which Dr. Sun regarded as his enemy. However, the Peking cabinet refused to ratify the agreement, and Ambassador Karakhan issued a three-day ultimatum demanding that it do so immediately, without further negotiation. Karakhan also engaged in a propaganda campaign in order to convince the Chinese public of the fairness of the agreement and of the Chinese government's inability to perceive China's true interests. The ultimatum and the propaganda simply stiffened the Chinese cabinet's attitude. On March 20, Dr. Wellington Koo replaced Dr. Wang and tried to bring Mr. Karakhan to further negotiations, while the Foreign Office sent telegrams to the provinces explaining its position and seeking support. Among other matters the telegrams called attention to the inconsistency of Soviet Russia's recognizing the sovereignty of China in Outer Mongolia while keeping in force Mongolian-Soviet treaties and maintaining a Russian minister in Urga. There was considerable public support for the Peking government's position, even among some of Dr. Sun's followers, but there was also a strongly stated body of opinion which favored Soviet Russia and opposed the Peking government. Various important provincial military leaders pressured Peking to sign. The full resources of the Chinese Communist Party were mobilized to help. It was in this tense situation that Borodin appealed to Dr. Sun for his support, too.

From Peking, Borodin sent a telegram complaining of the government's failure to accept Mr. Karakhan's unselfish proposals and intimating that Dr. Sun should use his influence on behalf of Soviet Russia. The telegram was published in the *Canton Gazette* on April 1 in a communiqué of the government in the South. That government, as expressed through its organs, was "in favor of reassuming relations with Russia upon the preliminary terms as agreed between Dr. C. T. Wang and L. Karakhan." [2] The agreement, in effect a treaty, was signed on May 31, 1924 after a few minor modifications. A few days later, Gregory Voitinsky, the Comintern delegate for China, called upon Dr. Sun at his home on Honam Island. He reminisced about the visit only nine months later, after Sun Yat-sen's death.[3] Though the Koumintang people in the South were not pleased with the signing of the treaty, which seemed an act of disloyalty to the southern government, Sun Yat-sen "spoke very openly and made it clear that he understood thoroughly the meaning of the treaty between the U.S.S.R. and the Chinese government, as well as the significance of it for the Chinese people in general." So Voitinsky eulogized.

In July, after Borodin had returned to Canton but while Mr. Karakhan was still unable to take possession of the Russian legation, the Kuomintang issued a manifesto giving full support to the treaty. The manifesto opened by recalling the party's historic struggle for China's freedom and independence and pointed to the political program adopted by the First Kuomintang Congress, which called for abolition of unequal treaties and for most favored nation treatment of countries which had given up special privileges in China. Soviet Russia, it asserted, had cast off imperialism and long since stated its intention to give up all special rights. The manifesto then berated the Peking "bogus government" for procrastinating over implementing the new relations with Soviet Russia, a matter of greatest concern and benefit to the nation. It contrasted Russia's generosity, arising from its revolutionary ideology, with the position of all other powers, whose treaties over the past several decades were all invasions of China's sovereignty. The present Sino-Russian treaty accorded with the principle of equality and mutual respect for sovereignity as explained by Mr. Borodin in his telegram from Peking to the Leader; he had stressed that its spirit was in full accord with the foreign policy announced in the Kuomintang's political program. Yet the Peking "bogus government, which temporarily holds the seat of power, still delays in carrying out the Treaty in deference to the powers which give it breath." Hence, "rather than say Russia recognizes the Peking bogus government . . . and thus enhances its international position, one should better say the Peking bogus government received Russia's recognition the more to expose its evils to the people and the world." The manifesto closed with the hope that the Chinese and Russian people would increasingly understand each other; but as for the Peking bogus government, the people should hoe it out! Even before the treaty was signed, the Leader had explained to Canton reporters his full understanding of it and had opposed not only the errors of party members who had not made a full investigation of its terms but also the indifference and irresponsibility of the populace. "Therefore the Party instructs its members to carry out the Political Program and advocates upright reason as the way to guide the people." [4]

As he recovered from his serious illness of May 1924,[5] Dr. Sun confronted a problem much more vexing than either Mr. Karakhan's difficulties with the diplomatic corps or with the government in Peking. He had to deal with a broad protest within his own party over the way in which the Communist members were acting.

Conflict over Communists in the Kuomintang

The conflict may justly be traced back to Lenin's famous Theses on the National and Colonial Questions, which he formulated for the Second Congress of the Communist International, held in July–August 1920. Lenin advocated that Communist parties in backward and colonial countries join in national-revolutionary movements but maintain and strengthen their separate organizations to prepare for a proletarian socialist revolution.[6] This basic strategy was, of course, elaborated and refined in the following years. Reluctantly the Chinese Communist leaders had agreed to have their party members join the Kuomintang, which would lead the national-revolutionary movement. The leaders had to define a strategy for this ambiguous role and communicate it to the membership and to the party's adjunct, the Chinese Socialist Youth Corps. Discovery of this confidential strategy and observation of its implementation aroused the animosity of some veteran Kuomintang leaders and many common members.

In Paris, where conflict between Communist and non-Communist Chinese students was emerging, Tseng Ch'i, a founder of the Young China Party, had his attention brought to a small booklet, *Secret and Final Decision of the Chinese Communist Party in Joining the Kuomintang*, which contained the resolutions on that matter (quoted above, pp. 149–50) voted on at the third Congress of the Chinese Communist Party in June 1923 and at the Second Congress of the Chinese Socialist Youth Corps in August. In February 1924, Mr. Tseng asked a son-in-law of Hsieh Ch'ih to take the pamphlet to Mr. Hsieh in Shanghai, which presumably he did.[7] Hsieh Ch'ih, a member of the recently elected Kuomintang Central Supervisory Committee, was also a veteran of the anti-Manchu struggles, a member of the first Parliament elected in 1913, and long a loyal follower of Sun Yat-sen.

According to another account,[8] a Kuomintang member who had joined the Communist Party showed Hsieh Ch'ih an issue of the Socialist Youth Corps' *Journal* which contained a series of reports and resolutions adopted at an enlarged meeting of the corps' Executive Committee, held at the end of March 1924. This set off the fireworks, first in Shanghai during the latter part of April and in May. Chang Chi, another member of the Kuomintang Central Supervisory Committee, joined in an investigation of Communists in the Kuomintang. He had been one of the active student leaders in Japan before the Republican Revolution, had helped to reorganize the T'ung Meng Hui into an open political party, and had been elected to the first Parliament also. At one time close to the Anarchists, he was one of Dr. Sun's links with intellectuals in Peking after the May Fourth Incident. Chang Chi became a friend of Maring, worked for the union of Communists and the Kuomintang, and sponsored Li Ta-chao, his fellow provincial, as the first Communist to join the Kuomintang under Dr. Sun's new policy. A lion of a man and a fighter, he was not to be trifled with. Apparently since November 1923 both Mr. Hsieh and Mr. Chang had become skeptical of the loyalty of Communists to the Kuomintang.[9]

The Youth Corps' *Journal* printed resolutions [10] on strategy in local work, such as concentrating on the seamen and railway workers in the Canton labor movement; on trying to become the heart of future farmers' corps in Shunte (the county south of Canton); and on influencing the student federation by working through the Kuo-

[233]

mintang Youth Bureau in Shanghai. Resolutions concerning the attitude of Youth Corps members in the Kuomintang cautioned against creating unnecessary conflict or competing for high-level positions. Instead, members were instructed to strive to induct farmers, workers, and middle school students so as to increase the number of revolutionists and to expand proletarian power in the Kuomintang. There followed a quotation of eight resolutions concerning the work and the attitude of Communist Party members in the Kuomintang,[11] which apparently were adopted by the Central Committee in a plenum after the Kuomintang's First Congress.

Why cooperate? the resolutions asked; and the answer was that under present economic conditions, China must pass through the national revolution of the People's livelihood, which was the Kuomintang's mission. But the Kuomintang's organizational discipline was lax and had prevented it from completing the national revolution speedily; hence the Communist party had decided that its members should join to encourage the Kuomintang to fulfill its task. Because the Kuomintang was undergoing reorganization, Communist Party members must not retain their old contempt for the Kuomintang but rather should assist in its progress. Though not entirely satisfied with the results of the Kuomintang Congress, Communists should be careful not to categorize as "Rightists" those members who were cool toward themselves, nor treat them disrespectfully; such actions would only create a Right faction. The correct strategy would be to try to convert Right into Left and not adopt an attitude which would drive Left to Right. To demonstrate cooperation, Communists must serve strenuously in Kuomintang work, but they must also find ways to guide its meetings and work. The Communist members in any sort of Kuomintang organization must carefully discuss methods of work for that organization and must educate comrades in correct procedure. "If our party comrades can fulfill their obligations and cause all Kuomintang members to fulfill theirs, this will make it truly become a party with organization and able to act, and our objective in joining the Kuomintang can then be achieved."

Communists should constantly propagandize the Kuomintang's

new declaration and not permit that party's members to disregard it. In selecting personnel for work in the other party's organizations, care must be exercised to pick competent and suitable Communists so as to earn the Kuomintang's respect and trust, and also help its progress. Finally, we will quote the last two resolutions, because they were among the ones later called to Dr. Sun's attention.

(7) Hereafter in all propaganda, publishing, people's organizations, and other concrete movements related to the national revolution, our party should use the Kuomintang name and do it as Kuomintang work. We can thereby conserve energy and talent, cause the Kuomintang to change and develop, and concentrate and enlarge the effect of our efforts. But in matters which we recognize as essential and in which the Kuomintang is unwilling to use its name, we will still do them as our party's individual activity.

(8) Naturally, while developing the Kuomintang organization, we may not arrest the development of our own party organization. But when we introduce new persons into our party we should select them very carefully. No one who does not thoroughly understand our party's ideology, strategy and discipline, nor earnestly desire to take up the duties of our party, should be lightly drawn into membership. If we draw in many weak elements, not only will the Kuomintang misunderstand our purposely drawing away their members, but it will cause our party organization gradually to grow lax and confused.

Armed with such information on how the Communists intended to use the Kuomintang, and with some knowledge of what they were doing,[12] Hsieh Ch'ih and Chang Chi set off for Canton early in June to impeach the rival party before Sun Yat-sen and other Kuomintang leaders. Even before they arrived an anti-Communist tide had risen in Canton.

Meanwhile, the leaders of the Chinese Communist Party were having second thoughts. They held a secret enlarged plenum of the Central Committee in Shanghai from May 10 to 15. The Comintern's Executive Committee had become concerned by Voitinsky's report that Communists working within the Kuomintang felt "an ideological alienation" from its members. According to a report from Borodin, "a great ideological disorder prevailed in the Kuomintang."

The task of the plenum was to redefine the role of Communists in the other party. A Resolution on the Work of Communists in the Kuomintang condemned a tendency toward dissolution within the Nationalist Party (right deviation), noted the struggle between Right and Left currents in the Kuomintang, and advocated that Communists work to strengthen the Left Wing. A Resolution on the Trade Union Movement condemned excessive Communist involvement in Kuomintang organizational work and suggested a shift of emphasis to propaganda work: Communists should "strive to become actual leaders of the propaganda departments of the Kuomintang." The resolution also demanded the creation of "fighting-ready trade unions of a purely class character" for the vanguard of the Chinese proletariat—railway workers and miners—and warned that "we should not aid the Kuomintang as an organization to permeate the ranks of the industrial proletariat." The Communist Party might assist the party in organizing unions of artisans and salesmen, and should place its members in the Kuomintang labor departments in order to influence "the unfolding of class struggle and to create the all-worker front." [13]

Chang Kuo-t'ao, who attended this enlarged plenum, remembers that all the participants worried about membership in the Kuomintang, which the Comintern continued to insist upon. The plenum agreed, though without enthusiasm, to support the Kuomintang Left Wing. It decided that only a few Communists should devote themselves to practical work within the other party and those few should avoid mere routine tasks. The majority should concentrate on work among the proletariat, peasants, and young intellectuals in order to expand the Communist Party.

Shortly after the plenum, Ch'en Tu-hsiu told Chang Kuo-t'ao that Wang Ching-wei and Chang Chi had called on him and protested the practice of having Communist fractions within the Kuomintang. To Ch'en's great embarrassment his two visitors showed him the resolutions on the matter discovered in the Socialist Youth Corps' *Journal*. They said they spoke for Hu Han-min and Hsieh Ch'ih as well in finding the system of fractions a violation of Li Ta-chao's statement at the recent Kuomintang congress that Communists joined the senior party as individuals and not as a party within a party. In reply, Mr. Ch'en contended that the purpose of fractions was to assure that comrades abided by Kuomintang decisions and took an active part in the work; there was no intention to struggle for power or harm the Kuomintang in any way. Yet Ch'en Tu-hsiu confessed to Mr. Chang that if he were a Kuomintang member, he, too, would oppose communist fractions in his party. He recognized that the solidarity of this influential group of Nationalist leaders on the issue—three of whom had favored the party reorganization and could not be considered rightists—had serious implications for the future. Yet, as Chang Kuo-t'ao remembered the conclusions of their long discussion, the two men agreed that it certainly would not be acceptable for the Communist Party to dissolve itself within the Kuomintang, nor would it give up fractions. Either the Kuomintang would tacitly accede to the fraction system or the Communist Party would have to withdraw its members, hoping for inter-party cooperation thereafter.[14]

Down in Canton, Dr. Sun's son, Sun Fo, and Huang Chi-lu, both members of the municipal Kuomintang office, proposed on June 1 that central party headquarters restrict Communist agitation.[15] When Chang Chi arrived from Shanghai he brought the conflict into the open in a public lecture, and Hsieh Ch'ih offered a draft report to the Central Executive Committee on June 14. On the same day, Chang Chi went to discuss the problem with Sun Yat-sen, and that evening Li Lieh-chün gave a dinner for Kuomintang leaders on both sides of the fence to try to harmonize matters; but such an issue could not be settled at a dinner table. After reading Hsieh Ch'ih's draft of the accusation, Dr. Sun asked that the matter be deferred till the return of Mr. Borodin, who was expected soon.[16]

Two days later, Sun Yat-sen formally inaugurated the Kuomintang's new military academy, which Soviet Russia had largely financed. Among those attending the inauguration were Chang Chi and a number of other party leaders who were soon to oppose him.

On June 18, Teng Tse-ju, Chang Chi, and Hsieh Ch'ih of the five-man Central Supervisory Committee, placed a formal "Impeachment of the Chinese Communist Party" before the Leader and the

Central Executive Committee. After its formal opening, the impeachment quoted from resolutions of the Second Congress of the Socialist Youth Corps and of the Third Congress of the Communist Party, which stressed their revolutionary goals in joining the Kuomintang, instructed their members to be united in word and action within the other party in order to maintain their organizational independence, to steer the Kuomintang toward Soviet Russia, and to recruit the best elements of the Kuomintang into their own organization.[17] The impeachment next quoted from the Youth Corps' *Journal* some of the resolutions briefed above, which all dated later than Li Tao-chao's profession at the First Kuomintang Congress that the Communist Party had no ulterior purpose in joining. It then quoted, without a source, an instruction to all Communist Party and Youth Corps members in the Kuomintang, without regard to its position, to advocate that the Peking government recognize Soviet Russia and sign the agreement negotiated between C. T. Wang and Karakhan. The impeachers next quoted from Li Ta-chao's statement to the Congress and contrasted it unfavorably with the secret documents of the Communist Party and Youth Corps.

The "Opinions" of the impeachers start quite temperately but grow steadily more heated.[18] They did not, they asserted, oppose the admission of Communists and Socialist Youth Corps members into the Kuomintang, nor were they criticizing individuals. But they considered it entirely improper that there should be a party within the party, yet that was exactly what those members organized into fractions were. The Communists had hoodwinked the Leader, which might be called shady and cruel in the extreme. Communist Party and Youth Corps members joining the Kuomintang as a body hoped in time, the impeachers charged, "to compel our party to implement what they adovcate," and they instanced the Communists' clamor for the bogus northern government to sign the agreement and restore relations with Soviet Russia. The impeachers especially objected to attempts by Communist fractions to use Kuomintang publications to publish their propaganda, as for example, in pushing the theory that "the national revolution of the bourgeoisie is not the final revolution". In a sup-

plement, the accusers pointed to the number of communists holding important positions in the Kuomintang Central Executive Committee; the fact that the two parties had, in reality, formed a joint
front for work among students, youth, women, workmen, and
farmers; and to the anomaly that the majority of officers sent out to
organize Kuomintang business were on the Communist register.

Fearing for their party's future, Teng Tse-ju, Chang Chi, and
Hsieh Ch'ih requested the Central Executive Committee to come to
a fundamental decision for the public good.

Sun and Borodin Try to Quiet the Issue

We have no exact information as to the manner in which Dr. Sun
handled this challenge to the policy of the Comintern of infiltrating
the Nationalist Party by Communists and young Socialists and attempting to make it a more militant leader of a national revolution.[19] We do know, however, that there was a great deal of politics
as Kuomintang leaders of various factions and persuasions attempted to influence the outcome of the controversy.[20]

When Mr. Borodin returned on about June 20, he first had a
meeting with the Canton Communists and a private dinner with
Sun Yat-sen. There is no published record of their crucial discussion, but by July 1 the rumor had reached Shanghai that Borodin
had subtly warned Dr. Sun in the following way: Communists had
joined the Kuomintang purely for the purpose of cordial and
friendly Sino-Russian relations. To make a reality of the plan for the
two orphaned countries to join hands, the Kuomintang must not
hinder the development of the Chinese Communist Party. That
would not be good for China's future, and Soviet Russia would
have to look for some other path of advancement.[21] This was a
rumor; by what route it reached Shanghai is unknown. But there it
was understood to imply that if the Kuomintang did not permit the
Chinese Communist Party to advance, then Soviet Russia would
make separate arrangements with the northern government.

The ground is somewhat firmer with respect to a discussion
which Hsieh Ch'ih and Chang Chi had with Mr. Borodin on June

25 at his residence in Tung-shan. Sun Fo acted as interpreter, and a Chinese record of the conversation has been published.[22] It was an acrimonious debate, with the Chinese side protesting Communist fractions and Borodin defending the idea of intraparty struggle as the way to strengthen the Kuomintang and form a strong center group. Chang Chi stated that previously he had favored the Communists joining the Kuomintang, but now he had changed his opinion. He believed that the natures of the two parties were so different that they could not intermingle, and he proposed that they travel separate roads. Borodin replied that the Third International believed that only the Kuomintang program was suitable for the Chinese Revolution, and hence had caused the Chinese Communist Party and the Socialist Youth Corps in their entirety to join the Kuomintang, and if any members rejected the order they would be considered in revolt. Then he said what must have sounded like a threat.

> If we ordered the Communists to leave, and the Communist Party perhaps to change its name but with its principles the same as those of the Kuomintang, this would merely disintegrate the revolutionary forces and the future would certainly be unfortunate.

The Chinese replied that they had not yet decided to advocate separation, but they could not permit the practice of fractions. The two sides argued over which of the parties had received the greater benefit from the coalescence. One of the Chinese expressed himself bluntly:

> The Chinese Communist Party originally had no weight because it was merely a messenger of the Third International. The latter was created by Russia and Russia's policy toward the Chinese revolution was to use Chinese communists in the Chinese Nationalist Party to manipulate it right or left. Russia considers the Chinese Communist Party its child but is still uncertain whether the Nationalist Party can be Russia's friend. This is our observation.

Borodin argued that all parties were divided into Right and Left factions. China could use the Kuomintang principles for a hundred years, he said, and if the Kuomintang were transformed into the Communist Party he would oppose it and quit Canton. To this, the interlocutors asked why then should there be a separate Communist Party? Borodin replied,

> The central offices of the Kuomintang have not been properly organized and cannot direct the party, nor can they yet regularly make proposals on problems of greatest concern to the country. Therefore the Communist Party cannot abolish its own organization. The Kuomintang relies on majority decisions and can freely drive out the communist members, but we hope it will not come to this.

The interview ended on this note. Neither side had given ground, and Borodin seems to have made the price of Soviet Russian cooperation clear: the Communist Party must remain in the Kuomintang yet keep its separate organization.

The pressing need for Russian assistance may have been conclusive in the ultimate decision of Sun Yat-sen and the Central Executive Committee. Since there are no published records of Dr. Sun's reasoning, and since the minutes of the Central Executive Committee meetings leading to the formal decision are still secret,[23] we can only state the outcome. Appended to the impeachment was the decision reached on July 3 at the fortieth session of the Executive Committee. Essentially, the committee decided to stand pat.

> Taking the political program and the declaration issued by the Congress as the standard, all who have entered the party and who display revolutionary determination and sincerely respect the real ideas of the Three Principles of the People shall be treated as party members, no matter what faction they belonged to previously. All who contravene the declaration and political program shall be punished according to regulations. Comrades of the party should not be suspicious but should still continue the former struggle.[24]

The committee also decided to issue a proclamation and to ask the Leader to convene a plenary session of the Central Executive Committee for a thorough discussion. A proclamation was issued on July 7 which restated this position in persuasive language.[25]

A single proclamation could hardly quiet the protests that were now coming from "pure" Kuomintang members in several cities against efforts of Communists in their midst to strengthen their own leadership in the revolution. From Peking came complaints that Communists in the Kuomintang had tried to convert a memorial meeting for May Fourth into a celebration of the birthday of Karl Marx; there were also complaints that the Communists had agitated for the Peking government to recognize Soviet Russia even without a treaty and had claimed, though falsely, that Dr. Sun had sent a telegram instructing Kuomintang members to join in that agitation. During July there were petitions from students in Peking against Communists who were manipulating a Kuomintang election; the students demanded the expulsion of the Communists. Fifteen anti-Communist petitions were sent to Dr. Sun or the Central Executive Committee from various Kuomintang units in Shanghai and Chekiang. One charged the Communists with rigging the elections in the party branch at Shanghai University, a Kuomintang institution with a notably radical faculty. Another petition accused three well-known Communists—Yün Tai-ying, Ch'ü Ch'iu-pai, and Shih Ts'un-t'ung—of stating that the northern government was responsible for China's foreign relations and so supporting its signature to the Sino-Soviet Treaty. Another Communist outrage petitioned against was the publication in a supplement to the Kuomintang newspaper, *Min-kuo Jih-pao,* of an essay advocating the independence of Mongolia. Conflict grew so intense in Shanghai that each side was accusing the other to Dr. Sun. Mao Tse-tung and nine other Communists working in the Kuomintang's executive headquarters there sent a telegram denouncing Yeh Ch'u-ts'ang, one of the most important Kuomintang leaders who, for his part, demanded the Communists be expelled. From Hankow came similar complaints. In Canton, at the formal establishment of the Kuomintang's municipal headquarters on July 6, Chang Chi made an anti-Communist speech, and Wang Ching-wei made an eloquent statement upholding the Three Principles of the People as the *only* ideology for China and refuting certain Communist contentions. There was thunderous applause, and many Communists walked out. In August, petitions from party members in Canton and Macao, both with several hundred signatures, requested that the Leader expel Communists from his party.[26]

Final Lectures on San Min Chu-i

Dr. Sun resumed his lectures on the Three Principles of the People on August 3, after a lapse of three months. The remarkable point about the first lecture on the People's Livelihood was its blunt refutation of Marxism. Dr. Sun had read a good deal about socialism and indicated in the lecture his knowledge of the history of socialist movements in Europe and their internecine conflicts. Though he praised Karl Marx as a great social philosopher, he forcefully opposed Marx's concept of class struggle as the motive force in historical development; he also countered the theory of surplus value; and he pointed out various ways in which Marx's predictions had proved incorrect. Marx, Sun said, was concerned with the pathology of society; his own prescriptions were to prevent the emergence of such problems. He countered Marx with the findings of Maurice William.[27]

That Dr. Sun devoted about half the lecture to discounting Marxism, at least for China, cannot have been unrelated to the controversy over Communist activities within his party. It led to a quarrel with Michael Borodin. According to one witness, after the lecture had been delivered in the auditorium of Kwangtung Normal College, Borodin, who had been in the audience, went to the office of the president of the college where Dr. Sun was resting. Borodin challenged him on many points, and Dr. Sun patiently answered, but Borodin was unsatisfied. After a half-hour debate the two men left unsmiling. Another observer said he had never seen Dr. Sun so furious.[28]

The next lecture on August 10 seemed more conciliatory. Dr. Sun began by setting aside theory, upon which it was so easy to disagree. He repeated his contention that the *min-sheng* principle and communism really were the same. "Communism is the ideal of People's Livelihood, and People's Livelihood is practical communism". He chided the extremists among Kuomintang veterans and native Communists for their quarrels and presented an ideological justification for their cooperation.

What is the present status of the social question in China? All the ideas and doctrines advanced by those who study the social question and advocate solutions are imported from Europe and America. . . . Nowadays the most up-to-date advocate the methods of Marx. Therefore, the majority of youth favor communism and want to see the methods of Marx adopted in China. . . . Their zeal is very good. They advocate a radical solution. To solve the political and social question they believe it necessary to strike at the roots, since without a radical solution nothing can be accomplished. Therefore they use their utmost powers to bring about the Communist Party to agitate China.

At present our old comrades of the Kuomintang have many erroneous ideas about the Communist Party, believing the Three Principles of the People are incompatible with communism.

Dr. Sun drew an analogy to the period before the revolution during which many T'ung Meng Hui members failed to emphasize all three principles, thought only of nationalism and the overthrow of the Manchus, or believed that democracy and the People's Livelihood would follow spontaneously. He argued that this unconcern with the two other principles had led to the failure of the republic, to the emergence of militarism, and to the vacillation of comrades on political and social questions.

Why do I dare say that our revolutionary comrades do not understand the Principle of People's Livelihood? It is because since the reorganization of the Kuomintang, many comrades, because of their opposition to the Communist Party, keep on saying that communism and the Three Principles of the People are dissimilar, that in China it is enough to practice the Three Principles, and that communism absolutely should not be admitted. But what is the Principle of People's Livelihood at bottom? . . . People's livelihood is the prime mover of all social movements; because it did not progress, social civilization did not develop, economic organization did not improve, and morality retrogressed to the extent of producing all kinds of injustice. For example, class struggle and the suffering of workers and such kinds of oppression are all due to the nondevelopment of the people's livelihood. All sorts of social abnormalities are the result, while the problem of people's livelihood is the cause.

Seen in this light, what is the Principle of People's Livelihood after all? It is communism, it is socialism. Therefore in regard to communism, not only can we not say that it is in conflict with the Principles of People's Livelihood, but [we must say] it is a good friend. . . . If communism is the good friend of the Principle of People's Livelihood, why do Kuomintang members want to oppose the Communist Party? The reason perhaps is that among Communist Party members also there are some who do not know what communism is and have often spoken against the Three Principles of the People, thereby arousing the ill-feelings of the Kuomintang. But those ignorant and reckless party members must not be charged against the entire [Communist] Party and its ideology; we may only call it their individual behavior. We certainly may not take the bad behavior of individual Communist Party members as the standard for opposing the Communist Party. . . . Then why did some of our comrades raise this problem? The reason is that they do not understand what the Principle of People's Livelihood is, do not know that it is communism, and that this sort of communistic system, which I have already lectured upon, did not originate with a discovery by Marx.[29]

Dr. Sun then described his favored scheme of equalization of property by two means—(1) taxation based on the owner's declared valuation of land and the government's right to purchase it at that value, and (2) government appropriation of unearned increment due to general socioeconomic improvement. This, he believed, would easily and simply solve the land problem, and was much fairer than the nationalization of property practiced in Europe and America, which was simply confiscation.[30] He then discussed the need for railway expansion and for the opening of new mines and factories, all of which would require borrowing foreign capital, but under a system of state capitalism. Dr. Sun began to sound once more like the planner of *The International Development of China*.

Setting the Communist Issue to Rest

Shortly after these two lectures, the Kuomintang's Central Executive Committee met in plenary session to deal with the controversy over Communist activities. In Canton there was an atmosphere of crisis, but for other reasons. The city had just escaped a serious flood. Early in August the government had been forced to rescind an order claiming eleven streets as public property when outraged citizens stormed police stations in protest. A strike of Chinese employees in the foreign concessions on Shameen had been underway

[245]

since mid-July, and pickets prevented Chinese workers from returning to their jobs in spite of the fact that Sun Yat-sen had approved an agreement with the concession authorities and tried to get its acceptance by the activist faction of his party. Rice stored in foreign-owned warehouses in the city itself could not be moved because the stevedores had struck in support of the Shameen workers. In July, the generalissimo had tried to get the mercenary forces out of Canton and ordered the arsenal to cease supplying them arms, but they had fastened even more strongly on the outlying towns and cities and were increasing their extortions. On August 7 the Merchants' Corps of Kukong drove the Yunnan mercenaries out of their city, and similar conflicts elsewhere seemed likely. Native bankers were refusing to accept at face value the new coins turned out in great quantities by the mint, partly because of a flood of similar but debased currency secretly minted by militarists. Notes issued by the Kwangtung finance commissioner a month before were worth only 30 percent, though mercenaries and officials were demanding that they be exchanged at full value. The Central Bank had just opened, but there was much doubt how readily its bonds and bank notes would be accepted.[31]

The most serious development was the discovery on August 9 that a Norwegian freighter, *Hav,* had arrived at Canton with a large consignment of arms for the Merchants' Corps.[32] Although the corps had obtained an import license from an official of the military government, Dr. Sun ordered the vessel seized, and one of his gunboats forced it to Whampoa, where the arms were unloaded and put under guard at the academy. On August 12, some 1,500 members of the Merchants' Corps forced their way into the Generalissimo's Headquarters to demand the return of their arms. They threatened a general strike if the arms and ammunition were confiscated. The amalgamated province-wide corps removed its headquarters to Foshan while the government stationed the Guards Army of Wu T'ieh-ch'eng at important points in Canton. This crisis soon overshadowed by far the conflict within the Kuomintang. It was time for closing ranks, not for splitting.

The Central Executive Committee plenum met on five days between August 15 and 23, with thirteen regular members and eight alternates present. Chang Chi and Hsieh Ch'ih attended as Central Supervisory members. Among the twenty-three, six were Communists—Yü Shu-te, T'an P'ing-shan, Yü Fang-chou, Han Lin-fu, Shen T'ing-i, and Ch'ü Chi'iu-pai. On August 19, 20, and 21 the committee took up the problem of Communists in the Kuomintang. Fortunately, a fairly detailed account of the discussions is available.[33] At the first meeting, Chang Chi opened debate by explaining the Central Supervisory Committee's impeachment and raising seven points which he believed the members of the Central Executive Committee should keep in mind. The spokesman for the Communist position was Ch'ü Ch'iu-pai, a young leader close to Borodin and an upholder of Comintern policy within his party. He discussed the compatibility of Marxism and the Three Principles of the People and also whether or not admission of the Communists into the Kuomintang was necessary for their cooperation. He then confronted the problem of party fractions, which had created suspicions of machinations; he said frankly that since there was a Communist Party its members within the Kuomintang must act in unison. The real issue should be whether they had violated the Kuomintang's declaration and regulations; if so, they should be disciplined since they had joined the Kuomintang as individuals. If the plenum should decide to separate the Communists from the Kuomintang, then it might well be said that the development of the Communist faction [34] was enough to erode the Kuomintang, but if it did not separate, then why should there be suspicion and jealousy of the Communist Party's growth, even its growth as a part of the Kuomintang? [35] This statement was, in effect, a challenge: either expel us or permit us to grow.

The Political Council, a small group of advisers to Dr. Sun which he set up at Borodin's suggestion on July 11, held its sixth meeting on August 20 and passed two resolutions to set before the plenum. Six persons were present: Dr. Sun, Hu Han-min, Liao Chung-k'ai, Ch'ü Ch'iu-pai, Wu Chao-shu (C. C. Wu), and Borodin.[36] One resolution dealt with the problem of the Communist faction within the Kuomintang, and the other with the question of the Kuomintang's connections with the world revolutionary movement. The idea of the latter was to set up an International Liaison Committee within the Political Council, which would be appointed by the Leader and keep contact with revolutionary movements of common people and oppressed races in various countries, and with the Third International. It would confer with the Third International on the method for affiliating the Chinese Revolution with the world proletarian revolutionary movement, and the method for effecting a liason— i.e., supervising—Chinese Communist activities that were related to the Kuomintang. The scheme here was to have a three-man commission to solve conflicts, with a member from each party and one from the Third International.[37]

In the next day's plenary meeting of the Central Executive Committee, Wang Ching-wei observed that there were three factions in regard to the Communist issue: those who believed cooperation with the Communists was harmful to the Kuomintang; those who considered it beneficial; and those who believed that a situation in which Communists straddled both parties was not harmful, but that secret fractions were bad. He asked that people note the difference between the Communist Party and its individual members. It was natural that Communists should guard the secrets of their party. Only if the Kuomintang had direct relations with the Third International could such misunderstandings be avoided and secrecy be discounted, according to Mr. Wang.[38] With seemingly little debate, the conferees passed the two resolutions which had been prepared for them by the Political Council, and the Kuomintang's membership thereafter was informed by an "Instruction on Questions Relating to Admission of Communists."[39] This instruction reaffirmed the policy of admitting Communists, and credited their party with special responsibility for the proletariat within the Kuomintang, which itself struggled to benefit all classes. After reviewing the matters raised in the impeachment submitted by the Central Supervisory Committee members, but essentially setting the charges aside, the instruction then recognized the need of the Communist Party for secrecy and explained the plan for setting up an International Liaison Committee to solve this problem. It exhorted the comrades to cooperate with each other to fulfill the national revolution.

Thus the decision to continue cooperation with the Communist Party on the basis of its members individually joining the Kuomintang seems to have been made by a small group of Dr. Sun's most favored colleagues, those in the Political Council, which he chaired and which Borodin advised. Continuation of Soviet Russian aid, though not mentioned in published portions of the debates nor in the resolutions, probably was a decisive consideration. But the decision had merits of its own in addition to the agreeable concept of including all revolutionaries in a single movement under the leadership of the Kuomintang. The Communists who had joined Dr. Sun's old party, ardent young patriots of a second revolutionary generation, were indeed contributing to its rejuvenation. Why drive them out?

And so the issue was closed—temporarily. It erupted again after Dr. Sun's death, but in the meantime it was obscured by the generalissimo's conflict with the Merchants' Corps, his next attempt to mount a northern campaign, and his trip to Peking.

Problems with the Merchant Community

The controversy between Sun Yat-sen's government and the Merchants' Corps over the arms which they had purchased and Sun had confiscated brought him into conflict also with the consular body at the end of August. In essence, the controversy was a struggle for power brought on by several factors. One was Dr. Sun's earlier introduction into Canton of extraprovincial mercenaries to drive out Ch'en Chiung-ming. The commanders thereafter fattened upon the city. Another was the heavy taxation occasioned by the wars against Ch'en and other rivals. A third, of later origin, was the Kuomintang's sympathetic attitude towards the Communist Party and encouragement of labor to organize unions independent of the old craft guilds, as well as fears among many Cantonese that Dr. Sun planned to organize a Bolshevist government or "introduce bolshevism", both of which fears he tried to allay. Yet the struggle had deeper roots than these and was not confined to Kwangtung. In many parts of China merchants were arming to resist the insatiable financial demands of the military. Many of the Canton corpsmen were hired toughs.

The Canton merchant community under the leadership of Ch'en Lien-po (Cantonese, Chan Lim-pak), who was comprador of the Hong Kong & Shanghai Banking Corporation's Canton branch, had been trying for months to strengthen their corps and to federate with all the local corps in Kwangtung. This effort was perceived by Dr. Sun and his supporters as a threat to their government. When the large shipment of arms arrived in Canton waters, Dr. Sun suspected Ch'en Lien-po of being in league with Ch'en Chiung-ming, and he soon began to suspect foreign involvement.[40]

The shipment of nearly 5,000 rifles and the same number of pistols and revolvers, with ample ammunition, had been purchased through a German firm in Hong Kong; it was procured in Belgium, stored in a government warehouse, and then shipped from Amsterdam on a Norwegian freighter; and it was consigned to a German firm in Canton. Furthermore, as Dr. Sun later revealed, the British consul in Canton (actually it must have been the acting consul general, Bertram Giles) informed him that several Englishmen had incited Ch'en Lien-po to buy the arms and oppose the government, and that further shipments were on the way. He said it was the work of only a few Englishmen, who could be punished, but that it was up to Dr. Sun to control the Merchants' Corps and Ch'en Lien-po.[41] What Mr. Giles did not reveal—and what he may not have known yet—was that the manager of the Hong Kong office of the Hong Kong & Shanghai Banking Corporation had arranged the financing and that the commissioner of customs in Canton, a Britisher, was implicated in the attempted arms smuggling. Even the British government was ignorant of these facts until October.[42]

After the arms were confiscated an intense and protracted struggle ensued in Canton. The leaders of the Merchants' Corps threatened a general strike unless their arms were returned. The chairman of the Chinese Chamber of Commerce, Ch'en Lien-chung, a brother of Lien-po, called at the various consulates to try to solicit their intervention, and the chamber sent telegrams to Chinese communities overseas presenting the merchants' side of the case; they also telegraphed the diplomatic corps and the inspector-general of customs in Peking, trying to win their support. The merchants began exerting economic pressure on the government which, for its part, brought troops back into Canton, sent in three companies of Whampoa cadets, mobilized the Guards Army under Gen. Wu T'ieh-ch'eng, and ordered the arrest of Ch'en Lien-po, who fled. By August 25, the merchants had called a general strike in Canton and nearby cities, though two Yunnanese generals, Fan Shih-sheng and Liao Hsing-ch'ao, were mediating. Dr. Sun ordered the strike to end immediately, declared martial law throughout the city, forbade the telegraph office to send out telegrams, and had the Canton police prevent citizens from taking valuables into Shameen for safety. On August 26 he apparently contemplated a bombardment and general attack upon Hsi-kuan (Cantonese, Saikwan), the most congested and wealthiest part of the city, to force the merchants to bend to his will, but most of his commanders reportedly opposed so drastic an action.[43] On August 28 he sent the gunboat *Yung Feng*, cleared for action, in a threat to bombard Hsi-kuan.[44] That same day, Eugene Chen called upon the French consul general to inform him that the authorities had decided to remove the barricades which the merchants had erected between Hsi-kuan and the rest of the city by using artillery; he warned that this might expose the side of Shameen that faced the city to some danger.[45]

At this critical juncture the foreign consular body intervened, sending the senior consul—the Japanese consul general Amau Eiji—to call on the civil governor, Liao Chung-k'ai, to warn him against bombarding the city in order to suppress the Merchants' Corps. Mr. Liao, just then in a late night conference at the headquarters of Gen. Yang Hsi-min, replied that the merchants had just agreed to a settlement, which was to take effect the next day.[46] On the morning of August 29, Consul General Giles, probably not having heard this, sent a despatch to Fu Ping-ch'ang, commissioner for foreign affairs, which harshly backed the warning of the previous evening by saying, "I am now in receipt of a message from the Commodore in Hongkong that, in the event of Chinese authorities firing upon the city, immediate action is to be taken against them by all British Naval forces available." [47]

This foreign intervention in a Chinese power struggle brought forth a strong protest from Dr. Sun, who put his name to a manifesto which charged British imperialism with supporting the rebellion of the comprador of the Hong Kong and Shanghai Bank, and called the threat in the British consul's dispatch tantamount to a declaration of war. It derided British concern over the "barbarity of firing on a defenseless city" as hypocrisy "in the light of the Singapore Massacre, Amritsar, and other atrocities in Egypt and Ireland." Dr. Sun repudiated the suggestion that his government could fire on a defenseless city, since the only section of Canton against which it might be compelled to take action was Hsi-kuan, the armed stronghold of the Ch'en Lien-po rebels.[48] In short, Sun held open the threat he might yet bombard. He also sent a public telegram of protest to Ramsay MacDonald, prime minister in Britain's Labour government.[49] But in the face of the British threat, Sun's weak government scarcely dared to act against the Merchants' Corps, if it had intended to.

Matters now were at a standstill. The strike had ended, but the merchants did not pay the required half-million and did not get their arms. Many generals were eager to acquire the power represented by those rifles, which Commandant Chiang guarded with the small force available at the academy. There were various proposals for their use: to distribute them among allied armies, to sell a part of them in order to finance the Kuomintang's new Training Regiment, and to sell them back to the merchants to finance Sun's planned Northern Expedition. During the next five weeks of continued negotiation and indecision, most of the arms remained at Whampoa, though some were distributed by Chiang upon Sun's orders.[50]

The foreign intervention probably added point to the anti-imperialist campaign which the Kuomintang launched with Dr. Sun's blessing on September 7, the anniversary of the signing of the Boxer Protocol in 1901. A rally and parade inaugurated "anti-imperialism week" and the party issued a proclamation in memory of the nation's humiliation. It called on all classes to unite with the Kuomintang to overthrow imperialism and the northern warlords. Banners urged the boycotting of British and American goods, and the overthrow of militarism, imperialism, and the consular body.[51] By now the antiimperialist and antimilitarist themes were the core of Kuomintang propaganda.

In an interview published the next day, Dr. Sun stressed the need for interclass unity to overthrow imperialism.[52] Appropriately, he began by denouncing the Boxer settlement. He termed the protocol "the Charter of World Imperialism in China . . . the instrument by which the whole country is reduced to a state that is worse than that of a colony." The object of the protocol was not to punish the Manchus but to enslave China by keeping her in a state of financial subjugation and to prevent her from industrial development, he averred. He derided the notion that the renunciation of the remainder of the indemnity by the imperialist powers, a matter then under consideration, was due to an awakened sense of international justice or magnanimity; it was "due in the first place to the success of the Russian Revolution which has set China an example of how a nation may free itself from the shackles of foreign aggression and injustice." [53] He stated once more his conviction that China's problems all stemmed from imperialism.

> The turmoil and poverty of this country, although in natural resources we are perhaps the richest in the world, is due to one cause, namely that our international status is worse than that of a colony. . . . Hence we have many masters, pursuing their sinister objectives in devious ways; some ruthlessly, some cunningly, some openly, some under the guise of benevolence, some supported by powerful navies to break into our house, some kindly propose to keep open our door. But all together Imperialism has but one aim—to keep us down economically and politically.

He then explained why "the industrial class" (but not the compradors), labor, farmers, and intellectuals all had a vital interest in national liberation and industrial development, and he called upon them "to unite in one comprehensive organization based on discipline and to assume leadership of the National Revolutionary movement in order to free the country from her present worse than colonial status."

Dr. Sun Launches His Final Northern Expedition

During the critical first week in September, Sun Yat-sen decided to launch a Northern Expedition from Shao-kuan, directed against the Chihli clique. By September 12 he had departed to that town, the railhead 140 miles from Canton near the mountainous northern border of Kwangtung.

Why did Dr. Sun undertake this campaign? In doing so he seemed to be abandoning everything that had been accomplished in Canton since his victory over Ch'en Chiung-ming the previous November: his reorganized and now functioning party, his Russian allies, and the party military academy which he had opened with pomp less than three months before. Dr. Sun started political preparations for an expedition against Ts'ao K'un and Wu P'ei-fu as early as June 1924, but why did he actually launch the expedition in September?

On September 9, in a letter to Chiang Kai-shek, Dr. Sun made an explanation in which he gave the "three vital reasons" why it was urgent and suitable to carry out the Northern Expedition. The first was the British threat.

During this strike, if we had delayed a day longer a conflict would surely have emerged and the objectives of the English gunboats would have been my headquarters, the gunboat Yung Feng and Whampoa, which could have been pulverized in a few minutes. We absolutely do not have the power to resist them. Although this time we fortunately escaped, later we may again take up the issue at a suitable time. This is the first reason why we cannot but evade death here and pursue life elsewhere. Second, the attack by our enemies in the East River is right now on the point of being incited, and if another situation like that at Shih-p'ai should occur, it is very difficult to conjecture who would get the benefit. Third is the greed and tyranny of the guest armies which produce all sorts of evil consequences. This is also a vital reason. For these three vital reasons we cannot continue to stay in this place another moment; therefore it is best to relinquish it quickly, leave completely, and plan a different road to life. The very best road to life now is through a Northern

Expedition. Furthermore, the Fengtien Army has gone through the pass, Chekiang may stand firm, men's hearts are all set upon overthrowing Ts'ao and Wu, and in the vicinity of Wu-Han there are troops under my influence. If we take advantage of this situation and struggle with determination, increasingly urge on and advance straight ahead, taking the battle field as our school, then the outcome is sure to be good . . .[54]

On the basis of this contemporary letter we can scarcely doubt that Dr. Sun was seeking to escape from a situation in Canton which he found intolerable. But there was an optimistic side too, advanced in the last sentence of the letter. He was reverting to an earlier strategy which involved getting to Peking through an alliance of major military factions opposed to the Chihli clique. The Soviet Russian strategy of a gradually built-up and mass-based nationalistic movement was, it appears, just too slow and troublesome for Sun Yat-sen. Furthermore, he had been through a very trying three months since his illness in May.

By September the national political pot was bubbling: another Chihli-Fengtien war was in the offing. General Wu P'ei-fu had been attempting to reunite China through a combination of political alliances and minor campaigns, and only Manchuria, Shansi, Chekiang, and the southernmost provinces of Kwangtung, Kwangsi, and Yunnan were outside the sphere of the Chihli clique. Hence, Chang Tso-lin, leader of the Fengtien clique, Lu Yung-hsiang, the military governor of Chekiang, and Sun Yat-sen in Kwangtung were allies, of a sort, against Ts'ao K'un, the president, and Wu P'ei-fu, his main prop. A contest for control of the rich prize of Shanghai had long been brewing between Ch'i Hsieh-yuan of the Chihli clique, who was military governor of Kiangsu, and Lu Yung-hsiang, who controlled Shanghai through a subordinate, Ho Feng-lin. General Ch'i was eager to get the city's opium and other revenues. By August, the military-political chessboard was so arranged that Ch'i Hsieh-yuan might safely go to war with Lu Yung-hsiang, who had enemies in all neighboring provinces. Chang Tso-lin and Sun Yat-sen were pledged to send troops to threaten the rear of these enemies and thus give indirect aid to Lu. In fact, Lu Yung-hsiang telegraphed Dr. Sun on September 4, asking for help.[55]

[255]

The Kiangsu-Chekiang war broke out early in September, and it seemed that a campaign from Kwangtung into southern Kiangsi might, at a minimum, prevent some Kiangsi forces from participating in the attack on Chekiang.[56] Even more important was the imminence of war between the armies of Wu P'ei-fu and Chang Tso-lin, the two mightiest military powers in China. With Wu's armies pulled northward to face the Manchurian army there might be some weakening of the southern Chihli flank, and thus a possible opportunity for Sun Yat-sen. On the other hand, if Sun's allies were defeated, then Kwangtung might really be in danger from the Chihli clique. Thus it appears that Dr. Sun was propelled into his northern campaign partly by his frustrations with conditions in Canton and partly by the possibilities arising from the larger political scene. One significant clue: by mid-September, Dr. Sun was again being referred to in announcements as "President." [57]

Organizing a military campaign required interfactional diplomacy, finance, logistics, and propaganda. The Canton base had to be left secure, and the attainment of this involved negotiations with Ch'en Chiung-ming and his generals on the East, and with T'ang Chi-yao, the powerful Tuchun of Yunnan on the West, to persuade them to leave hands off. Each of Sun's main allies in the North sent representatives to Canton, and he sent delegates North.[58]

It seems there was a good deal of opposition within Sun's own camp to his military adventure. Sun Fo resigned as mayor of Canton and left for Shanghai, but this may also have been a gesture of appeasement to the Canton merchants, for the mayor had been responsible—or rather, the vehicle—for much of the extra taxation imposed on the city to finance the Generalissimo's Headquarters.[59] Hu Han-min replaced Liao Chung-k'ai as governor and was to be the man in charge of the rear base. Dr. Sun requested the ever-faithful Liao to take charge of finance and supplies for the campaign, and Liao may have taken up these chores briefly, but on September 17 he resigned in frustration and disgust.[60] Chiang Kai-shek petitioned to resign his position as commandant of the military academy. Sun used great persuasion to try to win Chiang's support, but all he got for his campaign was one company of cadets as a personal guard.[61]

What position Borodin took is uncertain. He attended the meetings of the Political Council where the decisions to undertake the campaign were made, but he could scarcely have favored an enterprise so out of keeping with the revolutionary strategy he had been inculcating—unless he was glad enough to see Dr. Sun out of the city.[62] The Central Committee of the Chinese Communist Party was against the expedition, and Teng Chung-hsia voiced this opposition in an article in a new labor journal: "The Northern Expedition has nothing to do with the true revolution of national liberation and the unions and farmers associations should not get involved in it." [63] T'an P'ing-shan led the "Farmers' Army" to Shao-kuan in a show of support; but this "Army" consisted of the students of the second class in the Farmers' Movement Training Institute who were receiving field training. They only stayed ten days.

The expedition was preceded by numerous proclamations. In one of the first, dated September 10, Dr. Sun admitted the validity of many of the grievances of Canton citizens because of oppressive soldiers and greedy officials as well as the great burden of supporting the entire load of the revolution. The proclamation tried to draw a distinction between revolutionary principle and actual practice and promised to reform the practice. Specifically, Sun's declaration to the Canton people promised:

> (1) In the shortest possible time to transfer every army and actually start the Northern Expedition; (2) in order to entrust Kwangtung to the Kwangtung people, self-government will be put into actual practice; the Canton municipal government will be reorganized speedily and the mayor be elected by the people as the first step towards self-government for the entire province; (3) now vexatious levies and miscellaneous taxes are all abolished and the tax schedule will be separately fixed by the people's elected officials. The Revolutionary Government has already made up its mind to carry through these three points and the people of Kwangtung should know that, in the matter of revolutionary practice, the Revolutionary Government intends to follow the wishes of the people and bring about speedy reorganization.[64]

A proclamation on the objectives of the Northern Expedition issued by the Kuomintang on September 18 stressed the now dominant propaganda theme—the antiwarlord, antiimperialism theme.

The expedition was directed not only against Ts'ao K'un and Wu P'ei-fu but against all warlords and against the imperialism which supported them. Once imperialism had been overthrown, China could escape its position as a semicolony and create a free and independent state.[65]

The aging revolutionary leader made his headquarters in the Shao-kuan railway station while his soldiers were billeted in mat-sheds in the hills about the town. Hunan troops, withdrawn from the East River front to take part in the campaign, passed through Canton, where the American consul general observed that they presented "a deplorable appearance," poorly uniformed, equipped with antique rifles, and undernourished.[66] They had agreed to participate in the hope of getting back to their native province. Generalissimo Sun appointed the eminent Hunanese statesman T'an Yen-k'ai as commander in chief of the campaign. Various "guest armies" from Honan, Kiangsi, and Yunnan gradually assembled about Shao-kuan, but the Yunnanese forces under titular command of Yang Hsi-min, and the Kwangsi troops of Liu Chen-huan, which probably were the most objectionable to the citizens of Canton, would not participate in the expedition. By early October leading elements invaded southern Kiangsi.[67]

The expedition accomplished nothing significant. It was made irrelevant by three events which occurred in rapid succession in the middle of October—the defeat of Lu Yung-hsiang, the destruction of the Merchants' Corps, and Feng Yü-hsiang's coup d'état in Peking, which resulted in the overthrow of Wu P'ei-fu and the imprisonment of Ts'ao K'un.

General Lu Yung-hsiang was betrayed by his subordinates and fled to Japan on October 13 when his front against Ch'i Hsieh-yuan was collapsing. The Northern Expedition could do nothing to assist him.

Suppression of the Merchants' Corps

Negotiations between Dr. Sun's representatives and the merchant leaders for return of the arms seized from the steamer *Hav* continued throughout September without reaching a settlement. The generalissimo, desperately in need of funds for his Northern Expedition, asked $3 million from the merchants, but he also demanded a pledge of fealty from Ch'en Lien-po and insisted that the Merchants' Corps be subordinated to his government. Ch'en Lien-po issued a circular telegram on September 16, which declared his allegiance to Dr. Sun Yat-sen and stated, "I trust that the Generalissimo's magnanimity and leniency will forgive my past errors." But the merchants declined to pay $3 million nor to place the corps under the government's control. Instead they threatened another general strike, negotiated with Ch'en Chiung-ming, and reportedly offered to finance his return to Canton. Whether Ch'en could return, however, would depend primarily upon the Yunnanese mercenaries, whose commanders were courted by both sides.[68]

In this threatening situation General Li Fu-lin, who had succeeded Sun Fo as acting mayor of Canton, took up the negotiations. Early in October General Li worked out an agreement for the return of 5,000 rifles to the merchants, for which they would pay $200,000 and permit a city-wide assessment equivalent to one month's house rent. But the merchants also threatened a general strike to begin on October 10, presumably in case the arms were not returned. Dr. Sun accepted the settlement and, on the afternoon of October 9, ordered Chiang Kai-shek to send the arms to General Li for return to the merchants. This Chiang reported doing on the evening of October 9, but he told Sun he had withheld the ammunition against actual receipt of the $200,000. According to a public statement of the government's case, dated October 19, the rifles were handed over to General Li on the evening of October 9 in the presence of representatives of the Merchants' Corps, although at the last minute the Merchants' Corps suggested and the government agreed to deliver some ammunition and to hold back 1,000 of the rifles. The government charged that the merchants failed to carry out their side of the agreement but did not specify particularly what they had failed to do.[69]

Sun Yat-sen at Shao-kuan could not be intimately aware of the rapidly developing and volatile situation in Canton, yet he sent many instructions to his associates there, and some of these appear as mutually contradictory. On October 9, the same day that he accepted the settlement, he secretly telegraphed Chiang, requesting him to abandon Whampoa and bring all the arms and the cadets to Shao-kuan for the Northern Expedition. He repeated the request on October 10. Chiang replied that he was determined to defend the island to the death. He argued that they must not relinquish Canton but should weather the crisis, organize a brigade with the newly arrived Russian arms, and then solidify the base area. He begged Sun to return.[70]

Early on the morning of October 10, Sun sent a most urgent telegram to Hu Han-min, Yang Hsi-min, Hsü Ch'ung-chih, Liu Chen-huan, Ku Ying-fen, Chiang Kai-shek, Li Fu-lin, and Li Lang-ju, stating that the merchants' strike and the enemy's rebellious attack—i.e., by Ch'en Chiung-ming—were being launched at the same time, which was the result of too much leniency. If these events should really occur, Sun urged his colleagues to use the cadre and other students, together with the loyal braves of the Fu Army (i.e., Li Fu-lin's force), to go to the gates and exhort the merchants. If the merchants did not submit, then Sun begged his colleagues immediately "to make the goods stores public property." This action should be directed against those merchants in Hsi-kuan who had most opposed the government. At the same time, Sun added, "I request that you take goods which can be made into clothing [i.e., uniforms] and send them first to Shao-kuan." He urged his colleagues to act resolutely for the sake of the revolution's future.[71] When Sun sent this instruction, he may not have known whether the arms were still with Li Fu-lin and whether the strike was on or off, but Sun's instruction was a plain request to settle the issue with the Merchants' Corps by force if the merchants actually started a general strike. Exactly five days later force was used, but only after the merchants had defied the government concretely.

October 10, the day on which the merchants were to get back their arms, was also the Nationalists' great holiday. The Merchants' Corps threw a cordon across that part of the bund where their arms were to be unloaded from junks. At about 2:30 P.M. a Nationalist parade was marching down the bund carrying banners and shouting slogans. It was made up of a labor corps in blue uniforms and cadets in olive drab, followed by students, teachers, and school children. According to the American consul general, some, but not many, of the laborers and cadets were armed though Nationalist sources assert that all the paraders were bare-handed. The parade arrived at the spot where the Merchants' Corps was unloading its arms, and the parade leaders demanded the right to march straight along the bund. This the corps refused. Someone started shooting, and with this the Merchants' Corps opened a heavy fire on the laborers and cadets, who scattered and were hunted down. About a dozen paraders were killed, eight corpsmen were wounded, and many spectators were killed, wounded, or drowned in trying to escape the melee.[72]

This street battle heightened the tension between the merchants and the radicals among the Nationalists. The merchants immediately declared a general strike, asserting that less than half their arms and munitions had been returned. Streets were barricaded despite government orders to end the strike. According to a Kuomintang historian, the United Association of Merchants' Corps proclaimed that Ch'en Chiung-ming's army would attack soon, and that on October 12 the corps in Hsi-kuan and elsewhere put up posters advocating overthrow of the government. According to the American consul, the merchants appeared to be making a desperate effort to gain the support of Yunnanese troops with the object of ousting the Sun regime. On October 13 the government brought 5,000 troops into Canton from the East River front and ordered them to disarm the Merchants' Corps; it also declared martial law and ordered the shops to open immediately.[73] The conflict approached its climax.

On October 11 Sun Yat-sen appointed a revolutionary committee with himself as chairman and with six other members—General Hsü Ch'ung-chih, Liao Chung-k'ai, Wang Ching-wei, Chiang Kai-shek, Ch'en Yu-jen, and T'an P'ing-shan. He ordered the committee to pacify the Merchants' Corps. Yet at the same time he was urging

Chiang and others to give up Canton and come with their troops to Shao-kuan. Then he ordered Hsü, Liao, and the Yunnanese general, Chu P'ei-te to call upon Gen. Fan Shih-sheng in order to explain why the Merchants' Corps must be subdued and to beg his neutrality. The call was made, but Fan's actual role is in doubt, Some troops, particularly units of the Guards Army under Gen. Wu T'ieh-ch'eng, were sent back from Shao-kuan. On October 14, after troops had been brought in from the East River front, Sun ordered Hu Han-min to act for him as head of the revolutionary committee, appointed Liao its secretary and Chiang as head of the military committee, and these leaders, together with Borodin, prepared to attack.[74]

By fortunate chance, Borodin's report on a meeting of the revolutionary committee held on October 14, which settled the plan for suppressing the Canton Merchants' Corps that very night, is preserved and published.[75] The committee decided to raid and destroy the lair of "the Tigers," as the corps was called, in the Western suburb (Hsi-kuan). Several small units were placed under Chiang's control, a political department was set up with Wang Ching-wei in charge and Chou En-lai, Liao Chung-k'ai, and T'an P'ing-shan as his deputies, to "determine the actions of the Revolutionary Committee and the armed forces." But which of the armed forces would fight was very uncertain.

The attack began at dawn on October 15. Almost all available forces did participate in the combined assault. The Merchants' Corps had barricaded itself in the densely populated commercial section. Corpsmen fired down upon their assailants from the strong towers which pawn shops used for storing valuables. But the government had infiltrated Hsi-kuan with saboteurs, including barbers and unemployed laborers, who poured kerosene around buildings and set them afire to drive the corpsmen out. By nightfall much of the commercial sector was in flames and the corpsmen were completely defeated. Troops looted freely. The western suburb continued to burn, and some troops looted through October 16, until they were stopped by the government on threat of immediate execution. The corpsmen were disarmed, and their leaders fled to

Hong Kong or surrendered. Property losses due to the fires were huge, since somewhere between 600 and 1,100 buildings were burned and many others looted. This brief battle settled the power struggle between the merchant leaders and the Nationalists. Two companies of Whampoa cadets were in the fight; it was their first contribution to their party, though a minor one.[76]

In Kuomintang annals the suppression of the "merchants' rebellion" is a glorious victory. Among many residents of the city, however, the feeling against Sun Yat-sen was "bitter and full of hatred." As soon as some order had been restored, hundreds of Chinese began to bring their jewelry, specie, and other valuables into the British and French concessions on Shameen to put them into foreign banks for safety.[77]

The burning, looting, and civilian casualties further tarnished the reputation of Sun Yat-sen and the Kuomintang among those Chinese who were inclined to be hostile. Sun's enemies among Canton merchants immediately sent telegrams to Cantonese and other Chinese at home and abroad blaming Sun specifically for the devastation. One telegram received in America on October 17, signed by the Kwangtung volunteers, asserted that Sun had ordered the attack on the western suburbs of Canton with machine guns and bombardment and had authorized troops to loot and burn the city. The telegram called the situation "worse than ever since the Republic" and asked the recipients to "spread news and remit funds" for relief. On October 22, nine Cantonese associations in Shanghai sent out a circular telegram addressed to Cantonese associations in other Chinese cities and abroad, expressing their horror at the act "ordered by Sun Wen," and saying the nine associations had unanimously passed a resolution "to fix the 15th day of October as a day to remember Sun Wen's Burning and Wiping Out Our Market and Tyrannously Killing the Kwangtung People." The Canton government's official account of its suppression of the "rebellion," issued on the 19th and summarized above, was an attempt to counteract adverse opinion. The government also organized relief measures but had little success in persuading the Cantonese voluntarily to channel relief funds through its hands.[78]

Such was the atmosphere—triumph among the victors and hatred among the vanquished—when Dr. Sun returned to Canton on October 30. A week before, Gen. Feng Yü-hsiang had betrayed his superior, Wu P'ei-fu, in a coup d'état, which simply overturned the political chessboard in north China.

The second Chihli-Fengtien war was in its opening stages. Feng Yü-hsiang, with his crack troops, was supposed to hold the left flank in Jehol against Chang Tso-lin's Manchurian army. Suddenly, in a classic double cross, Feng brought his troops back to Peking by forced marches and seized the capital before dawn on October 23. Wu P'ei-fu was caught between the Manchurians at his front and Feng and his fellow conspirators at his rear. Unable to secure aid from his military associates in the Yangtze provinces, General Wu was forced to flee from Tientsin by sea and eventually made his way to Wu-Han. On November 2 Ts'ao K'un, whose presidential palace in Peking was surrounded by Feng's troops, announced his resignation, though he remained under arrest for two years.[79] Under these circumstances Dr. Sun's military campaign into the mountains of southern Kiangsi—more than a thousand miles away from the main theater—scarcely had any significance. Furthermore, a few days after the coup, General Feng and his allies may have invited Dr. Sun, though indirectly, to come to Peking to participate in national reunification. In two telegrams sent on October 27, Sun indicated his interest in going north; he hurried back to Canton on October 30, and on November 1, he received an invitation. By November 4 he had made public his intention to proceed northward.[80]

Dr. Sun's Purposes in Planning His Trip North

We have little information on Dr. Sun's reasons for deciding to go to Peking.[81] Presumably he wished to negotiate for a new, united government that would carry through the foreign and domestic policies he had recently been advocating. Probably he hoped to be the new president. To go would be a logical extension of the objectives he had in joining the alliance against Ts'ao K'un and Wu P'ei-fu. Yet if he went, what leverage would he have? Military power in

Chihli was balanced between the new Kuominchün, commanded by Feng Yü-hsiang in Peking, and the Manchurian army under Chang Tso-lin, controlling Tientsin. The Yangtze provinces were still the domain of the Chihli faction. In retirement, Tuan Ch'i-jui was being urged by Chang Tso-lin, and probably by Feng Yü-hsiang also, to take the position of chief executive.

Some of Dr. Sun's colleagues opposed his going because it would be dangerous and for other reasons. The Communist Party leadership first opposed and then endorsed the trip.[82] Borodin's position is uncertain. He attended the Political Council meeting on November 1 which decided upon the announcement that Dr. Sun would make regarding his departure for the North. It was decided that Sun should proceed as far as Shanghai where he would issue his proposals; if these were agreed to by those in power he would cooperate with them.[83] These plans sound very tentative. There was much indirect negotiation during the next several weeks, and Sun's departure was postponed several times.

On November 10, Dr. Sun issued a "Manifesto on Going North." This is virtually the last proclamation attributed to him directly, and it presents his dream for the nation in simple terms. The manifesto reaffirms the Three Principles of the People as the basis for solving the nation's problems. The program adopted at the First Kuomintang Congress was a maximum objective, but the minimum program for the present should include the rescinding of all unequal treaties and agreements imposed on China by the imperialist powers, and a clear definition of authority between the central and provincial governments. Six major benefits would then accrue:

(1) After China has achieved a status of international equality, the people's economy and productivity may be fully developed. (2) Industrial development will bring improvements in the rural economy, making it possible to meliorate the life of the toiling farmer. (3) Full expansion of productive power will improve the living conditions of the working class and heighten its solidarity. (4) Development of agriculture and industry will increase the people's purchasing power, and this will stimulate a flourishing commerce. (5) Questions of culture and education will not be lost in empty talk, for with economic development the need for knowledge and ability will increase, while the growth of national wealth will

[265]

make it easy to gather funds for cultural work and education, and this will be the beginning of the solution of the problems of unemployment and loss of schooling among intellectuals. (6) After abolition of the unequal treaties, China's laws can be made to prevail throughout the entire country, and when all foreign concessions are abolished there will be no place in which the plotting and sabotage of counter-revolutionaries can be based.

Sun then called for a National Assembly whose main task would be the unification and reconstruction of the country. But first there should be a preliminary conference of representatives of modern industrial bodies, merchant associations, educational associations, universities, the alliance of provincial student associations, trade unions, peasant associations, the military forces which had participated in the struggle against Ts'ao and Wu, and political parties. This conference should be kept small and meet soon, and to it the Kuomintang would submit its minimum proposals. Representatives to the National Assembly should be elected directly by the membership of the listed types of organizations.[84] The idea behind such a form of organization did not originate with the Kuomintang; ironically, Wu P'ei-fu had proposed just such a system for choosing delegates to a National Citizens Convention in August 1920, to reconstruct the national political system after the Chihli-Anfu War. Likewise the Chinese Communist Party had called for such an assembly in July 1923.[85]

The demand for a National Assembly elected by occupational and interest groups became the next great propaganda effort of the Kuomintang and the Communist Party. Such a body would be a complete break from the Western parliamentary form which the Chinese republic had tried in 1913. Presumably the scheme would appeal to a variety of organized and articulate sectors of the population, and such a preliminary conference and National Assembly might be more amenable to Dr. Sun's prescriptions than a reconvened old Parliament or than a reconstruction conference appointed by the northern victors. But as a means for bringing unity to a country where real power lay with military governors, commanders, and bureaucrats it was an impractical suggestion. Even the problem of deciding what groups might send representatives would be insoluble—who should decide? Sun Yat-sen insisted on this scheme to the end, but nothing came of it: he simply lacked the influence, not to mention the power, to make it prevail.[86]

On the very day of Sun's proclamation, Chang Tso-lin, Feng Yü-hsiang, Lu Yung-hsiang, and Tuan Ch'i-jui met in Tientsin to plan a new government, and the major Chihli military commanders in Central China issued a joint telegram supporting Tuan as chief executive.[87] All this was done without benefit of Dr. Sun's presence.

Russians by now were much in evidence in Canton. They were frequently seen at the Foreign Office or riding about in cars with Chinese officials. On November 7, the anniversary of the October Revolution, the local government showed solidarity by attending a reception at the Soviet consulate and by staging a parade of Chinese soldiers, laborers, and farmers' guards, in which Russian marines from the *Vorovsky* marched. After shouting slogans—"Down with Imperialism!," "Down with Capitalists!," "Long Live Soviet Russia!"—the paraders gathered in a public park to be addressed by Dr. Sun, Hu Han-min, Wu T'ieh-ch'eng, Wang Ching-wei, and staff members of the Soviet consulate. The American consul general observed that there was every evidence that the southern regime and the Soviets were very close.[88]

Dr. Sun also seemed to be trying to draw closer to the Japanese government. He had sent Li Lieh-chün, his current chief of staff, to Japan, where he stayed throughout October "to bring China and Japan to a true understanding." On October 13, Dr. Sun telegraphed Li to remain in Japan and propagandize for a great Asian alliance. Li rejoined Dr. Sun just before his departure for Shanghai. The American consul general noted on November 12 the recent great cordiality of southern officials towards Japan as compared to their conventional politeness towards British, French, and American representatives. The Japanese consul general frequently called on Hu Han-min and occasionally on Sun Yat-sen for "unofficial visits." When Dr. Sun sailed from Hong Kong, the only foreign official listed as seeing him off was the Japanese consul general there.[89]

What understandings were in the making seem not to be revealed in Kuomintang sources. Dr. Sun still had his Pan-Asian dream. He may have felt the need for Japanese assistance in future dealings with Tuan Ch'i-jui and Chang Tso-lin. He may even have wanted a counterweight to Soviet influence. But also, he was calling for the abrogation of all unequal treaties, and Japan was a chief beneficiary in China of these treaties. Could he win support of the Japanese government?

Departing from the Revolutionary Base

Before he could leave, Dr. Sun had many matters to attend to in Canton. Both the government and the Kuomintang were in disarray. It was important to leave his base in the charge of reliable people, but he was taking a number of close comrades with him. Dr. Sun appointed Hu Han-min deputy generalissimo; he was already governor of Kwangtung. T'an Yen-k'ai was put in charge of the Northern Expedition. The Leader allowed T'an P'ing-shan to resign from his post as head of the party's Organization Department and replaced him by another Communist, Yang P'ao-an, who had been secretary of the department, as acting head. He also appointed two other very active Communists from Kwangtung to the department, P'eng Pai and Juan Hsiao-hsien. Such appointments confirmed his determination to give responsible positions to the new blood in his party. These were key positions in view of the fact that the Kuomintang's Second Party Congress was scheduled for a few months hence. In the military sphere, the generalissimo named the force being created at Whampoa as the party army, appointed its officers, and named Liao Chung-k'ai as party representative. With the first shipment of Russian arms and the weapons seized from the *Hav,* the Training Regiment was now a real instrument. Dr. Sun appointed General Hsü Ch'ung-chih head of the party's Military Affairs Department with Chiang Kai-shek as secretary.[90]

November 12 was Dr. Sun's birthday; he was fifty-eight by Occidental reckoning. Since he was to depart the next day, a great lantern parade was organized by various bodies, including labor unions and student associations. He reviewed the parade, said to have numbered more than 20,000, from the upper story of the Kwangtung Finance Office. The next day, offices and schools were closed, pending his departure. The southern revolutionary was being given the greatest honors. He held separate conferences with the closest associates he was leaving behind, and then he and his young wife took a launch over to the gunboat *Yung Feng;* from its deck he said farewell to the civil and military officials gathered on the jetty. Then the *Yung Feng* steamed off carrying Dr. Sun and his party to Whampoa, where he bade goodbye to the officers, cadets, and troops. After a final meal with his companions, Dr. Sun sailed on his gunboat to Hong Kong, escorted by the Russian sloop *Vorovsky.* On November 14 he said final farewells before his ship sailed at noon for Shanghai. Besides his wife, he had a suite of eighteen persons, for this was an important mission.[91] How different this sailing was from his lonely flight some two years before!

The revolutionary leader had but four months to live. He left behind a strengthened party and a group of old comrades and young activists committed to carrying out his revolutionary program. The Kuomintang was beginning to activate mass organizations among farmers, workers, and students, and it was developing a strong propaganda appeal for Chinese patriots. Sun left an ineffective government which controlled neither the military power nor the financial resources of the area it claimed to rule. Yet foundations had been laid: the military academy, the beginnings of the party army, an operative Central Bank, and a modern municipal administration. He also left behind a "political-military aid mission"—to use a modern term—headed by two very talented Russians, Michael Borodin (who went north at the same time as Dr. Sun did) and Gen. Vasily K. Blücher, with their staffs of revolutionary experts and their ample financial resources. Yet it would take more than a year before Kwangtung could be unified, its fiscal resources centralized, its various armies politicized and brought into a rational structure, and an operative government could be created. Large political storms lay ahead before that revolutionary government could launch a military campaign with the intent of unifying and pacifying the country, which was Dr. Sun's dream.

CHAPTER NINE
The Final Quest

The last four months of Dr. Sun's life were a period of deep disappointment. When he left Canton he had less than one month of passable health left. On his final journey nothing seemed to work out as he hoped.

The Shanghai Stopover

Sun arrived in Shanghai on November 17 and returned to his home in the French Concession where he spent four busy days conferring with Kuomintang leaders and meeting representatives of Gens. Tuan Ch'i-jui, Ch'i Hsieh-yuan, Feng Yü-hsiang, and Hu Ching-i.[1] One of his first acts must have given him considerable satisfaction: he issued a blast at British arrogance. The *North China Daily News* had editorialized that he ought not be allowed to reside in Shanghai since his presence would destroy the city's neutrality. In retort, he reminded foreigners that their settlements were Chinese territory and that as guests they had better not meddle in their host's affairs. "If, therefore, foreigners should dare to oppose or obstruct my presence in Shanghai, I, with the support of my countrymen, am determined to take some drastic steps to deal with them. Be it remembered that we, Chinese people, are not to be trifled with so long as we dwell in our own territory." The time had come, he said, to abrogate foreign settlements in China.[2]

Dr. Sun's main purpose in Shanghai was to size up the situation in the North. His conferences were to determine when and under what conditions he would go to Tientsin to confer with the northern triumvirate, Chang, Feng, and Tuan.[3] Also, according to information reaching the British consulate, he made overtures for an alliance with the Yangtze valley *tuchüns*, who were almost all members of the Chihli clique.[4] Nothing seems to have come of this effort; in fact, Ch'i Hsieh-yuan at Nanking headed a list of *tuchüns* issuing a second circular telegram demanding that Tuan Ch'i-jui accept the top position in Peking. Next day, on November 20, Tuan announced that he was going to the capital as provisional chief executive to organize a provisional government, and that within a month he would convene a reconstruction conference of provincial delegates, which would give birth to a National Assembly.[5] This was vague enough, perhaps, to leave open the door for Dr. Sun's scheme of a conference composed of representatives of occupational groups and for a similar National Assembly, which Dr. Sun described at a meeting of Chinese newspaper reporters at his home. The purpose of his trip north, he told them in a fiery speech, was to promote such an assembly, to eliminate the twin evils of the militarists and the imperialists who support them, and to abolish the unequal treaties.[6]

Dr. Sun sailed for Japan on November 21, en route to Tientsin. In a shipboard interview with a Japanese correspondent he said his purpose in going to Peking was to create an atmosphere favorable for the convening of a broadly representative people's assembly. "Although there is a rumor that I am to assume the Presidency in Peking, I have no idea, at least for the present, of taking up that position," he declared. "I would rather remain as I am, because of my belief that China today badly wants a man who is capable of creating and unifying strong public opinion and I think I am just the man she wants." He added that his main hope was to persuade the powers to give up their concessions and other unjust privileges. He planned to stop only in Kobe since there would not be time, so he said, to go to Tokyo.[7]

The Japanese Interlude

The visit to Japan was a mixture of warm public reception with full press coverage of interviews and speeches, and studied neglect by the Japanese government. The aging leader spent six days in Kobe, from November 24 to 30.[8] Judged by his speeches, the purpose of the trip was to win Japanese support for the abolition of the unequal treaties. He pressed his old theme of Pan-Asianism and of Japan's duty as the younger brother to aid the elder brother, China, to win full independence. For this Japan would win not only China's undying gratitude but also the benefit of greatly increased trade. Some of the press interviews were bitterly anti-Western in general and anti-British in particular, but he praised Soviet Russia for having magnanimously given up all special rights that the tsars had acquired. Japan should follow the Kingly Way and do the same.[9] For a Chinese student audience Sun described the plan for a new kind of National Assembly and urged his listeners to bombard the government with telegrams demanding its convocation.[10] He was in high form: these public presentations were his last great burst of pyrotechnics before the flame of life began to flicker. The Japanese public responded enthusiastically.

Though Sun had sought an invitation, the Japanese government did not invite him to Tokyo.[11] By contrast, two representatives of Tuan Ch'i-jui were received by the Japanese prime minister and foreign minister, as well as by other dignitaries. As Jerome Ch'en put it pithily, "This was not the kind of treatment one country would normally accord to a visiting potential president of another."[12] Nevertheless, members of the Kenkyukai group in the House of Peers visited him, and he was well treated by the head of the Kawasaki Shipbuilding Company, an old friend.[13] He also saw, and may have stayed with, Toyama Mitsuru, the power behind the Black Dragon (or Amur River) Society, a supernationalist and one-time behind-the-scenes patron of Dr. Sun.[14] His former friend, Inukai Ki, now minister of communications, did not accept Sun's invitation to see him in Kobe, but sent a vice-minister in his place. And there were several officers from the Ministry of War and General

Staff who came to pay respects.[15] In these private conversations, Dr. Sun apparently was seeking Japanese official support for the abolition of the unequal treaties, financial assistance, and—here we speculate—for help in Peking for his presidency. But he was asking too much; nor would he, as a quid pro quo, confirm in perpetuity Japan's rights and interests in Manchuria.[16] It appears he left Japan empty-handed.

No sooner had Sun Yat-sen arrived in Tientsin on December 4, 1924, than he fell ill. It was a sickness which could only grow more serious. During most of December he was confined to his bed, until his attendants decided to take him to Peking for better medical treatment. After due preparations had been made for his entry into the capital, the Leader was taken there by a special train on the last day of the year. He was met at Ch'ien-men station by a large throng which he was too ill to address, and then taken to the Hotel de Pekin where he is said to have made a brief speech. This was his last public appearance. Although attended by several physicians, his condition grew steadily worse. On January 26 he entered the hospital of Peking Union Medical College and underwent an operation. It was discovered that cancer had reached the liver and was incurable. The next day his three physicians announced the verdict, "malignant tumor." Thereafter daily bulletins reported his condition. Dr. Sun stayed in the hospital for about three weeks and then was moved, on February 18, to the home of Ku Wei-chün (Dr. V. K. Wellington Koo). He was attended by his wife, his son, and many of his closest followers. At about 9:30 A.M. on Thursday, March 12, Dr. Sun's life flickered out.

Final Political Maneuvers

Even as he approached the end, politics, as always, swirled around him. In Tientsin he had several discussions with his old quasi-ally, Chang Tso-lin, and also received delegates from Tuan Ch'i-jui and Feng Yü-hsiang. Dr. Sun had come north on the invitation of these men in the hope of unifying the country through political agreement. But the northern militarists were deeply suspicious of each other; they were tough politicians who would use Dr. Sun if they could but would not be used by him. An example of their behavior can be found in the fate of the scheme for a new kind of National Assembly. On December 19, though bedridden, Dr. Sun appointed many persons throughout the country as propagandists for the plan, but shortly thereafter Tuan Ch'i-jui announced the details of a reconstruction conference to be made up of military leaders, politicians, and notables invited by the Peking government.[17] There were some negotiations before Dr. Sun's illness became critical, and his last political act was to dictate a compromise message to Tuan on January 17, insisting that the conference include delegates from occupational organizations, and that power of final decision on national policy matters must be left to his proposed National Assembly. When this plea failed, the Kuomintang Central Executive Committee resolved and ordered that no party members should attend the reconstruction conference.[18]

What hopes did Dr. Sun have of abolishing the unequal treaties? When he arrived in Tientsin, the diplomatic corps was calling upon the new provisional chief executive to recognize the validity of all existing treaties as the price for recognition of his government; this was always its position when a change of Chinese presidents occurred. Dr. Sun was reportedly furious when Tuan agreed,[19] but that decision was inescapable given the financial dependency of the central government upon the powers. And what about Sun's pro-Russian and anti-Western posture? His speeches in Japan embarrassed some of his colleagues and perhaps Dr. Sun, himself. There were several indications of this unease. In mid-December the leading members of the Kuomintang issued a statement explaining that Sun Yat-sen and the Kuomintang were not in sympathy with bolshevism and communism, and that their friendly attitude toward Soviet Russia was entirely due to its repudiation of tsarist aggression and its conclusion of new treaties with China on the basis of equality.[20] At about the same time the chief of staff of the Japanese garrison in Tientsin briefed the other foreign staff officers, reporting that Dr. Sun had stayed with Toyama Mitsuru in Kobe. There Mr. Toyama had advised him to drop his antiforeign policy, and

Dr. Sun had replied that abolition of extraterritoriality and unequal treaties was a mere slogan to hold the Kuomintang together; he realized the plan's impracticality and had no intention of putting it into effect. He was not enamored of bolshevism.[21] This, of course, is third-hand information, but why should a Japanese officer pass it on to his colleagues?

An emissary of Chang Tso-lin told the British minister in Peking, Sir Ronald Macleay, that General Chang had warned Dr. Sun, on his arrival in Tientsin, against his association with Bolshevists, and had told him that if he persisted it would lead to a break between them. According to Chang's intermediary, Dr. Sun had seemed impressed.[22] On December 19 Eugene Chen called upon Sir Ronald to attempt to explain Dr. Sun's Kobe speech, which he said had been distorted through double translation. Sun did not mean to tear up the treaties, only to create a determination among his countrymen to make the reforms necessary to secure aboliton of extraterritoriality, rendition of concessions, and tariff autonomy. Mr. Chen said frankly that Dr. Sun and his party believed in friendship with Soviet Russia, but he was not antiforeign nor anti-British. He asked if the British minister would receive Dr. Sun "for the purpose of clearing up misunderstandings between us."[23] Two weeks later, after Dr. Sun had arrived in Peking, Mr. Chen called at the American legation to explain away "Bolshevik activities" in Canton.[24]

All this seems to be tactical maneuvering in hopes of quieting foreign uncertainties about Dr. Sun's intentions in case he should be part of a new government; these maneuvers were carried on, of course, before the gravity of his illness was realized.

Michael Borodin's role during the northern trip is obscure. He left Canton at the same time as Dr. Sun, probably first going to Shanghai.[25] Apparently he then went to Peking, arriving before Dr. Sun, and he either escorted him there from Tientsin or met him on arrival.[26] By early January, the American minister, Dr. Schurman, understood that Borodin was Dr. Sun's constant companion.[27] This information tells us nothing about the advice on tactics he offered, if he did so at all.

Dr. Sun's national prestige seems to have grown during the trip north—or so it is my impression. During the latter part of October his name had been purposely besmirched in Cantonese communities because of the burning and looting of the main commercial center of Canton by troops under his orders. But as he moved north he was met by enthusiastic crowds in Shanghai, Kobe, Tientsin, and then in Peking, when he was already mortally ill. The turnouts were no doubt organized by advance men, but nevertheless the greeters seemed genuinely appreciative of the southern revolutionary. By that time he was supported by more effective publicity than before. But the main reason why Dr. Sun's prestige was on the rise—if that is a fair appraisal—was what he stood for in public: national unity, peace, and bringing the foreigners' privileged position in China to an end. In short, "Save China!"—the old, old cry! Patriotic Chinese responded positively.

As the news of Dr. Sun's incurable illness spread,[28] many of his closest associates journeyed to Peking to be with him. Some were already there. Yet other important followers, such as Hu Han-min, Liao Chung-k'ai, Hsü Ch'ung-chih, and Chiang Kai-shek, remained in Kwangtung where the military situation was dangerous. On January 26, when the gravity of Dr. Sun's condition was confirmed, Wang Ching-wei was the only member of the Kuomintang Political Council in Peking. Five other notables were coopted to join him in an emergency Political Council consisting of Yü Yu-jen, Wu Ching-heng (Wu Chih-hui), Li Yü-ying (Li Shih-tseng), Ch'en Yu-jen (Eugene Chen), and Li Ta-chao. Two were members of the Central Executive Committee and two of the Supervisory Committee. Eugene Chen was not in either body but was prominent in Kuomintang publicity work and had accompanied the Leader on his journey from Canton. Others were added as they arrived in Peking. Mr. Borodin served as adviser; he was one of the few permitted to see Dr. Sun at his sickbed.[29] This group decided to request a last testament from the Leader when the time was more auspicious.[30] They waited nearly a month.

The Revolutionary Leader's Final Testament

On February 24, after Dr. Sun had been moved to a private residence and his condition was deteriorating rapidly, a small committee approached him, with the approval of his wife, Soong Ch'ingling, to request his final instructions. The group consisted of his son, Sun Fo, his wife's elder brother, Sung Tzu-wen (T. V. Soong), her elder sister's husband, K'ung Hsiang-hsi (H. H. Kung), and Wang Ching-wei. It could not have been easy for Chinese to ask a dying leader for his final testament. Accounts of what transpired depend primarily upon reports by Wang, delivered nearly a year later. Unless someone took down the conversation, the words quoted by Wang must be thought of as artifacts. Dr. Sun is supposed to have warned his followers of the dangers and temptations that would face them after his death, and Wang supposedly assured him of their constancy. He then asked for Dr. Sun's instructions. The Leader replied that he had already written many books and asked what further they wanted him to say. At this, Wang offered to read the draft of a testament which they had drawn up. If Dr. Sun approved, he could sign it; but if he wished to modify it, Wang would act as his recorder. Dr. Sun consented to listen, and after hearing the 145 words which make up the testament, is said to have nodded assent and then exclaimed, "Good! I thoroughly approve."

It appears that later, for reasons of propriety, it was given out that Dr. Sun dictated the testament and that Wang Ching-wei was merely the scribe. Wu Chih-hui is the authority for the statement that the draft had already been approved by a meeting of the Political Council before being submitted to the Leader.[31]

Wang Ching-wei also produced the draft of a private will. This bequeathed Dr. Sun's books and papers, personal possessions and house, to his wife. Dr. Sun approved this draft also, but he did not sign either document at that time. The signing took place on March 11, with Dr. Sun's wife guiding his faltering hand. Wang Ching-wei signed as copyist and several of Dr. Sun's relatives and long-time followers added their signatures to the two documents as attestants. Photographic copies were given out to the press shortly after Dr. Sun's death the next morning.[32]

There are different translations of the political testament, which has come to be known as The Leader's Will, but they vary only in shades of meaning:

> For forty years I have devoted myself to the cause of the National Revolution, the object of which is to raise China to a position of independence and equality. The experience of these forty years has convinced me that, to attain this goal, the people must be aroused and that we must associate ourselves in a common struggle with the peoples of the world who treat us as equals.
>
> The Revolution has not yet been successfully concluded. Let all our comrades follow my writings—The Plans of National Reconstruction, the Fundamentals of National Reconstruction, The Three Principles of the People, and the Manifesto of the First Congress of Representatives—and make every effort to carry them into effect. Above all, my recent declaration in favor of holding a National Convention of the People of China and abolishing the unequal treaties should be carried into effect as soon as possible.
>
> This is my last will and testament.
>
> March 11.   Sun Wen

For many Chinese this has become a sacred document, known as Tsung-li's Testament. The Kuomintang leaders in Peking soon resolved that as the opening ceremony of every party meeting all in attendance should stand for a reading of the Leader's Testament. They sent an order to party headquarters in Canton, and the first such ceremony was held there on April 23, 1925.[33] It has been followed in all formal Kuomintang meetings ever since. Thereafter, reading of the testament at Monday morning ceremonies became required practice in governmental offices under the Nationalist government. Sanctification of the testament was thus the first step in the sanctification of Sun Yat-sen, himself, a process which more and more obscured the real man.

Still another paper appeared at Dr. Sun's bedside on March 11, a letter of farewell to Soviet Russia. This was in English, prepared by Eugene Chen in consultation with Borodin, according to later Kuomintang accounts. Mr. Borodin's own report to Moscow tells that the dying man kept repeating, "Only if the Russians continue to help . . . Only if the Russians continue to help." [34] T. V. Soong read the draft of the letter to Dr. Sun, and he was asked to sign it. Given the circumstances, many leading members of the Kuomintang declined to treat it with the respect they accorded to the testament.[35] No one signed as witness, and the letter was not given to the press with the two wills. It was first published in *Pravda* on March 14 and released in China by a Rosta despatch from Peking on March 17. The despatch began, "Feeling the approach of his death, Dr. Sun Yat-sen, on the 11th of this month, called the members of the Central Executive Committee of the Kuomintang and had the following letter drafted to the Central Committee of the U.S.S.R., signing it with his own hand." Rosta's text read as follows:

To the Central Executive Committee of the Union of Soviet Socialist Republics:

My dear Comrades,

As I lie here, with a malady that is beyond men's skill, my thoughts turn to you and to the future of my party and my country.

You are the head of a Union of free republics which is the real heritage that the immortal Lenin has left to the world of the oppressed peoples. Through this heritage, the victims of imperialism are destined to secure their freedom and deliverance from an international system whose foundations lie in ancient slaveries and wars and injustices.

I am leaving behind me a party which I hoped would be associated with you in the historic work of completely liberating China and other exploited countries from this imperialist system. Fate decrees that I must leave the task unfinished and pass it on to those who, by remaining true to the principles and teachings of the Party, will constitute my real followers.

I have, therefore, enjoined the Kuomintang to carry on the work of the national revolutionary movement in order that China may be freed from the semi-colonial status which imperialism imposed upon her. To this end I have charged the party to keep in constant touch with you; and I look with confidence to the continuance of the support that your Government has heretofore extended to my country.

In bidding farewell to you, dear comrades, I wish to express the fervent hope that the day may soon dawn when the U.S.S.R. will greet, as a

friend and ally, a strong and independent China and the two allies may together advance to victory in the great struggle for the liberation of the oppressed peoples of the world.
    With fraternal greetings.[36]

After Dr. Sun's passing, several other messages were sent and declarations made by the elements of the tripartite alliance working for the Chinese national revolution—the Kuomintang, the Comintern, and the Chinese Communist Party. Some Kuomintang leaders in Peking, using the name of the Central Executive Committee, wired to Stalin and Zinoviev pledging to continue Sun Yat-sen's work and appealing for continued support. Stalin, for the Central Committee of the Russian Communist Party, and Zinoviev for the Comintern, wired reassurances. In an open letter, the Central Committee of the Chinese Communist Party pledged full support to the Kuomintang on behalf of the Communist Party itself, the Chinese workers and peasants, the world proletariat, and all parties associated with the Comintern.[37]

The death of Dr. Sun Yat-sen was a political event of national importance. His followers were determined to secure the greatest possible honor to his memory and the largest possible advantage to the causes he had espoused. They demanded official holidays in mourning, the assignment of public funds for memorial expenses, and the renaming of parks in his honor. Some of the ambiguities of Dr. Sun's career were reflected in the controversies that soon emerged over the uses to be made of his name.

Dr. Sun had been baptized a Christian. It was reported by Christians among his relatives and followers that before his death he had stated clearly, and wished it to be known, that he died a Christian. His widow and son decided he should have a Christian funeral. Yet some among his influential followers were fiercely anti-Christian; they linked the Christian religion in China with imperialism and naturally opposed a Christian service. The wishes of the family prevailed, and the first service—a private one—was a Protestant service held in the great hall of the Peking Union Medical College on March 19. It was conducted by the Reverend Liu T'ing-fang (Timothy Lew), with testimonial speeches by Hsü Ch'ien and

K'ung Hsiang-hsi which emphasized Dr. Sun's Christian convictions as well as his revolutionary ones.[38]

Professor L. Carrington Goodrich attended the service and sang in the double male quartet. He kindly permitted the following account, written the same day, to be quoted from his diary:

> As the choir filed down the chapel corridor to the bower of flowers by the altar the place was hushed save for the tones of the preacher reading in Chinese from the Scriptures. The casket draped in a Kuo Min Tang flag was placed below the dais beneath the flowers and under a large picture of Dr. Sun, showing him clad in the simple garb of a commoner. Then followed prayer by Dr. Tsu, a simple testimony by Dr. Lew, songs by the congregation, by a contralto soloist, and by a double male quartet. All these were effective enough, but the remarkable features of the service were the addresses of the Hon. George Hsu, former minister of justice, and Mr. K'ung Hsiang-hsi, whose wife is the sister of Madame Sun, and who has long been connected with Christian institutions in China. . . .
>
> Mr. Hsu in limpid Mandarin outlined the beliefs of his friend, and in one quotation after another showed how deeply Sun had been actuated by the spirit and teachings of Christ. "He was a revolutionist; so am I." "He came to save the poor, and the unfortunate, and those in bondage. So have I also tried to do." "He decried the traditions maintained by the lawmakers of Judea, and plead for universal brotherhood. It is because of similar shackles that bind China that I have made my crusade. It is because the organized Church has been so divided and divisive that I have long given up my membership in the church, but I believe in Christ and his teachings and have endeavored to make them my own." Mr. K'ung was more brief, but he was equally outspoken: "Just a day or so before his death Dr. Sun called me to his bedside, and taking both my hands in his, said: "You're a Christian and so am I. I wish to tell you something I have always felt which you will understand. Just as Christ was sent by God to the world, so also did God send me."

Immediately after this Christian service, Dr. Sun's coffin was moved to the park adjacent to the imperial palace buildings. Those drawing and escorting the hearse represented other groups symbolically claiming Dr. Sun as theirs—his Kuomintang followers, dressed in formal gowns and black satin jackets, his student admirers with banners, and his Russian supporters. Ambassador Karakhan took a role of prominent mourner and members of the

Russian embassy formed part of the inner chain around the coffin. In the park itself, loudspeakers gave out a recording of one of Dr. Sun's Canton speeches on the Principle of Nationalism. The coffin was draped with the Kuomintang flag. During the next two weeks thousands upon thousands passed the bier to extend their respects to the revolutionary leader. On the second of April the coffin was transported to a beautiful temple in the Western Hills, awaiting its future removal to Nanking.

Dr. Sun's followers also arranged impressive memorial services in cities throughout China and in several foreign countries.[39] These lasted until April 12. These memorial services were an outpouring of respect for an indomitable idealist who had devoted his life to his country. The processions and public meetings, the written and verbal tributes, the enshrined pictures of Dr. Sun and the half-masted flags did honor to a frustrated patriot, whose dreams for China were only gradually being fulfilled half a century later.

Conclusions

Inevitably this study has presented an exterior view of Sun Yat-sen. His sentiments and motives emerge from a written record—his own writings and the recorded observations of many who knew him. So far as we know he did not leave an intimate diary, and he wrote most of his published letters to effect a desired result; they do not necessarily reveal his inner sentiments and convictions. Nor should we forget the myth making that began immediately after his death and the censorship that still conceals some of the record. Still, a picture of a man like no other—a man with particular talents, concerns, and hopes—presents itself to us. The picture of Sun Yat-sen may not be entirely clear, but it is unmistakably his.

One strong impression of the youth and the man is his intellectual curiosity. The Kwangtung village lad suddenly plunged into the strange environment of an Anglican missionary school in Hawaii, the student in a foreign medical school in Hong Kong, the fugitive, reading for months in the British Museum library, the refugee in Japan and the wanderer on three continents, and then the economic planner and political philosophizer in Shanghai—during all these phases Sun Wen eagerly absorbed knowledge and expanded his horizons. He read widely when not involved in his activist role, and he loved to engage visitors from abroad in discussion of foreign affairs. In his later years international relations, Western political systems, and foreign economic conditions interested him particularly. Yet reading his speeches and public writing leaves one with the feeling that much of this knowledge was super-ficial.

Another impression is of his dogged determination. In 1894 the recent Chinese graduate in medicine pitted himself against a Man-chu regime that had ruled his country for 250 years, and he per-sisted in this struggle for seventeen years in spite of terrible dis-couragements and repeated setbacks. Between 1913 and 1924 he set himself against Yuan Shih-k'ai and each successive government in Peking, and organized three rival regimes far away in the South. Such single-minded pursuit of remote goals required tremendous self-confidence, devotion, and conviction of the rightness of his cause. These qualities he surely had.

From most reports, Dr. Sun had a magnetic personality. Many Western visitors who had no particular reason to revere him were impressed by his sincerity, the simplicity and directness of his speech, and the low-keyed passion with which he held to his con-victions. Of course he had his detractors too, those put off by his impractical schemes and his egoism. He had a strong appeal to his countrymen, apparently due both to his engaging personality and to the causes he supported. Anti-Manchuism and antiimperialism both became very popular issues. He won the devotion of diverse groups.

In his years of exile, his fellow migrants from Kwangtung in com-munities throughout Southeast Asia, Canada, and America received him warmly and many helped him generously. They knew he hoped to improve conditions at home, and he assured them that a progressive government would enhance their own status abroad. They could take pride in being Chinese and would no longer be second-class. He seems never to have lost his magnetic appeal for the overseas Chinese. Patriotic students admired him when revolu-tionary sentiment flared hot in the 1900s; they lionized him as pro-visional president and on his triumphal tours in 1912. During the last years of his life he fired them by his speeches against foreign privilege and his opposition to military rule. Modern, educated Chinese respected his cosmopolitanism and progressive outlook, though some considered him an impractical idealist given to large talk and few accomplishments. Revolutionaries of various factions accorded him honor as first among them, and within his own party his position as leader was seldom challenged. He had an inner circle of devoted followers and a larger group he could call upon for special services. Yet probably it was not easy to be his disciple, and we really do not know what the psychological relationships were between him and those closest to him. There has been much idealization of such relationships; a clear example is the romanticized picture of the reciprocal devotion between Chiang Kai-shek and the Leader.

Dr. Sun's personal life was simple. Though he constantly pursued money, it appears that he kept for himself only so much as he needed for a modest maintenance. He dispensed large amounts, financing revolts, paying salaries of secretaries and emissaries, subvening publications, enticing members of Parliament, and bringing military commanders over to his side. He used such expenditures to forward his causes; it was money for the power to have his way. The only constraint on his uses of money to achieve his goals, it seems, was the perennial shortage of it.

Again and again we observe ambivalences in Dr. Sun's behavior. He was devoted to China, there can be no doubt of that, and he hoped to rejuvenate his country with help from abroad. Yet to gain this help he offered concessions which could only have strengthened the foreign grip on the country. During his latter years he became particularly sensitive to foreign domination and likened China to a colony with many masters, yet as late as mid-1923 he seemed willing to offer large economic concessions in Kwangtung to British business. Early in 1924 he still toyed with the scheme for a militarily enforced foreign tutelage of the entire country.

His attitude toward domestic power holders seems ambiguous. He detested Tuan Ch'i-jui when he brought China into World War I and contracted loans from Japan (Sun's side also joined the war and sought war loans), but he was keen to ally with Tuan and his faction when the Anhwei general was at odds with Peking. He professed a low opinion of Chang Tso-lin as a bandit and hireling of Japan, and yet he courted him for financial help and military alliances. In late 1921, and again in 1922 when a refugee in Shanghai, Dr. Sun flirted with both the great northern power factions, Chihli and Fengtien—the issue being, which would agree to put him in the presidency.

Then there is the matter of upholding constitutionalism. The only constitution he could have been upholding in 1917 was the provisional one that he had promulgated just before retiring from the presidency in March 1912. Yet this had been superceded by much further drafting in an elected Parliament and by another provisional constitution promulgated by Yuan Shih-k'ai in 1914. By the time of his election as "Extraordinary President" in 1921, there was the draft constitution which the Peking government promulgated in 1919. Whatever the murky constitutional situation, Sun pretended that an election by some 230 members of a Parliament whose term had expired made him president of the Chinese Republic de jure.

A way to explain these and similar ambiguities is to believe that Dr. Sun saw ends as justifying means. His end was the betterment of the country, and he saw himself as the agent to achieve this betterment. This, of course, is an exterior view again. Quite likely Sun was not concerned with a need for consistency, though occasionally he was called upon to explain his deviations.

In recalling Dr. Sun's vision for China, one can emphasize its progressive character or one can focus upon the impracticality of many of his schemes. He wanted to move China into the twentieth century and up to its rightful place at the head of the procession of nations. He wanted whatever was the latest in political practice or material progress for China—immediately. He drew up ideal schemes of government, combining Western and Chinese elements. He planned audaciously for China's economic transformation. He wanted a better life for all classes and hoped to prevent the abuses of capitalism and avoid the interclass conflicts he observed abroad. He believed in the power of education and wished to spread enlightenment.

Yet most of his plans were very impractical. To give an example: more than half a century later China has produced nowhere near the mileage of railroads he planned to build in ten years when director of railway planning under Yuan Shih-k'ai. Who but an egoist would press such fantasies as *The International Development of China* upon the public? Impractical though his plans generally were, he had a much larger vision for China than most other leaders of his day.

Dr. Sun berated his countrymen for having allowed China to fall behind the West in material accomplishments and scientific knowledge, though he expressed no doubts about the inherent superiority of Chinese civilization. He employed the popular defensive arguments that most Western achievements were elaborations of earlier Chinese discoveries and that China was still superior in matters of the spirit, human relations, and political philosophy. For all these self-assurances, one may sense, nevertheless, that Sun Wen was terribly torn between his pride in China and his admiration for the West. It was psychologically unbearable to him that his country should be so poor, backward, and ignorant (by Western standards), be patronized and exploited by foreigners, and be surpassed by "the younger brother," Japan. His intense and lasting concern for his country's political reformation and economic development might be explained as psychologically compulsive. One cannot help wondering about the deeper reasons for his endless pursuit of foreign assistance to solve his and China's problems. Was he driven by an inner necessity? And what were the effects on his psyche of his almost constant failure to receive foreign help?

He did not look to any one power to save China. As we have pointed out, he solicited them all. Before 1917 he pinned his greatest hopes on Japan; then during the war years and into the early twenties he looked to the United States; and, briefly, he prospected Germany. Even as he moved into his "Soviet alliance" he tried to keep lines open for American, British, and Japanese assistance. Very likely he did not want to become overly dependent upon one patron. With respect to Soviet Russia, he made it clear repeatedly that he did not favor bolshevism for China and that he admired the new Russia because it treated China as an equal. Other powers were welcome to do the same.

In retrospect, it seems that most Westerners in China who knew of Sun Yat-sen did not understand his appeal to his countrymen. Most of them were there to make money or save souls; they had little chance for detached observation or assessment. Furthermore, most foreigners were beneficiaries of the unique privileges embodied in the treaty system; they were unlikely to favor their abolition. Some friendly journalists sensed Sun Yat-sen's appeal, but on the whole the foreign press did not appreciate this troublemaker. Western governments did not take him seriously except when he created separatist regimes in the South that seemed to increase political turmoil. Those responsible for China policy in Western governments failed to recognize Sun's relationship to the growing tide of Chinese nationalism, and during his last years some thought him a demagog who whipped nationalism up. The Japanese were more discerning; they had much better information and, after all, Japan was the most direct target of Chinese nationalism from 1915 onward. A few perceptive Russians saw the nationalistic tide as a powerful force to be channeled against the capitalist powers. Such men as Joffe, Karakhan, and Borodin encouraged Dr. Sun to play up these nationalistic passions.

We have called Sun Yat-sen a "frustrated patriot" because most of his career was marked by discouragement in his efforts to achieve patriotic goals. He had two great successes, one of which he did not live to see. His triumph was to have initiated and nurtured a movement that succeeded many years later in overthrowing Manchu despotism and establishing a republic. In this effort he had many associates who contributed money, issued propaganda, and organized revolts, but this does not diminish his important, and at times inspiring, role among the revolutionaries. Sun Wen had his moment of recognition and glory as provisional president of the new republic in 1912. His second great success was in leading the Kuomintang's reorganization in 1924. This set it on the way to becoming an effective instrument for the seizure of political power several years after his death. This complex task, too, had the help of many comrades, Russian assistance, and the cooperation of the Chinese Communist Party, which added fresh nationalistic fire and social revolutionary dimensions to the movement. All deserve their due.

The disappointments were endless. Revolt after revolt against the Manchus failed. To raise money for revolution was painfully difficult. The republic turned out to be a complete disillusionment, stolen—so Dr. Sun later came to believe—by that autocrat, Yuan Shih-k'ai and corrupted by bureaucrats, militarists, and self-seeking politicians. The dreams of railway development with foreign loans came to nothing and nothing grew from his elaborate plans for China's economic transformation. No foreign government recognized any regime he headed, not even the provisional revolutionary government in Nanking. They waited for Yuan Shih-k'ai. The revolutionary leader tried to block loans to Yuan's government and other governments in Peking without success. Foreign governments paid no heed to the advice he offered so freely.

Dr. Sun did enjoy three coups in gaining foreign financial assistance, each of which served the donor country's political aims. The Japanese government lent him money through a cover agent in 1916 so he could join those opposing Yuan Shih-k'ai's monarchical scheme, and Germany probably financed his work against Tuan Ch'i-jui's plan to bring China into World War I on the Allied side, a policy which Sun strongly opposed. Yuan's death ended the first effort and the main result of German aid was a rival regime in the South in which Dr. Sun participated for less than a year. The third contribution, by Soviet Russia, was more substantial. Soviet Russia did assist him to organize a revolutionary movement that would be directed against the powers and the government in Peking—a government which Russia recognized and with which she maintained diplomatic relations.

Administrations in Canton did show modernizing achievements under Sun Yat-sen's son, the mayor, but the generalissimo's headquarters bled the city to support his wars. His alliances with northern military cliques brought him no nearer to Peking, and his military campaigns toward the Yangtse were failures. One such failure was due to the betrayal, as it is indelibly presented in history, of a man he considered a disciple, Ch'en Chiung-ming; and Sun had the deep satisfaction of organizing a punitive campaign that drove General Ch'en from Canton.

All of Sun Wen's hopes to get the presidency in Peking so he could restore a constitutional government—whether by negotiation, alliances, campaigns, or foreign assistance—came to nought. When he finally arrived at the capital on the last day of 1924 he was dying of cancer.

His is a somber story of shattered dreams. But it is a record shown by history and not one that Dr. Sun could foresee as he launched each new plan. He probably was borne along by the support of his wife and colleagues, by signs of popular approval and partial successes, and by the expectation of accomplishment ahead. Yet for a man to persevere against so many discouragements suggests that he was sustained by an enduring confidence both in his causes and in himself. He was working for his dream of China, and this is why his compatriots revere him.

List of Abbreviations Used in Notes

CWR	*China Weekly Review.*
CYB	*China Year Book.*
FER	*Far Eastern Review.*
FRUS	U.S. Department of State. *Papers Relating to the Foreign Relations of the United States.*
GBFO	Great Britain, Foreign Office.
HTCH	*Hsiang-tao Chou-pao.*
Kao, *Chronology*	Kao Yin-tsu, comp. *Chung-hua Min-kuo Ta Shih Chi.*
KFCC	Sun Yat-sen. *Kuo Fu Ch'üan Chi.*
KFNPttp	*Kuo Fu Nien P'u Tseng Ting Pen.*
KMWH	*Ko-ming Wen-hsien.*
Li, TJKTCT	Li Yün-han. *Ts'ung Jung Kung tao Ch'ing Tang.*
Mao, CKSHS	Mao Ssu-ch'eng, comp. *Min-kuo Shih-wu Nien i-ch'ien chih Chiang Chieh-shih Hsien-sheng.*
NCH	*North China Herald.*
NYT	*New York Times.*
Su-ch'ing, KCTCYM	Su-ch'ing. *Kung-ch'an Tang chih Yin-mou Ta Pao-lu.*
Tsou, CKKMTSK	Tsou Lu. *Chung-kuo Kuomintang Shih Kao.*
USDS	U.S. Department of State.

Notes

Titles of articles and chapters in Chinese, Russian, and Japanese are given in translation; book titles are given in transcription and translation.

INTRODUCTION

1. The largest untapped source for the present volume is that in Japanese. See, for example, the extensive bibliography on Sun published in *Shisō* No. 396 (1957, no. 6): 79–93, and the extensive bibliography compiled by Ch'en P'eng-jen of Japanese writings concerning Sun Yat-sen in Huang Chi-lu, ed., *Yen-chiu Chung-shan Hsien-sheng ti Shih Liao yü Shih Hsüeh* [Historical Materials and Historical Studies on Sun Yat-sen], (Taipei: Chung-hua Min-kuo Shih Liao Yen-chiu Chung-hsin, 1975), pp. 469–517. I was most fortunate to have the assistance of Mrs. Lea Kisselgoff and Mrs. Lydia Holubnychy, who abstracted for me many items of recent Russian scholarship on the period of Dr. Sun's cooperation with Soviet Russia. Scholars in the People's Republic of China seem absorbed in problems of identifying Sun Yat-sen's class background and in defining the historical stage represented by the 1911 revolution, both in procrustean Marxist categories; naturally they eulogize Sun's cooperation with the Communist Party and his support for the masses toward the end of his career. Mainland historians have also published much data on revolutionary personalities and movements leading to 1911. See, for example, the eight-volume compendium, *Hsin-hai Ko-ming* (Shanghai: Jen-min Ch'u-pan She, 1957). Such work is outdone in volume by the vast compendia published in the Republic of China.

2. Li Yün-han, "Comments on Biographical Writings Concerning Sun Yat-sen," in Huang Chi-lu, ed., *Yen-chiu Chung-shan Hsien-sheng ti Shih Liao yü Shih Hsüeh,* pp. 199–231, and Chiang Yung-ching, "A Comparison of Various Editions of *The Collected Works of Sun Yat-sen* and an Introduction to the New Edition," in ibid., pp. 125–61.

3. Li Yün-han, "Comments on Biographical Writings Concerning Sun Yat-sen."

4. Philip C. Huang, *Liang Ch'i-ch'ao and Modern Chinese Liberalism* (Seattle: University of Washington Press, 1972), p. 176, n. 33, points out that Japanese police records

contain some 3,000 pages of reports on Liang Ch'i-ch'ao during his stay in Japan. Doubtless the Japanese police were reporting likewise on Dr. Sun. The reports are in Nihon Gaimushō, "Kakumeitō kankei" [Pertaining to the Revolutionary Party], in *Kakkoku Naisei Kankei Zasshū: Shina no Bu* [Miscellaneous Collection Pertaining to the Domestic Affairs of Foreign Countries: China], vols. 1–4. Unpublished Documents.

5. Interview, Dr. V. K. Wellington Koo with Professor C. Martin Wilbur and Mrs. Crystal Seidman, December 14, 1972, on file with the Chinese Oral History Project, East Asian Institute, Columbia University, pp. 10931, 10933. Dr. Sun visited young Mr. Koo at his rooms in Hartley Hall on two successive evenings, probably between November 8, 1909 and January 18, 1910.

6. James Cantlie and C. Sheridan Jones, *Sun Yat Sen and the Awakening of China* (New York and London: Fleming H. Revell Co., 1912), pp. 4, 24–25, 31, 56–57. Dr. Cantlie hoped, in writing as he did, to counteract the disparagement of Sun which he read in news reports by "China experts" after Sun's inauguration as provisional president in January 1912.

7. Li Lu-chao to C. Martin Wilbur, October 25, 1974.

8. Nathaniel Peffer, "One of Asia's Three Great Moderns. The Enigma of Sun Yat-sen, Maker of the Chinese Republic, Without Honor Save in History," *Asia* (August 1924): 591–94, 657–58.

CHAPTER ONE   MOLDING INFLUENCES AND THE CAREER LINE

1. Harold Z. Schiffrin, *Sun Yat-sen and the Origins of the Chinese Revolution* (Berkeley and Los Angeles: University of California Press, 1968), p. 31. The account of Sun's early life in these paragraphs is taken from Dr. Schiffrin's scholarly study.

2. See Sun Yat-sen, *Kuo Fu Ch'üan Chi* [The Collected Works of Sun Yat-sen], rev. ed., 6 vols. (Taipei: Chung-kuo Kuomintang Central Executive Committee, 1961), 3: 241–43, for a summary of the address given to Chinese students in Hong Kong University on February 20, 1923. There are numerous collections of Sun Yat-sen's works. I have used this because it is relatively complete and is convenient. There is, however, a later edition in 11 volumes with different pagination. Hereafter, I cite my source as KFCC.

3. Schiffrin, *Sun Yat-sen,* pp. 27–29, 34–40, 41.

4. Chün-tu Hsüeh, "Sun Yat-sen, Yang Ch'ü-yün, and the Early Revolutionary Movement in China," *Journal of Asian Studies* 19 (1960): 309; Lo Hsiang-lin, "The Story of the Founding of the Hsing Chung Hui," *China Forum* 1, no. 2 (July 1974): 143.

5. The list of members who joined between November 24, 1894 and September 2, 1895, and a record of income and expenditures, are given in *Ko-ming Wen-hsien* [Documents of the Revolution], compiled by Lo Chia-lun (Taipei: Committee for the Compilation of Materials on the Party History, Central Executive Committee of the Chung-kuo Kuomintang, 1953–), 3: 288–90. (Hereafter this multivolume series is cited as KMWH, with page numbers running consecutively through the volumes.) Another account of the founding of the Hsing Chung Hui is given in Lo Chia-lun

and Huang Chi-lu, comps., *Kuo Fu Nien P'u Tseng Ting Pen* [A Chronological Biography of the Father of the Country, Enlarged and Collated], 3d ed., 2 vols. (Taipei: Committee for the Compilation of Materials on the Party History, Central Executive Committee of the Chung-kuo Kuomintang, 1969), 1: 60–62. (Hereafter this third edition is cited as KFNPttp.) One of the compilers provides an interesting account of how this work developed. See Huang Chi-lu, "Experiences in Enlarging and Collating the *Chronological Biography of the Father of the Country*," in Huang Chi-lu, ed., *Yen-chiu Chung-shan Hsien-sheng ti Shih Liao yü Shih Hsüeh*, pp. 101–05. Among the photographic reproductions at the beginning of volume 1 is a picture of a certificate for one share of stock in The Commercial Union of China, signed by Y. S. Sun as president, and dated "Jan 22nd 1895." Lo in "The Story of the Founding," p. 136, says that a share was worth $10, so this may have been one of ten shares owned by Li To-ma, who subscribed $100. A ten-dollar share was to be repaid by $100 after the revolution succeeded. Out of the sales, Sun took $100 in cash and $1,004 was converted into a letter of credit worth HK $2,000. KMWH, 3: 290.

6. Schiffrin, *Sun Yat-sen*, pp. 56–97, especially p. 68. Chün-tu Hsüeh, "Sun Yat-sen," and *Huang Hsing and the Chinese Revolution* (Stanford: Stanford University Press, 1961), pp. 29–31.

7. Hsüeh, "Sun Yat-sen," p. 312, n. 26, quoting Ch'en Shao-pai and Hsieh Tsuan-t'ai (who wrote under the name of Tse Tsan Tai); their accounts were first published in 1929 and 1924, respectively.

8. Ibid., p. 313.

9. The exception seems to be the case of the T'ung Meng Hui early in 1912, when Dr. Sun had already been installed as provisional president of the Chinese Republic, and it was thought inappropriate for him to head the T'ung Meng Hui as well. Wang Ching-wei was elected head but did not take up the office. Shortly thereafter, Sun, who had given up the provisional presidency, was elected president of the reorganized T'ung Meng Hui. The reorganization was followed by the establishment of an open political party, the Kuo Min Tang, which had a directorate of nine, of which Dr. Sun was one. On September 3, 1912, this directorate elected him its head, but he delegated the work to Sung Chiao-jen, the moving spirit and chief architect of the new party. See K. S. Liew, *Struggle for Democracy: Sung Chiao-jen and the 1911 Revolution* (Berkeley and Los Angeles: University of California Press, 1971), pp. 157, 177.

10. Hsüeh, *Huang Hsing*, p. 31. Professor Hsüeh overlooked stops at Shanghai at the end of August 1900, in December 1902, and again in October 1905, though on two of these occasions Dr. Sun may have stayed aboard his ship in the harbor.

11. The earliest photos I have seen of Dr. Sun wearing a Chung-shan jacket date from his provisional presidency during the first months of 1912. See Cantlie and Jones, *Sun Yat Sen*, facing p. 64, and Frederick McCormick, *The Flowery Republic* (London: John Murray, 1913), facing, p. 258. This appears to be a completely unadorned military uniform. However, there is a photograph of Sun wearing a tropical suit with a Chung-shan-like collar when visiting in Malaya c. 1908. See Su Hsi-wen, *Kuo Fu Sun Chung-shan Hsien-sheng Hua Chuan: A Pictorial Biography of Dr. Sun Yat-sen* (Hong Kong: Chung-wai Wen-hua Shih-yeh Yu-lang Kung-ssu, 1965), p. 36. Fic-

tionalized paintings of Dr. Sun show him wearing such a uniform as early as 1905. See Chia-luen Lo, *The Pictorial Biography of Dr. Sun Yat-sen* (Taipei: Historical Archives Commission of the Kuomintang, 1955), p. 46.

12. Sun Yat Sen, *Kidnapped in London, Being the Story of My Capture by, Detention at, and Release from the Chinese Legation, London* (Bristol: J. W. Arrowsmith, 1897); photographic reprint, with a foreword by Kenneth Cantlie (London: China Society, 1969). The kidnapping story is interestingly reconstructed by Lyon Sharman in her valuable biography, *Sun Yat-sen: His Life and Its Meaning* (New York: John Day Co., 1934), pp. 45–51. Lo Chia-lun made a careful study of the documents of the case, described in KFNPttp, pp. 78–86. Schiffrin, *Sun Yat-sen*, pp. 99–139, devotes most of a chapter to the story, having dug up even more documentary information.

13. Schiffrin, *Sun Yat-sen*, p. 129 and Sharman, *Sun Yat-sen*, pp. 47–48. Mrs. Sharman emphasizes the Christian aspect, whereas the more skeptical Professor Schiffrin infers that Sun dressed up the account to appeal to his Christian audience. However, he accepts the idea that as a result of the escape, Sun believed he had a God-given destiny. Text of the letter in KFCC, 5: 15–16, and a full translation in John C. H. Wu, *Sun Yat-sen: The Man and His Ideas* (Taipei: The Commercial Press, 1971), pp. 110–113.

14. Schiffrin, *Sun Yat-sen*, pp. 130–32, quoting from Sun Yat Sen, "China's Present and Future: The Reform Party's Plea for British Benevolent Neutrality," *Fortnightly Review* n.s. 61 (March 1, 1897): 424–40.

15. See Key Ray Chong, "Cheng Kuan-ying (1841–1920): A Source of Sun Yat-sen's Nationalist Ideology?" *Journal of Asian Studies* 28 (February 1969): 247–67; and Yen-p'ing Hao, *The Compradore in Nineteenth Century China* (Cambridge: Harvard University Press, 1970), pp. 193, 202–06. Dr. Chong discusses the theory that Sun contributed ideas to Cheng.

16. Benjamin Schwartz, *In Search of Wealth and Power: Yen Fu and the West* (Cambridge: Harvard University Press, 1964), passim for Yen's translations; Y. C. Wang, *Chinese Intellectuals and the West, 1872–1949* (Chapel Hill: University of North Carolina Press, 1966), pp. 193–228 on "The Political Thought of Yen Fu and Liang Ch'i-chao" and pp. 339–49, 355–61, where Dr. Wang traces many of Sun's ideas to Yen and Liang.

17. Harold Schiffrin, "Sun Yat-sen's Early Land Policy," *Journal of Asian Studies* 16 (August 1957): 549–64. For a broader account of the developing revolutionary ideology between 1895 and 1905, see Chiang Yung-ching, "Development of Revolutionary Discussions in the Days of Hsing Chung Hui," *China Forum* 1, no. 2 (July 1974): 147–99.

18. There are many sources on this brief cooperation and then competition. Lo Jung-pang, ed., *K'ang Yu-wei: A Biography and a Symposium* (Tucson: University of Arizona Press, 1967), pp. 180–84, 191, 193–200 and valuable notes, particularly pp. 253, 257–61, 267–72; Chang P'eng-yuan, *Liang Ch'i-ch'ao yü Ch'ing Chi Ko-ming* (Taipei: Academia Sinica, Institute of Modern History, 1964), pp. 119–39; Ting Wen-chiang, *Liang Jen-kung Hsien-sheng Nien P'u Ch'ang-pien Ch'u Kao* (Taipei: Shih-chieh Shu Chü, 1959), p. 83 ff.; Schiffrin, *Sun Yat-sen*, pp. 158–67, 183–90; Li Chien-nung, *The Political History of China, 1840–1928*, transl. and ed. Ssu-yu Teng and Jeremy Ingalls

(Princeton: Van Nostrand, 1956), pp. 179–80; Joseph R. Levenson, *Liang Ch'i-ch'ao and the Mind of Modern China* (Cambridge: Harvard University Press, 1953), pp. 58–66.

19. KFNPttp, pp. 102, 106–08, 112–13; Marius B. Jansen, *The Japanese and Sun Yat-sen* (Cambridge: Harvard University Press, 1954), pp. 68–74; Li Yün-han, "Dr. Sun Yat-sen and the Independence Movement of the Philipines (1898–1900)," *China Forum* 1, no. 2 (July 1974): 201–24.

20. The revolt is described in Schiffrin, *Sun Yat-sen*, pp. 224–48.

21. Hsüeh, *Huang Hsing*, pp. 38–77; Schiffrin, *Sun Yat-sen*, pp. 345–66. Harold Z. Schiffrin, "The Enigma of Sun Yat-sen," in *China in Revolution: The First Phase, 1900–1913*, ed. Mary Clabaugh Wright (New Haven: Yale University Press, 1968), pp. 443–74, 462–74; Liew, *Struggle for Democracy*, pp. 45–84. Dr. Liew is particularly pointed on the matter of intraparty conflicts.

22. Schiffrin, "The Enigma," pp. 469–70. The quotation is from the British minister in Peking, Sir John Jordan.

23. KFNPttp, pp. 356–404, October 10–December 21, 1911 (when Sun reached Hong Kong) is full of the revolutionary developments in China but has relatively little about Dr. Sun's activities, and only a couple of items to show that he even attempted to communicate with the leadership in China. Unless all records are lost, it seems he was not really in close touch with the leaders in the field.

24. Sun Yat-sen, *Memoirs of a Chinese Revolutionary: A Programme of National Reconstruction for China* (1918; reprint ed., Taipei: China Cultural Service, 1953), p. 173. The date of Sun's passing through St. Louis was about October 14, 1911. The *New York Times* for October 13, carried a story from Hankow, dated October 12, about the revolt in the Wu-Han cities and reported that "Dr. Sun Yat-sen, leader of the anti-Manchu party, if plans do not miscarry, is to be elected President." (The *New York Times* is hereafter cited as NYT.)

25. Cantlie and Jones, *Sun Yat Sen*, p. 61.

26. *Times* (London), November 17, 1911, p. 5.

27. KMWH, 1: 1 and KFCC, 4: 143–44. The first source dates the telegram by the Chinese lunar calendar as ninth month, twenty-second day, which converts to November 12, 1911 by the Western solar calendar. However, both sources say the telegram was sent from Paris, as does KFNPttp, p. 395, which does not date it but places it after November 21. Supposedly Dr. Sun reached Paris on November 20 or 21. KFNPttp, p. 393, is based upon the research of Chang Fu-jui, who studied French newspapers and journals of this period. See Chang Fu-jui, "Hsin-hai Ko-ming Shih ti Fa-kuo Yü Lun" [Public Opinion in France at the Time of the 1911 Revolution]; abridged translation by Ho Chen-hui in *Chung-kuo Hsien-tai Shih Ts'ung-k'an* 3 (August 1960): 45–77, p. 56. The *Times* (London), November 22, 1911, p. 5, says Sun left London for China on Monday, which was November 20. A second difficulty with the November 12 date is that the invitation from the Shanghai revolutionary military governor, Ch'en Ch'i-mei, to other military governors to send delegates to a conference in Shanghai was issued on November 13 (KMWH, 1: 3). Chün-tu Hsüeh and

K. S. Liew accept the November 12 date for Dr. Sun's Paris telegram (Hsüeh, *Huang Hsing*, p. 124; Liew, *Struggle for Democracy*, p. 135 and note 51). I believe the telegram was sent from Paris between November 21 and 24.

28. This point is developed by Hsüeh, *Huang Hsing*, pp. 119–30 and Liew, *Struggle for Democracy*, pp. 135–36.

29. Earnest P. Young, "Yuan Shih-k'ai's Rise to the Presidency," in Wright, *China in Revolution*, pp. 419–42, traces the steps toward the decision to offer Yuan the presidency; see especially pp. 421–22. "But from mid-November onward, there seemed never to have been any serious doubt that, if he would arrange for Manchu abdication, he would be leader of the new republican order. Qualifications about constitutional limitations and sites for the capital were afterthoughts and were never urged with enthusiasm by the majority of Southern leaders." Hsüeh, *Huang Hsing*, p. 134 says that "It was almost the unanimous opinion of the revolutionary leaders that should Yuan Shih-k'ai come over to their side, he should be offered the presidency as a reward. . . . The offer to Yuan was reaffirmed by Sun Yat-sen after he had been elected President." Professor Hsüeh cites a telegram, Sun to Yuan, dated December 29, 1911, reprinted in KFCC, 4: 144.

30. KFNPttp, pp. 435–37 and 465; Hsüeh, *Huang Hsing*, pp. 135–36. The provisional president's maneuvers during this period are well covered in John Gilbert Reid, *The Manchu Abdication and the Powers, 1908–1912* (Berkeley: University of California Press, 1935), pp. 270, 274–78, based mainly on official British sources. It is clear that the powers favored Yuan Shih-k'ai.

31. Sun to Teng Tse-ju, April 18, 1914 in KFCC, 5: 171–72, partially translated in Hsüeh, *Huang Hsing*, p. 166.

32. Isaac F. Marcosson, "The Changing East: Sun Yat-sen and South China," *The Saturday Evening Post* 195 (November 25, 1922): 20–21, 98–105. In a letter to Georgi Chicherin, Soviet chief commissar for foreign affairs, dated August 28, 1921, Sun Yat-sen said that he gave up the presidency on the advice of friends whom he trusted completely and who had a better knowledge than he of China's international situation. Now, said Dr. Sun, his friends admit that his retirement was a big political blunder comparable to Lenin's being superceded by Kolchak, Yudenich, or Wrangel! Xenia Joukoff Eudin and Robert C. North, *Soviet Russia and the East, 1920–1927: A Documentary Survey* (Stanford: Stanford University Press, 1957), pp. 219–221.

33. Cantlie and Jones, *Sun Yat-sen*, p. 65, a facsimile of Sun's letter on stationery of the President's Office, Republic of China, Nanking, March 12, 1912.

34. On Sun's decision to go north, Hsüeh, *Huang Hsing*, p. 140. The *North China Herald*, August 24, 1912, p. 513, has a long description of Sun's delayed sailing, while he awaited Huang Hsing. Huang was practically forced by his friends to remain behind for fear he would be executed in Peking as two southern generals had been. (The *North China Herald* is hereafter cited as NCH).

35. NCH, August 31, 1912, pp. 603, 604, 606.

36. The formation of the new party is well described by Liew, *Struggle for Democracy*, pp. 173–77; also KFNPttp, pp. 481–82.

37. NCH, August 31, 1912, p. 604.

38. Hsüeh, *Huang Hsing,* p. 142, quoting from KFCC, 4: 223 and *Min-li Pao* of September 6, 1912. NCH, September 7, 1912, p. 698, reports that Yuan had urged Sun to telegraph Huang.

39. Hsüeh, pp. 141–42, quoting *Min-li Pao* for October 7, 1912, p. 2. This is not mentioned in KFNPttp, but the speech is found in KFCC, 3: 83–85.

There is a strange item in the *New York Sun,* September 24, 1912, purportedly a statement "dictated" by Dr. Sun to the correspondent of the *Sun* in Nanking on August 27, 1912. The preliminary paragraph by the correspondent states that the former president had returned to Nanking "from his latest trip to Peking" on the previous evening, and gone to his home on Upper Shang Fei Road. The next morning he received the correspondent at his town office, where he dictated the statement which he wished particularly to be addressed to the American press and public.

Dr. Sun is made to say "I have within a few hours returned from a visit to the capital; the city which, if foreign journalists are to be credited, I hardly dared visit because of the personal danger I would run! . . . During my visit to President Yuan in June . . ."

The difficulty is, there is no evidence that Sun left Peking before his trip to Kalgan on September 6, nor did he see President Yuan in June. The purported statement in the *Sun* is reprinted in full as an appendix in the American edition of Cantlie and Jones, *Sun Yat Sen,* pp. 241–52, and part is quoted by Sharman, *Sun Yat-sen,* pp. 149–51. Mrs. Sharman thinks the wording might have been "the facile English of some deft collaborator, but the too-great-faith of it was Sun Yat-sen's." The intent of the statement was to reassure readers in America that China was not about to fall apart in struggles between north and south, and so to set at rest rumors of Sun's opposition to Yuan Shih-k'ai. The entire story, if not the statement, was a deception by the *Sun's* correspondent.

40. Hsüeh, *Huang Hsing,* p. 143; George T. Yu, *Party Politics in Republican China: The Kuomintang, 1912–1924.* (Berkeley and Los Angeles: University of California Press, 1966), p. 105; Liew, *Struggle for Democracy,* pp. 172–80 does not discuss Sun's attitude toward Yuan, except in the sense of his hope that through the British parliamentary system the president would be controlled by a responsible cabinet.

41. Hsüeh, p. 141, quoting from the president's mandate in *The China Year Book, 1913,* p. 525. (*The China Year Book* is hereafter cited as CYB.)

42. In a leading article on Sun Yat-sen's railway plans, the *North China Daily News* pointed out that he would have little success in negotiating loans for his railway corporation since only government-secured loans were feasible; it hinted that Yuan Shih-k'ai was tricking Dr. Sun in granting him autonomous authority. NCH, September 28, 1912, p. 873.

43. NCH, September 21, 1912, pp. 819–20 and 831. The American minister to China, W. J. Calhoun, took a cynical view of Yuan's financial and titular grants to Dr. Sun; he thought them a political accomodation to win Sun's support. He took the same view of accomodations made to Huang Hsing and Ch'en Ch'i-mei. He deprecated Sun's organization of a staff and employment of Chinese and foreign assistants to go

abroad with him "on his hunt for the 'golden fleece'." USDS 893.00/1505, dispatch, Peking, Calhoun to Secretary of State, November 12, 1912. Albert Maybon, *La République chinois* (Paris: A. Colin, 1914), pp. 143–46, takes a disparaging view of Sun's railway organization. He visited Sun's office early in 1913 but gained the impression that all the activity there created an illusion of power without substance. In Shanghai, he says, no one doubted that Dr. Sun was the victim of a hoax by Yuan Shih-k'ai.

44. KFNPttp, pp. 476–77, a talk with reporters in Shanghai on June 25, 1912; full text in KFCC, 4: 476–79. Urianghai (*Wu-liang-hai*) is Tannu-Tuva, west of Lake Baikal.

45. KFNPttp, pp. 477–78; KFCC, 3: 49–50.

46. KFNPttp, pp. 483–485.

47. Ibid., p. 488. Wang telegraphed back on about September 18 that his discussions in France were encouraging. Dr. Wellington Koo remembers calling upon Dr. Sun in his office in Shanghai, and being shown maps of China covered with railways. Dr. Sun was counting on raising money from the West, mainly the United States and the United Kingdom, coming, he hoped from the banking consortium. Dr. Koo was "impressed by his enthusiasm and really his desire to sort of do something concrete for the country. Having given up his presidency of the Republic to Yuan Shih-k'ai, he showed himself very interested in some constructive work for China." Koo-Wilbur interview, pp. 10933–36.

48. George Bronson Rea, *The Breakdown of American Diplomacy in the Far East*, n.p., n.d. [Shanghai, 1919?], pp. 39–43; and George Bronson Rea, *The Case for Manchoukuo*, (New York and London: D. Appleton-Century Co., 1935), pp. 77–78. Mr. Rea approved President Wilson's refusal to support American participation in the reorganization loan and says he called upon him to thank him in Dr. Sun's name, but he was disappointed not to have been able to swing a railway construction loan. He says he returned to Europe in an attempt to secure separate loans from British, French, and German bankers for separate railways in order to prevent domination of the system by any one country. Apparently nothing came of his efforts, perhaps because it was well understood that Dr. Sun no longer had any authority in railway matters.

49. Sharman, *Sun Yat-sen*, pp. 155–158, including a Reuter's dispatch of March 2, on plans for a Sino-Japanese Commercial Trust Company, to be capitalized at £1 million and interesting itself principally in railway construction. A more detailed and better-sourced account of Sun's Japanese tour and negotiations is in Jansen, *The Japanese and Sun Yat-sen*, pp. 158–62. Also, KFNPttp, p. 497.

50. KFNPttp, p. 490. In Sun Yat-sen, *The International Development of China* (1920; reprint ed., Taipei: China Cultural Service, 1953), pp. 209–19, there is an appendix containing the "Preliminary Agreement Providing for the Financing and Construction of the Railway from Canton to Chungking with Extension to Lanchow" which was made at Shanghai on July 4, 1913 between the Chinese National Railway Corporation and Messrs. Pauling and Company, ltd. of 26 Victoria Street, London, S.W. The Chinese text is in KFCC, 2: 265–71. There is no indication that the agreement was signed by anyone. Later Dr. Sun referred to this contract as a model "since it

was the fairest to both parties and the one most acceptable to the Chinese people of all contracts ever made between China and foreign countries." See *The International Development of China,* p. 7, from the introduction, which was first published in English in the *Far Eastern Review* for June 1919 and republished as Sun Yat-sen, "International Development of China," in *Public* 22 (December 6, 1919): 1134–35.

51. Jerome Ch'en, *Yuan Shih-k'ai,* 2d rev. ed. (Stanford: Stanford University Press, 1972), pp. 129–31; Li, *The Political History of China,* pp. 286–88; Liew, *Struggle for Democracy,* pp. 191–92; Hsüeh, *Huang Hsing,* pp. 152–54; KMWH, 6: 721–38, and vol. 42 (entire volume) for detailed accounts of the assassination, evidence, and trial.

52. Ch'en, *Yuan Shih-k'ai,* pp. 125–29; Li, *The Political History of China,* pp. 288–90.

53. NYT, May 25, 1913, section 3, p. 5, reprinting text of a statement sent by Sun Yat-sen from Shanghai and printed in Paris, May 9. This campaign is discussed below.

54. Hsüeh, *Huang Hsing,* pp. 156–161; Yu, *Party Politics,* pp. 114–15; Ch'en, *Yuan Shih-k'ai,* pp. 134–36. Documents of the "Second Revolution" are assembled in KMWH 44.

55. KFNPttp, pp. 530, 536. Sun left Shanghai on August 2 and went first to Taipei. He arrived in Japan on August 8 or 9. Hsüeh, p. 218, n. 1, cites a NYT dispatch from Moji, dated August 8 reporting Sun's arrival.

56. The problems of historical interpretation are well discussed by Hsüeh, *Huang Hsing,* pp. 153, 155, 160–61 and notes.

57. This topic is thoroughly covered in Edward Friedman, *Backward Toward Revolution: The Chinese Revolutionary Party* (Berkeley: University of California Press, 1974).

58. KFNPttp, p. 567 has the marriage as October 25, 1914, basing the date on a Japanese source which relies on a statement in Linebarger's biography of Dr. Sun; but that dates it October 25, 1915! Paul Linebarger, *Sun Yat-sen and the Chinese Republic* (1925; reprint ed., New York: AMS Press, 1969), p. 355. Mr. Linebarger knew Dr. and Mrs. Sun socially, and she may have been the source of the date as well as the photograph of the couple at about the time of their marriage, shown opposite p. 328. Lyon Sharman pointed out the ambiguity concerning the marriage year, stating that Chinese sources say 1914, others, 1915. The Japanese press learned of the marriage in early January, 1916 and the *New York World* published the fact in a story on February 16 together with a dispatch from Berkeley, expressing the skepticism of Sun Fo, a student there; Sharman, *Sun Yat-sen,* p. 180. That the marriage could have been kept from the Japanese press for more than a year as well as from Dr. Sun's only son, seems unlikely.

I am convinced that 1915 was the year because of a letter Dr. Sun wrote to Mrs. James Cantlie, dated October 17, 1918, in which he told her that his marriage took place three years before in Tokyo. Since his letter was written near the wedding anniversary it seems unlikely he would have been a year off. See Neil Cantlie and George Seaver, *Sir James Cantlie, a Romance in Medicine* (London: J. Murray [1939], p. 119. In December 1914, Dr. Sun wrote James Deitrick, "I have no English secretary at present. My lady secretaries, both sisters, the elder one Miss Eling Soong has just married, and the younger one Miss Rosamonde Soong went back to Shanghai lately. So I have to do the English writing myself." Sun Yat-sen, *10 Letters of Sun Yat-sen, 1914–1916* (Stanford: Stanford University Libraries, 1942), letter postmarked December 25, 1914. This is scarcely the way he would write of a person he had recently married. In letters written to Mrs. Cantlie and Mr. Deitrick we find a change of address sometime between March 19, 1915 and November 18, 1915, which could be explained by his move after the marriage. Dr. Hollington K. Tong confirms this hypothesis by stating that Dr. and Mrs. Sun moved to a new address in Aoyama after the marriage in 1915, following a brief stay in the home of Toyama Mitsuru. Sun Yat-sen, *The Vital Problem of China,* preface, p. ix. According to Sun's biographer in *Biographical Dictionary of Republican China,* ed. Howard L. Boorman and Richard C. Howard, 4 vols. (New York: Columbia University Press, 1967–1971), Dr. Sun and his first wife had not been divorced when he married Miss Soong. See *Biographical Dictionary* 3: 185.

59. An illuminating account of Dr. Sun's first administration in Canton is the M.A. thesis and East Asian Institute Certificate Essay by Carol Tyson Reynolds, "Sun Yat-sen and the Constitution Protection Movement, 1917–1918" (Columbia University, 1971). Dr. Sun left Canton on May 21, 1918. See KFNPttp, p. 730.

60. This is the conclusion reached in Joseph T. Chen, *The May Fourth Movement in Shanghai* (Leiden: E. J. Brill, 1971), pp. 23, 58, and 197; Chen counters the assertions of several later Kuomintang writers. Josef Fass attempts to demonstrate an influence of the New Culture and May Fourth movements upon Sun, but can cite very little evidence; Josef Fass, "Sun Yat-sen and the May-4th-Movement," *Archiv Orientální* 36, no. 4 (1968): 577–84.

61. Leonard Shihlien Hsü, *Sun Yat-sen: His Political and Social Ideals* (Los Angeles: University of Southern California Press, 1933); Tsui Shu-chin, "The Influence of the Canton-Moscow Entente upon Sun Yat-sen's Political Philosophy," *The Chinese Social and Political Science Review* 18 (April–October 1934); Wang, *Chinese Intellectuals and the West,* pp. 320–61; Chester C. Tan, *Chinese Political Thought in the Twentieth Century* (Garden City, N.Y.: Doubleday, 1971), pp. 116–61; Wu, *Sun Yat-sen,* pp. 280–369. Of the more recent works, Professor Tan's study is most judicious, Professor Wang's is critical, and Dr. Wu's is adulatory.

62. Hsiang Ta-yen, "Annotations for the Newly Published Pieces of Dr. Sun Yat-sen's Holograph Letters to his Son." *China Forum* 2, no. 1 (January 1975): 206–21, with the four letters in Chinese reproduced photographically on pp. 155–63.

63. Mr. Li Lu-chao to C. Martin Wilbur, October 25, 1974. I am skeptical that Dr. Sun, as a Chinese, did not take tea, but perhaps the superstrong British tea is meant.

64. Information from Professor Fang Chao-ying.

CHAPTER TWO   FINANCING REVOLUTION

1. Shelley Hsien Cheng, *The T'ung-Meng-Hui: Its Organization, Leadership and Finances, 1905–1912* (Ann Arbor, Mich.: University Microfilms, 1962). This was Dr. Cheng's Ph.D. dissertation at the University of Washington. The fourth chapter, pp. 162–219, concentrates on fund raising, summarized in three tables, after p. 206.

2. Professor Jen Yu-wen estimates that Sun Mei contributed about three-quarters of a million dollars for the cause. Jen, "The Youth of Dr. Sun Yat-sen," in Jen Yu-wen and Lindsay Ride, *Sun Yat-sen: Two Commemorative Essays* (Hong Kong: University of Hong Kong Centre of Asian Studies, 1970), p. 15.

3. Schiffrin, *Sun Yat-sen*, pp. 103, 218, 325; KFCC, 5: 82–85, Letters from Sun to Wu Chih-hui written in 1909, probably in October; abstracted in KFNPttp, p. 290. Henry Bond Restarick in *Sun Yat-sen, Liberator of China* (New Haven: Yale University Press, 1931), p. 128, relates that in 1917 Sun's brother wished to be appointed governor of Kwangtung in return for all the money he had contributed. After a quarrel, Sun paid his brother off with $20,000. No source is given for this statement, but Bishop Restarick gained much of his information from reminiscences of Sun's former supporters in Honolulu. In late 1917, Sun was grand marshal of a military government in Canton.

In the following discussion, when dollar figures are mentioned, the currency will be specified if given in the source.

4. Boorman and Howard, *Biographical Dictionary of Republican China*, 1: 73–77. KFNPttp, p. 209; Sun Yat-sen, *Memoirs of a Chinese Revolutionary*, p. 166. Cheng, *The T'ung-Meng-Hui*, p. 213, n. 39, mentions contributions by Mr. Chang of Fr30,000 (US $5,788 or ¥11,576) in 1906, and HK$5,000 shortly after; he probably was the "comrade" Sun referred to in a letter to Wu Chih-hui in 1909 as giving $50,000, KFCC, 5:85. Chang joined the T'ung Meng Hui and supported Dr. Sun's efforts after the revolution of 1911–12; he was a member of the Chung-hua Ko-ming Tang, allowing his name to be used as director of the finance department. Jermyn Chi-hung Lynn, *Political Parties in China* (Peking: Henri Vetch, 1930), p. 35, asserts that Chang gave Sun more than two and a half million dollars in all, but offers no source for his statement.

Charles Jones Soong (Sung Chia-shu), a well-to-do Christian, met Dr. Sun in about 1894. Later they became close friends when Dr. Sun came to Shanghai at the end of 1911. According to Mr. Soong's daughter, Ch'ing-ling, he supported Sun Yat-sen for years, but she does not say when this was. After Dr. Sun married Miss Soong, her father broke all relations with his friend and disowned his daughter, according to her account. See Edgar Snow, *Journey to the Beginning* (New York: Random House, 1958), p. 89, as related by Mme Sun in about 1930.

5. Cheng, *The T'ung-Meng-Hui*, pp. 190–92.

6. Ibid., pp. 45–48. He received a very high rank, and tried to get a new constitution adopted by the lodges of the Hung Men that would have brought about its merger with his "Chinese Revolutionary Army," but that was unsuccessful until much later.

7. By 1903 there were 11 head offices and 103 branch associations of the China Reform Association in Canada, the United States, Mexico, and Central and South America, with a claimed membership of several hundred thousand. By 1906 there were nearly 200 branch associations now extended to Australia, Penang and Singapore, and the Dutch East Indies. This was far more than the Hsing Chung Hui or the T'ung Meng Hui succeeded in organizing and, furthermore, many of Sun's followers were won over by K'ang Yu-wei and Liang Ch'i-ch'ao. The association set up a com-

mercial corporation in 1903 to engage in banking, mining, land speculation, rice brokerage, street car lines, hotels, and restaurants in China, Hong Kong, Malay, Canada, and the United States. Sales of stock reached a value of $598,760 and the corporation did set up businesses in Hong Kong, Mexico, and the United States. Lo Jung-pang, *K'ang Yu-wei*, pp. 195, 258–61, 269, 275.

8. Cheng, *The T'ung-Meng-Hui*, pp. 48, 64, n. 159; 105–06; 151–52, nn. 11–13.

9. Ibid., p. 207, table 1.

10. KMWH, 3: 277.

11. Cheng, *The T'ung-Meng-Hui*, pp. 46, 48.

12. Restarick, *Sun Yat-sen*, p. 67. The notes were signed by Sun Wen, president, and Gnone Hap, treasurer.

13. KFNPttp, p. 205. This says bonds up to #135 were issued. If this means they were sold, at $250, the income would have been $33,750; but the source, Feng Tzu-yu, seems ambiguous.

14. Wang Gungwu, "Sun Yat-sen and Singapore," *Journal of the South Seas Society* (Chinese title, *Nan-yang Hsueh Pao*) 15 (December 1959): 59, citing Sun's letter of September 30, 1905 to Ch'en Ch'u-nan. Ch'en (locally known as Tan Chor Lam) was an early supporter of Dr. Sun and became chairman of the local branch of the T'ung Meng Hui, organized in February 1906.

15. Cheng, *The T'ung-Meng-Hui*, pp. 193–95, and 207, table 1.

16. Jansen, *The Japanese and Sun Yat-sen*, p. 127, based upon two important Japanese sources. The period referred to is 1910–11.

17. Wang, "Sun Yat-sen and Singapore," pp. 61–62. The letter is given in KFCC, 5: 36–39, quotation on p. 38.

18. Ibid., pp. 62–63; KFCC, 5: 52–53, quotation on p. 53. The currency is not specified.

19. Cheng, *The T'ung-Meng-Hui*, p. 196. Sun described the plan briefly in a letter dated May 7, 1911 in KFCC, 5: 129. Probably it was a spin-off from the syndicate which Dr. Sun, Homer Lea, and Charles Beach Boothe set up in March 1910. This is discussed below.

20. Cheng, *The T'ung-Meng-Hui*, p. 197. The regulations of the bureau are in KFCC, 6: 246–48.

21. Charles B. Hager, "Doctor Sun Yat Sen: Some Personal Reminiscences," *The Missionary Herald* (April 1912), reprinted as appendix in Sharman, *Sun Yat-sen*, p. 386.

22. Cheng, *The T'ung-Meng-Hui*, pp. 44–48. Some additional information on Sun's 1904 visit to the United States is found in Hsü Shih-shen, "Important Source Materials Not Printed in *Kuo Fu Ch'üan Chi*," in Huang Chi-lu, ed., *Yen-chiu Chung-shan Hsien-sheng ti Shih Liao yü Shih Hsüeh* [Historical Materials and Historical Studies on Sun Yat-sen], pp. 164–71.

23. Wang, "Sun Yat-sen and Singapore," p. 64. The Chinese in Singapore did contribute a great deal to the revolutionary causes between 1902 and 1911, as seen in a chart in Li En-han, "Historical Materials and Historical Studies for the Study of Sun Yat-sen in Southeast Asia," in Huang Chi-lu, ed., *Yen-chiu Chung-shan Hsien-sheng ti Shih Liao yü Shih Hsüeh*, pp. 292–94.

24. Ibid.; letter printed in KFCC, 5: 72–74, quotation on p. 73.

25. KFNPttp, pp. 321–33. A drive in Malaya to finance the uprising brought in $47,906.67, according to Png Po Seng, "The Kuomintang in Malaya," *Journal of Southeast Asian History* 2, no. 1 (March 1961): p. 6. The more complete account is in Hsüeh, *Huang Hsing*, p. 86, based upon a variety of sources. He estimates that the total sum raised for this revolt approached HK$190,000, and describes the fund raising of Huang Hsing and Teng Tse-ju. Dr. Cheng, *The Tung-Meng-Hui*, pp. 186–95 and p. 207, table 1, believed that at least HK$210,000 were spent on the revolt plus some HK$20,000 spent to care for members of the demobilized force. His breakdown differs from that of Dr. Hsüeh.

26. Sun Yat-sen, *Memoirs of a Chinese Revolutionary*, p. 175; KFNPttp, p. 406. Hsüeh, *Huang Hsing*, p. 131. Dr. Cheng, *The T'ung-Meng-Hui*, pp. 199–201, details large amounts subscribed by wealthy Chinese in Southeast Asia after the revolution seemed successful. He says that when Dr. Sun went to Nanking on January 1, 1912, to accept the provisional presidency he took with him HK$300,000 to pay the troops of the revolutionary army. However, this sum may have been a combination of contributions from overseas Chinese and Japanese loans.

27. Cheng, *The T'ung-Meng-Hui*, p. 190.

28. See note 7 above (this chapter), and Cheng, pp. 204–05.

29. Schiffrin, *Sun Yat-sen*, pp. 109, 325. Wang Gungwu, "Chinese Politics in Malaya," *China Quarterly* no. 43 (July/September 1970): 8, 11, speculates on the issues which brought support for Dr. Sun's cause. Y. C. Wang remarks on the importance of minority status and discriminatory practices in fueling the nationalism of overseas Chinese; Wang, *Chinese Intellectuals*, p. 338.

30. Hu Han-min, probably in 1912 when he was military governor of Kwangtung, withdrew sums from the provincial treasury to repay money borrowed for the two Canton uprisings of 1911. See Chiang Yung-ching, "Hu Han-min Hsien-sheng Nien P'u Kao," *Chung-kuo Hsien-tai Shih Ts'ung-k'an* 3 (1960): 145.

31. NCH, October 19, 1912, p. 176, "Criticism of Dr. Sun."

32. Rea, *The Case for Manchoukuo*, p. 74. Mr. Rea tried to place the loan, on behalf of Yuan's minister of finance, Chou Tse-chi with William Salomon and Company, but was blocked by the State Department. Later, apparently in September or October 1912, the Peking government arranged a loan in London. NCH as cited in n. 31.

33. Samuel C. Chu, *Reformer in Modern China: Chang Chien, 1853–1926* (New York: Columbia University Press, 1965), pp. 76–77.

34. Ibid., p. 77; Hsüeh, *Huang Hsing*, p. 131 (he credits the negotiations to Huang); Jansen, *The Japanese and Sun Yat-sen*, pp. 146–47.

35. Jansen, *The Japanese and Sun Yet-sen*, p. 147; he thinks ¥3 million may have been advanced. Also Hsüeh, *Huang Hsing*, p. 131; Sharman, *Sun Yat-sen*, p. 134.

36. Liew, *Struggle for Democracy*, pp. 143–44; Hsüeh, *Huang Hsing*, p. 131; Rea, *The Case for Manchoukuo*, pp. 75–76. Mr. Rea says he was the intermediary in trying to place a loan.

37. Cheng, *The T'ung-Meng-Hui*, pp. 199–201 and chart on p. 208. Most of the money was sent during the first few months after the Wuchang revolt.

38. Ibid., p. 200.

39. KMWH, 5: 579–80, 587–89. Letters of Sun to Teng, April 8 and October 20, 1914.

40. KMWH, 49: 1. This was called to my attention by Professor Gilbert Chan. There is an even more exact figure in a telegram from Dr. Sun to the Merchants' Association of Surabaja, which he learned had telegraphed the government claiming it had lent him $2.2 million. The total he had received, he said, was ¥1 million in loans from Japanese merchants; and from overseas Chinese, $1,744,318.2 in Japanese yen and English—i.e., Hongkong?—dollars. Of this latter amount, two Chinese from Surabaja had sent nineteen collective contributions to Tokyo, totalling ¥16,240 and another had sent "English dollars" 2,700 for which receipts had been given by the party finance office. He denied having received a cent from the Surabaja Merchants' Association. KFCC, 4: 273–74, telegram dated Jan. 30, 1917.

41. KMWH, 48: 79–84 has a series of letters from Mr. Liao.

42. KMWH, 5: 663, from Feng Tzu-yu, *Ko-ming I Shih*. Lin Sen was president and Feng Tzu-yu vice-president of the party in the United States. On Huang Hsing's role in smoothing relations among fund raisers in America, see Hsüeh, *Huang Hsing*, p. 178, and Yu, *Party Politics*, pp. 133–35. In KFCC, 4: 232–60, there are scores of telegrams from Sun appealing for funds or directing their use for the anti-Yuan campaign. Also KMWH, 48: 85–129 for much more detail.

43. The above cited newsletter (KMWH, 49: 1) states that there are reports that the government had paid back US $600,000 but in fact had not paid a cent, due to opposition from provincial officials. However, Lynn, *Political Parties in China*, p. 43 says the matter was settled by the president instructing the governor of the Bank of China to remit $600,000 to Dr. Sun.

44. Restarick, *Sun Yat-sen*, p. 122. Bishop Restarick further states that receipts in Honolulu show a total of more than $15,000, the remittances sent by Luke Chan, and the receipts signed by Sun Wen and his treasurer. Unfortunately, the writer did not report the dates of these receipts.

45. KMWH, 49: 300–324 for monthly accounts; pp. 344–52 gives much detail about several fund-raising campaigns in Burma, with each donor in each locality listed. The total came to about HK$10,000. These items were called to my attention by Mrs. Carol Reynolds.

46. Ibid., pp. 324–38.

47. Ibid., pp. 300–301; Li, *The Political History of China*, pp. 390–94 on the conference, which broke down in September 1919.

48. KFCC, 5: 384–89. This gives a budget. Part of the letter explaining the purpose is translated in Wang, *Chinese Intellectuals,* pp. 333–34.

49. KMWH, 51: 369–389. There was to be a graduated series of honors for those who contributed from $200,000 down to $100, and appropriate awards to successful solicitors as well.

50. Tsou Lu, *Chung-kuo Kuomintang Shih Kao,* 2d ed. (Taipei: Commercial Press, 1965), pp. 453–56. (*Tsou Lu, Chung-kuo Kuomintang Shih Kao* is hereafter cited as Tsou, CKKMTSK).

51. Ibid. We deduce that the round number donations were made in China, for contributions from abroad are given in figures with fractional amounts depending upon how much the foreign currency brought in "Shanghai Foreign Dollars," that is, "Mex." San Francisco led (rounded figures $2,748), followed by Canada ($2,258), Penang ($1,258), and Cuba ($950), but Chinese in the Philippines, South Africa, and Australia remitted in the hundreds of dollars, other centers sending more modest amounts.

52. KMWH, 52: 414–26, taken from Teng Tse-ju, *Chung-kuo Kuomintang Er-shih Nien Shih-chi.*

53. KFNPttp, pp. 912, 926, September 22 and November 17, 1922.

54. KMWH, 52: 419–26. There is a mysterious item, "dime silver" still not returned. I speculate this was silver owned by the Canton mint, which may have been spirited away.

CHAPTER THREE   THE SEARCH FOR FOREIGN AID AGAINST THE MANCHUS

1. Schiffrin, *Sun Yat-sen,* p. 92, quoting a dispatch from Byron Brenan written early in November 1895, shortly after the plot was defeated. The factual basis for this and the next paragraph is Professor's Schiffrin's reconstruction of the Canton plot, especially pp. 71–92.

2. Ibid., pp. 130–32, from the *Fortnightly Review,* March 1, 1897, pp. 424–40.

3. Schiffrin, *Sun Yat-sen,* p. 201. The whole episode is treated in one chapter, pp. 177–213.

4. Jansen, *The Japanese and Sun Yat-sen,* reconstructs the story from a Japanese perspective, with emphasis upon Japanese political leaders, continental expansion, and a particular group of Japanese adventurers, *shishi.* Japanese help for Sun Yat-sen in the early period is treated in three chapters, pp. 59–130. Schiffrin, *Sun Yat-sen,* deals with Sun's Japanese connections in four chapters, pp. 140–178, 214–54, and 300–366. He describes the development of Chinese student radicalism, much of it in Japan, in other chapters. He deals with matters after the founding of the T'ung Meng Hui in Schiffrin, "The Enigma of Sun Yat-sen." A useful recent Chinese work is Ch'en P'eng-jen, *Sun Chung-shan Hsien-sheng yü Jih-pen Yu-jen* [Mr. Sun Yat-sen and his Japanese Friends] (Taipei: Ta-lin Book Store, 1973). This contains translations of writings in Japanese about Sun, many by his Japanese friends. A useful listing of Sun's various periods of residence in Japan is provided in Ch'en P'eng-jen, "A Chro-

nology of Sun Yat-sen's Visits to Japan (Preliminary Draft)," in Huang Chi-lu, ed., *Yen-chiu Chung-shan Hsien-sheng ti Shih Liao yü Shih Hsüeh* [Historical Materials and Historical Studies on Sun Yat-sen], pp. 518–43.

5. Jansen, *The Japanese and Sun Yat-sen*, pp. 54–58 presents a biography of Miyazaki up to the time of his meeting with Dr. Sun. Other Japanese mentioned here are also given biographical treatment. Another useful work is Ch'en Ku-t'ing, *Kuo Fu yü Jih-pen Yu-jen* [Sun Yat-sen and his Japanese Friends] (Taipei: Yu Shih Book Store, 1965). This has biographies of some twenty Japanese with whom Sun had relations, in some cases quoting from his correspondence or their reminiscences. Quotations from letters by Sun are abbreviated, in some cases seemingly to conceal embarrassing material, as in a letter to Ōkuma Shigenobu of May 11, 1914.

6. Jansen, *The Japanese and Sun Yat-sen*, pp. 68–74 has an account of the Philippine undertaking. Hirayama Shū stated long after that Sun used the profits from the sale of Japanese arms to the Philippines as his capital for starting a newspaper in Hong Kong. Hirayama Shū, "T'an-shang Chien Fei-li-pin so Kou Hsieh Tan Shih" [A Discussion of Borrowing the Weapons and Munitions Purchased by the Philippines], in *Chung-hua Min-kuo K'ai Kuo Wu-shih Nien Wen-hsien,* series 1, vol. 9, *Ke-ming chih Ch'ang-tao yü Fa chan–Hsing Chung Hui* (Taipei: Chung-hua Min-kuo K'ai Kuo Wu-shih Nien Wen Hsien, 1963), p. 604.

7. The Huichow revolt is reconstructed in Schiffrin, *Sun Yat-sen,* pp. 214–54. In a letter to Wu Chih-hui in October 1909, Dr. Sun mentioned the ¥5,000 given by Japanese; KFNPttp, pp. 291–92. The eulogy is in Sun, *Memoirs of a Chinese Revolutionary,* as quoted by Jansen, p. 96. Facing his page 118 is an inscription honoring Yamada Yoshimasa, the martyr, composed by Dr. Sun on his visit to Tokyo in 1913.

8. Schiffrin, *Sun Yat-sen,* pp. 307–08, 313.

9. Ibid., pp. 280–81.

10. Jansen, *The Japanese and Sun Yat-sen,* p. 121.

11. KFNPttp, p. 234, basing itself on Feng Tzu-yu, gives a figure of ¥5,000, while Jansen, *The Japanese and Sun Yat-sen,* p. 123, gives ¥70,000 basing this on a Japanese collection of stories and biographies of Japanese adventurers in East Asia. According to this account, ¥10,000 of the money was used to give Dr. Sun a great farewell banquet, but the amount was made up by a Japanese broker.

12. On this controversy, see Hsüeh, *Huang Hsing,* pp. 52–53, and Liew, *Struggle for Democracy,* p. 72.

13. Jansen, *The Japanese and Sun Yat-sen,* facing p. 119 for a photo-copy of the document.

14. According to a history of the *Genyōsha,* an early liberal movement, Japanese contributed over ¥250,000 to Sun's movement before 1911. Cited by Jansen, *The Japanese and Sun Yat-sen,* p. 141, but without substantiating details.

15. J. Kim Munholland, "The French Connection that Failed: France and Sun Yat-sen, 1900–1908," *Journal of Asian Studies* 32 (November 1972): 77–95. A more extended study is that of Dr. Jeffrey Barlow. He permitted me to read part of his dissertation on Sun Yat-sen and France, which I did after having written the following account.

16. Munholland, "The French Connection," p. 78.

17. Ibid., p. 79. The report of the interview is dated 7 October. KFNPttp, p. 128 has Sun arrive in Taiwan on September 28. It mentions no side trip to Hanoi but is vague on Sun's activities until his arrival back in Tokyo from Taipei on November 16.

18. KFNPttp, p. 150.

19. KFNPttp, p. 150 has Sun leave Japan for Annam via Hong Kong on Dec. 13, 1902 and has him arrive in Hanoi in December. George Soulié has an account of Sun's surreptitious stop in Shanghai to secure a permit from the French consulate to enter Indochina, at which time M. Soulié, a judge in the mixed court, arranged for his escape by stalling a request of a Chinese official for Sun's arrest until he got safely back aboard his French boat. George Soulié de Morant, *Soun Iat-senn* (Paris: Librairie Gallimard, 1932), pp. 113–14. This work has many mistakes in dating and much of it is a translation of Sun's *Memoirs of a Chinese Revolutionary*.

20. Munholland, "The French Connection," pp. 79–80.

21. Cheng, *The T'ung-Meng-Hui*, p. 35; Schiffrin, *Sun Yat-sen*, pp. 302–03. KFNPttp seems to have very little information on this stay in Hanoi.

22. KFNPttp, p. 162.

23. Munholland, "The French Connection," p. 82.

24. Marianne Bastid, "La Diplomatie française et la révolution chinoise de 1911," *Revue d'histoire moderne et contemporaine* (1969): 228, n. 4. This statement is not sourced.

25. Munholland, "The French Connection," pp. 80–87; KFNPttp. pp. 203–04 for the shipboard conference, which is also mentioned by Sun in *Memoirs of a Chinese Revolutionary*, p. 159. Unfortunately, Professor Jean Chesneaux sheds no new light upon Dr. Sun's French connections in his popular biography, *Sun Yat-sen* (Paris: Le Club Français du Livre, 1959), pp. 116–19.

26. KFNPttp, pp. 209–10. Hu I-sheng was a cousin of Hu Han-min and his account is presented here.

27. Ibid., pp. 213–14.

28. Munholland, "The French Connection," p. 87 for the circumstances.

29. Cheng, *The T'ung-Meng-Hui*, p. 174. One of his sources states that M. Leoni was a politician in Paris where the bonds were printed, p. 213, n. 36.

30. KFNPttp, pp. 208 and 212 has him leave for Europe in the winter, and sail from Marseilles on his journey back on March 4, 1906. However, he was in Singapore from February 16 to the end of the month, according to Wang, "Sun Yat-sen and Singapore," p. 60. Professor Wang does not give his dating evidence at this point, but his careful research inspires credence. Cheng, *The T'ung-Meng-Hui*, p. 174 mentions this mysterious visit to France, believing the purpose was to sell bonds.

31. Munholland, "The French Connection," p. 88, based on the consul's report of 22 April 1906. Dr. Sun was in Hong Kong harbor on April 16 and back in Tokyo by April 28, according to KFNPttp, p. 213.

NOTES TO PAGES 63-66

32. Munholland, "The French Connection," p. 88, based on Canton to governor-general of 15 June 1906. It is not clear that Sun was in Tonkin at that time.

33. Ibid., p. 89. Judging by the dates of the reports (22 January and 7 February 1908) at the time of Sun's expulsion, they may have been justifications for earlier inaction.

34. Cheng, The T'ung-Meng-Hui, pp. 220-36, and Hsüeh, Huang Hsing, pp. 65-68.

35. Bulletin d'École française d'Extrême-Orient 7 (1907): 442-54. Besides a digest of the speech, the article translates in part Sun's Ko-ming Fang-lüeh and anti-Manchu propaganda in an eighty-four-page pamphlet, Ko-ming Hsien-feng.

36. Munholland, "The French Connection," pp. 89-90.

37. The battle is well described in Hsüeh, Huang Hsing, pp. 66-68, and Cheng, The T'ung Meng-Hui, pp. 232-36. Cheng is the source for the report of Sun's arms shipment. See also KFNPttp, pp. 257-59.

38. Munholland, "The French Connection," p. 91.

39. Cheng, The T'ung-Meng-Hui, pp. 180, 235. Dr. Cheng was uncertain whether the sum was in Hong Kong dollars or francs, a difference of ten or four million in U.S. dollars.

40. Ibid., p. 175. The bonds were later released and sent to Sun's new headquarters in Singapore. When the police learned of their existence, Sun burnt them to avoid difficulties.

41. Ibid., pp. 180, 214, n. 54, which cites many letters from Sun. KFNPttp, p. 277 with date October 28, 1908, where Sun is trying to raise $8,000 (Singapore?) for traveling expenses.

42. KFNPttp, pp. 286, 288. There are only a few lines on his French stay, which lasted to July 21. Wu, Sun Yat-sen, p. 132, says the loan was almost negotiated.

43. Cheng, The T'ung-Meng-Hui, p. 181, based upon Sun's letters.

44. KFNPttp, pp. 324-25, December 28, 1910 to January 3, 1911. Dr. Sun had taken a fine suite in a Paris hotel, and explained to Chang Chi that to be in a large hotel was important for consultations with the political world.

45. Ibid., pp. 393-97, November 21 to November 24, 1911. In Memoirs of a Chinese Revolutionary, p. 175, Sun mentioned seeing M. Clemenceau, who was not prime minister in 1911, but he was at the time Sun was writing the memoirs. KFNPttp, p. 397 mentions several French notables Sun saw, as does Lo Hsiang-lin in Kuo Fu yü Ou Mei chih Yu-hao [Sun Yat-sen and his European and American Friends] (Taipei: Chung-yang Wen Wu Kung-ying She, 1951), pp. 116-17. Professor Lo devotes a brief chapter to Sun and Clemenceau.

46. Bastid, "Le Diplomatie française," p. 244, based upon a report to the Foreign Ministry of the Sun-Simon meeting in Paris on November 23. Sun left France the next day. On that day, November 24, an emissary from Sun, one Binko Hou, called on the Foreign Office and was told by Berthelot that the French government's attitude toward the revolution would depend upon the guarantees offered to its nationals. Bastid, p. 238, based upon report in the French archives.

[310]

47. Ibid., p. 238; Reid, *The Manchu Abdication and the Powers,* pp. 253, 410, n. 100.

48. Sun, *Memoirs of a Chinese Revolutionary,* pp. 170–71; Bastid, "La Diplomatie française," p. 228.

49. Key Ray Chong, "The Abortive American-Chinese Project for Chinese Revolution, 1908–1911," *Pacific Historical Review* 41 (1972): 54–70. The unpublished dissertation of Thomas William Ganschow, *A Study of Sun Yat-sen's Contacts with the United States Prior to 1922* (Ann Arbor, Mich.: University Microfilms, 1971), provides important additional details.

50. Biographical sketch in *Dictionary of American Biography,* s.v., "Lea, Homer." I have not seen a much quoted study by Frederic L. Chapin, "Homer Lea and the Chinese Revolution" (A.B. honors thesis, Harvard University, 1950).

Homer Lea was born in 1876 and was undersized and hunchbacked. As a student at Stanford University he became interested in China, studied the language, and sought out Chinese acquaintanceships. Thus he became friendly with the San Francisco branch of the Chinese Reform Association, K'ang Yu-wei's organization, which sent him to the Far East in 1900 to assist K'ang in a planned revolt (Sharman, *Sun Yat-sen,* pp. 89–91). He was in K'ang's entourage in the summer of 1900, promoting a scheme to attack Canton from Macao with an army of 25,000 Chinese, officered by Americans, but nothing came of the plan (Schiffrin, *Sun Yat-sen,* pp. 206–07, citing a report of the governor of Hong Kong, August 3, 1900). Professor Chong says that Dr. Sun met Homer Lea in Tokyo in 1901 when Lea was returning to California (Chong, "The Abortive Chinese-American Project," p. 55) but this seems difficult to square with Sun's account of their meeting, probably in 1904, as though it was the first occasion. Sun was addressing a meeting of Chinese when he saw an undersized, pale-faced, intelligent-looking American, who was a stranger to him. After the meeting the stranger came up to offer his services to Dr. Sun's cause, and the next day Sun sought him out and said he would appoint Lea as his chief military adviser, if ever he should have the official power to do so (Sharman, *Sun Yat-sen,* pp. 126–27 quoting Sun Yat-sen, "My Reminiscences," in the *Strand Magazine,* March 1912. Mrs. Sharman placed the incident in 1909 or after, which is implausible). Dr. Sun did not date this meeting, but Lo Hsiang-lin and Sun's official biographers make it 1904 (Lo, *Kuo Fu yü Ou Mei chih Yu-hao,* p. 97; KFNPttp, p. 299), and it probably was in San Francisco during May or June (deduced from Sun's activities at that time in Sharman, *Sun Yat-sen,* pp. 82–83 and Schiffrin, *Sun Yat-sen,* pp. 327, 332). About this time, Lea became involved in training Chinese young men as cadets for K'ang's movement and took on the title of general. He accompanied K'ang on a tour of the United States in the summer of 1905, reviewing the cadet corps with him in Philadelphia and New York, and possibly acting as a spy for Dr. Sun (Sharman, *Sun Yat-sen,* pp. 90, 93; Lo, *K'ang Yu-wei,* pp. 271–72, who does not give a source for the suspicion of Lea as a spy for Sun).

Also Huang Chi-lu, *Kuo Fu Chün-shih Ku-wen—Ho-ma Li Chiang-chün (Ch'u Kao)* for a biography of Lea and his relations with Dr. Sun.

51. Arthur W. Hummel, ed., *Eminent Chinese of the Ch'ing Period,* 2 vols. (Washington: U.S. Government Printing Office, 1943–44), 1: 402–05 for a biography under the mandarin romanization, Jung Heng (1828–1912). Yung Wing wrote an autobiog-

raphy, *My Life in China and America* (New York: Henry Holt and Co., 1909) but it carries his story only to 1901 and the index does not even list Sun Yat-sen.

52. Chong, "The Abortive American-Chinese Project," pp. 56–64. The first evidence of interest in Sun, in a letter Allen to Boothe, January, 21, 1909, from which there are quotations on pp. 64–65.

53. Ibid., pp. 61, 64.

54. KFNPttp, p. 299.

55. Chong, "The Abortive American-Chinese Project," p. 67, quoting letters, Allen to Boothe, March 4 and 14, 1910. Apparently Allen revealed his opinion of Sun only after he learned that Lea and Boothe were to meet him.

56. Sun received Lea's invitation on February 21; because of other duties he could not have left till after February 28 (KFNPttp, pp. 299, 301).

57. Yung to Boothe and Lea, March 4, 1910, cited in Chong, "The Abortive American-Chinese Project, p. 65, n. 33. Apparently Yung Wing did not accompany Sun to the West Coast, so the appeal presumably was separate from the planned conference.

58. The documents of the conference are dated March 14, but the meetings might have lasted for several prior days.

59. Because I have not examined the Boothe papers, the following is reconstructed from Mr. Huang Chi-lu's study of them, summarized in KFNPttp, pp. 301–06, and the article by Professor Chong, also based upon them. See Huang, *Kuo Fu Chün-shih Ku-wen*, pp. 48–56.

60. These may be Chinese cadets that were trained in the United States during 1905 and later; see above, note 50.

61. Translated into Chinese in KFNPttp, pp. 301–06.

62. From Huang Hsing's letter to Sun of May 13, 1910, we gather that the concession area was in the French-leased territory of Kwangchowan. There a place had been found for several thousand men who could be disguised as farmers. Hsüeh, *Huang Hsing*, p. 79.

63. Chong, "The Abortive American-Chinese Project," p. 65 and n. 34.

64. Ibid., p. 66, and nn. 35, 36.

65. Ibid., p. 67. Boothe mentioned this evidence to Allen to persuade him to try again to raise money. Later Dr. Sun asked for the oaths to be returned to him and apparently they were; Ibid., p. 69.

66. Ibid., p. 66, based on Yung to Boothe, March 28, 1910.

67. The offer is found in Jansen, *The Japanese and Sun Yat-sen*, pp. 143, 255, n. 25, based upon a copy of the letter in Chapin, *Homer Lea*, p. 140. The second letter is the first in a series of 11 communications from Sun to Lea between March 24, 1910 and October 13, 1912, recently published. See Lü Fang-shang, "A Brief Account of the Homer Lea Papers" [In Chinese] in Huang Chi-lu, ed., *Yen-chiu Chung-shan Hsien-*

sheng ti Shih Liao yü Shih Hsüeh, pp. 417–68. Sun's letters to Lea, and 11 written to Mrs. Lea from June 27, 1912 to February 11, 1922, are reproduced in this article in English.

68. KFNPttp, p. 312; Hsüeh, *Huang Hsing,* pp. 79–82.

69. KFCC, 5: 98, dated March 24, 1910.

70. Chong, "The Abortive American-Chinese Project," p. 67, Sun to Boothe, April 5, 1910.

71. Ibid.

72. KFNPttp, pp. 313–14.

73. Chong, "The Abortive American-Chinese Project," p. 67, Allen to Boothe, June 23.

74. KFNPttp, pp. 317–18. Sun instructed Boothe, when sending a remittance to use Sun's personal name, Chung-shan. There are three letters from Sun to Lea written from Penang and dating August 11, September 29, and November 7, 1910, all of which reveal Sun's planning and need for funds, in Lü Fang-shang, "A Brief Account of the Homer Lea Papers," pp. 442–47.

75. Chong, "The Abortive American-Chinese Project," p. 68; and Lü Fang-shang, "A Brief Account of the Homer Lea Papers," pp. 445–47.

76. Chong, "The Abortive American-Chinese Project," p. 68.

77. Ibid., pp. 68–69, Boothe to Charles B. Hill, February, 7, 1911 and Boothe to Sun, April 13.

78. I am indebted to Professor Thomas William Ganschow for this information. He discovered Sun's note to Knox in the latter's papers. Details in Ganschow, *A Study of Sun Yat-sen's Contacts with the United States Prior to 1922.*

79. KFNPttp, p. 365, October 15 in Chicago and p. 372, October 20 in New York.

80. In the English version of his autobiography printed as *Memoirs of a Chinese Revolutionary* in 1918 (Taipei edition, 1953), pp. 174–75, Sun describes his success in dealing with London bankers, who he said he approached through his English friend. In the Chinese version (KFCC, 1: 48, and 2: 97), he names Homer Lea. The English version has many errors, and romanization sometimes is unintelligible.

81. The phrase is that of Lyon Sharman in *Sun Yat-sen,* p. 127.

82. Wang, "Sun Yat-sen and Singapore."

83. Schiffrin, "The Enigma of Sun Yat-sen," pp. 471–72.

84. Ibid., p. 471, n. 101, citing a Foreign Office dispatch, Grey to Jordan, November 14, 1911, enclosing the memorandum submitted by Dawson the previous day. Professor Schiffrin says this was the day *after* Sun and Lea had left for Paris, but KFNPttp, p. 393 has them arrive in Paris November 21. The *Times* (London) November 22, 1911, p. 5, says "After a ten days' visit to London *incognito* Dr. Sun Yat Sen left on Monday (Nov. 20) for China." This is its only contemporary reference to Sun's presence in London.

85. J. O. P. Bland and E. Backhouse, *Recent Events and Present Policies in China* (London: William Heineman, 1912), p. 283. These British journalists were very well informed and had close connections with the British legation in Peking.

CHAPTER FOUR ATTEMPTS TO HARNESS FOREIGN POWER

1. Sun used the deception in Yokohama in 1895 and again in 1897 in *Kidnapped in London*. On March 9, 1904 he swore to a deposition that "to the best of my knowledge and belief" he had been born in Oahu on November 24, 1870. Sharman, *Sun Yat-sen*, p. 79–80; Schiffrin, *Sun Yat-sen*, p. 327.

2. The *New York Times* carried a description of the Sun home in an article based upon reports by an American businessman, A. Masters MacDonell; NYT, July 15, 1917, section 6, p. 7. A photograph of the house may be seen in KMWH, 51, front matter. This shows the gardens and rear of the house as it was in May 1921 during ceremonies celebrating Dr. Sun's inauguration as president in Canton. Linebarger, *Sun Yat-sen*, p. 356 has a description of the home; its emphasizes Dr. Sun's simple life, abstinence from smoking and alcohol, and sparing diet. The Shanghai home is now a shrine. Pictures of the house and grounds, the reception rooms, study (with glass-covered bookcases and the dynastic histories), dining room, bedroom and sun porches are presented in Sui Hsüeh-fang and Hsü Ta-kang, *Sun Chung-shan Hsiensheng Ku Chü* [Mr. Sun Yat-sen's Former Dwelling] (Shanghai: Jen-min Ch'u-pan She, [1958]).

3. Inventories of Sun's book purchases in Japan during the 1913–16 period show his range of interests: there are works in popular philosophy and ethics by Bertrand Russell, Rudolph Eucken, and Friedrich Nietzsche; four volumes on the French Revolution; a work on capitalism by J. A. Hobson; one on elements of English law and another on municipal life and government in Germany; Havelock Ellis's *Man and Woman*; a work on psychical research; and four apparently inspirational works by Orison Swett Marden, *Every Man a King, Miracle of Right Thought, He Can Who Thinks He Can*, and *The Secret of Achievement*. The sales slips are preserved in the Kuomintang archives in Taiwan. Wu, *Sun Yat-sen*, pp. 196–97.

Professor Arthur N. Holcombe of Harvard visited Dr. Sun's home in 1928 and leafed through some of his books. He examined Sun's notations on the pages of Oliver Wendell Holmes's essay, "The Common Law" and observed that he had read with care Pollock and Maitland's *History* and other books "dear to the hearts of western lawyers and students of the science of government." Arthur N. Holcombe, *The Chinese Revolution: A Phase in the Regeneration of a World Power* (Cambridge: Harvard University Press, 1930), pp. 19–20. Edgar Snow visited the house in about 1930 and wrote of the excellent English and Chinese library. Snow, *Journey to the Beginning*, p. 83.

4. George Sokolsky, "The Reminiscences of George Sokolsky" (Manuscript, Columbia University Oral History Research Office, in the Oral History Collection of Columbia University (1956, 1963).

5. Lo, *Kuo Fu yü Ou Mei chih Yu-hao*, devotes chapters to eighteen of Sun's Western friends and mentors.

6. Nora Waln, *The House of Exile* (Boston: Little, Brown, 1942), pp. 203–05, based upon her personal observation of "returned students" in Canton.

7. See a digest of his *Fortnightly Review* article of 1897 in Schiffrin, *Sun Yat-sen,* pp. 130–32. In speeches after he resigned his provisional presidency, he advocated an "open door policy" for foreign investments, with control retained by China. See KFNPttp, pp. 484, 487, 489, September 5 and 26, October 12, 1912. He was proud of the contract drawn up with the Pauling Company in July 1913 for the construction of a railway from Canton to Chungking, which he considered entirely fair to both countries. See chapter one, note 50.

8. Jansen, *The Japanese and Sun Yat-sen,* pp. 146, 256, n. 38.

9. Ibid. Hsüeh, *Huang Hsing,* credits the second loan to Huang, with Chang Chien as guarantor, while Chu, *Reformer,* p. 77, apparently credits the loan to Chang Chien's personal efforts alone.

10. Jansen, *The Japanese and Sun Yat-sen,* pp. 147, 256, n. 39, on the confusion over whether money was actually paid.

11. Ibid., p. 147; Hsüeh, *Huang Hsing,* pp. 131–32. Chang Chien vigorously protested when he heard of this proposed reorganization of Han-yeh-p'ing to give the Japanese a controlling hand. Chu, *Reformer,* pp 77–79. USDS 893.6351/4 dispatch, Peking, Reinsch to Secretary of State, February 28, 1917, has an important collection of documents provided by Dr. J. C. Ferguson concerning the Han-yeh-p'ing Company, and details of this proposed loan, which the Chinese head of the company, Sheng Hsuan-huai, was under pressure from Sun Wen and Huang Hsing to negotiate and sign—reportedly under threat of death from General Huang! Mr. Sheng evaded conclusion of the loan by making it contingent upon the approval of the republican government, which turned out to be the government under Yuan Shih-k'ai, which did not give approval, so the documents imply.

12. Liew, *Struggle for Democracy,* pp. 143–44, makes a point of the rivalry among regimes to raise loans. Earlier, Sung Chiao-jen had planned to sell to Japan the sole agency rights for antimony produced in Hunan. Liew, p. 83. Bland and Blackhouse, *Recent Events and Present Policies,* p. 252, on the variety of public properties offered for mortgage.

13. Bland and Backhouse, *Recent Events and Present Policies,* pp. 366–67.

14. USDS 893.00/1187 and 1211, dispatches, Peking, Calhoun to Secretary of State, February 16 and 20, 1912, enclosing dispatches of C. D. Tenney from Nanking, February 8 and 10. Mr. McCormick apparently was a friend of Secretary Knox and carried a message from him to Chinese leaders concerning American and Japanese cooperation in respect to China. He interviewed Dr. Sun in Nanking, and later wrote a book about his experiences in revolutionary China, *The Flowery Republic,* in which Dr. Sun figures frequently. Professor Jansen's account of Japanese intrigues with the revolutionaries does not include the offer of an alliance, except through the State Department source, and he considers this a misunderstanding. See, Jansen, *The Japanese and Sun Yat-sen,* pp. 152, 256, n. 60.

15. Jansen, *The Japanese and Sun Yat-sen,* p. 162; USDS 893.00/1659, dispatch, Shanghai, Consul General Amos P. Wilder, to Legation, Peking, April 1, 1913. Wilder believed Sun would appear foolish for having "thrown himself into the arms of Japan," since the masses of Chinese distrusted the Japanese.

16. A discussion of the negotiations for the loan is in Ch'en, *Yuan Shih-k'ai,* pp. 125–29 and Li, *The Political History of China,* pp. 288–90. The terms are given in KMWH, 6: 748–58.

17. KFNPttp, pp. 506–09.

18. The *Times* (London), April 28, 1913, p. 6.

19. The text of the telegram in Cantlie and Seaver, *Sir James Cantlie,* pp. 111–12. This work reprints a number of letters from Dr. Sun and his wife to the Cantlies from January 1912 to August 1921. Sir James and his wife tried to influence public opinion and prominent persons, but without success. The *Times* (London) quoted Sun's telegram to Cantlie, on May 3 (p. 3).

20. NYT, May 25, 1913, section 3, p. 5, reprinting text of a statement sent by Sun Yat-sen from Shanghai and printed in Paris, May 9.

21. Jansen, *The Japanese and Sun Yat-sen,* pp. 162–64, which describes a variety of private Japanese initiatives on Sun's behalf against Yuan in May and June, 1913.

22. The *Times* (London) May 10, p. 16 and May 14, p. 5.

23. USDS 893.00/1683, dispatch, Peking, Chargé d'Affairs Williams to Secretary, May 4, 1913, inclosing letter, Amos P. Wilder, U.S. Consul General, Shanghai, dated May 1. Mr. Wilder left out the name of his informant, the interviewer.

24. Jansen, *The Japanese and Sun Yat-sen,* pp. 165–66 and Hsüeh, *Huang Hsing,* p. 218, n. 101.

25. Sun Yat-sen, *Sun Wen Hsueh-shuo,* appendix to chapter six, in KFCC, 2: 68, and Sun, *Memoirs of a Chinese Revolutionary,* p. 116. A superior translation based upon the original letter to Huang Hsing is provided by Chün-tu Hsüeh in *Chinese Studies in History* 7, no. 3 (Spring 1974): 10. The letter was dated February 4, 1915, and does not mention any concessions Dr. Sun might have been willing to make to Japan in return for an alliance.

26. Quoted from the translation in Sun, *The Vital Problem of China,* (1941; reprinted., Taipei: China Cultural Service, 1953), p. 141. The letter was found in Ōkuma's papers after his death, but I do not know whether this was the source of the translation cited. A text of the letter was leaked and published in June 1914. See Jansen, *The Japanese and Sun Yat-sen,* pp. 188–89, 215, nn. 37, 38. I do not find the letter in KFCC, and it is only mentioned in KFNPttp, p. 550.

What purports to be the text of this letter to Ōkuma appears in Saggitarius [pseud.], *The Strange Apotheosis of Sun Yat-sen* (London: Heath, Cranton Ltd., 1939), pp. 58–62.

27. Jansen, *The Japanese and Sun Yat-sen,* pp. 192–93, 262, nn. 50, 51. The letter is found in the microfilmed files of the Japanese Foreign Office. (Gaimusho: Meiji-

Taisho Documents, 1.6.4.1. Exposures 5546–53), and the sample treaty is quoted by Jansen in English translation.

Mrs. Sharman discussed another alleged document which appeared in the press in April 1915, while negotiations concerning the Twenty-One Demands were underway. This "contract" stipulates a sum of money and number of rifles to be supplied to Dr. Sun by certain named Japanese, to be secured by ¥10 million worth of bonds to be issued by Sun Yat-sen. The Japanese were also to provide a volunteer force to assist Sun, and conditions of pay and employment were included in the contract. In return, after the occupation of Chinese territory by a joint Chinese and Japanese force, "all industrial undertakings and railway construction and the like not mentioned in treaties with other foreign powers, shall be worked with joint capital together with the Japanese." As soon as a new government is established, it will recognize all of Japan's demands as settled and binding. The document ends with the statement that the articles were signed in February and that the first installment of ¥400,000 had been paid. Sharman, *Sun Yat-sen*, pp. 190–99.

Mrs. Sharman, tentatively concluded that this may have been a genuine agreement, but only on the assumption that it dates from February 1914, and not 1915, considering it incredible that Dr. Sun would have proposed such a contract as late as February 1915, when China was aroused by Japan's demands on Peking. This deduction has little force now, in view of the sample treaty dated March 14, 1915 in the Japanese Foreign Office files.

28. Albert A. Altman and Harold Z. Schiffrin, "Sun Yat-sen and the Japanese: 1914–16," *Modern Asian Studies* 6, pt. 4 (October 1972): 391–93. Dr. Schiffrin interviewed Mr. Kuhara in December 1963 and saw the receipts. The first, and largest loan, is recorded in a published collection of Japanese Foreign Office documents; ibid., n. 37. The Japanese Cabinet made a decision on March 7, the day before the loan to Wang T'ung-i, to support every anti-Yuan faction, through quasi-civilian agencies. Kuhara also advanced a loan of ¥1 million to Yuan's old rival, the former viceroy of Kwangtung-Kwangsi, Ts'en Ch'un-hsuan, who was in Japan. Another agent advanced ¥1 million to a Manchu royalist, who had an army in North China.

Wang T'ung-i apparently was a naval officer, for shortly after receiving this loan he was back in Shanghai where Dr. Sun instructed him to be in command of naval vessels in a planned coup, and to coordinate his efforts with Ch'en Ch'i-mei. KFNPttp, p. 632 for April 16, 1916.

29. Altman and Schiffrin, "Sun Yat-sen," pp. 396–99.

30. Hsüeh, *Huang Hsing*, p. 181, based upon unpublished private papers. The telegram is not found in any of Sun's collected works.

31. Sun, *10 Letters of Sun Yat-sen*. These date from August 14, 1914 to November 24, 1916. In addition, the Special Collections Department of Stanford University Libraries has in the extensive James Deitrick Papers and the Sun Yat Sen Collection two letters from Sun to Deitrick dated November 30, 1914 and February 5, 1915, and telegrams from Sun to Deitrick dated January 1 and 27, 1915 and July 1, 1916. There are also some twenty letters from Deitrick to Sun dating from July 11 to November 4, 1912, but no corresponding letters from Dr. Sun. Also from the Deitrick side there

are copies of two letters to Sun, dating November 28, 1914 and March 14/27, 1915, and telegrams from January 9, 1915 and June 30, 1916. Yet it is clear from the correspondence that several letters and telegrams are not in the files.

I am much indebted to Patricia J. Palmer, manuscripts librarian, Department of Special Collections, The Stanford University Libraries, for arranging to supply me with copies of correspondence between the two men not already published in *10 Letters*.

Professor Li Yün-han, a staff member of the Kuomintang archives in Taiwan, kindly sent me copies of five letters from Deitrick to Sun, found in the archives, and dated December 12 and 30, 1914, January 9 and 30, and March 14/27, 1915 (the latter also in the Stanford collection). A handwritten note on the margin of the letter of January 9 gives the clue making it possible to decode some of the secret telegrams in the Stanford collection. See n. 38, below.

Professor Thomas William Ganschow studied the papers in the Deitrick collection at Stanford and included an interesting chapter in his dissertation, *A Study of Sun Yat-sen's Contacts with the United States*, pp. 125–59. He is expanding his study for publication.

32. *Who's Who in America, 1912–13* and later issues to 1917. According to *International Cable Register of the World 1912*, "Pridstream" was the cable address of the Atlantic-Pacific Railway, of which Mr. Deitrick was vice-president, and also for a company in Nicaragua, named Blufields, Managua and Rio Grande. According to the biographical note in the Stanford Library inventory of the Dietrick papers, he was known to be deceased by 1932. The quotation is from a letter, Dietrick to Sun, Sept 2, 1912. All the 1912 letters appear to be from London.

33. Lü Fang-shang, "A Brief Account of the Homer Lea Papers," pp. 457–58.

34. S. to D., August 14, October 12 and 19, 1914.

35. S. to D., August 14, and October 19, 1914.

36. S. to D., August 14, and D. to S. December 30, 1914.

37. S. to D., November 30, and D. to S. November 28, 1914.

38. S. to D., November 20, 1914 and open cable January 1, 1915. Secret cable, D. to S., January 9, 1915 and letter of the same date.

The two men used the *Western Union Telegraphic Code* published by the International Cable Directory Company in 1900. For secret communication they picked the appropriate code numbers or words to convey the message and then ascended thirty-two places in the code book.

39. D. to S., December 30, 1914. Secret cable S. to D., January 27, and letter, S. to D., February 5, 1915.

40. Letter, S. to D., February 5, 1915. This also quotes Sun's cable on the Chautauqua proposal.

41. D. to S., March 14/27, 1915.

42. S. to D., November 18, 1915, and May 27, 1916. Secret cable, D. to S., June 30, and open cable, S. to D., received July 1 in San Fransisco.

43. Letters, S. to D., July 5 and November 24, 1916. The latter, which is the last in *10 Letters*, was to be delivered by Mr. Robert Norman, "a confidential friend of mine." Later, Mr. Norman served as legal adviser to Dr. Sun.

44. Details of the diplomatic story are revealed in Madeleine Chi, *China Diplomacy, 1914–1918* (Cambridge: Harvard University Press, 1970) pp. 115–19.

45. KFNPttp, p. 666. Chinese text in KFCC, 6: 32–93. The source for the statement that Sun gave his ideas to Chu, who then drafted the work, is not stated in KFNPttp. However, in a letter to Li Tsung-huang on May 23, 1917, Sun Wen writes of this book as having been written by Chu Chih-hsin and recommends it for reprinting. See KFCC, 5: 262–63. Mr. Gary Glick informs me that a Japanese translation appeared in August 1917, with a preface by Dr. Sun's friend, Inukai Ki, and with Chu Chih-hsin as author. This was not for sale. It is difficult to say when the work began to be attributed to Sun as author. Dr. S. T. Leong apparently has seen a copy dated 1918 in which Sun Yat-sen is so given. Sow-Theng Leong, "Sun Yat-sen and Bolsheviks," *Transactions of the International Conference of Orientalists in Japan* 14 (1969): 41. The earliest version in an American library seems to be 1928 and is attributed to Sun. Apparently the first English translation was published in 1941 under the Wang Ching-wei regime, with the title *China and Japan: Natural Friends—Unnatural Enemies; a Guide for China's Foreign Policy* (Shanghai, China United Press, 1941). This had a foreword by President Wang Ching-wei, and was edited by T'ang Leang-li. A search through three guides to periodical and public affairs publications fails to show that any part of the work was published in English in 1917.

Chu Chih-hsin's essay, sponsored by Dr. Sun and later attributed to him, probably completed in April or early in May 1917, is a strange book. Its main theme is clear: China should stay out of the war. Strongly hostile toward England, the writer seemed sympathetic toward Germany, which in his view had been the least aggressive of the powers toward China. Russia was seen as the most dangerous, though at the very time of writing the Russian war effort was collapsing and revolution was underway. The book gives a favorable view of Japan's intentions and opposes the effort of "the pro-American group" to bring China into the war so that the United States would protect her against her neighbor. China and Japan had a common culture and depended upon each other economically, and should also be natural allies against Russian aggression.

The writer's geopolitical speculations now seem embarrassing in the light of actual developments during and after the war. Using considerable reference to European history and colonial policy, he attempted to demonstrate deductively what would happen to China as a result of the war. British machinations presented the greatest danger. In case of victory, England would give Russia its way in China in order to divert Russia from India. In case of stalemate, England might suddenly ally with Germany and give Germany freedom in the far East for the same reason. Whatever happened during the war, England would be compelled thereafter to ally either with Russia or Germany; and in either case China would be sacrificed for the preservation of the Indian colony. America as a protector was unreliable: it would never antagonize a strong world power for the sake of a country in which it had no interest—the case of Korea being clear evidence.

Yet the writer was not hostile to the United States. Of all the powers he saw it as the least anxious to exploit China. What he objected to was an attempt by China to play off America against Japan and Japan against America. His positive conclusion was that China should befriend Japan and also endeavor to prevent any conflict between Japan and the United States. Preventing such conflict would leave Japan free to accomplish her mission of aiding China to develop itself.

> The relationship between China and Japan is one of common existence or extinction. Without Japan, there would be no China; without China, there would be no Japan. For the sake of establishing a lasting peace between the two countries, no trifling cause should be permitted to disturb their friendship.

(KFCC, 6: 88; *The Vital Problem*, p. 124.) America's geographical position prescribed her to be China's natural friend. China should rely on these two friendly states for capital, technical advice, and raw materials, the writer concluded. Japan could be of greater assistance because of her similarity to China in language and race, but from a political point of view, China was related to America as pupil to tutor, both being democratic countries. Hence, the three Pacific nations should cooperate. By their concerted effort disarmament might someday be effected and permanent peace be secured for the world.

In October 1914, Dr. Sun had been furious at Chu Chih-hsin's independence in raising funds and not remitting them through him in Tokyo, but they were soon reconciled. See Friedman, *Backward Toward Revolution*, pp. 73–74, 85, 90. When Chu died tragically on September 21, 1920, Sun was bereft. His death "is like the loss of my right and left hands," he wrote. See Boorman and Howard, *Biographical Dictionary of Republican China*, 1: 443.

As this essay was being written, Dr. Sun was angling for a loan from Russia. When he learned of the March 1917 revolution he wondered whether it would still be possible to get a Russian loan with Chinese mines as security. See KFNPttp, p. 667, March 27, 1917, for Sun's annotation.

46. KFCC, 4: 271–72 (misdated January). The telegram was published in the *China Press* on March 8, and partially in Wu, *Sun Yat-sen*, pp. 257–58. The telegram was much criticized in the Chinese press and the Western press in China. See NYT, March 13, 1917, p. 1, and FER, April 1917, pp. 402, 407.

47. Josef Fass, "Sun Yat-sen and the World War I," *Archiv Orientální* 35 (1967): 115–20, including long excerpts from the text of the German secret report. This is cited and discussed in Li Kuo-ch'i, "Some Records in the German Archives . . ." (See note 56 below).

48. USDS 893.00/2842, dispatch, Canton, Heintzleman to Reinsch, April 28, 1918. Sun's letter of March 18 stated,

> I take this opportunity unhesitatingly to affirm that hitherto I have never received funds from German sources. In my present movement I am actuated solely by the desire to restore the Constitutional Government to China and to give our people the benefits and blessings of democratic institutions.

A report to the British Foreign Office of July 14, 1917 said a "most reliable" source indicated that Sun had received 2 million taels from Germany in early May, but a notation of August 5 states that while Great Britain had definite proof of a German approach to Sun, the Foreign Office had no proof how that approach was received. Reynolds, "Sun Yat-sen," pp. 20–21, citing Foreign Office documents.

49. USDS 893.00/2707, dispatch, Canton, Heintzleman, August 6, 1917. KFNPttp, p. 677, for Sun's gift of $300,000 on June 27 to Adm. Ch'eng Pi-kuang, who then brought seven warships to Canton.

50. USDS 893.00/2631, telegram from Sun Yat-sen with notations. See Chi, *China Diplomacy*, pp. 118, 124 on the attitudes of Wilson and Lansing.

51. USDS 893.00/2709, dispatch, Canton, Heintzleman, August 14, 1917, describing a private conversation with Dr. Sun; 893.00/2719, same, September 7, reporting a call on the consulate by Hu Han-min at the instance of Dr. Sun. Earlier, Mr. Heintzleman reported that he had been reliably informed through several sources that the Japanese consul general had called upon Dr. Sun on August 2 and that a Japanese of the local branch of the Bank of Taiwan called on Dr. Sun with a letter from the consul, offering to make a loan. USDS 893.00/2708, dispatch, Canton, Heintzleman, August 9, 1917. Whether Sun's government was able to arrange loans from Japanese banks, business firms or individuals is uncertain. I could find no reference to such in KMWH, 49 and 51, which contain considerable detail on the financing of the military government.

52. Proclamation in KFCC, 4: 88; Tsou, CKKMTSK, pp. 1017–08. According to Mr. Heintzleman, a resolution pertaining to war with Germany passed the Parliament at Canton on September 13, which "tolerates" a state of war. After further debate on September 22, the wording was changed to "recognizes the existing state of war." Forty-nine out of sixty members present passed this resolution. See USDS, 893.00/2725, dispatch, Canton, Heintzleman, September 27, 1917.

53. Ibid. New information on Sun's "Constitution Protection Movement" is presented in Chiang Yung-ching, "New Materials on Constitution-Protection in the *Military Government Gazette*," in Huang Chi-lu, ed., *Yen-chiu Chung-shan Hsien-sheng ti Shih Liao yü Shih Hsüeh*, pp. 237–63.

54. USDS 893.00/2726, 2728–29, and 2730. The counselor of the Chinese legation in Washington called at the Department of State on November 2, 1917 with the information that the southern government was sending a large shipment of its bonds to Honolulu for sale to sympathizers, and asking the department to take steps to stop the sales. Mr. Frank P. Lockhart did the staff work in the State Department to alert the Treasury, Justice, and Labor Departments and the Post Office to stop the importation and sale, particularly in Honolulu, Seattle, and San Francisco. On learning that Sun Fo and two other persons had left Canton for the Philippines to sell bonds, the State Department wrote to the War Department on November 26, 1917 suggesting that the secretary of war "may possibly wish to take steps to prevent the sale of these bonds or the future importation of bonds in the Philippine Islands."

55. KMWH, 49: 324–38 has a record of bonds issued to various persons for sale in China and abroad, giving the impression that some $15 million worth were sold. By contrast the record of funds received and dispersed by the finance bureau of the Military Government from September 28, 1917 to June 30, 1918 is quite precise, and shows many contributions large and small from overseas Chinese. Ibid., pp. 301–23.

56. Professor Li Kuo-ch'i cites the documents in the German Foreign Office archives on this affair in "Te-kuo Tang-an chung Yu-kuan Chung-kuo Ts'an-chia Ti-i-tz'u Shih-chieh Ta-chan ti Chi Hsiang Chi-tsai" [Some Records in the German Archives Concerning China's Entry into the First World War], *Chung-kuo Hsien-tai Shih Chuan-t'i Yen-chiu Pao-kao*, no. 4 (Taipei: Chung-hua Min-kuo Shih-liao Yen-chiu Chung-hsin, 1974), pp. 317–43.

57. Sun, *The International Development of China*, pp. v, 1–2, 7.

58. Ibid., pp. 4–5.

59. Ibid., pp. 220–24, printing the letter, Reinsch to Sun, March 17, 1919. Later Dr. Reinsch sent copies of the plan to the Secretary of State. USDS 893.60/9–10, June 9, 1919. Minister Reinsch was interested enough to send Paul P. Whitham, special commissioner of the Department of Commerce, to inspect the proposed northern deep-sea port area. He found a suitable site. Then Reinsch discussed the idea with the governor of Chihli, other provincial leaders, and some members of the Peking government, who greatly favored the project, which was to be known as the Great Northern Port, exactly Sun's name for it! Paul S. Reinsch, *An American Diplomat in China* (Garden City, N.Y.: Doubleday, Page & Co., 1922), p. 233. Dr. Reinsch left Peking on September 13, 1919, having resigned his position.

60. The Hendrick Christian Andersen papers in the Library of Congress include four letters from Dr. Sun and two enclosures, and seven copies of letters to him from Mr. Andersen. Andersen was an American sculptor who lived in Rome; his scheme was to develop a "World Centre of Communications, a City of Peace," and he pressed his plans upon various world leaders. See *Who's Who in America, 1918–1919*, s. v. Andersen, Hendrick Christian." Quotation from Andersen to Sun, April 16, 1919.

61. Sun, *The International Development of China*, pp. 225–26, letter from William C. Redfield, Secretary of Commerce, to Sun Yat-sen, May 12, 1919; and p. 227, letter from General Caviglia (i.e. Enrico Caviglia, Italian minister of war), May 17, 1919; and Cantlie and Seaver, *Sir James Cantlie*, p. 120, quoting Sun to Lady Cantlie, March 20, 1919, in which he says he has sent copies to each member of the Cabinet of the British government. However, this could only have been the preliminary version. We speculate that Dr. Sun also sent a copy to his acquaintance, Georges Clemenceau, the French prime minister. Later he tried through Lady Cantlie to persuade Marquis Curzon (George Nathaniel Curzon of Kedleston) to write an introduction for the British edition of the work, but was turned down. Cantlie and Seaver, *Sir James Cantlie*, p. 112.

62. FER, 15 (March, June, and August 1919); 16 (April, June, October, and November 1920); this omits program 5, 6, and conclusion. Dr. Sun took over without credit drawings for the Great Northern Port, planned by a group of Chihli officials and businessmen, which appeared in FER, 16 (January 1920): 15–17. Ideas for improving the port of Shanghai were taken from "Report of the Future Development of Shanghai Harbor," issued in April 1918 by the Whampoo Conservancy Board, according to FER, 15 (September 1919): 584.

The first edition of the work as a book was printed by The Commercial Press, Ltd., Shanghai, 1920. This has a preface by Sun Yat-sen dated July 20, 1920, but the month of publication is uncertain. There is a microfilm copy of this edition in the State Department Decimal File: USDS 893.00/4002. It was sent with a card, "Compliments of Sun Yat Sen." MacMurray ordered that the book be filed with no acknowledgement. This discourtesy seems to have typified Dr. MacMurray's attitude toward Dr. Sun. Another edition was published in Shanghai in May 1921, for which Dr. Sun wrote a preface on April 25. The book was also published in London and New York by G. P. Putnam & Sons in 1922, probably toward the end of the year. I use the Taipei reprint for convenience. It appears to be complete and authentic.

63. Dr. Sun thanked five named friends (several were YMCA secretaries) for giving "great assistance in reading over the manuscripts with me." *International Development of China*, p. vi, preface dated Canton, April 25, 1921. For *Chien-she* appearance, see KFNPttp, p. 762 and Tsou, CKKMTSK, pp. 556–57.

64. Sun to Andersen, March 29, 1920 in which Dr. Sun says he is sending five copies of his third program.

65. Sokolsky, "Reminiscences" p. 25; Thomas W. Lamont, *Across World Frontiers* (New York: Harcourt, Brace and Co., 1951), pp. 241–42. The date was about April 5, 1920. I have not found a contemporary report by Mr. Lamont on this interview, but it is clear that the strongest impression which he retained was this request to finance an army "from one supposed to be China's great exponent of peaceful leadership and of democratic processes in place of military ones," as he puts it.

The only nearly contemporary report by Mr. Lamont on his Shanghai visit which I have found mentions his talk with southern leaders, who begged him not to make a loan that would strengthen the Peking government, but he does not name them, nor mention his talk with Dr. Sun. See USDS 893.51/2829, cable from Morris, U.S. embassy Tokyo, May 14, 1922, for Lamont, who used the American diplomatic facilities.

Miss June Y. Mei searched the Lamont papers at the Baker Library, Harvard University, on my behalf, but found nothing that even mentions Sun Yat-sen. His name does not appear in the appointments diary of the Lamonts' China trip, nor is he mentioned in a summary of the trip which Mr. Lamont wrote in May 1920, for government use, assessing the political and economic situation in China.

66. Sun, *The International Development of China*, p. 208.

67. KFCC, 5: 380–82, translated in Sun, *The Vital Problem of China*, pp. 143–47. See also a letter to Sun's friend, Miyazaki Torazō in October 1920, in KFCC, 5: 418.

68. USDS 793.94/1090, dispatch, Peking, Ruddock to Secretary of State, July 27, 1920. A copy of the draft of this letter was kept in George Sokolsky's papers and a photo-reproduction was kindly given to me by Mr. Donald Feurstein, Mr. Sokolsky's son-in-law. It is a typewritten draft with corrections in Dr. Sun's own hand, and while originally dated "Shanghai, June 10, 1920" there is written upon the top the date July 10, 1920, and "The following letter has been addressed to General Tanaka, Minister of War, by Dr. Sun Yat Sen." Presumably this was added by Mr. Sokolsky, who on occasion passed information about Dr. Sun to the American consulate in Shanghai. Whether the letter was sent to General Tanaka is unclear, but I have no doubt it expressed Dr. Sun's feelings at the time.

69. USDS 893.5043/1, dispatch, Canton, Huston, June 28, 1922.

70. USDS 893.00/2901, cablegram, Shanghai, Sun Yat-sen to President Wilson, November 19, 1918, and correspondence, Wilson to Lansing and reply. Wilson did not wish to be drawn into correspondence with Dr. Sun, "much as I have sometimes sympathized with his professed principles and objects." Lansing concurred and told the president of "very ugly stories" about Dr. Sun.

71. Reinsch, *An American Diplomat in China*, p. 334.

72. U.S. Department of State, *Papers Relating to the Foreign Relations of the United States, 1921*, 1: 337–42, (hereafter cited as FRUS). The incident caused a great flap in the department, with messages back and forth about what to do with the inconvenient letter. See USDS 893.00/4239.

73. USDS 793.94/1238. President Sun's letter was dated September 16, 1921.

74. FRUS, 1921, 1: 325, printing part of 893.00/3817, dispatch, Peking, Charles R. Crane, February 28, 1921. In the part printed, the legation reports what associates of Dr. Sun allegedly felt about his "impractical and grandiose schemes" and his "great personal vanity." In the North he was regarded at best as an impractical idealist. But what was not printed was the statement that many regarded him "as an unscrupulous adventurer more than willing to intrigue with the Japanese and the Anfu Party, sacrificing the interests of the nation to his own ends." The dispatch went on to describe the revulsion of feeling against his plans to start another military campaign against the North, since he had stated that it could be conducted without funds, the troops subsisting upon the resources of the country being traversed.

75. USDS 711.93/62, telegram, Ma Soo to President Harding, March 3, 1921, and marginal notation, dated 3/9.

76. USDS 893.00/3998, letter, Geo. B. Christian, Secretary to the President, to Henry P. Fletcher, Under Secretary of State, July 27, 1921, inclosing letter from Ma Soo, and letter of reply from Mr. Fletcher.

77. USDS 893.00/4080, memorandum of the Division of Far Eastern Affairs, Department of State, September 28, 1921, dictated by N. T. J. and signed by MacMurray regarding "Self-Constituted Constitutional Government of China at Canton." 893.00/4171, letter, Ma Soo to Charles Evans Hughes, Chairman of the Washington Conference, December 7, 1921, and referred to FE on December 12. The letter submits a list of points for the conference prepared by the Ministry of Foreign Affairs, Canton. It called, first of all, for withdrawal of recognition of the Peking government by the powers and recognition of the government of President Sun Yat-sen. This would lead to the unification of China. It then outlined a series of points to restore China's full sovereignty and lost rights. E. T. Williams had a six-page comment, which accepted various of the points with qualifications, but denied that "a proper national government already exists at Canton" because the Parliament elected in 1912, which elected Sun as president in 1921, had already outlived its term of office and furthermore was a "rump" Parliament.

78. USDS 893.602 Sh 1/1–21.

79. USDS 893.602 Sh 1/11, taken from the *Chicago Daily News*, September 1, 1921 and Sh 1/21, a copy from the U.S. Department of Commerce, April 15, 1922, both apparently supplied by Mr. Shank.

80. This conclusion is based only on the record in the State Department, and might be modified by evidence from other sources. I have found nothing from the Chinese side.

81. USDS 893.156R11, dispatch, Canton, Bergholz to Secretary of State, October 11, 1921.

82. USDS 893.156R11/1, letter, Wilbur J. Carr [Department of State] to Leon Allen Bergholz, January 23, 1922.

83. USDS 893.156R11/4–17, various. Dr. Sun learned, naturally, that the State Department was blocking his efforts to get American enterprise to Canton for developmental purposes. After returning to the city in February 1923, he did not establish a government claiming to head the republic. In a conversation on April 14 with the new consul in charge, R. P. Tenney, he referred to the failure of the scheme for port development with the Rabbitt firm. Now he intended to get capital from other countries, and the Japanese, he said, were very anxious to invest at Canton. He wondered whether the U.S. consulate could assist in inducing American capital to enter the field in such a way that approval or disapproval of the U.S. government would be unnecessary. USDS 893.00/4988, dispatch, Canton, Tenney to Secretary of State, April 14, 1923.

84. Marcosson, "The Changing East: Sun Yat-sen and South China," pp. 101–02.

85. Josef Fass, "Sun Yat-sen and Germany in 1921–1924," *Archiv Orientální* 31 (1968): 134–48, citing German Foreign Office archives.

86. USDS 761.93/258, dispatch, Hong Kong, William H. Gale to Secretary of State, September 24, 1922; NCH, October 7, p. 3. The *Telegraph* provided a translation and then reprinted the entire story as a pamphlet.

87. Fass, "Sun Yat-sen and Germany," p. 139.

88. NCH, October 7, 1922, p. 9, quoting Reuter, Berlin, September 29.

89. NCH, October 7, 1922, p. 9; USDS, 761.93/260, dispatch, Shanghai, Cunningham to Secretary of State, October 2, 1922, enclosing news clippings. Underlining in the above quotations were in Dr. Sun's official statement.

CHAPTER FIVE GROPING TOWARD SOVIET RUSSIA

1. Li Yün-han, *Ts'ung Jung Kung tao Ch'ing Tang* [From the Admission of the Communists to the Purification of the Kuomintang], 2 vols. (Taipei: China Committee on Publication Aids and Prize Awards, 1966), 1: 108–20 on Sun's interest in Soviet Russia and in socialism. (This is hereafter cited as Li, TJKTCT).

2. The text of the telegram is not contained in KFCC, nor is it mentioned in KFNPttp, though Tsou Lu mentions it in CKKMTSK, p. 342. According to Leng, Shao-chuan and Norman D. Palmer, *Sun Yat-sen and Communism* (New York: Frederick A. Praeger, 1960), p. 48, the telegram had to be sent through intermediaries. Part of it is quoted in S. L. Tikhvinsky, *Sun Yat-sen: On the Occasion of the Centenary of his Birth (1866–1966)*. (n.p., n.d., Novosti Press Agency Publishing House, [1966]), p. 23; and it is indirectly quoted in S. L. Tikhvinsky, *Sun Yat-sen and Problems of Solidarity of the Peoples of Asia*, Twenty-sixth International Congress of Orientalists:

Papers Presented by the USSR Delegation (Moscow, 1963), p. 5, referenced to *Izvestia*, July 5, 1918. Dr. Sun arrived in Shanghai on June 25, after a brief visit to Japan; if he sent the telegram from there as Tsou Lu says, the effort to contact Lenin came about the end of June 1918.

3. Tikhvinsky, *Sun Yat-sen: On the Occasion*, p. 23; Jane Degras, *Soviet Documents on Foreign Policy*, vol. 1. *1917–1924* (London: Royal Institute of International Affairs, 1951), pp. 92–93, from *Izvestia*, March 9, 1919.

4. Allen S. Whiting, *Soviet Policies in China, 1917–1924* (New York: Columbia University Press, 1954) pp. 269–71 for an English text of the first Karakhan Manifesto, and pp. 28–33 and notes for discussion of its emendation and Russian denial of the disputed passage. *Hsin Ch'ing-nien* 7, no. 6 (May 1920) carried a Chinese translation of the original manifesto, from either French or English (pp. 1239–41 of Japanese reprint edition), and a collection of responses from fifteen organizations or federations, and editorials from nine newspapers and journals, all commending Soviet generosity (pp. 1241–67).

5. Sokolsky, "Reminiscences," pp. 18–20.

6. USDS 761.93/142, dispatch, Shanghai, Cunningham, March 30, 1920. In his "Reminiscences," Sokolsky said that Popoff came to Shanghai in 1919 at the time of the student strike—i.e., in May or June—and that he saw him frequently. The name was an assumed one.

7. M. A. Persits, "The Eastern Internationalists in Russia and Some Questions of the National-Liberation Movement (1918–July 1920)," in *Komintern i Vostok; Bor'ba za Leninskuiu Strategiiu i Taktiku v Natsional'no Osvoboditel'nom Dvizhenii* [Comintern and the East; the Struggle for the Leninist Strategy and Tactics in the National Liberation Movement]. (Moscow: Glav. Red. Vost. Lit., 1969), pp. 87–89. The late Mrs. Lydia Holubnychy provided me with this information.

8. Tikhvinsky, *Sun Yat-sen: On the Occasion*, pp. 26–27, and Tikhvinsky, "On Sun Yat-sen's Attitude," pp. 74–75. The date of publication is given as July 13, 1920. According to Professor Tikhvinsky, Dr. Sun was unable to send his reply direct to Moscow, and routed it through Ma Soo in New York, who forwarded it to M. Litvinov in Copenhagen. The incident is not mentioned in KFNPttp nor is Sun's telegram found in KFCC.

9. Sokolsky, "Reminiscences," part 1, p. 23. Mr. Sokolsky remembered that he translated the telegram and helped Sun prepare his reply.

10. Eudin and North, *Soviet Russia and the East*, pp. 218–19, translated from *Pravda*, March 15, 1925, p. 2. The date of the meeting may be inferred as between October 29, when Ch'en Chiung-ming's troops retook Canton, and November 25, when Dr. Sun sailed from Shanghai for that city. Tikhvinsky, *Sun Yat-sen: On the Occasion*, p. 28 for the last quotation. Whether this was Voitinsky's only meeting with Dr. Sun in Shanghai is unclear.

11. Katsuji Fuse, *Soviet Policy in the Orient* (Peking: Enjinsha, 1927), pp. 225–26; Ts'ui Shu-ch'in, *Sun Chung-shan yü Kung-ch'an-chu-i* (Hong Kong; Asia Press, 1954), pp. 21–22. Fuse, a well-informed Japanese journalist, mentions dissemination of So-

viet propaganda in the organ *Ch'ün Pao* and the establishment of a Russian language course in the Canton Higher Normal College, moves similar to those undertaken by Voitinsky and his team in Shanghai in 1920. *Ch'ün Pao* was supported by Ch'en Chiung-ming and edited by three young Chinese Communists, Ch'en Kung-po, T'an P'ing-shan, and T'an Chih-t'ang. See Ch'en Kung-po, *The Communist Movement in China: An Essay Written in 1924*, ed. C. Martin Wilbur (New York: Octagon Books, 1966), pp. 7–8. Ch'en mentions two Russian agents coming to Canton in the guise of merchants and getting in touch with the group. Fuse offers the text of a memorandum of agreement between Alexieff and Sun in March 1921. Ts'ui Shu-ch'in, who gives no sources, says that Alexieff called upon Sun but denies there was any agreement. In S. L. Tikhvinsky, "On Sun Yat-sen's Attitudes toward Soviet Russia, 1917–1925," in *Voprosy Istorii* no. 12 (1963): 77, it is mentioned that Dr. Sun drew his information on Soviet Russia from the Rosta office opened in Canton in 1921. According to Marc Kasanin, a member of the mission of the Far Eastern Republic to Peking, headed by M. I. Yurin in 1920–21, his friend, A. E. Khodorov, who headed the Rosta office in Peking, went south where he met Sun Yat-sen and talked with him about Russia, the revolution, and the Far Eastern Republic, and on his return to Peking told his friend of the meeting. Marc Kasanin, *China in the Twenties*, trans. Hilda Kasanina (Moscow: Central Department of Oriental Literature, 1973), p. 108. This probably was in the summer of 1921.

Holubnychy, "The Comintern and China," pp. 43–44, quotes from an article by M. A. Persits, based upon archives, in *Sun Yat-sen, 1866–1966*, pp. 357–58, which says the authorities of the Far Eastern Republic had established contacts with Sun's representatives "and were giving him material support."

12. Quoted in Eugene Chen, "Sun Yat-sen—Some Memories," CWR 43 (December 19, 1927): 76. This may be a reprint of Mr. Chen's article of the same title in the *People's Tribune*, Peking, Special Memorial Issue, March 12, 1926, which I have not seen.

13. Eudin and North, *Soviet Russia and the East*, pp. 219–21, translated from *Bolshevik* no. 19 (October 1950): 46–48 and elsewhere. The text is not found in KFNPttp nor in KFCC.

14. Ruth T. McVey, *The Rise of Indonesian Communism* (Ithaca: Cornell University Press, 1965), pp. 13–34, for Sneevliet's activities in Indonesia and his expulsion; pp. 57–60 for his participation in the second Communist International congress; and p. 77 for his arrival in China. Unfortunately, Dr. McVey was led astray on the date of Maring's meeting with Dr. Sun in Kweilin by errors in C. Martin Wilbur and Julie Lien-ying How, *Documents on Communism, Nationalism, and Soviet Advisers in China, 1918–1927* (New York: Columbia University Press, 1956). Also Dov Bing, "Sneevliet and the Early Years of the CCP," *China Quarterly* 48 (October/December 1971): 681–82.

15. A. I. Kartunova, "The Comintern and Some Questions on the Reorganization of the Kuomintang," in *Komintern i Vostok: Bor'ba za Leninskuiu Strategiiu i Taktiku v Natsional'no-Osvoboditel'nom Dvizhenii* (Moscow: Glav. Red. Vost. Lit., 1969), p. 302. Kartunova states that Maring spent nine days in Kweilin and had three talks with Dr. Sun, apparently basing her statement upon Comintern archives. I am indebted to Mrs. Holubnychy for this information. In contrast, Teng Chia-yen, in "Ma-ting Yeh

Tsung-li Shih Chi" [A True Account of Maring's Visit to the Leader], KMWH, 9: 1409–11, says that Maring spent only three days in Kweilin and saw Dr. Sun twice. Teng was in Kweilin and had charge of hospitality for Maring, according to his reminiscent account. The compilers of KMWH add a note that they have seen no detailed records of the talks, but provide some further information based on secondary sources. Ibid., pp. 1411–13. Dov Bing, "Chang Chi and Ma-lin's First Visit to Dr. Sun Yat-sen," *Issues & Studies* 9, no. 6 (March 1973): 57–62, dates the Maring's stay in Kweilin from December 23 to January 1, 1922.

16. Bing, "Sneevliet and the Early Years of the CCP," pp. 681–82 uses a variety of Maring's writings and interviews dating from 1925 and 1935 when treating the Kweilin meetings; he also cites one manuscript report dating July 11, 1922, prepared by Maring for the Comintern, "Bericht des Genossen H. Maring für die Executive." This most authoritative account of Sneevliet's visit with Sun is translated in Helmut Gruber, *Soviet Russia Masters the Comintern* (Garden City: Anchor Press/Doubleday, 1974), pp. 369–72.

17. Teng, "Ma-ting Yeh Tsung-li Shih Chi," says he participated in the second meeting and recounts Dr. Sun's rejection of the idea of an alliance with Russia. When Mr. Teng wrote his account is not indicated.

18. Yu, *Party Politics in Republican China,* p. 163. Dr. Yu is more categorical than two official Kuomintang accounts of the meeting, those in KMWH, 9: 1409–13 and KFNPttp, pp. 853–55, but he used two sources I have not seen.

19. Teng, "Ma-ting," p. 1411. There is a curious item in the State Department archives which cannot be verified. The American consul general in Hong Kong transmitted a confidential document on alleged terms of a secret agreement between Sun Yat-sen and the Soviet government of Russia, which had been handed to Mr. Gale by the chief of the Intelligence Department of the Hong Kong government and which was headed "Joint Naval and Military Report Dated 3rd January 1922." There is a twenty-one line quotation of the purported agreement, after which the document states, "The above is a summary of the agreement between Soviet Russia and Sun Yat Sen sent by the latter's delegates on the 26th December 1921." This is exactly the time that Maring was with Dr. Sun in Kweilin, and it is not impossible that British intelligence agents in Canton acquired a copy of a letter through an enemy of Dr. Sun. The text appears to be a translation and it is as follows:

> The Soviet Government of Russia declare that they will assist the Chinese Republic to fight for her integrity, allowing no third nation to extend her forces into the interior. The Soviet Government will assist the South China Republic with any available equipment so that she may wage any nation [sic] which tries to check her progress or invade her territory. The development of the South China Republic had been much checked by the Japanese. Observing this, the Soviet Government of Russia had been much [these three words are struck out, obviously a typing error] will work with the South China Republic to exclude all possible Japanese interests in South China Republic. The Soviet Government would also like to bring about a complete Chinese Republic and therefore must assist the South China Republic to win the Civil War so that China can be unified. When China is uni-

fied, all the Soviet troops will withdraw from Chinese territory and open the Siberian territory for trade. After all the above movements have veeb [been] satisfactorily carried out, a big Republican movement to join all the weaker nations in the Far East bordering on the Pacific will be sent [sic] in motion. The Authorities working for this are trying to get all the weaker nations, especially China, to succeed the strong monarchical [sic] movement.

See USDS 761.93/238, dispatch, Hong Kong, Gale to Secretary of State, March 24, 1922.

20. Tsou, CKKMTSK, p. 342 and Wang Ching-wei "Political Report," p. 3855; also Conrad Brandt, *Stalin's Failure in China, 1924–1927* (Cambridge: Harvard University Press, 1958), pp. 26–27 quoting from Ssu-ma Hsien-tao, *Pei Fa Hou chih Ko P'ai Ssu Ch'ao* (Peiping, 1930), p. 45, a secondary source. In the first sources Dr. Sun is said to have telegraphed this conclusion to Liao Chung-k'ai while in the last he is reported to have told it to Mr. Liao on his return to Canton.

21. KFCC, 3: 233–35. The speech was given on January 4, 1922, in Kweilin at a reception tendered by residents from Kwangtung.

22. A Russian version of the letter was published in *Dokumenty Vneshnei Politki SSSR*, 5: 83–84, kindly translated for me by Mrs. L. Kisselgoff. Whether Dr. Sun ever received this second Chicherin missive is unclear. There is no record of its receipt in KFNP, nor have I found it mentioned in Chinese accounts of his life.

23. Whiting, *Soviet Policies in China*, pp. 78–86 offers a condensed account of the congress based upon primary sources. He mentions only one Kuomintang delegate, who was listed by the name Tao, presumably a pseudonym. The "Brief History of the Chinese Communist Party" speaks of Kuomintang members in the plural, but it mentions only Chang by name. See Wilbur and How, *Documents*, pp. 57–58. S. A. Dalin and Chang Kuo-t'ao, who attended the congress, both mention Chang Ch'iu-pai as a Kuomintang delegate. S. A. Dalin, "The Great Turn: Sun Yat-sen in 1922," in *Sun Yat-sen, 1866–1966; Sbornik Statei, Vospomananii, Materialov* [Sun Yat-sen, 1866–1966; a Collection of Articles, Reminiscences, and Materials] (Moscow: Glav. Red. Vost. Lit., 1966), p. 281; this was abstracted by Mrs. Holubnychy. Chang Kuo-t'ao, *The Rise of the Chinese Communist Party, 1921–1927: Volume One of the Autobiography of Chang Kuo-t'ao* (Lawrence, Kan.: The University Press of Kansas, 1971), pp. 188 ff. KFNP has no record of Dr. Sun appointing Chang Ch'iu-pai as a Kuomintang delegate to the Congress of Toilers; his name first appears in the index to KFNPttp for September 6, 1922.

24. Whiting, *Soviet Policies in China;* Wilbur and How, *Documents*, p. 58, where the "Brief History of the Chinese Communist Party" is explicit about the unfavorable impression caused by conditions in Russia and the rudeness of young Chinese Communists.

25. Dalin, "The Great Turn," pp. 255–57. The first talk was April 29 and the last meeting was June 12 or 14. None of this is mentioned in KFNP.

26. Dalin, "The Great Turn," p. 272.

27. Ibid., p. 269.

28. Ibid., p. 276.

29. Ibid., p. 281. It was at this time that Chang Ch'iu-pai, according to Dalin, was campaigning in Canton for an alliance with Soviet Russia.

30. Ibid., pp. 283–85.

31. KFCC, 4: 518–19, "The Attitude which Should be Taken in Foreign Relations. A Conversation with his Staff Aboard the Gunboat Mo-han, at Canton, August 9, 1922." Sun's discourse is given in literary Chinese and hence is not a verbatim record.

CHAPTER SIX THE DYNAMIC SETTING FOR ALLIANCE WITH RUSSIA

1. KFNPttp, p. 860 concerning the arrival in Kweilin of Chang Tso-lin's delegate on February 12, 1922, and p. 862 on a delegate from Tuan Ch'i-jui arriving in Canton on February 20. How negotiations with Wu P'ei-fu were conducted is not said.

2. The vice-minister for foreign affairs in the Canton government, Dr. C. C. Wu, went to Mukden to negotiate, and on his return told the American vice-consul in charge about the agreement. Chang Tso-lin would support Dr. Sun as president and Liang Shih-yi as premier, and Tuan Ch'i-jui would be vice-president. USDS 893.00/4336, dispatch, Canton, Jonston to Secretary, April 4, 1922.

   In an interview with Rodney Gilbert in Canton, Wu T'ing-fang, the foreign minister of the southern government, explained that "we tried to come to an understanding with Wu, but could get nowhere near agreement . . . [but] we had little difficulty in getting on common ground with Chang Tso-lin's representative." He added, "Whoever comes to an understanding with us will have to agree that he [Dr. Sun] be provisional president pending the convocation of a parliament and regular elections. We should make no further stipulations." Rodney Gilbert, "Dr. Wu Ting-fang Speaks Out Plainly," NCH (April 29, 1922), pp. 327–30, with the dateline Canton, April 12. In his interview with Isaac Marcosson in mid-May, Dr. Sun explained his alliance with Chang Tso-lin, "because he had an army and the desire to bring about unification . . . I would have effected the same deal with Wu P'ei-fu." Marcosson, "The Changing East: Sun Yat-sen and South China," p. 101. Mrs. Bonnie Lawrence led me to these references through her essay, "Sun Yat-sen, Ch'en Chiung-ming and the Coup d'État of June 16, 1922" (M. A. thesis, Columbia University, 1971). See a somewhat different reconstruction of the terms of the alliance in Li, *The Political History of China*, pp. 413, 420.

3. Kao Yin-tsu, comp. *Chung-hua Min-kuo Ta Shih Chi* [A Chronological Record of the Chinese Republic] (Taipei: World Book Co., 1957); pp. 95–96 for relevant events of May and June 1922. (Hereafter this work is cited as Kao, *Chronology*.) See also Li, *The Political History of China*, pp. 414, 421–22.

4. KFCC, 4: 29–32; also NCH, June 17, 1922, p. 804. "As Chief Executive of the sole *de facto* as well as *de jure* governing body of this country that is fully constituted at this moment," the manifesto said, "I have the honour to remind the Treaty Powers of their repeated pledge of non-interference in our present internal struggles and to

request them to observe the same in spirit as well as in the letter." This was subscribed:

Sun Yat-sen/ By the President
Wu Ting-fang/ Minister of Foreign Affairs.

5. USDS 893.00/4576, dispatch, Canton, Huston, June 22, 1922.

6. USDS 893.00/4493, telegram, Peking, Schurman, June 25, repeating telegram from Huston, Canton, June 23, 1922; and telegram from State to Amlegation, Peking, June 26 in reply. The American minister recommended that the consular body in Canton neither mediate nor provide good offices, for he regarded Dr. Sun as "the one outstanding obstacle to reunification." He added, "Now that nothing remains but the elimination of Sun Yat Sen, not victorious but defeated, it would seem that the undertaking should be left to the Chinese Government if Chen Chiung Ming can not or will not accomplish it." Frank P. Lockhart drafted the reply: "Department is unwilling that Consul at Canton should participate in any plan of mediation. Your views in this regard have the Department's unqualified approval."

7. USDS 893.00/4623, dispatch, Schurman to Secretary of State, July 28, 1922, enclosing Dean's circular, No. 191 dated July 7, containing dispatch of Consul General J. W. Jamieson, senior consul, Canton, June 28.

8. Ibid. Other terms concerned good treatment for Dr. Sun's followers and a sanctuary for his expeditionary force somewhere along the Kiangsi border.

9. USDS 893.00/4656, dispatch, Peking, Tenney to Secretary of State, August 12, 1922. Mr. Norman requested the American consul to arrange for an American gunboat, mentioning that the Japanese had already offered such assistance. The American consul turned this request down, and Mr. Norman then approached the British consulate, which arranged for the *Moorhen* to take Dr. Sun to the *Empress of Russia* and passage to Shanghai.

10. KFCC, 4: 32–35, dated August 15, 1922; NCH, August 19, 1922, p. 511, as carried by Reuter's, dated August 17. The Chinese version seems strongly directed toward restoring Dr. Sun's "face" and heaping bile on Ch'en Chiung-ming; it pledges to take those who uphold the Republic as friends and those who are disloyal to it as enemies. The Western version differs in some other details.

11. USDS 893.00/4651, dispatch, Shanghai, Cunningham to Secretary of State, August 22, 1922. On August 17, Mr. Cunningham reported that Gen. Ts'ao K'un was seeking an alliance with Sun against Wu P'ei-fu. Sun was to be president and Ts'ao the vice-president, and Chang Tso-lin was said to be agreeable. USDS 893.00/4652. There was, indeed, rivalry within the Chihli clique between the factions of Ts'ao and Wu, and General Ts'ao did entertain hopes of becoming president, but it seems unlikely that Ts'ao would actually enter an alliance against Wu. A rumor of the sort Mr. Cunningham forwarded, based upon the statement of "a rather well informed person," might have been intended to sow suspicions or to exert political pressure.

12. NYT, August 19, 1922, p. 5, datelined Shanghai, August 18.

13. NYT, August 22, 1922, p. 15; *Times* (London), August 25, p. 7; datelined Shanghai, August 24.

14. This is a main theme in articles on China in The *New York Times* at this time.

15. See Kao, *Chronology*, p. 103.

16. Sun to Reinsch, August 26, 1922, Paul S. Reinsch Papers, now in the State Historical Society of Wisconsin, Madison.

17. J. B. Powell, "Sun Wants U.S. to Take Up All of China's Debts," *Chicago Daily Tribune*, August 25, 1922, p. 4. Also "Sun Would Transfer China's Debt to U.S.," NYT, August 25, 1922, p. 15.

18. Wu's delegate in Shanghai was Gen. Sun Yueh. The politician Sun Hung-i was an intermediary between the two sides. Hsu Ch'ien and Chang Chi were among Sun Yat-sen's representatives for discussions with Wu. The whole topic is well discussed in a chapter of the forthcoming book on Wu P'ei-fu by Professor Odoric Wou.

19. CWR, September 23, 1922, p. 136, for a report that on September 4, Wu P'ei-fu ordered Hsiao Yao-nan, the Tupan of Hupei, to send Sun Yat-sen $100,000 to relieve his financial distress. An alliance against Chang Tso-lin was being formed "according to information received in Hankow." KFNPttp, p. 910 for word of Chang's secret contribution.

20. KFNPttp, pp. 906, 910, 913, August 21, September 17, and end of September 1922, for negotiations to open the way for part of the defeated northern expeditionary army to take Fuchow; pp. 903, 910–12, August 3, September 10 and 22, for negotiations with Chang Tso-lin and a draft plan for cooperation among the three factions against Chihli.

21. See KFCC, 5: 456–516, beginning September 5, 1922 till end of December, for letters to such commanders as Ch'en Chia-yu, Chu P'ei-te, Chang K'ai-ju, Yang Hsi-min, Lu Ti-p'ing, Liu Yü-shan, and Chiang Kuang-liang.

22. Bing, "Sneevliet and the Early Years of the CCP," pp. 685–89 and Dov Bing, "Was There a Sneevlietian Strategy?" *China Quarterly* no. 54 (April/June 1973): 350–52 (This was written to defend the earlier *China Quarterly* article, which had been attacked by A. C. Muntjewerf, in *China Quarterly* no. 53. The strategy Maring advocated was that members of the Communist Party join the Kuomintang and carry on revolutionary work within it, but without giving up their separate party identity.

23. The instructions were, "The Central Committee of the Communist Party of China according to the decision of the Presidium of Comintern of 18 July must remove its seat to Canton immediately after receiving this note and do all its work in close contact with Comr. Philips." Signed by Voitinsky for the Far Eastern Section of the Comintern and dated Moskou, July 1922. McVey, *The Rise of Indonesian Communism*, p. 79, and Bing, "Sneevliet and the Early Years of the CCP," p. 688, n. 58. "Philips" was Sneevliet/Maring's public name on this trip to China. It is surprising that Maring and Voitinsky knew so little of the coup d'etat of June 16 that they were ready to order the Central Committee of the Chinese Communist Party to move to Canton. Or did they think Ch'en Chiung-ming in control was fine?

24. Bing, "Sneevliet and the Early Years," p. 690 says Maring met Sun in Shanghai on August 25, 1922, citing a variety of later sources, several of which do not give the

date nor identify Maring. On August 30 Sun wrote to Chiang Kai-shek telling him that a representative had come bringing a letter inquiring about Far Eastern problems, which Sun had answered point by point. It is generally assumed that the writer of the letter was Joffe, and it is possible that its bearer was Maring. KFNPttp, pp. 907–08, August 25 and 30. This does not specify Maring as the person Joffe sent to call upon Sun.

25. Dr. Bing enthusiastically presses Maring's central role, but everything he cites concerning Maring's talk with Sun and about the Hangchow plenum is in the class of later reminiscences.

26. "The Brief History of the Chinese Communist Party," an inside account completed in the latter part of 1926, has the Chinese Communist Party taking the initiative in approaching Dr. Sun after his arrival in Shanghai with a proposal for interparty cooperation "while promising him all kinds of assistance." It then details steps toward the agreement. See Wilbur and How, *Documents*, pp. 61–62. Chang Kuo-t'ao, who had reason to learn the details but whose account is reminiscent, says that Ch'en Tu-hsiu, Li Ta-chao, and Maring each called upon Dr. Sun separately; but he has this happen after the West Lake plenum of the Central Committee, which he apparently misdates as on August 10, 1922. Chang, *The Rise of the Chinese Communist Party*, p. 260. There is a great deal more scholarly literature on this subject.

27. According to Chang Kuo-t'ao, ibid., those first inducted were Ch'en Tu-hsiu, Li Ta-chao, Ts'ai Ho-sen, and Chang T'ai-lei, and they were sponsored by Chang Chi. KMWH, 8: 1040–41 for Ch'en's appointment to the committee.

28. S. L. Tikhvinsky, *Sun Yat-sen: Vneshnepoliticheskie Vozzreniia i Pracktika* [Sun Yat-sen: His Views on Foreign Policy and His Practice] (Moscow: "Mezh. Otn.," 1964), pp. 264–66. I am indebted to Mrs. Holubnychy for a translation.

29. Tikhvinsky, *Sun Yat-sen: On the Occasion*, p. 30.

30. The letter appears in many collections, some in abbreviated form. A photographic reproduction is in Sun Yat-sen, *Sun Chung-shan Hsien-sheng Shou-cha Mo-chi* [Reproductions of Mr. Sun Yat-sen's Handwritten Letters] (n.p., n.d.), pp. 5–6. See also KFCC, 5: 453–54.

31. Wang Yü-chün, *Chung-Su Wai-chiao ti Hsü-mo: Ts'ung Yu-lin tao Yo-fei* [The Prelude to Sino-Soviet Relations: From Yurin to Joffe] (Taipei: Academia Sinica, Institute of Modern History, 1963), p. 335–39, for names of members of Joffe's mission.

32. Sun Yat-sen, *Sun Chung-shan Hsien-sheng Shou-cha Mo-chi*, pp. 2–3; KFCC, 5: 495–96. This letter is extensively though loosely translated in S. I. Hsiung, *The Life of Chiang Kai-shek* (London: Peter Davies, 1948), pp. 160–61.

33. A. I. Kartunova, "Sun Yat-sen—a Friend of the Soviet People," in *Voprosy Istorii KPSS* 9, no. 10 (October 1968): 32. This gives the text of the letter, with two omissions of unspecified length, as found in Russian translation in the Central Party Archives in the Institute of Marxism-Leninism, Moscow. I am indebted to Mrs. Holubnychy for a translation back into English.
The letter begins with a sensational passage in view of the fact that Sun Yat-sen and Chang Tso-lin were allies and both Chang and the Peking government were

resisting turning over control of the Chinese Eastern Railway to the Soviet government. A frustrated Joffe had made an ominous threat in a note of November 14; this denied the rumored concentration of Russian troops on the Manchurian border and alleged Red Army preparations to occupy the railway zone, since "the Red Army needs no preparations to occupy the CER." (Whiting, *Soviet Policies in China*, p. 194). Dr. Sun wrote:

> Dear Lenin,
>
> I am taking use of an opportunity in order to write you in brief about an important matter . . . [ellipsis in Kartunova's text] You could be able to force Chang Tso-lin, within limits of wisdom, to do whatever is necessary for the safety of Soviet Russia.
>
> If you follow such a policy, not only would you be able to avoid a dangerous reaction against you in China but you would also be helping me to create conditions which would facilitate and accelerate a joint work of Russia and China.

34. Kartunova, "Sun Yat-sen," p. 31; Tikhvinsky, *Sun Yat-sen: On the Occasion*, p. 31. The date of Chang Chi's trip to Peking is confused because he gave several different dates in later reminiscences. It seems, however, that he arrived after December 5, since a letter of that date from Chiao I-t'ang in Peking to Sun Yat-sen mentions Chang's expected arrival. Wang, *Chung-Su Wai-chiao ti Hsü-mo*, p. 449.

35. Chang Chi, *Chang Po-ch'uan Hsien-sheng Ch'üan Chi* (Taipei: Chung-yang Wen Wu Kung-ying She, 1951), pp. 195–96. However, this much quoted reminiscence comes from a speech by Chang Chi on September 21, 1941. An even later reminiscence, a secondhand account, is Chang Kuo-t'ao's statement that the purpose of Chang Chi's mission was to induce Soviet Russia to help the Kuomintang by supplying arms via Outer Mongolia for military action against the Peking government. Chang Kuo-t'ao, "Wo-ti Hui-i" *Ming Pao* no. 8, p. 89; or, for a less specific statement on the desired Soviet military assistance, Chang, *The Rise of the Chinese Communist Party*, 1: 267. Joffe is said to have replied that there was no possibility of carrying out this plan.

36. Lydia Holubnychy, "The Comintern and China, 1919–1923" (M.A. thesis, Columbia University, 1968), p. 71. Mrs. Holubnychy provides much detail on Soviet Russian and Comintern policies towards China. Favorable Russian attitudes towards Wu P'ei-fu are pointed out by Whiting, *Soviet Policies in China*.

37. Eudin and North, *Soviet Russia and the East*, pp. 343–44, and Jane Degras, *The Communist International, 1919–1943: Documents*, vol. 2, 1923–1928 (London: Oxford University Press, 1960), pp. 5–6. Bing, "Sneevliet and the Early Years of the CCP," pp. 692–93 for Maring's trip to Moscow.

38. NCH, October 7, 1922, p. 9.

39. FER, October 1922, pp. 603–06. Mr. Rea mentioned his long friendship with Dr. Sun; he does not, however, mention discussions with him at this time.

40. CWR, December 16, 1922, p. 88 from the *Japan Advertiser* of November 26. An independent translation of this interview—Japanese to German to English—is found in B. Nicolaevsky, "Russia, Japan, and the Pan-Asiatic Movement to 1925," *Far Eastern Quarterly* 8 (1949): 275–76. I do not find this interview in KFCC. Dr. Sun's pro-Ger-

man sentiments at the beginning of the war are confirmed in Jansen, *The Japanese and Sun Yat-sen,* pp. 206–09.

41. GBFO 371/9181/F946 [F946/12/10], dispatch, Barton, Shanghai, January 22, 1923 to H. M. Chargé d'Affaires, Peking. Sir Sidney Barton reports a call on him by Eugene Chen on January 19, when Mr. Chen told him of attending Dr. Sun's dinner for Mr. Joffe the previous evening. Other accounts of meetings in KFNPttp, p. 946 for January 22; and NCH, January 27, p. 243.

42. R. A. Mirovitskaia, "The First Decade," in *Leninskaia Politika SSSR v Otnoshenii Kitaia* [The Leninist Policy of the USSR with Regard to China] (Moscow: Nauka, 1968), pp. 25–26, based upon archives of the USSR Ministry of Defense. Kindly abstracted for me by Mrs. Holubnychy.

43. Holubnychy, "The Comintern in China," pp. 94–95, based upon I. Ermashev, *Sun Yat-sen* (Moscow: "Molodaia Gvardiia," 1964). Though appearing to quote from Joffe and Sun, Ermashev's work gives no sources. It was edited by Professor S. L. Tikhvinsky, a specialist on Sun Yat-sen.

44. GBFO F902/650/10, "Secret Report on Activities of M. Joffe in Shanghai," March 24, 1923. A few months later A. I. Gekker selected the first group of Russian military officers to go to China to serve with Dr. Sun.

45. Ibid. It is not clear whether the intelligence agents expected the Soviet aid to come after recognition, or was contingent only upon the agreement to give recognition later.

46. The statement apparently first appeared in the *China Press* of January 27, 1923. USDS 761.93/305, dispatch, Shanghai, Cunningham, Jan. 27 to Peking, Schurman, containing a clipping. The *New York Times* for January 27 carried a digest in an Associated Press article from Shanghai dated January 26, the date the declaration was issued. A Chinese translation was published in the Shanghai *Min Hsin Jih-k'an* on January 28, apparently the first Chinese version. Li, TJKTCT, pp. 145–47 and 158, n. 47. A Chinese text appeared in *Tung-fang Tsa-chih* 20, no. 2 (January 25, [sic], 1923): 9–10, together with a photograph of Mr. Joffe. Other sources, NCH, February 3, p. 289, or CYB 1924/5, p. 863.

47. According to Whiting, *Soviet Policies in China,* p. 204, the version of the agreement published in Russia left out the passage on the unsuitability of communism and sovietism in China.

48. Extensively translated in Euden and North, *Soviet Russia and the East,* pp. 231–37.

49. Quoted in part in Chiang Yung-ching, *Pao-lo-t'ing yü Wuhan Cheng-ch'üan* [Borodin and the Wuhan Regime] (Taipei: China Committee for Publication Aids and Prize Awards, 1964), p. 3. It is not clear whether Sun's letter to Chang still exists; it does not appear in KFCC, 5, among the many letters Sun wrote to political personalities at this time. It is noteworthy how scanty are the documents concerning the Sun-Joffe negotiations published by Kuomintang authorities.

50. NYT, January 28, 1923, I, pt. 2, 5: 7 and 8.

51. KFNPttp, p. 951. T'ang Leang-li, Ch'en Kung-po, and Fuse Katsuji provide bits of information but nothing substantial. T'ang Leang-li, *The Inner History of the Chinese Revolution* (London: George Rutledge and Sons, Ltd., 1930), pp. 157–58; Ch'en Kung-po, "Wo yü Kung-ch'an Tang," in *Ch'en Kung-po Chou Fu-hai Hui-i-lu Ho Pien* (Hong Kong; Ch'un-ch'iu Ch'u-pan She, 1967), p. 46; Fuse, *Soviet Policy in the Orient*, p. 200.

52. A. I. Kartunova, "Sun Yat-sen and Russian Advisers; Based on the Documents from 1923–1924," in *Sun Yat-sen, 1866–1966: Sbornik Statei, Vospominanii, Materialov* [Sun Yat-sen, 1866–1966; a Collection of Articles, Reminiscences and Materials] (Moscow: Glav. Red. Vost. Lit., 1966), p. 17; and Kartunova, "Sun Yat-sen—a Friend of the Soviet People," p. 34. Both abstracted by Mrs. Holubnychy.

53. KFCC, 4: 35–37; NCH, January 27, 1923, p. 215; NYT, January 26, p. 19; USDS 893.00/4883, Shanghai, Cunningham, to Secretary, January 27, 1923.

54. GBFO 371/9181/F649 [F649/12/10], dispatch, Barton, Shanghai, January 17, 1923 to Peking; GBFO 371/9181/F946 [F946/12/10], dispatch, same, January 22, 1923. GBFO 405/240 Confidential (12289), *Further Correspondence Respecting China*, Part 88, January–June 1923, no. 62 [F1107/12/10], Sir R. Macleay, Peking, February 28, 1923 to the Marquess Curson of Kedleston. The date of the interview is not given, but Mr. Macleay was in Shanghai from February 1 to 12.

55. Johnson to MacMurray, February 16, 1923 (the day of his talk with Eugene Chen), Nelson T. Johnson Papers, Library of Congress, Washington, D.C., based upon notes kindly given me by Dr. Dorothy Borg. Mr. Johnson summed up his view of the southern revolutionaries: "These people appear to me to be dreamers of that type that cannot make their dreams come true."

56. KFNPttp, p. 955; NCH, February 24, 1923, p. 500; Boorman and Howard, *Biographical Dictionary of Republican China*, 2: 75–76; NYT, February 20, p. 33. Dr. Sun's host was Yang Hsi-yen.

57. GBFO F67/12/10, Colonial Office to Foreign Office, January 8, 1923, enclosing Governor Stubbs's cable of January 7, in which he presented his plan to prevent Dr. Sun's return to Canton; GBFO 371/9223/F564. Paraphrase of a telegram from the governor of Hong Kong to secretary of state for colonies, February 20, 1923. In the minutes to this telegram concerning Dr. Sun's visit, Victor Wellesley found Stubbs "singularly naive" and Sir William Tyrrell thought him "not a very good judge of men." F. Ashton-Gwatkin found the account of Dr. Sun's change "not altogether convincing. Perhaps he wants to raise a loan in Hong Kong."

58. GBFO 371/9181/F1268 [F1268/12/10], dispatch, Macleay, Peking, March 10, 1923, enclosing notes by G. R. Hallifax, undated.

59. KFCC, 3: 241–43 for a summary of the address; also reported in NYT, February 21, p. 9. Even the normally hostile *North China Daily News* thought it a fine speech and commended the government of Hong Kong for giving Dr. Sun a big reception. NCH, March 10, p. 633, the "Leader" for March 6. Jen Yu-wen, "The Youth of Dr. Sun Yat-sen," appendix, pp. 21–22, reproduces clippings from *China Mail* (Hong

Kong) for Tuesday, February 20, 1923, carrying an account of the speech and its enthusiastic reception.

60. NYT, July 22, 1923, Section 7, p. 5. The date of the interview is not stated, but it was held at the heavily guarded Agricultural College, which was Dr. Sun's headquarters from March 2 till April 3. Dr. Brockman was a senior secretary of the International Committee of the YMCA.

61. GBFO 371/9181/F 1426 [F1426/1/10], enclosing dispatch, Jamieson, Canton, March 7, 1923.

62. GBFO 371/9181/F 1520, records of a conversation between Mr. S. F. Mayers and Sun Yat-sen, Canton, March 13, 1923, and with Liang Shih-yi, Hong Kong, March 16, 1923.

63. NCH, March 24, p. 587. When Sir James Jamieson paid a return call on Dr. Sun on March 20, Sun pointedly asked him if he had noted this speech on the necessity of cultivating good relations with Hong Kong and on the linking up of the Canton-Kowloon and the Canton-Hankow lines. Jamieson carried away "a distinctly favorable" impression from the talk. GBFO 371/9181/F 1574 [F1574/1/10], transmitting dispatch, Jamieson, Canton, March 21, 1923.

64. NYT, April 2, 1923, p. 2.

65. FER, 19, no. 5 (May 1923) with portrait of Dr. Sun, facing p. 287. This statement is not found in KFCC, 4, Proclamations.

66. GBFO 371/9181/F 1464 [F 1464/12/10], a series of communications dating May 9–18; and GBFO 371/9181/F 1628 [F1628/12/10], telegram, Macleay, Peking, May 28, 1923, transmitted to Colonial Office, June 4.

67. R. A. Mirovitskaia, "Mikhail Borodin (1884–1951)," in *Vidnye Sovetskie Kommunisty—Uchastiniki Kitaiskoi Revolutsii* [Outstanding Soviet Communists—The Participants in the Chinese Revolution] (Moscow: Akad. Nauk SSSR, Institut Dal'nego Vostoka, "Nauka," 1970), pp. 22–40, p. 24, based upon Soviet archives, and noted for me by Mrs. Holubnychy.

68. A. I. Cherepanov, *Zapiski Veonnogo Sovetnika v Kitae; iz Istorii Pervoi Grazdanskoi Revolutsionnoi Coiny, 1924–1927* [Notes of a Military Adviser in China: From the History of the First Revolutionary Civil War In China, 1924–1927], vol. 1 (Moscow: Academy of Sciences of the USSR, Institut Norodov Azii, "Nauka," 1964), pp. 6–7, 11. There is a "draft translation" of vol. 1 by Alexandra O. Smith, ed. Harry H. Collier and Thomas M. Williamson (Tapei: [U.S. Army] Office of Military History, 1970). I was privileged to have parts of the Russian work abstracted by Mrs. L. Kisselgoff and Mrs. L. Holubnychy. As a historical source, General Cherepanov's work must be used with care and some skepticism as to its political judgments. Some stated facts are clearly incorrect. The draft translation, unfortunately, has many errors. Hereafter this work is referred to as Cherepanov, *Zapiski*, and Draft Translation.

69. According to A. C. Muntjewerf, who had access to the Sneevliet papers in Amsterdam, the documents prove he was in Canton in May 1923, and she gives dates

from May 7 onward. There are other letters from him in June. See A. C. Muntjewerf, "Was there a 'Sneevlietian Strategy'?" *China Quarterly* no. 53 (January/March 1973): 165–66 and notes. In a reminiscent talk with Harold Isaacs in August 1935, Sneevliet remembered that on May Day 1923, he addressed a public meeting in Canton. Harold R. Isaacs, "Documents on the Comintern and the Chinese Revolution," *China Quarterly* no. 45 (January/March 1971): 108.

70. Ibid.

71. Kartunova, "The Comintern and Some Questions," pp. 304–05, quoting from Maring's letter of May 14, 1923.

72. Ibid., a letter of May 31. These were abstracted by Mrs. Holubnychy.

73. V. I. Glunin, "Comintern and the Formation of the Communist Movement in China (1921–1927)," in *Komintern i Vostok*, p. 258, gives the date as June 10–19, 1923. There is an extensive literature on this congress but very little primary documentation. Chang Kuo-t'ao, in *The Rise of the Chinese Communist Party*, 1: 296–316, discusses the debates with some rancor.

74. This is a digest of six "most important resolutions of the Third Congress" as given in "A Brief History of the Chinese Communist Party," as translated in Wilbur and How, *Documents*, p. 66.

75. Derived from the discussion in Chang Kuo-t'ao as just cited.

76. *T'an-ho Kung-ch'an Tang Liang Ta Yao-an* [Two Important Cases of Impeachment of the Communist Party] (n.p.: Kuomintang Central Supervisory Committee, September 1927), pp. 15–16; reprinted in KMWH, 9: 1279–80. The authenticity of this resolution is not in question.

77. Ch'en Tu-hsiu, *Kao Ch'üan Tang T'ung-chih Shu* [A Letter to All Comrades of the Party], December 10, 1929, as translated in *Chinese Studies in History* 3, no. 3 (Spring 1970): 224–50, 227.

78. Karakhan's appointment was announced on July 27 but presumably his selection was made some weeks earlier. The two men left Moscow on August 2, but Borodin reached Peking later than Karakhan, say in mid-September, after a stopover in Manchuria.

79. Pichon P. Y. Loh, *The Early Chiang Kai-shek: A Study of His Personality and Politics, 1887–1924* (New York: Columbia University Press, 1971), pp. 86–87 for a digest of Chiang's letter of July 13, 1923.

80. Mao Ssu-ch'eng, *Min-kuo Shih-wu Nien i-ch'en chih Chiang Chieh-shih Hsien-sheng* [Mr. Chiang Kai-shek before 1926] (n.p., n.d. [original edition, 1936]), p. 218. I have used the edition referred to as Mao B, in the work of Professor Loh, just cited. The book is often referred to as "Chiang Kai-shek's Diary." (Hereafter it is cited as Mao, CKSHS.)

81. Mao, CKSHS, p. 218. Biographies of Shen and Chang are in Boorman and Howard, *Biographical Dictionary*, but I have hunted in vain for biographical information on Mr. Wang. Aside from several mentions of him on the trip to Russia in "Chiang's

Diary," he is listed in KMWH, 10: 1468 as Kuomintang party representative in the First Training Regiment of the Whampoa Military Academy, before but not during the first eastern expedition of February–March 1925. Elsewhere I have seen him listed on the staff of Whampoa Military Academy as "Western Language Secretary." His alternate name was Wang Tsung-shan, according to scholar friends of mine in Taiwan, and he was said to have been editor of a Chinese newspaper in Canada sometime in the 1920s. He was living in Taiwan in 1970.

82. Whiting, *Soviet Policies in China*, p. 243. Karakhan showed the letter to Louis Fischer, who copied it and published part of it in his autobiography, *Men and Politics* (New York: Duell, Sloan and Pearce, 1941), p. 138. Mr. Fischer permitted Mr. Whiting to copy it from his files.

83. A. N. Kheifets, *Sovetskaia Diplomatiia i Narody Vostoka, 1921–1927* [Soviet Diplomacy and the Peoples of the Orient, 1921–1927] (Moscow: "Nauka," 1968), pp. 148–49.

84. Kartunova, "Sun Yat-sen and Russian Advisers," pp. 176–80. The dates of these meetings are confirmed in "Chiang's Diary," Mao, CKSHS, pp. 223, 231, but Chiang's account of his mission is extremely lacking in hard details. The diary account is presented in Hsiung, *The Life of Chiang Kai-shek*, pp. 175–79; and President Chiang, himself, gave another account in his *Soviet Russia in China: A Summing-up at Seventy* (New York: Farrar, Straus and Cudahy, 1957), pp. 19–23.

85. Kartunova, "Sun Yat-sen and Russian Advisers," pp. 179–80, citing a Soviet document.

86. Mao, CKSHS, pp. 222–34.

87. This resolution and Chiang's anger at reading it are mentioned in Mao, CKSHS, p. 234. It was published forty-five years later in *Kommunist* (Moscow) 45, no. 4 (March 1969): 12–14, and an English translation was issued by the Soviet news agency Novosti, New York, in April 1969. It is discussed below.

88. Chiang, *Soviet Russia in China*, p. 22; date from Mao, CKSHS, p. 233.

89. CYB 1924/5, pp. 850–53.

90. KFCC, 5: 558.

91. Fass, "Sun Yat-sen and Germany in 1921–1924."

92. Tikhvinsky, *Sun Yat-sen: On the Occasion*, p. 34. Elsewhere Professor Tikvinsky dates the telegram as September 8.

93. USDS 761.93/376, dispatch, Tientsin, Huston, September 15, 1923. This is not the sending date because the item providing the quotation came from the *North China Star*, October 6, reprinting a Rosta release datelined Peking, October 5. Professor Tikhvinsky also quotes from this telegram, evidently retranslating from the Russian; he dates it September 16.

94. Tikhvinsky, as just cited, pp. 35–36, quotations taken from USSR *Foreign Policy Documents*, 6: 435–36, presumably retranslated from the Russian. There may have

been two letters from Dr. Sun on the same day, for Professor Tikhvinsky did not use any part dealing with Chiang's mission, while Louis Fischer in copying from the letter provided by Mr. Karakhan did not quote the part used by Tikhvinsky.

95. USDS 893.00/5303. Mr. Norman's letter of September 18, 1923 was sent by John L. McNab to Senator Samuel M. Shortridge, who sent it to the secretary of state, Charles Evans Hughes.

96. NCH, October 6, 1923, p. 11, quoting the letter from Sun to Hotung of September 27.

97. USDS 893.00/5270. The recipient, Jackson H. Ralston, forwarded only part of Norman's letter on November 12, so the date of writing is not available.

98. KFNPttp, pp. 991 and 994, July 16 and August 7 for T'an's appointments. Kao, *Chronology*, pp. 125–31 and NCH, July–October, 1923, for the campaign.

99. I have gathered scattered information on the financing of this war in "Problems of Starting a Revolutionary Base: Sun Yat-sen in Canton, 1923," *Bulletin of the Institute of Modern History, Academia Sinica* (Taipei) 4, pt. 2 (1975): pp. 1–63.
   In the period April to September 1923 the Canton municipal finance office paid to the Generalissimo's Headquarters the sum of $3,975,465.94, according to published accounts in *Lu Hai Chün Ta-yüan-shuai Ta-pen-ying Kung-pao* [Gazette of the Army and Navy Generalissimo's Headquarters] 12 vols. (Reprint ed., Taipei: Committee for the Compilation of Materials on the Party History, Central Executive Committee of the Chung-kuo Kuomintang, 1969), 5: 2291–2307; 2495–2501 for day-by-day accounts for October and November 1923. Other volumes contain more accounts.

100. KFNPttp, pp. 1013–14; KFCC, 4: 95, 432 (for texts in Chinese); NCH, October 20, p. 155, dispatches from Canton, October 10; and GBFO 405–241 *Further Correspondence Respecting China*, 12469, no. 42 [F3405/12/10] containing text of telegram from Dr. Sun to Sir R. Macleay, British minister in Peking.

101. The letter was dated September 23. Karakhan showed a copy of it to Louis Fischer in Moscow, and Mr. Fischer typed out a copy, which Allen S. Whiting then copied from Fischer's file and published in *Soviet Policies in China*, p. 244. Fischer in *Men and Politics*, p. 138, says the letter was dated Moscow, September 23, 1923. This is unlikely, since Karakhan was already in Peking, but the stationery might have been printed with the Soviet Foreign Office letterhead. Actually, it is only a presumption that Borodin handed the letter to Sun. There seems to be no reference to it in the Kuomintang archives, but apparently they have been sanitized.

102. The attitude in the American State Department is typified in a statement by Frank P. Lockhart of the Division of Far Eastern Affairs written to William Phillips, under secretary of state, dated June 9, 1922, transmitting a dispatch from J. C. Huston, the American consul general in Canton who, in reporting his interview with Dr. Sun on April 29, remarked upon his pretentions and irrationality. Said Mr. Lockhart, "Sun is a serious obstacle in the way of the unification of China. He demonstrated this only a few days ago when he declined to accept Wu Pei Fu's proposals for the unification of the country and the settlement of various factional disturbances. I doubt it would be possible to suggest any solution of the trouble in China which

would be satisfactory to Sun." USDS 893.00/4402, dispatch, Canton, Huston, May 2, 1922 and attached memorandum, FPL to Mr. Phillips, June 9, 1922. Mr. Phillips subscribed, "Thanks. Very Interesting. WP."

Dr. J. V. A. MacMurray, head of the Far Eastern Division, endorsed this view a year later in forwarding to the secretary of state a memorandum prepared in the division. This pointed out that Sun's government, while advocating peaceful reunification of China, abolition of military governors, and disbandment of troops, was in actual practice engaged in warfare and "is one of the most potent factors of dissension in China." USDS 893.00/5286, memorandum and letter to secretary of state, November 19, 1923.

103. In the introduction to *The International Development of China*, Dr. Sun emphasized that negotiations with the Chinese government should be made only after a development plan had won the approval of the Chinese people, warned against trying to "do everything with the Chinese government alone," and offered the contract he had negotiated with the Pauling Company years before as a model. Sun, *The International Development of China*, p. 7.

104. Akira Iriye, *After Imperialism: The Search for a New Order in the Far East, 1921–1931* (Cambridge: Harvard University Press, 1965), pp. 47–51 discusses attitudes of the governments of the United States, Great Britain, and Japan toward Sun and the Kuomintang, focusing upon late 1924. His first two chapters discuss the policy of the powers toward China from 1922 to 1925 in the framework of results of the Washington Conference. Dorothy Borg, *American Policy and the Chinese Revolution, 1925–1928* (New York: American Institute of Pacific Relations, 1947), pp. 2–13 provides valuable background on the American position toward China in the period 1919–25, but with little reference to Dr. Sun.

CHAPTER SEVEN   WORKING WITH RUSSIAN AID

1. USDS 893.00/5318, dispatch, Canton, Jenkins, November 24, 1923, gives a total of 38,000 troops available to Sun Yat-sen against Ch'en Chiung-ming, "but may be exaggerated." The same figures in CWR, December 15, p. 113 quoting "well informed sources in Canton." On December 11, Hin Wong listed nine units of allied armies in Canton. CWR, December 29, 1923, p. 184. See also a list in KMWH, 10: 1430. A detailed and disparaging account of the military forces defending Canton at about the end of 1923 is provided by General A. I. Cherepanov, one of the first Russian military advisers sent to Canton, in his memoir published forty years later, but based partly upon contemporary Russian documents. Cherepanov, *Zapiski*, and Draft Translation, pp. 21–25.

2. On August 16, 1923, Sun wrote his minister of finance that he would need these funds in September. KFCC, 5: 555–56. On Sun's military financing, see Wilbur, "Problems of Starting a Revolutionary base." Since writing that article I have seen a collection of twenty-five orders by Dr. Sun for payments to various generals under his military government and totaling hundreds of thousands of dollars during 1923. See Hsü Shih-shen, "Important Source Materials Not Printed in *Kuo Fu Ch'üan Chi*," pp. 171–76.

3. Canton, Municipal Government, *Kwang-chow Shih Shih Cheng Pao-kao Hui-k'an, 1923* [Report of the Canton Municipal Government for 1923] (Canton: Municipal Government, February 1924), chart following p. 102; and Hin Wong in CWR, March 8, 1924, p. 58 and March 29, p. 176. On salt revenues, see CWR, February 2, 1924, p. 352, based upon Reuters from Peking (probably meaning the British legation as the source), which reports that salt revenues collected by the Canton authorities between May 1923 and the end of the year amounted to $2,828,000. Provincial revenues derived from information given by T. V. Soong to George Sokolsky, "A Visit to Hongkong and Canton," NCH, April 24, May 1, and May 6, 1926; and annual provincial figures in KMT archives, 444/19, *Ts'ai-cheng Pao-kao.*

4. NCH, October 27, 1923, pp. 254–55, "The Appalling State of Canton."

5. NCH, December 8, 1923, p. 659.

6. Liao Chung-k'ai's report to a meeting of Kuomintang comrades in Shanghai, December 9, 1923 on the situation in Canton, KMWH, 8: 1086; and *Chung-kuo Kuomintang Chou-k'an* no. 6 (December 30, 1923): p. 4, a telegram from Liao reporting from Shanghai; and ibid., no. 9 (February 24, 1924).

7. Text of two speeches in KFCC, 3: 258–69. See the picture of Dr. Sun and eighty-three other conference members in Lo, *The Pictorial Biography of Dr. Sun Yat-sen,* p. 101. On October 20, Sun addressed a meeting of the national YMCA conference in Canton, in which he revealed that the main subject of the recent Kuomintang conference had been how to weed out undesirables. He praised the character-building work of the YMCA, considered its organization a model, and urged it to train citizens in self-government. KFCC, 3: 269–81.

8. Fischer, *The Soviets in World Affairs,* 2: 636. For example, accounts of the Canton municipal finance office of money turned over to the Generalissimo's Headquarters for the months of April to September 1923 show an average of more than $660,000 per month. See *Lu Hai Chün Ta-yuan-shuai Ta-pen-ying Kung-pao,* 5: 2291–307.

9. I am indebted to the late Mrs. Lydia Holubnychy for much information on Borodin's life. She used a variety of Russian and English sources including a brief autobiography published in 1931. See also, USDS 861.44/2, dispatch, Rega, Coleman, August 24, 1927, transmitting biographical data, including a translation of Borodin's biography in the Moscow magazine, *Ogonek;* and NYT, September 3, 1953, p. 21 (obituary) and July 1, 1964, p. 5, on Borodin's rehabilitation.

10. N. Mitarevsky, *World Wide Soviet Plots* (Tientsin: Tientsin Press, n.d. [1927]), pp. 130–31. Ellipses and parenthesis in the quotation are as given. Mitarevsky was associated with the commission appointed by the Peking government to examine and translate documents seized in the raid on the Soviet embassy compound on April 6, 1927. The book attempts a systematic disclosure of Soviet activities in China based upon these documents, but in his exposition, Mitarevsky often does not identify the documents precisely or quote them completely. The book is valuable, however, because many quoted documents are not available in other collections. On the authenticity of the documents seized in the raid, see Wilbur and How, *Documents on Communism, Nationalism and Soviet Advisers in China,* pp. 8–37. In the case of the present item in Mitarevsky, there are strong grounds for deducing its reliability,

since no foreign forger in Peking in 1927 could have known that Borodin brought greetings from Karakhan; that early in October 1923, Dr. Sun still had hopes for the northward movement of his troops—that is, T'an Yen-k'ai's invasion of Hunan—; that he was awaiting word of the negotiations of his representative in Moscow—i.e., Chiang Kai-shek; nor could he have imagined Dr. Sun's specific hope to base himself on Mongolia.

The date of this meeting is not stated, but Dr. Sun gave a dinner for Borodin on October 9, at which he enquired extensively about the Russian munitions industry, according to Borodin's report mentioned in Kartunova, "Sun Yat-sen and Russian Advisers," p. 181.

11. Minutes of meetings with Communists or mixed radical groups on October 11, 13, and 17 are in Mitarevsky, *World Wide Soviet Plots*, pp. 132–33. The romanization of names of Communists have been corrected. Mitarevsky could scarcely have fabricated the names of the first Communists with whom Borodin met in Canton, T'an P'ing-shan, Juan Hsiao-hsien, and Fu Yun-yu (whom I have not identified), nor have known that Ch'en Tu-hsiu was in Shanghai at this time. He also mentions Guerman and Poliak attending the October 11 meeting. Iakov Guerman and Vladimir Poliak were the first two Russian military officers to arrive in Canton; both were there by that date.

12. GBFO F3569/650/10, dispatch, Peking, Macleay, October 30, 1923, enclosing dispatch from Jamieson, Canton, October 20. This tells of the arrival in Canton of the Soviet trade delegation, including Messrs. M. M. Borodin, Woldemar Pollak, Johann Kermann, and K. A. Stoianovitch, "accompanied by some twenty more of their fellow countrymen." (I am skeptical of the number of "fellow countrymen" as stated.) It incloses an article from the *Canton Daily News* of October 20, 1923, quoting Borodin's interview with a Chinese reporter; same in GBFO 228/3565 12423/23/4. The actual date of the interview is uncertain. The Shanghai *Shang Pao* reported from Canton, October 19, Borodin's answers to a Chinese reporter's questions, which appears to be the same interview. This was reprinted in the Communist journal, *Hsiang-tao* [The Guide] no. 45 (November 7, 1923), and is presented in translation in Warren Kuo, *Analytical History of Chinese Communist Party*, Book One (Taipei: Institute of International Relations, 1966), pp. 105–06.

13. Minutes of the meeting as given in Mitarevsky, *World Wide Soviet Plots*, p. 133. Cherepanov gives an extended account of Borodin's proposals for reorganization of the Kuomintang during his first weeks in Canton, but says nothing about his meetings with Communists. Cherepanov, *Zapiski*, 1: 31–37, Draft Translation, pp. 37–44.

14. KFNPttp, p. 1016, citing telegram in KFCC, 4: 433.

15. KFNPttp, p. 1018, citing *Kuomintang Chou-k'an* no. 1 (November 25, 1923). This journal, of which there were eight issues before the First Kuomintang Congress is valuable for the activities of the Provisional Central Executive Committee in preparing for the congress. I read issues 2–8 at Toyo Bunko in 1969; they are also available on microfilm.

The larger committee consisted of Hu-Han-min, Teng Tse-ju, Lin Sen, Liao Chung-k'ai, T'an P'ing-shan, Ch'en Shu-jen, Sun Fo, Wu T'ieh-ch'eng and Yang

Shu-k'an; the alternates were Wang Ching-wei, Li Ta-chao, Hsieh Ying-pai, Ku Ying-fen, and Hsü Ch'ung-ch'ing.

16. Mao, CKSHS, p. 229, October 26, 1923, quoting from Chiang's letter to Chicherin.

17. Tsou, CKKMT, pp. 448–49, n. 4; KFNPttp, p. 1017, which leaves out the last sentence about yoking and mounting Russia!

18. Chronological details in KFNPttp, pp. 1016–32, based on extensive use of historical accounts. There is much confirmatory detail in CWR, NCH, and Canton American consular reports, USDS 893.00/5271, 5272, and 5318, dating November 14, 16, and 24, 1923.

19. The urgency of the military situation is shown in a series of telegrams from Sun to various commanders from October 25 to November 12, 1923, in KFCC, 4: 434–38. Rodney Gilbert, "Military Operations in 1923," in CYB 1924/5, pp. 914–19, asserts (p. 915) that the Yunnanese troops besieging Huichow were bought off with $400,000 through the intermediation of Ch'i Hsieh-yuan, *Tuchun* of Kiangsu, and a member of the Chihli clique, which supported Ch'en Chiung-ming. Gilbert states that the reason Ch'en could not capture Canton was that his troops foolishly attacked the retreating Yunnanese, who turned on them and drove them off. See also NCH, December 15, 1923, p. 733, where Gilbert says the Chihli organization had already spent $1,200,000 on Ch'en Chiung-ming's campaign. USDS 893.51/4444, telegram, Peking to Secretary, December 9, 1923 for an explanation of the bribery and its failure.

20. NCH, November 17, 1923, pp. 444–46, "The Struggle for Canton," a series of reports from Canton, Hong Kong, and Peking from 31 October to November 15.

21. Mitarevsky, *World Wide Soviet Plots*, pp. 137–38. Here it is misdated as November 13, 1924, instead of 1923, which may be explained by the fact that the Russian dispatches were not always dated by year and the files discovered in the Peking raid soon became mixed. The error of a year shows that Mitarevsky was not closely familiar with Canton events. The account Borodin gave to Mr. Fischer in 1929 makes it clear that it was 1923, and since he gave exact dates for this and a subsequent meeting with Dr. Sun (November 13 and 16), it appears he had available a diary or other records. Fischer, *The Soviets in World Affairs*, pp. 636–38. Mitarevsky is confirmed (except on the year) in Cherepanov, *Zapiski*, 1: 37–43, Draft Translation, pp. 43–53. This gives more detail, obviously based upon Borodin's documents.

22. Fischer, *The Soviets in World Affairs*, pp. 637–38. There is no record of this in KFNPttp.

23. Eudin and North, *Soviet Russia and the East*, pp. 244–46; Degras, *The Communist International . . . Documents*, 2: 25–26.

24. KFCC, 3: 281–90, November 25, 1923, partially translated in Teng and Fairbank, *China's Response to the West*, pp. 264–67.

25. The speech was transcribed by T'an P'ing-shan and published in the second issue of *Kuomintang Chou-k'an*. Li, TJKTCT, p. 189, n. 124. Borodin wrote favorably of this speech to Voitinsky, a colleague in the Comintern, according to Kartunova,

"The Comintern and Some Questions", p. 308. The letter was written January 4, 1924 from Shanghai.

26. Sun Yat-sen, *Sun Chung-shan Hsüan Chi*, 2 vols., (Peking: Jen-min Ch'u-pan She, 1957), 2: 467–71, and review by Harold Schiffrin and Fang Chao-ying in *Journal of Asian Studies* 17 (February 1958), 262–65; mentioned in Leng and Palmer, *Sun Yat-sen and Communism*, p. 78. In Borodin's account, quoted by Cherepanov, *Zapiski*, 1: 42–43, Draft Translation, p. 52, Sun is pictured as telling Borodin on November 16 about the letter he was writing "to my friends in the Japanese Cabinet" urging Japan to recognize Soviet Russia.

27. Adelaide Mary Anderson, *Humanity and Labour in China; An Industrial Visit and Its Sequel (1923 to 1926)* (London: Student Christian Movement, 1928), pp. 45–47. She called on Dr. and Mrs. Sun on November 25, 1923 and gives a charming picture of their modest home on Honam.

28. KMWH, 8: 1078–79 for the most important work of the Provisional Executive Committee from records preserved in the Kuomintang archives in Taiwan; pp. 1079 for text of the proclamation, and of the draft party program dated November 20, 1923. The proclamation is translated in Milton J. T. Shieh, *The Kuomintang: Selected Historical Documents, 1894–1969* (New York: St. John's University Press, 1970), pp. 73–74.

29. Evidently Borodin did not attend all the meetings. In KFNPttp, pp. 1020–34, he is listed as present in four out of eight meetings for which attendants are given. After attending the eleventh meeting on November 27, he left for Shanghai with Liao Chung-k'ai.

30. "Petition to Impeach the Communist Party, Presented by the Kwangtung Branch of the Chung-kuo Kuomintang and Tsung-li's Criticisms and Explanations" in *T'an-ho Kung-ch'an Tang Liang Ta Yao-an*, pp. 1–11 and KMWH, 9: 1271–73. The signers were Teng Tse-ju, Lin Chih-mien, Tseng K'o-ch'i, Huang Hsin-ch'ih, Chu Ch'ih-ni, Huang Lung-sheng, Teng Mu-han, Chao Shih-chin, Lin Ta-ts'un, Wu Yung-hsin, and Ch'en Chan-mei.

31. For a biography of Teng Tse-ju see Boorman and Howard, *Biographical Dictionary*, 3: 257–59. Most of my information on the others comes from KFNPttp, which is indexed.

32. Sun Wen's handwritten reply in *T'an-ho Kung-ch'an Tang Liang Ta Yao-an*, also summarized in KFNPttp, p. 1037. It is translated in Conrad Brandt, Benjamin Schwartz, and John K. Fairbank, *A Documentary History of Chinese Communism* (Cambridge: Harvard University Press, 1952), pp. 72–73. (I have slightly altered their translation.)

33. The Military Government's side of the controversy is summarized in KFNPttp, pp. 1040–47. See CYB 1924/5, pp. 849–57 for the documents from both sides; FRUS, 1923, 1: 551–79, and 1924, 1: 409–16 for many dispatches and instructions on the American side; FRUS, 1921, 1: 491–505, for an earlier attempt of Sun's government to acquire customs revenues. GBFO 405/241 and 244, confidential. *Further Correspondence Respecting China*, July–December 1923 and January–June 1924, contain dis-

patches on the British side. For some background see Stanley F. Wright, *The Collection and Disposal of the Maritime and Native Customs Revenue since the Revolution of 1911* (Shanghai: Inspectorate General of Customs, 1925), pp. 45–47, 148–50, and 167–69; pp. 185, 186 for 1919 and 1920 payments to the Canton Military Government. NCH and NYT carried numerous news articles on the developing crisis.

34. CYB 1924/5, p. 854.

35. Based upon Macleay's dispatch from Peking, December 21, 1923 to the Marquess Curson of Kedleston, GBFO 405/244, just cited, item no. 21 [F779/3/10], which summarized the developments and inclosed important documents. This dispatch was not received till March 13, 1924, long after the crisis was over.

36. NCH, December 8, 1923, p. 665, Reuters dispatch, Canton, December 4.

37. USDS 893.51/4432 and supplement, and 893.51/4436; same in FRUS, 1923, 1: 561–62. The Navy Department instructed the chief of the Asiatic fleet to concentrate available ships at Canton and take necessary measures short of actual warfare.

38. USDS 893.00/5324, dispatch, Shanghai, Cunningham, December 6, 1923, inclosing clipping from the *North China Daily News*, same date, with Mr. Green's account of the interview on December 4. Also NYT, December 6, 1923, p. 16. NCH, December 15, pp. 769–70 carried the account at greater length.

39. USDS 893.51/4516, dispatch, Canton, Jenkins, December 10 to Peking, Schurman, in which Jenkins reports that Maurice Cohen, Dr. Sun's bodyguard, told his friend, an American vice-consul, that "Sun won't fire a shot." NYT, December 7, p. 17, carried a story from London based upon a Hong Kong dispatch, reporting that Dr. Sun promised the British commander in chief and the French admiral, noninterference with the customshouse "if the measures you take are sufficient to prevent me." On December 15, Mr. Norman, Dr. Sun's American legal adviser, told the American consul general that Dr. Sun "promises not to follow up with any forcible action for the present." USDS 893.51/4463 and FRUS, 1923, 1: 532.

40. Texts in CYB 1924/5, pp. 854–55, and FRUS 1923, 1: 568–69. The reply was dated December 12, but time of delivery was left to the discretion of the senior consul in Canton.

41. FRUS, 1923, 1: 572.

42. Ibid., pp. 571, 574, and NYT, December 19, 1923, p. 2 on demonstrations; USDS 893.51/4520, dispatch, Canton, Jenkins, December 18, on Norman's report. This also encloses Dr. Sun's appeal to the American people.

43. NYT, December 20, p. 4. Text of such a letter in KFCC, 5: 560 and KFNPttp, p. 1047, but dated December 30.

44. USDS 893.51/4471–77 for incoming telegrams beginning December 20 to end of the year, some arguing that the case is like the Boston Tea Party.

45. CYB 1924/5, pp. 855–57.

46. NYT, December 22, p. 3.

47. USDS 893.51/4521, dispatch, Canton, Jenkins to Schurman, December 20, on rumors being spread by Eugene Chen and "other extremists among Dr. Sun's ad-

herents"; 893.00/5348 containing dispatch, Canton, Jenkins, December 28 with sample of propaganda; and GBFO 371/10249/F26 [F26/26/10] on the Foreign Office critique of Governor Stubbs for his intervention between Sun Yat-sen and the diplomatic body, and Stubbs's spirited defense.

48. KFCC, 3: 308–18, dated December 21; partial abstract in Tan, *Chinese Political Thought in the Twentieth Century*, pp. 144–45, which stresses Sun's holding up the West as a model. The date of the speech was December 22.

49. USDS 893.00/5348, dispatch, Peking, January 9, 1924 transmitting dispatch of Canton, Jenkins, December 28, 1923, enclosing a report of the meeting by Professor R. C. Brownell. According to this report, Eugene Chen later tried to smooth away Dr. Sun's "erratic statements," making it appear that he had not been talking seriously in all he said about relations with Russia and India. However, Dr. Sun gave an interview to Grover Clark sometime in December, in which he expounded his theory of the coming war of the oppressed peoples of the world against the oppressors. After the victory in this war, China would be free and take a leading place in world civilization. The one chance for avoiding the catastrophe of such a war would be for the dominant powers to change their attitude toward China and treat her justly in every way. He spoke at length about the present Russian government and remarked that Russia and China were natural allies, who together would make a practically impregnable combination. Grover Clark, "World Revolutionary Talk," *Peking and Tientsin Times*, January 19, 1924, a clipping in USDS 761.93/445, dispatch, Tientsin, Huston, January 24, 1924.

50. GBFO 405/244, confidential. *Further Correspondence Respecting China*, January–June 1924, item 24 [F568/568/10], Peking, Macleay, January 10, 1924, transmitting a resume of Sun's remarks, provided to Macleay by the counselor of the U.S. legation. The ultimate source is not stated, but there are enough differences from the other statement to make it appear to be a separate account.

51. Schurman to The President, Peking, April 8, 1924, Papers of Jacob Gould Schurman in Cornell University Libraries, Ithaca, N.Y. p. 10. A copy was kindly provided me by Dr. Dorothy Borg. It gives a most unflattering picture of Dr. Sun.

52. USDS 861.01/793, telegram, Peking, Schurman to Secretary of State, February 16, 1924.

53. USDS 893.51/4519, telegram, Peking, Schurman to Secretary of State, January 29. He did not mention the proposal in his dispatch of January 8, which concerned mostly the customs crisis. USDS 893.51/5405.

54. NYT, January 12, 1924, p. 1. When queried on the story, the secretary of state refused to comment, but it was pointed out "in official circles" that the American government was "not prepared to push the cause of any faction in China," NYT, January 14, p. 3.

55. I could find no dispatch on the subject; the proposal is not mentioned in FRUS; and Minister Schurman did not mention it in his letter to President Coolidge, just cited. Furthermore, in December 1926, the American minister to Peking had a search made of the legation files but could find no report of Dr. Sun's proposal. See next note.

56. Late in 1926, Hallet Abend, in a series of articles on Canton, reported Dr. Sun's proposal to Dr. Schurman and its neglect. Dr. J. V. A. MacMurray, then the American minister, who had been head of the Far Eastern Division of the State Department in 1924, did not recall any report about the proposal, and after a fruitless search of the legation files he wrote Douglas Jenkins, who had accompanied Dr. Schurman on the visit to Dr. Sun. Mr. Jenkins replied on January 12, 1927, that he had not written a memorandum on the interview because he thought Dr. Schurman would do so. He then recalled what he remembered about it, ending the account with the sentence quoted. Copies of the letters are in the JVA MacMurray Papers in the Princeton University Library, Princeton, N.J., and were kindly provided me by Dr. Borg.

As he recalled in his autobiography, Hallet Abend had gotten the story from "an ousted Canton official" then in Hong Kong. I suspect this was C. C. Wu, who had participated in the Sun-Schurman interview. Mr. Abend said he followed up by pressing Consul General Jenkins for confirmation. Sun's purported plan called for joint military occupation of all provincial capitals by the invited powers, and military control of all railways, rivers, ports, and telegraph. Experts from the United States and Europe should work in China for five years to advise on military matters, railways, finance, flood control, public health, education, etc. with both the central and provincial governments. In the fifth year of the tutelage, national and provincial elections would be held and then control would gradually be handed over to the leaders chosen by the people. Mr. Abend believed (probably erroneously) that full details were in the State Department files and that Washington had sounded out several European capitals but that nowhere was the proposal seriously entertained. Hallet Abend. *My Life in China, 1926–1941* (New York: Harcourt, Brace & Co., 1943), pp. 23–25. This was called to my attention by Professor Yoshihiro Hatano.

Mrs. Sharman also describes Dr. Sun's proposal to Minister Schurman, though she dates it in the spring of 1923, which cannot fit Dr. Schurman's travel schedule. She does not indicate how she learned the details but believes it was seriously made. Sharman, *Sun Yat-sen*, p. 250.

57. KFCC, 4: 526; KFNPTttp, p. 1051, where dated January 12, 1924.

58. Sharman, *Sun Yat-sen*, p. 253. She does not give the source of the quotation, but was, herself, very close to the YMCA in China.

59. There is an extensive literature on the First Kuomintang Congress. Official minutes were printed in Canton in 1924, as *Chung-kuo Kuomintang Ch'üan-kuo Tai-piao Ta-hui Hui-i-lu* (n.p., n.d. [Canton, 1924]), 66 pp. A copy is in the Library of Congress. Toyo Bunko in Tokyo has *Chung-kuo Kuomintang Ch'üan-kuo Tai-piao Ta-hui T'e Hao* [Special Edition on the National Congress of the Kuomintang], no. 3 (Canton, January 30, 1924), which has much information on the first two days of the congress. My main source is KMWH, 8: 1077–1100 on preparations; 1100–1160 for lists of delegates, election of central committees, opening and closing speeches by Dr. Sun, texts of main resolutions, proclamation, program, party constitution, and day-by-day agenda. Based upon archives, this Kuomintang publication is quite selective in what it reveals about the congress. KFCC, 3: 340–64 gives texts of eight speeches by Dr. Sun. The main events are summarized in KFNPttp, pp. 1053–70.

60. USDS 893.00/5375, dispatch, Canton, Jenkins, to Secretary of State, January 23, 1924. Karakhan's telegram is found in Chinese in KFNPttp, p. 1058.

61. KFNPttp, pp. 1060, 1063, and 1065 for the telegrams.

62. KFCC, 3: 348. This speech is translated in Sun Yat-sen, *Fundamentals of National Reconstruction* (Taipei: China Cultural Service, 1953), pp. 156–64.

63. Ibid., 353–56. A similar report of the speech is in Cherepanov, *Zapiski*, 1, Draft Translation, pp. 82–84. It seems that the two are derived from separate transcripts.

64. Cherepanov, *Zapiski*, 1: 67–71, Draft Translation, pp. 85–92. Cherepanov states that his account quotes Borodin's notes; I presume they were written at the time.

65. As printed in KMWH, 8: 1125–36, the declaration includes the program. The opposition of Tai Chi-t'ao and Hu Han-min to the more radical proposals of Borodin, and his subsequent hatred for Tai, are discussed by Herman Mast III and William G. Saywell, "Revolution Out of Tradition: The Political Ideology of Tai Chi-t'ao," *Journal of Asian Studies* 34, no. 1 (November 1974): 85.

66. This is problematic because it is not known exactly when certain individuals joined the Chinese Communist Party. I count five of the appointed delegates as Communists—Shen T'ing-i, Yü Shu-te, Ch'en Tu-hsiu, T'an P'ing-shan, and Li Ta-chao; and the following fifteen elected delegates (in the sequence listed in KMWH, 8: 1101–02)—Lin Tsu-han, Lo Mai (real name Li Wei-han), Hsia Hsi, Yüan Ta-shih, Mao Tse-tung, Liu Po-lun, Hsüan Chung-hua, Han Lin-fu, Yü Lan-chu (Fang-chou), Ch'en Ching-hu, Wang Chin-mei, Liu Fen (Po-ch'ui), T'an K'o-min, Li Lung-chih (Li-san), Liao Kan-wu. However, it is uncertain that all attended. For example, Chang Kuo-t'ao was elected as a delegate from Peking, and attended one day's meetings, but is not listed; and he says that Ch'en Tu-hsiu, who is listed, remained in Shanghai during the congress. Chang, *The Rise of the Chinese Communist Party*, 1: 327–34.

67. Cherepanov, *Zapiski*, 1: 78–79, Draft Translation, 99–100.

68. The text in Li's own band and a printed version are given in KMWH, 9: 1243–54. It has been partially translated in Chiang, *Soviet Russia and China*, pp. 26–28.

69. Accounts of the debate, based upon minutes of the congress are in Chiang, "Hu Han-min Hsien-sheng Nien P'u Kao," p. 200; and Li, TJKTCT, pp. 176–82. Both summarize some of the speeches. Also Cherepanov, *Zapiski*, 1: 79–81, Draft Translation, pp. 102–04.

70. KMWH, 8: 1146–47, chapter 13 of the constitution.

71. Ch'en, *The Communist Movement in China*, p. 125, appendix 4, "The Decisions of the Second Congress of the Communist Party of China 1922": (6) Decision concerning the Labor Union Movement and the Chinese Communist Party, Number 18.

72. KMWH, 8: 1105. It is fair to point out that T'an, Shen, and Lin had worked with Sun before joining the Communist Party.

73. KMWH, 8: 1161–63; KFNPttp. pp. 1070–71; Tsou, CKKMTSK, pp. 401–02, for some differences. Some bureaus were added and then dropped, and the Investigation Bureau—a sort of secret intelligence arm?—was abolished, 'tis said.

74. KFNPttp, pp. 1060–62 gives an account of Sun's method of lecturing and his revision of the transcripts. He described his method in the preface to the first series,

dated March 30, 1924. See KFCC, 1, texts, page 1. *Chung-kuo Kuomintang Chou-k'an* began publishing the lectures in issue no. 11, March 9, 1924, and running through no. 30, July 20 with the sixth lecture on democracy. The work has been translated several times into English. The most reliable translation is that of Paschal M. d'Elia, S.J., *The Triple Demism of Sun Yat-sen* (Wuchang: The Franciscan Press, 1931). The reader should beware of abridged versions.

75. For a very different emphasis in selection see, Wu, *Sun Yat-sen*, chapter 12 on "The Principle of Nationalism."

76. Quotations from KFCC, 1: 8, 9.

77. Borodin was still in Canton on the date, February 9, 1924.

78. KFCC, 1: 38 for quotations.

79. Ibid., pp. 65, 66.

80. Ibid., p. 72.

81. Obviously this is an inadequate summary of the six lectures on democracy in KFCC, 1: 73–175 and d'Elia, *The Triple Demism of Sun Yat-sen*, pp. 211–400. The orations mentioned are in KFCC, 3: 372–417.

82. KFCC, 1: front matter, pp. 1–15 in Sun Wen's own hand. Also, Sun, *Fundamentals of National Reconstruction*, pp. 9–16, with texts in Chinese and English translation.

83. Kartunova, "Sun Yat-sen and Russian Advisers," p. 181, quotes a December 1923 report from Borodin on the good relations he had established with Dr. Sun: "In all of my speeches I stressed the extreme importance of the leading role of Sun Yat-sen in the national-revolutionary movement in China, and by doing so I was proving to him our wishes to strengthen his position as a leader."

84. Tsou, CKKMTSK, p. 449, n. 7; Tsui, "The Influence of the Canton-Moscow Entente," CSPSR 20 (April 1936): 110–111; and Li, TSJKTCT, pp. 264–66.

85. Tsou, CKKMTSK, pp. 447–48, and 457–58, nn. 20, 21. Tsou estimates that in the first half of 1924, party expenses ran above $30,000 per month, and he gives a long list of subsidies from the party, mostly for journals. Eugene Chen categorically denied that the Soviet government or its representatives had promised or paid any money to Dr. Sun or the Canton government. See his written answers to questions by the *Hong Kong Telegraph*, published March 20, 1924, as reported by Jenkins to Schurman, March 24 in USDS 761.93/467.

86. C. Martin Wilbur, "Forging the Weapons: Sun Yat-sen and the Kuomintang in Canton, 1924," mimeographed (New York: East Asian Institute of Columbia University, 1966), pp. 72–77, based primarily upon Mao, CKSHS; KMWH, 10: 1429–70, 11: 1764–76 (a chronology); Cherepanov, *Zapiski*, 1, pp. 90–107, Draft Translation, pp. 115–32. Also Roderick L. MacFarquhar, "The Whampoa Military Academy," [Harvard] *Papers on China* 9 (August 1953): 146–72; Richard B. Landis, "The Origins of Whampoa Graduates Who Served in the Northern Expedition," reprint from *Studies on Asia 1964* by Modern Chinese History Project, Far Eastern and Russian Institute University of Washington, Reprint Series No. 19; and F. F. Liu, *A Military His-*

tory of Modern China 1924–1949 (Princeton: Princeton University Press, 1956), pp. 8–24.

87. Mao, CKSHS, p. 250 for the resignation. Liu, *A Military History*, p. 9, asserts, but without a substantiating source, that at the first meeting on February 6, Chiang and the Soviet advisers differed substantially on the curriculum and management of the academy, so Chiang indignantly resigned in protest. However, Mr. Liu has a serious anachronism in stating that Galin and Borodin made the Russians limit their demands, for Galin did not arrive in Canton till October 1924.

Professor Loh's careful study shows that Chiang was dissatisfied with many aspects of the Canton situation when he resigned, and he would not return till satisfied in various demands. Loh, *The Early Chiang Kai-shek*, pp. 90–96. Cherepanov, *Zapiski*, 1, pp. 85–86, Draft Translation, pp. 110–111, speculates on Chiang's reasons, but the treatment is drenched with a hostile bias.

88. Mao, CKSHS, pp. 253, 272; quotation from Loh, *The Early Chiang Kai-shek*, p. 96.

89. Mao, CKSHS, p. 288. The Provincial Finance Office, the Canton municipal government and the Army Estimates Office were each to contribute $5,000 per month, and the Public Safety Bureau, $15,000. Yü Fei-p'eng, a member of the preparatory committee and later second in charge of the academy's military supply department, states that monthly running expenses were set at $30,000. See his "Reminiscences on the Founding of Whampoa Military Academy," in KMWH, 10: 1453.

90. *The National Revolutionary Army. A Short History of its Origins, Development and Organization*. This is a translation of a Soviet document found in the Soviet military attaché's office in Peking on April 6, 1927. Its latest date is March 1926, and it was written in Canton to survey the work of the Russian military advisers from 1923 on. The translation was printed in GBFO 405/255, confidential. *Further Correspondence Respecting China*, October–December, 1927, no. 6, enclosure 2. It is also found in GBFO 371/12440 [F8094/87/10]. The statement is on p. 5 of the version in confidential print. Fischer, *The Soviets in World Affairs*, 2: 640. Mitarevsky, *World Wide Soviet Plots*, p. 39, quotes from a letter from Moscow, March 17, 1925 to Peking, which stated that Galen had been given R100,000 for the upkeep of the school for two months, but this was when the academy had grown.

91. Cherepanov, one of the first three Russian instructors, mentions other arrivals by name in his *Zapiski*, 1, pp. 107, 111, Draft Translation, pp. 140, 146.

92. The ceremonies are described in KFNPttp, pp. 1094–95, and Mao, CKSHS, pp. 298–99; the speech is printed in KFCC, 3: 428–39.

93. A brief biography of Pavel Andreevich Pavlov is in A. V. Blagodatov, *Zapiski o Kitaiskoi Revolutsii 1925–1927 gg* [Notes on the Chinese Revolution, 1925–1927] (Moscow: Academy of Sciences of the USSR, Institute of Oriental Studies, "Nauka," 1970), p. 120. Mrs. Holubnychy made an abstract translation of this work for me.

94. NCH, June 21, 1924, p. 480 lists Mr. Govoroff and Mr. and Mrs. Borodin and child sailing from Shanghai for Canton on the S.S. *Linan* on June 15. If this is correct, they could have not attended the opening ceremonies at Whampoa. KFNPttp, p. 1104 lists the Russian, "Kao-ho-lo-fu," as advisor to the military council, appointed on July 11.

95. Pavlov's work is described in Cherepanov *Zapiski*, 1, pp. 100 and 105–07, Draft Translation, 131–32, and 137–40. The drowning was reported in NCH, July 26, 1924, p. 129, and CWR, August 9, p. 338. Dr. Sun ordered a public funeral.

96. The first name and patronymic were taken from the names of his sons, Zoya and Vsevold, and the surname from his wife, Galina. See Kasanin, *China in the Twenties*, p. 177.

97. There is much conflicting information on the quantity of the arms. A note in Mao, CKSHS, p. 336 says the shipment, which the Generalissimo's Headquarters had agreed to purchase, included mountain cannon, field guns, rifles and pistols, heavy and light machine guns, and ammunition for all. In Chiang, *Soviet Russia in China*, p. 257, it is stated that during 1924 "when our revolutionary government in Canton was threatened by a revolt, we accepted Soviet Russia's proffered military aid, totalling some 3,000 tons of material." The contemporary press in Hong Kong mentioned 2,000 rifles and seven field pieces, or 5,000 rifles and five field guns, according to a personal communication from Professor Walter Gourlay. Wang Po-ling, an important Whampoa figure, remembered long after that there were 8,000 rifles with 500 rounds for each. Liu, *A Military History*, p. 14. George Sokolsky learned in March 1926 that the first shipment consisted of 12,000 rifles and 40 field pieces—all free of charge. Sokolsky, "A Visit to Hong Kong and Canton." Cherepanov in *Zapiski*, 1, pp. 110–11, Draft Translation, p. 146, lists nine of the new officers; he says the ship arrived October 8, 1924.

98. See Sun's handwritten instructions to Chiang on October 3, when he learned the Russian vessel was nearing Canton, in Mao, CKSHS, p. 335; KMWH, 10: 1481–82; KFCC, 5: 571.

99. KFNPttp, p. 1108 for the appointment of Soong, and p. 1111 for the appointment of trustees. NCH, August 23, p. 287 for the announcement of capital, and KFCC, 3: 447–52 for the speech of August 16, 1924. It is translated in Sun Yat-sen, *Fundamentals of National Reconstruction*, pp. 165–175. A recent Russian scholar gave the exact figure, Ch $10 million, as the amount Moscow agreed to grant the Canton government as a loan to establish the Central Bank. See Ermashev, *Sun Yat-sen*, p. 295. I am indebted to Mrs. Holubnychy for this information.

I doubt that the claimed capital actually was transferred to Canton, because it would have to be moved through international monetary channels, which would not escape the notice of the foreign diplomatic and banking community. In September 1924, the American consul general in Canton, Douglas Jenkins, learned from the manager of the International Banking Corporation that the Soviet group in Canton had received remitances of HK $250,000 during the past eight weeks. He was unable to trace the money beyond its recipients, Mr. Vladimir Poliak and Mr. A. N. Gilko, except that $30,000 was recently paid by Mr. Poliak to the Central Bank. Mr. Jenkins believed the money was used to buy furniture and fixtures for the head office; he doubted that the bank's capital had been subscribed and said it was known to have little funds. USDS 893.00B/125, Canton, Jenkins, September 18, 1924 to Edward Bell, chargé in Peking.

100. For resistance and then acceptance of the bank's note issue, see NCH, August 30, p. 333; CWR, September 6, p. 26, and November 15, p. 348.

101. Translated in Eudin and North, *Soviet Russia and the East,* pp. 344–46; also Degras, *The Communist International,* 2: 25. Italics in original. This directive did not reach Canton in time for the Chinese Communist Party Congress. The directive is independently translated and discussed in Holubnychy, "The Comintern and China," pp. 105–14.

102. See above, pp. 176–77, 192, 208.

103. Biographies of Lin Po-ch'ü, whose *hao* was Tsu-han, in Boorman and Howard, *Biographical Dictionary,* 2: 377–79, and Donald W. Klein and Anne B. Clark, *Biographic Dictionary of Chinese Communism, 1921–1965,* 2 vols. (Cambridge: Harvard University Press, 1971) 1: 567–73. Boorman and Howard give 1882 as the date of Lin's birth, while Klein and Clark give 1886.

104. KFNPttp, p. 1084, gives the dates of P'eng Su-min's nomination as April 14, 1924 and appointment as April 17, 1924. P'eng died on or before August 11, 1924 and was succeeded by Li Chang-ta, who was then succeeded by Huang Chü-su on October 20. Huang was apparently forced out, and one of Dr. Sun's last appointments was to put Liao Chung-k'ai in charge of the bureau on November 11, 1924. See KFNPttp, pp. 1113, 1141, 1149, 1152.

105. Biographies of P'eng Pai (or P'ai) in Boorman and Howard, *Biographical Dictionary,* 3: 71–73; Klein and Clark, *Biographic Dictionary,* 2: 720–24; and Eto Shinkichi, "Hai-lu-feng—The First Chinese Soviet Government," *China Quarterly* nos. 8 and 9 (1961 and 1962): 160–83, 149–81. Peng's "Report on the Haifeng Peasant Movement" has been translated by Donald Holoch in *Seeds of Peasant Revolution, Report on the Haifeng Peasant Movement by P'eng P'ai* (Ithaca: Cornell University China-Japan Program, 1973).

P'eng Pai was twenty-seven years old when he became secretary of the bureau. After the split between the Kuomintang and the Chinese Communist Party, he was arrested on August 24, 1929 in the Shanghai International Settlement and turned over to national government authorities, who executed him on August 30. He died a martyr for the Communist cause when not yet thirty-three years old.

106. This sharply condenses Lo Ch'i-yüan, "Pen Pu I Nien Lai Kung-tso Pao-kao Kai-yao" [Abbreviated Report of the Past Year's Work of this (Farmers) Bureau], *Chung-kuo Nung-min* no. 2 (February 1926): 147–207 and no. 3 (March 1926): 155–59. Lo Ch'i-yüan (or Lo I-yüan as the name is given by some) was a Communist and succeeded P'eng Pai as secretary of the bureau.

This report, prepared for the Second Kuomintang Congress, provides many important details on the famers' movement, though rather little for the period before Dr. Sun's departure. P'eng, Lo, and Juan Hsiao-hsien were the "big three" of the farmers' movement in Kwangtung until about mid-1926. For a biography of Lo, see Boorman and Howard, *Biographical Dictionary,* 2: 427–28. He was captured and executed in July 1931 when about thirty-eight years old.

107. Lo, "Pen Pu I Nien Lai," p. 174.

108. Chou Fu-hai, who was a Communist in 1924, alleges that the entrance examinations for the first class were read in the home of T'an P'ing-shan and that those of non-Communists were rejected immediately. Chou Fu-hai, "T'ao-ch'u-la Ch'ih Tu

Wu-Han chih Pao-kao" [Report of My Escape from the Red Capital, Wu-Han] (originally published in 1927), reprinted in *Ch'en Kung-po Chou Fu-hai Hui-i-lu Ho Pien* (Hong Kong: Ch'un-ch'iu Ch'u-pan She, 1967), p. 150. Tsou Lu makes the same assertion in Tsou, CKKMTSK, p. 407.

109. Lo, "Pen Pu I Nien Lai," pp. 167–86. There is great detail on students of the second class, their curriculum, and their training activities, for Mr. Lo was director of that session of the Institute.

110. *Chung-kuo Kuomintang Chou-k'an* no. 36 (August 31, 1924), and KFCC, 3: 460–64. Parts of the speech are abstracted in Hsü, *Sun Yat-sen: His Political and Social Ideals,* pp. 23–24.

111. Chung-kuo Kuomintang, "Ko-ming Cheng-fu tui-yü Nung-min Yün-tung Ti-i-tz'u Hsüan-yen" [First Proclamation of the Revolutionary Government on the Farmers' Movement] in *Chung-kuo Kuomintang Chung-yao Hsüan-yen Hui-pien* [A Collection of Important Announcements of the Chung-kuo Kuomintang] (n.p.: Tang I Yen-chiu Hui, May 1929), pp. 347–51. Dated in table of contents as June 19, 1924. Lo, "Pen Pu I Nien Lai," p. 159, says the Kuomintang Farmers' Bureau proclaimed a constitution for associations in July 1924, but I have not found it. A much more elaborate constitution was adopted by the Kwangtung provincial farmers' association at its founding congress in May 1925, but by then there had been considerable development in the movement.

112. *Kwangtung Nung-min Yün-tung Pao-kao* [Report on the Kwangtung Farmers' Movement] (n.p.: n.p., October 1926), p. 124. The report gives considerable detail about how the Chinese Communist Party Farmers Committee directed the apparatus, but it mainly concerns periods after November 1924.

113. KFNPttp., p. 1104. Other members of this Kuomintang committee were Ku Ying-fen, Kan Nai-kuang, and P'eng Pai. Borodin's continuing interest in the farmers' movement is well established.

114. *Chung-kuo Kuomintang Chou-k'an,* no. 42, from Roy Hofheinz, Jr., "Peasant Movement and Rural Revolution: Chinese Communists in the Countryside 1923–1927" (Ph.D dissertation, Harvard University, 1966), p. 68.

115. The above information and what follows in the next paragraph is based upon my study of the beginnings of the farmers' movement in Kwangtung, a manuscript on deposit in the China Documentation Center, International Affairs Library, Columbia University, which brings together a variety of scattered information for the period up to May 1925, when the Provincial Farmers' Association was established.

116. Kwang-ning, which is discussed here, and Hai-feng county, when P'eng Pai was able to return on the heels of the first eastern expedition and revive his suppressed associations in March 1925.

117. The following abbreviates nine pages of the above manuscript. The principal sources are Ts'ai Ho-shen, "Chin Nien Wu I chih Kwangtung Nung-min Yün-tung" [The Kwangtung Farmers' Movement on May First This Year], HTCP, no. 112 (May 1925): pp. 1030–36, section five, entitled "A Reminiscence of the Kuang-ning Farmers' Tide"; *Kwangtung Nung-min Yün-tung Pao-kao,* pp. 64–83, 98–100; and *Ti-i-tz'u Kuo-*

nei Ko-ming Chan-cheng Shih-ch'i ti Nung-min Yün-tung [The Farmers' Movement during the Period of the First Revolutionary Civil War] (Peking: Jen-min Ch'u-pan She, 1953), pp. 139–47. Professor Hofheinz also devoted a chapter to this situation in his dissertation.

118. This is charged by Tsou Lu, who says that Borodin created a special military unit made up of troops from several extra-provincial forces and the armored car unit of the generalissimo's palace which he sent to assist the Kwang-ning farmers' association against the local *min t'uan*. However, he does not date this. He says that thereafter Borodin often used this force to oppose *min t'uan* that were fighting farmers' associations. Tsou, CKKMTSK, p. 408. A Communist source, *Kwangtung Nung-min Yün-tung Pao-kao*, p. 81, states that it was at Borodin's suggestion that troops were sent by Canton to Kwang-ning, but within the time frame of its narrative this seems to come after Borodin left Canton about mid-November 1924 (see below).

119. The most frequently cited source on this congress is Teng Chung-hsia, *Chung-kuo Chih-kung Yün-tung Chien Shih* [A Brief History of the Chinese Labor Movement] (Moscow: 1930, and many times reprinted. n.p.: Hua Chung Hsin Hua Shu-tien, April 1949), pp. 52–58. Teng was one of the Communist organizers. Chang Kuo-t'ao gives a reminiscent description in *The Rise of the Chinese Communist Party*, 1: 226–38. A very different account is given in a Kuomintang compilation, *Chung-kuo Lao-kung Yün-tung Shih* [A History of the Chinese Labor Movement] 5 vols. (Taipei: Chung-kuo Lao-kung Fu-li Ch'u-pan She, 1959), 1: 201–02. There is a judicious reconstruction in Chesneaux, *The Chinese Labor Movement*, pp. 185–87.

120. Descriptions of Canton labor conditions prior to 1923 are given in the works cited above. In addition I have used for this paragraph two most interesting contemporary works: G. C. Denham, "Anarchism and Communism in Canton and its Connection with the Labour Movement," GBFO 371/8040 [3215/2646/10], with covering letter dated Shanghai, July 25, 1922. This has four appendices, on the Canton Socialist Young Men's Association, Anarchist societies, labor societies, and Chino-Korean societies. Mr. Denham was an intelligence officer. Written independently is a fine dispatch from J. Calvin Huston, American consul general in Canton, "The Recent Rise of Labor Unions and the Growth of Chinese Socialism in Canton under the Aegis of the Kuo Ming Tang." USDS 893.5043/1, Canton, June 28, 1922.

There is a valuable list of Kwangtung and Canton labor organizations formed up to 1927, with brief descriptions in Jean Chesneaux, *Les Syndicats chinois 1919–1927* (Paris: Mouton, 1965), pp. 27–35.

121. Information on Hsieh in Huston's despatch, cited in the previous note. The two were acquainted. Hsieh studied at Columbia in 1915 and also at the Rand School in New York. He had an American wife, formerly Miss Hurd. Huston transmitted a copy of a letter Hsieh had written to the American Socialist Party, apparently late in 1921, giving an account of his life and work since leaving the United States in 1916. He was forty years old in 1922.

122. Huston's dispatch, pp. 13–15 and Denham, "Anarchism and Communism," appendix A. According to Chow Tse-tsung, *Research Guide to the May Fourth Movement* (Cambridge: Harvard University Press, 1963), p. 111, Hsieh Ying-pai presided at this founding meeting on March 14, 1922.

123. See above, p. 174.

124. Among those who left Canton in the summer of 1922 over this conflict were Huang Huan-t'ing, Ma Chao-chün, Hsieh Ying-pai, and Ch'en Ping-sheng.

125. For example, on May 5, 1923, labor unions joined in a great celebration of Sun's return, bypassing Labor Day in favor of the second anniversary of his inauguration as president in 1921. In October, Canton unions publicly protested Ts'ao K'un's inauguration as president in Peking and his recognition by the foreign powers. In December, during the Customs Crisis, some Canton unions joined in demonstrations supporting Sun and sent telegrams appealing to workers in foreign countries that had sent gunboats to Canton. See NCH, May 12, 1923, p. 363; May 19, passim; CWR, November 3, 1923; and NCH, January 12, 1924.

126. See below, p. 233 and n. 10 for chapter 8.

127. *Chung-kuo Lao-kung Yün-tung Shih*, 2: 289–90 for a description of Liao Chung-k'ai's preparation, the parade, and pp. 290–97 for Dr. Sun's speech. Also KFCC, 3: 418–25. An abstract appears in Hsü, *Sun Yat-sen*, pp. 21–22. Strangely, KFNPttp completely skips this May Day activity. Léon Wieger, *Chine moderne*, 5 (Hsien-hsien [Hopei]: n. p. 1924), pp. 267–70, gives an account of May Day meetings at Canton and other cities, translates a song for that day and a labor song.

128. NYT, May 14, 1924, p. 11: May 15, p. 19; May 16, pp. 10, 18 (editorial); May 17, p. 3 (denial); NCH, May 17, p. 246; May 24, pp. 286, 287; CWR, May 17, 1924, p. 435; USDS 893.44 Sun Yat-sen/1, Peking, Bell, to Secretary of State, May 15, 1924. Sun went to White Cloud Mountain to recuperate on May 21, 1924 and returned on May 27, recovered. See KFNPttp, pp. 1089–90.

129. *Kwang-chow Shih Kung-jen Tai-piao Hui Chüeh-i-an* [Resolutions of the Conference of Workers' Delegates of Canton City] (Canton: Labor Bureau of the Central Executive Committee of the Chung-kuo Kuomintang, May 1924). There are sixteen resolutions and the speech given by Dr. Sun on May Day. Pictures are dated May 1 and 8, which may indicate the dates of the conference. Seen in the Kuomintang archives, no. 447/155. See also, Chesneaux, *The Chinese Labor Movement*, p. 246.

130. *Chung-kuo Lao-kung Yün-tung Shih*, 2: 299–300.

131. Teng, *Chung-kuo Chih-kung*, p. 95 asserts that it had great influence. Chesneaux considered the conference to mark a turn for the trade union movement in South China, basing his judgment on a 1924 article by Voitinsky. See Chesneaux, *The Chinese Labor Movement*, pp. 246–47. McVey, *The Rise of Indonesian Communism*, p. 217 and notes, paints a disparaging picture of the conference based on accounts by Tan Malaka, who attended as an Indonesian delegate.

132. The name in Chinese is Fan Hung T'ai. A monument was erected to his memory in Canton in January 1925, with an inscription written by Hu I-sheng. Translations of the eulogy are given in NCH, May 9, 1925, p. 229, and Wieger, *Chine moderne*, 6: 162–63. On the bomb incident see NYT, June 20, 1924, p. 1; June 21, 1924, p. 15; NCH, June 28, p. 486.

133. On the background of the strike and details concerning it, see GBFO 371 F3481/19/10, "Report by Commodore, Hong Kong, for July 1924," sent to Foreign Of-

fice, October 14, but dated August 7, before the strike was settled; also a large file from the Foreign Office F259/259/10 sent to the Colonial Office, and filed under 129/490 CO 4303. American consular reports in USDS 893.5045/39–46, telegrams and dispatches from Jenkins in Canton, July 14–August 19, 1924; and 893.00/5468, 5469, 5470, and 5474, telegrams, Peking, Bell to Secretary of State, July 17, 19, 23, and August 1, 1924. NYT, July 20, 1924, p. 3; July 24, p. 3; NCH, July 19, p. 82; July 26, p. 128; August 2, p. 168; August 9, p. 206; August 16, pp. 241 and 247; August 23, p. 289; CWR, August 2, 1924, p. 313; August 9, pp. 340 and 346; August 23, pp. 415 and 416; August 30, p. 253; Chesneaux, pp. 247–48; Teng, cited, pp. 94–95; *Chung-kuo Lao-kung Yün-tung Shih*, p. 317. The two Chinese accounts stress the anti-imperialist character of the strike.

134. Details on the strike committee come from NCH, August 9, p. 206, and pieced together from sources cited above. I have found no list of its members. The following individuals are mentioned in Western sources: Eugene Chen as an envoy of Sun and a writer of English language propaganda; C. C. Wu, representing Dr. Sun; and Tan Lai-t'ing (an associate of Li Fu-lin) and Ma Chao-chün, apparently representing the strikers, negotiating with Colonel Grosse, chairman of the British muncipal council; Wang Ching-wei and Tse Ying-po [Hsieh Ying-pai], identified by NCH (August 16, p. 243) as leaders of the "Communist wing" of the Kuomintang [!] allegedly controlling the strike; and Sun Yat-sen himself, in the role of final mediator (NCH, August 23, p. 289).

CHAPTER EIGHT   FRUSTRATIONS AND THE NEW HOPE

1. For details of negotiations and text of the final treaty, see Whiting, *Soviet Policies in China*, pp. 221–35, 276–82.

2. USDS 893.00/5423, dispatch, Canton, Jenkins, April 2, 1924; quotation from CWR, April 19, p. 271, item dated Canton, April 5.

3. Eudin and North, *Soviet Russia and the East*, pp. 218–19. Voitinsky was in Canton for the Pacific Transport Workers' conference, which opened June 17, according to McVey, *The Rise of Indonesian Communism*, pp. 217, 443, n. 82. The reminiscences appeared in *Pravda*, March 15, 1925, p. 2.

4. KFCC, 4: 120–22, dated only July 1924.

5. See p. 223 and n. 128 of chapter seven.

6. Eudin and North, *Soviet Russia and the East*, pp. 63–65, 68–70, and Whiting, *Soviet Policies in China*, pp. 42–58.

7. Li Huang, "Autobiography," trans. Lillian Chu (Chinese Oral History Project, East Asian Institute, Columbia University, 1970), p. 191. Mr. Li was a close friend of Mr. Tseng in Paris at the time.

8. Su-ch'ing [pseud.], *Kung-ch'an Tang chih Yin-mou Ta Pao-lu* [Conspiracy of the Communist Party Exposed] (Canton: San Min Chü-lo Pu, n.d. [preface August 27, 1924]), pp. 25, 70, mentions Sung Ching-ya as the one who showed *Chung-kuo She-hui-chu-i Ch'ing-nien T'uan T'uan-k'an* no. 7 (April 11, 1924), to Hsieh Ch'ih. I have not seen that journal, which is extensively quoted in the book by Su-ch'ing. This re-

markably interesting work details the development of the controversy, apparently from inside information. (Hereafter cited as Su-ch'ing, KCTCYM.)

9. Li, TJKTCT, p. 227.

10. Su-ch'ing, KCTCYM, pp. 6–14. Some of the resolutions appeared as the second main item in *T'an-ho Kung-ch'an Tang Liang Ta Yao-an*, the impeachment submitted by Teng Tse-ju, Chang Chi, and Hsieh Ch'ih, all reprinted in KMWH, 9: 1278–86, cited here for its convenience.

11. The impeachment quoted only three of the eight, numbers 4, 7, and 8, the most damaging ones.

12. Professor Li Yün-han devotes most of his fifth chapter to Communists' activities within the Kuomintang that veteran members found objectionable. Li, TJKTCT, pp. 267–302.

13. Glunin, "Comintern and the Formation of the Communist Movement in China," pp. 268–69.

14. Chang, *The Rise of the Chinese Communist Party*, 1: 341–46.

15. KFNPttp, p. 1092.

16. Su-ch'ing, KCTCYM, pp. 15, 20. Those at the dinner were Wang Ching-wei, Hu Han-min, and Liao Chung-k'ai, who in varying degrees favored the Russian orientation and admission of the Communists; and Chang Chi, Feng Tzu-yu, Liu Ch'eng-yü, and Sun Fo, who were skeptical or opposed. Tai Chi-t'ao's position is uncertain, but later he became a leader among anti-Communists.

17. KMWH, 9: 1279–80. The impeachment is briefed in KFNPttp, pp. 196–98.

18. KMWH, 9: 1283–84.

19. The official Kuomintang chronological biography of Dr. Sun simply leaves out all details except final decisions. What follows is largely based on Su-ch'ing, KCTCYM, published in Canton almost immediately after the controversy was settled.

20. It is difficult to classify Kuomintang leaders according to their attitudes on the problem *at that time*. "Su-ch'ing," at various points in his narrative identifies their tendencies as follows:

Anti-Communist (in varying degrees): Teng, Chang, and Hsieh, Chang Ch'iu-pai, Chang Chih-pen (all members or reserve members of the two Central Committees), and Feng Tzu-yu, Sun Fo, Liu Ch'eng-yü, Ma Chao-chün, Hsieh Ying-pai, Chu Nai-pin, and Hsü Ch'ing-ho.

Taking a neutral position: Lin Sen, Li Lieh-chün, and Yü Yu-jen (all Central Executive Committee members).

Opposing action against the Communists: Hu Han-min, Wang Ching-wei, Liao Chung-k'ai, and Tai Chi-t'ao (all Central Executive Committee members).

Sun Yat-sen's position was crucial, and he opposed strong action against them.

In addition, there were ten Communists in the Central Executive Committee or its reserve list, but I believe only T'an P'ing-shan and possibly Ch'ü Ch'iu-pai were in Canton at the time.

21. Su-ch'ing, KCTCYM, pp. 34–35. KFNPttp does not mention Borodin's return or a private meeting with Dr. Sun.

22. KMWH, 9: 1286–91. A rather free translation is in Warren Kuo, *Analytical History of Chinese Communist Party*, 1: 396–402.

23. Su-ch'ing, KCTCYM mentions a number of meetings of the Central Executive Committee, but they are not listed in KFNPttp. Minutes of all Central Executive Committee meetings between the First and Second Congress have been printed in Taiwan but are still considered secret; my efforts to get a copy were unavailing.

24. KMWH, 9: 1286.

25. KFCC, 4: 117–18; summarized in KFNPttp, p. 1102.

26. Li, TJKTCT, pp. 319–24, documented from petitions preserved in the Kuomintang archives; Su-ch'ing, KCTCYM, pp. 59–84 for texts of fifteen Shanghai petitions: Ibid., pp. 40–43 for the meeting to open Canton municipal headquarters.

27. KFCC, 1: 176–98, and specifically on William, p. 186. Maurice William published *The Social Interpretation of History, a Refutation of the Marxian Economic Interpretation* in 1921. Later he wrote *Sun Yat-sen Versus Communism*, in which he claimed that Dr. Sun was converted from bolshevism by reading his book sometime between the lectures on nationalism and the ones on the People's Livelihood. This is refuted by Sharman, *Sun Yat-sen*, pp. 277–283, and Tan, *Chinese Political Thought in the Twentieth Century*, p. 136.

Professor Lo Chia-lun discovered that in a transcript of this lecture corrected by Dr. Sun, there is a crucial difference in wording in the introductory paragraph from that found in printed versions. In the latter, Dr. Sun is made to say, "The Principle of People's Livelihood is socialism, it is communism, it is utopianism." In the hand-corrected version the text says, "So the principle of *min sheng* is used to take the place of socialism. Also it is used to encompass all the problems of socialism. This is the scope of the definition of *min sheng*." See Allen S. Whiting, "A New Version of *San Min Chu I*," *Far Eastern Quarterly* 14 (1955): 91.

28. Tsou Lu, *Hui-ku-lu* [Reminiscences], 2 vols. (Nanking: Tu-li Ch'u-pan She, 1946, reprint, 1947), 1: 152–53, and Li, TJKTCT, p. 266. Mr. Huang Chi-lu told me on December 14, 1973, of observing Dr. Sun's anger at Borodin. Mr. Tsou was president of Kwangtung University, which included the Normal College, and it was probably in his office that the controversy broke out; but it is doubtful that he could have understood the discussion in English. How Borodin learned so quickly what Sun Yat-sen had said in Chinese is unexplained.

29. KFCC, 1: 206, 208.

30. Ibid., p. 211. On Sun's ideas on land equalization see Schiffrin, "Sun Yat-sen's Early Land Policy."

Whether Dr. Sun let this identification of communism and socialism with his *min sheng* principle stand is not mentioned in Whiting, "A New Version of *San Min Chu I*."

31. Based on reports by journalists in Canton in NCH, July 26, p. 130; August 2, p. 166; August 23, p. 415; CWR, August 30, p. 453.

32. I wrote an extended account of the Merchants' Corps incident in *Forging the Weapons*.

33. Li, TJKTCT, pp. 324–31, quoting from the minutes and listing those attending. Others were Tsou Lu, T'an Chen, Li Lieh-chün, Liao Chung-k'ai, Wang Fa-ch'in, Hu Han-min, Po Wen-wei, T'an Yen-k'ai, Ting Wei-fen, Wang Ching-wei, and En-k'o-pa-t'u as regular members, and Chang Wei-fen, Pai Yün-t'i, Fu Ju-lin, and Li Tsung-huang as alternates. Dr. Sun is not listed as attending.

34. The term used is *p'ai*, which can mean party, clique, or faction; it is not *t'uan*, which I have translated as "fraction," a Bolshevist technical term.

35. Li, TJKTCT, pp. 326–27.

36. KFNPttp., p. 1118.

37. KFNPttp., p. 1114. This was a scheme of Hu Han-min, but seems not to have resulted in anything effective. Chiang, "Hu Han-min Hsien-sheng Nien P'u Kao," pp. 204–05; Chiang, *Pao-lo-t'ing yü Wu-Han Cheng Ch'üan*, pp. 8–9.

38. Li, TJKTCT, pp. 328–29.

39. Reprinted in KMWH, 16: 2773–76, and partially in Li, TJKTCT, pp. 330–31. A different resolution said to be the result of this plenum is quoted in part in T. C. Woo, *The Kuomintang and the Future of the Chinese Revolution* (London: George Allen & Unwin, 1928), pp. 165–66; also summarized in Wilbur and How, *Documents*, pp. 151–52.

40. General accounts of the Merchants' Corps incident are given by Tsou, CKKMTSK, pp. 1093–95; Mao, CKSHS, p. 318 ff.; KMWH, 10: 1470–83; KFNPttp., p. 1111 ff.; Li, *The Political History*, pp. 464–65; and CYB 1925/26, pp. 849–50. USDS 893.113H29/1–5 is a series of telegrams and dispatches from the American consul general in Canton, Douglas Jenkins, about the seizure of the arms from the *Hav*, and details about the method of purchase. I provided considerably more detail on the incident in *Forging the Weapons*. The most extensive account, strongly biased in favor of the merchants, is Hua Tzu Jih-pao, comp., *Kwangtung K'ou Hsieh Ch'ao* [The Kwangtung Weapons Appropriation Storm] (Hong Kong: Hua Tzu Jih-pao, 1924). It has pictures of most of the principals involved.

41. Dr. Sun's statement was made in Kobe on November 25, 1924 to a Kuomintang group. He did not say when the British consul gave this information nor that it was given to him personally, but rather, "to us." KFCC, 3: 501. KFNPttp., p. 1112 converts this into a personal conversation, but I have seen no evidence that Dr. Sun saw the acting British consul general during any of this time.

42. GBFO 371/10240 [F3443/15/10] dispatch from Sir R. Macleay in Peking dated 6th September 1924, and inclosing Bertram Giles's dispatch from Canton of 21 August, which contains very damaging information about the involvement of important Britishers. The minutes written in the Foreign Office show the dismay and incredulity of these officials with the revelations.

43. NCH, August 30, 1924, pp. 332, 333; September 6, p. 376; CWR, August 30, pp. 445–56; September 6, pp. 26–27. The NCH article for September 6, under the title "Sun Yat-sen and his Generals," attributed to a Chinese correspondent and dated Canton, August 29, describes a meeting of the Military Council on August 26, in which Dr. Sun allegedly called for a bombardment of Hsi-kuan. It gives the opposition positions of Gens. Hsü Ch'ung-chih, T'an Yen-k'ai, Yang Hsi-min, and Fan Shih-sheng. Only Gens. Liu Chen-huan and Fan Chung-hsiu favored his proposal. Dr. Sun is said to have withdrawn from the meeting in great anger when his suggestions were overruled. No meeting of the Military Council is listed for August 26 in KFNPttp nor in Mao, CKSHS, but neither source is complete.

44. NCH, September 6, p. 376.

45. GBFO 371/10297 [F3656/3656/10], dispatch, Giles, Canton, August 29, 1924 to Macleay.

46. USDS 893.000/5650 encloses dispatches from Jenkins, the American consul general in Canton, dated from September 2 to 18, 1924. That of September 2 contains a copy of the memorandum of the Japanese consul general describing his call on Governor Liao and the terms of the settlement worked out by Gens. Fan Shih-sheng and Liao Hsing-ch'ao. The Japanese consul general, on behalf of the consular body, stated verbally "(1) That in the event of foreign persons or property being injured, they [the consular body] would hold the government responsible; (2) that they protested against the barbarity of firing on a defenseless city; (3) that in the event of injury to foreign persons or property they would take whatever measures they deemed desirable."

47. USDS 893.00/5650, Jenkins's dispatch of September 6, quoting Giles to Fu, captioned "H.B.M. Consulate General, Canton, 29th August, 1924." Also CWR, September 20, p. 92, and NCH, September 20, p. 459, for texts of warning, correctly dated. (Most Chinese sources incorrectly date Giles's warning as August 27.) Giles did not report his action to Macleay in Peking until H.M. minister telegraphed him for an explanation. Officials in the British Foreign Office considered Giles's action quite unwarranted and authorized Macleay to reprimand him. GBFO 371/10244 [F3043/19/10, F3044/19/10 and F3127/19/10], telegrams from Macleay to Foreign Office and minutes.

48. USDS 893.00/5650, cited. The manifesto, dated September 1, was published in the *Canton Gazette* on September 4. The prose is unmistakably that of Eugene Chen. For Chinese versions, KMWH, 10, 1479–80 or KFCC, 4: 44–46. Mr. Chung Shing, speaker of the Kwangtung assembly, sent a telegram to the dean of the diplomatic corps in Peking expressing appreciation for the consular warning. NCH, September 20, p. 459. The merchants' committee at Foshan sent their appreciation to Bertram Giles for "this act of humanity." CWR September 27, p. 133.

49. GBFO 371/10244 [F3004/19/10]. The minutes show the Foreign Office officials decided to ignore the telegram. KFCC, 4: 440–41 has a telegram from Sun Wen to MacDonald dated September 10, but the one received by the Foreign Office was dated September 1 and arrived on September 2.

50. For arms distribution see Mao, CKSHS, pp. 324, 326, August 23, September 8 and 12.

51. KFNPttp, p. 1124 states that the decision to stage an antiimperialist week was made by the Political Council on September 3, in a meeting at which only Dr. Sun, Ch'ü Ch'iu-pai, Wu Choa-shu, and Borodin were present. The Kuomintang proclamation is in KFCC, 4: 130–134. The rally, parade, and slogans are described in USDS 893.00/5650, Peking, Bell, September 20, 1924, forwarding a series of dispatches from Consul General Jenkins in Canton. Peking also had its "Humiliation Day" program. USDS 893.00/5596, dispatch, Bell, Peking, September 10, transmitting a threatening antiforeign leaflet.

52. USDS 893.00/5650, just cited. The text of the interview as published in the *Canton Gazette* on Monday, September 8, may have been touched up by Eugene Chen, Dr. Sun's English language secretary, for in places it bears his distinctive style.

53. Part of the American share of the indemnity had been returned to China nine years before the Russian Revolution, though its use was specified for fellowships and later to support Tsinghua College.

54. Mao, CKSHS, pp. 326–27; abbreviated in KFNPttp, 1062. Shih-p'ai is a town a few miles east of Canton. Perhaps the reference is to Ch'en Chiung-ming's near victory in November 1923. In a dispatch of September 6, Mr. Jenkins stated the belief that Dr. Sun was anxious to get away from Canton. USDS 893.00/5650; also /5729.

55. KFNPttp. p. 1124. This was the day after the Political Council decided, on September 3, to issue the proclamations of the Northern Expedition and the transfer of the Generalissimo's Headquarters to Shao-kuan. For military orders see KMWH, 10: 1484–91.

56. KFNPttp, pp. 1124–25 gives the alliance and the attack upon Lu Yung-hsiang as the first of four reasons why Sun decided on the military campaign. See also Li, *The Political History*, pp. 463–70. NCH has many pages on the Chekiang-Kiangsu war and useful chronologies, September 27, p. 494; October 4, p. 9; October 18, p. 96.

57. USDS 893.00/5729, dispatch, Canton, Jenkins, September 17, 1924.

58. Detailed information on the negotiations in my *Forging the Weapons*, pp. 95–96, 145, n. 13.

59. USDS, 893.00/5729, just cited, suggested that Sun Fo was selected as a scapegoat. In his farewell statement, he said that between April 1923 and June 1924 the Canton municipality contributed no less than $10 million in support of the miitary authorities.

60. KFNPttp, p. 1142 for appointments. Liao's telegram of resignation is reprinted in Liao Chung-k'ai, *Liao Chung-k'ai Chi* (Peking: Chung-hua Shu-chü, 1963) pp. 188–90. Liao inveighed against the splitting up of finances amongst the generals so that "orders of the Finance Minister don't go beyond the office door." Plenty was collected in opium and other taxes to cover military expenses, he said, but the problem was to unify finances, and this was beyond his powers, so he resigned. According to KFNPttp, p. 1133, Liao was so upset that he gave up all positions except work at

party headquarters and political training at Whampoa. I suspect this indicates a policy rift between Sun and Liao.

61. Mao, CKSHS, pp. 329–30.

62. There are undated reports from Borodin in Mitarevsky, *World Wide Soviet Plots,* p. 134, most disparaging of Sun Yat-sen, calling him "very backward," judging very badly in political matters; "he considers himself the hero and the others the mob, while in China he is simply an enlightened little satrap." Borodin stated that "in one of our last conversations" Sun compared himself to Confucius and hoped that his followers would cling to him with the same loyalty as Confucius's disciples showed to their master. Unfortunately, "last conversation" might mean "final," or it might mean "latest."

63. Jean Chesneaux, *The Chinese Labor Movement,* p. 503, n. 122. The passage is quoted in the French version. Ch'ü Ch'iu-pai reported the Central Committee's opposition in his monograph, *Chung-kuo Ko-ming chung chih Cheng-lun Wen-t'i* [Controversial Questions in the Chinese Revolution] (first published in April 1927) 2d ed. ([Shanghai?]: Chinese Communist Party, June 1928), p. 165. I am indebted to Dr. Bernadette Li Gentzler for this reference.

64. KFCC, 6: 48–50. More of the proclamation is translated in Li, *The Political History,* pp. 463–64. See also clippings from *Canton Gazette* in USDS 893.00/5729, dispatch, Canton, Jenkins, September 17, 1924.

65. KMWH, 10: 1489–91, and Shieh, *The Kuomintang: Selected Documents,* pp. 87–90.

66. USDS 893.00/5743, dispatch, Canton, prepared September 30, 1924.

67. Accounts of the expedition are given in KMWH, 10: 1484–98; *Pei Fa Chan Shih* [A History of the Northern Punitive War] 4 vols. and KFNPttp, p. 1128 ff. There are greatly varying reports on the numbers of troops assembled for the campaign.

68. From NCH, September 27, p. 501 (four reports from Canton and Hong Kong of September 18, 19, and 21); October 4, p. 14 and 16 (September 21); USDS 893.00/5730, dispatch, Canton, Jenkins, September 23; and 893.00/5743, just cited.

69. Series of telegrams and letters between Sun Yat-sen at Shao-kuan and Chiang Kai-shek at Whampoa or Canton, dated October 9 and 10 in Mao, CKSHS, pp. 338–43; and in KFCC, 4: 443 and 5: 571–74. The government stated its case in a self-justifying document. See NCH, November 1, p. 186.

70. Mao, CKSHS, pp. 339–40, where Sun's order is placed on October 9, and Chiang's reply on the same date. KFCC, 5: 571, gives a telegram from Sun to Chiang on October 10 making the same request, in case the merchants really struck the next day. The exchanges leave no doubt of Sun's determination to pursue the Northern Expedition and Chiang's determination to hold Whampoa. Hollington K. Tong, *Chiang Kai-shek,* rev. ed., (Taipei: China Publishing Co., 1953), pp. 546–47, makes the same interpretation: Chiang defied Sun and refused to come to Shao-kuan. "At the present time, I have decided not to move from here a single step. . . . It is my urgent wish you will return to the capital. This really holds the key to our success or failure . . ." Sun wired Chiang, "You must not linger on, because I will not return

to rescue Canton. You must grasp the opportunity and act resolutely. You must not hesitate."

71. See telegram in KFCC, 4: 443, dated 7–9 A.M., October 10. The telegram as quoted in Mao, CKSHS, p. 342 and KFNPttp., p. 1138 is rewritten to leave off the instructions to make public property of the shops and send clothing material to Shao-kuan; their texts merely say, "then go a step further and deal with them."

72. This account is based upon Jenkins's reports of October 11 and 13, USDS 893.00/5609 and 5776. His report of the battle itself came from an American eyewitness. The government's statement of October 19 (NCH, November 1, p. 186) describes the parade of several thousand young students, boys, and girls, their teachers, laborers, military cadets, "of course, unarmed." For later Nationalist accounts, KMWH, 10: 1471; Tsou, CKKMTSK, p. 1094. Two accounts appeared in NCH, October 18, p. 107, both with the dateline October 10, but that of the Eastern News Agency (Japanese) appears to be garbled.

73. Tsou, CKKMTSK, pp. 1094–95; USDS 893.00/5609 and /5776, cited; and 893.00/5620, Canton telegram, October 14.

74. KFNPttp, pp. 1138–40 and Mao, CKSHS, pp. 243–47. Borodin's report (see below), which probably was writen on the morning of October 14, has the revolutionary committee elected by the responsible labor party, in the South—that is the Kuomintang—at a meeting October 14, with Sun elected chairman and his deputy— that is Hu Han-min—given only the right to speak, i.e., not to vote. This casts a different light upon who was giving orders, a question which could be solved only with more adequate archival evidence than is publicly available.

75. Wilbur and How, *Documents,* pp. 170–73, document 11, "Borodin's Report on the Revolutionary Committee." For a discussion of the formation of the committee, from which Sun excluded Hu Han-min, theoretically the most important official at Canton, following Borodin's advice and going against that of Chiang Kai-shek, see ibid., pp. 156–57.

76. Accounts of the fighting from the Nationalist side are found in Ch'en Hsün-cheng's essay in KMWH, 10: 1470–73; Tsou, CKKMTSK, pp. 1095; and *Pei Fa Chan Shih,* 1: 116–17. The following cables and dispatches from the American consul general give on-the-spot reports: USDS 893.00/5620, 5623, 5777, 5798, dating October 15 through 23. Jenkins gives convincing details concerning incendiarism by government troops and looting. He transmitted an estimate of 600 buildings (later revised to 1,100) burned, at a value of HK $30 million. Other graphic accounts are given in NCH, October 18, p. 107; October 25, pp. 143–44. The government's official statement of October 19 blamed the Merchants' Corps for firing first and said the fires were due either to the fighting or to "incendiarism of bad characters." It stated that according to police reports about 490 houses were burned, admitted some looting by "bad characters and troops," and minimized the number of noncombatants hurt. The statement also charged that many of the corpsmen were disbanded soldiers, discharged policemen, city ruffians, and bad characters, hired for $12 per month, and that some were bandits and men sent from Ch'en Chiung-ming's forces. This is the earliest such assertion I have seen; but given the practices of the times, it seems credible.

The regular troops reported as entering the fight were those of Gen. Chang Ming-ta (Second Kwangtung Division), Wu T'ieh-ch'eng, Li Fu-lin, some Yunnan troops, unspecified, and, by inference, some Hunanese. See KMWH, 10: 1470–73; NCH, October 25, p. 144. Chiang Kai-shek's name appears only in later Nationalist accounts.

Estimates of property losses range from $50 million by spokesmen for the Merchants' Corps to about $1.5 million by the Canton police.

Cherepanov, *Zapiski,* 1: 115–16, Draft Translation, pp. 151–54, has an account strongly biased against Chiang Kai-shek, part of which is based on memory, part apparently upon records. Gen. V. K. Blücher (Galen), who was in Canton by late October 1924, wrote about the role of Whampoa cadets in guarding the arms and opposing their return to the merchants, but does not mention their participation in the battle on October 15. See article by A. L. Karunova, "Blücher's 'Grand Plan' of 1926," trans. Jan J. Solecki, *China Quarterly* no. 35 (July/September 1968): 21, quoting Blücher's undated account.

77. USDS 893.00/5777 and 5798, reports from Canton, Jenkins, October 18 and 23.

78. USDS 893.00/5675, a letter sent from the China Society of America in New York to the Department of State quoting the merchant volunteers' telegram, received October 17. NCH, October 25, p. 143.

79. The best reconstruction of this plot and the behind-the-scenes role of Japan, is found in James E. Sheridan, *Chinese Warlord: The Career of Feng Yü-hsiang* (Stanford: Stanford University Press, 1966), pp. 130–48. Sheridan gives no suggestion that Sun Yat-sen was involved in the plot nor knew anything about it.

80. KFCC, 4: 444–45, and USDS 893.00/5699, 5702, and 5709, transmitting telegrams from Canton. On the very day of Feng's coup d'etat, Dr. C. T. Wang, who had participated in its planning, called upon the American chargé d'affairs at Peking and informed him that there would be a new government by committee, which would invite Chang Tso-lin, Sun Yat-sen, Tuan Ch'i-jui, and other prominent leaders to a round table conference, with the object of unifying China. USDS 893.00/5673, Tientsin, October 24, telegram Gauss to Secretary of State, transmitting radio message from chargé d'affairs at Peking, October 23. I am not sure whether Sun was first invited or fished for an invitation to go to Peking. The telegrams in KMWH, 10: 1506 suggest that he sought the invitation.

81. Jerome Ch'en addressed himself to this question in "Dr. Sun Yat-sen's Trip to Peking, 1924–1925," pp. 75–99.

82. Tsou Lu records that "not a few" party officials opposed Sun's departure. See Tsou, CKKMSTSK, p. 1196; Li, TJKTCT, pp. 345–47, on the opposition by some of Dr. Sun's colleagues in North China. Consul General Jenkins learned from a "reliable source" on about October 29 that Hu Han-min thought it inadvisable for Sun to go to Peking; he got rumors on November 3 that "some of Sun's advisers still strongly opposed his going north." USDS 893.00/5812, dispatch, Canton, Jenkins, October 29, and 893.00/5709, telegram, Peking, November 6, transmitting Canton telegram of November 3.

Chinese Communists seem to have been divided on the issue. Ts'ai Ho-shen, editor of the party's major journal, *Hsiang-tao Chou-pao,* expressed opposition in the issue of October 29, but two weeks later had changed his position. The Communist

Party endorsed the trip on November 21. HTCP, nos. 89, 91 and 92, October 29, November 14 and 21, pp. 736, 757, 765–67. However, by November 14 Sun had already departed Canton. Later Communist sources reveal the initial Communist opposition. Ch'ü, *Chung-kuo Ko-ming chung chih Cheng-lun Wen-t'i*, p. 165, says that the Central Committee opposed Sun's trip to the North. Ch'en Tu-hsiu is said to have stated the same in his political report to the Fifth Chinese Communist Party Congress. See Pavel Mif, *Chin-chi Shih-ch'i chung ti Chung-kuo Kung-ch'an Tang* [The Chinese Communist Party in Critical Days] (Moscow: Sun Yat-sen University, 1928), p. 24. Chang Kuo-t'ao records the continued opposition of Communist Party members in Peking almost to the time of Dr. Sun's arrival. Chang, *The Rise of the Communist Party*, 1: 379–84. A student in Shanghai University at the time reminisces about disputes among Communist cadre there. See A. G. Krymov [T'ing Sheng], "The Last Trip of Sun Yat-sen," [in Russian] in *Sun Yat-sen, 1866–1966: Sbornik Statei, Vospominanii, Materialov*, pp. 290–92.

83. KFNPttp, p. 1145.

84. KFCC, 4: 50–54, dated November 10 and signed Sun Wen. Abstracted in KFNPttp, pp. 1150–51; English version published in the *Canton Gazette*, November 13, 1924, and found in USDS 893.00/5845, dispatch, Canton, Jenkins, November 15; translation in Shieh, *The Kuomintang: Selected Historical Documents*, pp. 95–99. A good summary in NCH, November 22, 1924, p. 302.

85. Wu P'ei-fu, *Wu P'ei-fu Hsien-sheng Chi* [The Collected Works of Mr. Wu P'ei-fu] (Taipei: Ta Chung Shu-chü, 1960), pp. 348–350. I am indebted to Prof. Odoric Wou for calling this fact to my attention. Central Committee of the Chinese Communist Party, "Second Manifesto . . . July 1923."

86. The Kuomintang used this system of a convention of delegates chosen from occupational groups to ratify a national constitution in 1931, and the Chinese Communist Party used the scheme in 1949 to ratify the Common Program and the establishment of the People's Republic. In both cases the party dominated most of the organizations represented.

87. Kao, *Chronology*, p. 157; Sheridan, *Chinese Warlord*, p. 147.

88. USDS 893.00/5742, telegram, Peking, November 11, 1924, transmitting Canton, November 10; and /5844, Canton, November 12, Jenkins to Secretary of State, describing the parade, the slogans, and mentioning Sun's address. KFNPttp and Mao, CKSHS simply leave out November 7, nor do I find the speech in KFCC or a mention of November 7 in its chronological table. An account of the parade, the slogans, and a list of the speakers appeared in the *Canton Gazette*—then an organ of the Canton government—on November 8. See CWR, November 22, p. 375. In his report, "Present Political Situation in the Canton Consular District," Consul General Jenkins estimated that Soviet Russia was represented by forty to fifty individuals in Canton, plus others at Whampoa, and still others instructing new officers and drilling recruits. USDS 893.00/5875, dispatch Canton, November 28, 1924. I am skeptical of such a large number at this date.

89. On Li Lieh-chün, see NCH, September 27, p. 501; October 11, p. 60; October 18, p. 96; and November 8, p. 221. KFNPttp, p. 1140, based on the draft of Sun's tele-

gram to Li. Li left Tokyo on November 6 and is listed as chief of staff in Sun's suite sailing from Hong Kong on November 14. KFNPttp, p. 1154, which also mentions the Japanese consul general's send-off. On Japanese closeness to the southern regime, USDS 893.00/5844, dispatch, Canton, Jenkins, November 12, 1924.

90. KFNPttp, pp. 1147–52.

91. Ibid., pp. 1152–55 for the farewell ceremonies and list of Dr. Sun's suite. Whether all traveled with him is uncertain.

CHAPTER NINE   THE FINAL QUEST

1. KFNPttp, pp. 1155–59 for the Shanghai stopover.

2. NCH, November 8, 1924, p. 224, a "Leader." Sun's retort, NCH, November 22, p. 303; KFCC, 4: 527. The possibility that Dr. Sun would not be permitted to land in Shanghai caused Wang Ching-wei on November 11 to telegraph Li Shih-tseng in Peking, asking him to go to the diplomatic corps and protest, and also to telegraph secretly to the French consul general in Shanghai to ask him to protect Sun. This statement is also quoted in "Saggitarius," *The Strange Apotheosis of Sun Yat-sen*, p. 116. The chapter dealing with Dr. Sun's northern trip is extremely hostile, as is the entire work. "Saggitarius" was H. G. W. Woodhead, according to information from Professor Jerome Ch'en.

3. NCH, November 22, p. 303.

4. GBFO 371/10917/F281 [F281/2/10], dispatch, J. T. Pratt, Shanghai, November 22.

5. Kao, *Chronology*, p. 158 for November 19 and 20.

6. KFCC, 3: 480–91; briefed in KFNPttp, pp. 1157–58.

7. NCH, November 29, p. 346, interview with an Eastern News Agency representative. A quite different interview with a Japanese journalist before sailing is given in KFCC, 3: 531. KNWH, 10: 1502–23 for many statements and telegrams by Dr. Sun during his trip north.

8. The stay in Japan is covered in KFNPttp, pp. 1160–66, stressing the great welcome, stream of visitors, and speeches, which are abstracted.

9. A collection of Sun's speeches in Shanghai and Japan as recorded by Huang Ch'ang-ku was published in Canton in March 1925. Sun Yat-sen, *Sun Chung-shan Hsien-sheng yu Shanghai Kuo Jih-pen chih Yen-lun*. See also, KFCC, 3: 491–522 for the speeches and KFCC, 4: 531–42 for the press interviews. Most were translated in Sun, *The Vital Problem of China*, pp. 147–174. Jansen, *The Japanese and Sun Yat-sen*, pp. 210–12; and 264, n. 15 for an interview which was definitely anti-British in tone.

10. KFCC, 3: 491–95.

11. Ch'en, "Dr. Sun Yat-sen's Last Trip to Peking," p. 90.

12. Ibid.

13. GBFO 405/247/No. 11 [F167/2/10], confidential. *Further Correspondence Respecting China* (January–June 1925), dispatch, Eliot, Tokyo, December 11, 1924, a report on Sun's visit to Kobe. Also, Sun, *The Vital Problem of China*, preface by Hollington K.

Tong, Chinese ambassador to Tokyo in 1953, p. x, which says the Japanese government considered preventing Dr. Sun from landing in Kobe, but that he was spirited ashore by Matsudaira Kajaso, the president of the Kawasaki Shipbuilding Company.

14. Dispatch by Eliot, just cited. On Toyama, see Jansen, *The Japanese and Sun Yat-sen*, pp. 34–41 and passim.

15. Dispatch by Eliot, cited.

16. Ibid., as reported by Baron Shidehara, the foreign minister.

17. KFNPttp, pp. 1169–70; Kao, *Chronology*, p. 161, December 24 and 30. CWR, February 21, pp. 335–36 has a list of about 150 invited persons. It included Dr. Sun and half a dozen well-known Kuomintang figures, but also Ch'en Chiung-ming, Yeh Chü, Hung Chao-lin, Lin Hu, and Teng Pen-ying, who were all his military opponents in Kwangtung.

18. KFNPttp, pp. 1176–77. The document is translated in Hsü, *Sun Yat-sen*, pp. 153–57. On January 30 the Kuomintang Central Executive Committee resolved and ordered that no party member should attend the reconstruction conference. KFNPttp, p. 1180–81. The conference was scheduled to open on February 1, 1925.

19. KFNPttp, p. 1169.

20. GBFO 405/247/No. 22 (F592/194/10), confidential. *Further Correspondence Respecting China* (January–June, 1925), dispatch, Macleay, Peking, December 29, 1924.

21. Ibid. Also GBFO 371/10248/F327 (F4327/19/10), telegram, Macleay, Peking, December 20. There is a two-day gap in KFNPttp during the Kobe stay, which Dr. Sun might have spent with Mr. Toyama.

22. GBFO 405/247/No. 22, just cited. Chang Tso-lin had expressed his concern about Dr. Sun's close association with bolshevism to the American chargé on November 29, and wanted the diplomatic corps to adopt a definite stand "in regard to the Bolshevik question" before Sun arrived in Peking. USDS 893.00/5804, telegram, Peking, Mayer, December 1, 1924.

23. GBFO 405/247/No. 22, cited.

24. FRUS, 1925, 1: 724.

25. According to Blücher's diary, by November 18, 1924, Borodin was no longer in Canton. An entry for December 1 on a talk between Blücher and Liao Chung-k'ai, indicates that Borodin would attend to the matter of a subsidy for the magazine *Chien-she* in Shanghai and for another magazine in Peking. M. F. Yuriev, a modern Russian scholar with access to Soviet archives, says that Borodin accompanied Sun when he left Canton. M. F. Yuriev, *Revolutsiia 1925–1927 gg. v Kitae* [The 1925–1927 Revolution in China] (Moscow: "Nauka," 1968), p. 83. However, Borodin is not listed in Dr. Sun's party in KFNPttp, p. 1154, nor as an arriving passenger on the *Shinyo Maru* in Shanghai, in NCH, November 22, 1924, p. 344. (However, this lists only Dr. and Mrs. Sun Yat-sen but no members of his Chinese staff). The P & O steamer *Mantua* picked up passengers in Hong Kong, including "Mr. and Mrs. Broden, Mr. Gilko, Mr. E. Chen," listed in that sequence, and other named foreigners, and arrived in Shanghai on the same day as the *Shinyo*. See NCH, November 22, p. 344. Mr. Gilko

might be A. N. Gilko, who served as the Soviet consul in Canton, and Mr. E. Chen could be Eugene Chen. However, it is strange that if Borodin arrived in Shanghai about the same time as Dr. Sun, this was not picked up by the alert press. It is also possible that Borodin came north on the *Vorovsky*, but I found no evidence in NCH that it stopped in Shanghai. The late Mrs. Holubnychy provided me with the information from Russian sources.

26. USDS 893.00/6003, Peking, Schurman, January 5, 1925; but NCH, January 10, p. 45, says Borodin called on Dr. Sun at Hotel de Pekin on December 31.

27. USDS 893.00/6003, just cited.

28. German and Japanese doctors attending Dr. Sun suspected cancer even before he left Tientsin, according to Hollington K. Tong, preface to Sun, *The Vital Problem of China*, p. xi. On January 5, the British minister in Tokyo cabled that a source he trusted confirmed that Dr. Sun was suffering from cancer. GBFO 371/10916/F44 [F44/2/10]. The *New York Times* reported on January 4, 1925 that Dr. Sun would be operated on for liver trouble. NYT, January 4, p. 3. The official announcement signed by three physicians after the operation, and dated January 27, stated that a malignant tumor had been found. NCH, January 31, p. 173. Thereafter there were daily bulletins on his condition. On February 3 the physicians informed Dr. Sun of his real condition, which he took calmly. NCH, February 4, p. 213. Other reports and daily bulletins in NCH, February 14, p. 256; February 21, p. 297; February 28, p. 338; March 7, p. 382.

29. KFNPttp, pp. 1178–79, based on Wang Ching-wei's report to the Second Kuomintang Congress in January 1926. Chang Kuo-t'ao gives an interesting reminiscent account of the meetings and problems discussed. He says that Borodin attended regularly, and that he, himself, was in the council from its formation. Chang, *The Rise of the Chinese Communist Party*, 1: 384–96. Ma Hsiang, one of Dr. Sun's bodyguards, reminisced that at the time of Sun's operation only four persons were admitted to him, Borodin, Sun Fo, K'ung Hsiang-hsi, and Sung Tzu-wen (T. V. Soong). (Information from Mrs. Holubnychy, based on a Russian translation of Ma's reminiscences.) However, according to KFNPttp, pp. 1182 and 1179, Sun Fo arrived in Peking only on February 2 while Mr. Soong sailed from Hong Kong to join Dr. Sun on January 29. (Based on Hong Kong newspaper reports.) T'ang Leang-li says Borodin did not see Dr. Sun between January 26 and March 11, the day before his death. T'ang, *The Inner History*, p. 195.

30. KFNPttp, pp. 1190–92, from Wang Ching-wei's report to the second Kuomintang Congress.

31. KFNPttp, p. 1191, n. 28. A careful study of the circumstances of the reading and signing of the wills is Jerome Ch'en, "The Left Wing Kuomintang—a Definition," pp. 557–63.

32. The two wills were published in photographic reproduction in *Kuo Wen Chou Pao* vol. 2, no. 9 (March 15, 1925) as a frontispiece; a clearer reproduction of the political testament is given as a frontispiece for vol. 2 of KFNPttp (and earlier editions).

33. Kuomintang archives 1–3/1, Minutes of the Central Executive Committee, seventy-sixth/seventy-seventh meetings, April 20 and 23, 1925.

34. M. S. Kapitsa, *Sovetsko-Kitaiskie Otnosheniia* [Sino-Soviet Relations] (Moscow: Gospolitizdat, 1958), p. 144, quoting directly from the Archives on the Foreign Policy of the USSR. Information from Mrs. Holubnychy.

35. KFNPttp, p. 1196, but no source for this account is given.

36. USDS 893.00/6198, dispatch, Peking, Ferdinand Mayer, April 11, 1925, containing a clipping from the *Far Eastern Times*, March 18, with the Rosta dispatch, dated Peking, March 17. Since the original draft was in English, this is presumably the version read to Dr. Sun and reportedly signed by him. (There is no signature attached to this.) A polished version appeared in NYT, May 24, 1925, VIII, p. 6. Still other versions arise from its translation into Chinese and then back into English. S. Tikhvinsky presents an English text translated back from the Russian version published in *Pravda* on March 14, probably the first printing. Tikhvinsky, *Sun Yat-sen: On the Occasion*, pp. 58–59. An English text was printed in *International Press Correspondence* vol. 5, no. 20 (March 19, 1925): 286.

37. The Peking-Moscow exchanges were published in *International Press Correspondence*, cited; the Chinese Communist Party declaration in HTCP no. 107 (March 21, 1925): 890, under the date March 15. The messages are summarized in Wilbur and How, *Documents*, p. 159.

38. Sharman, *Sun Yat-sen*, pp. 309–10; CWR, March 28, 1925, p. 116; L. Wieger, *Chine moderne*, tome 6 (1925): 170–71.

39. CWR, March 21 through April 25, mentions many of these services, including one in New York at International House on March 22, 1925 with John Dewey, Paul Myron Linebarger, and Alfred Shao-ke Sze among the organizers.

Bibliography

Titles of articles and chapters in Chinese, Russian, and Japanese are given in translation; book titles are given in transcription and translation. In the bibliography, the names of Chinese authors have been alphabetized in Western style.

Abend, Hallet. *My Life in China, 1926–1941.* New York: Harcourt, Brace & Co., 1943.

Altman, Albert A., and Schiffrin, Harold Z. "Sun Yat-sen and the Japanese: 1914–16." *Modern Asian Studies* 6, pt. 4 (1972): 385–400.

Andersen, Hendrick Christian. Hendrick Christian Andersen Papers. Library of Congress, Washington, D.C.

Anderson, Adelaide Mary. *Humanity and Labour in China: An Industrial Visit and Its Sequel (1923 to 1926).* London: Student Christian Movement, 1928.

Bastid, Marianne. "La Diplomatie française et la révolution chinois de 1911." *Revue d'histoire moderne et contemporaine* (1969): 221–45.

Bing, Dov. "Chang Chi and Ma-lin's First Visit to Dr. Sun Yat-sen." *Issues & Studies* 9, no. 6 (March 1973): 57–62.

———. "Sneevliet and the Early Years of the CCP." *China Quarterly* no. 48 (October/December 1971): 677–97.

———. "Was There a Sneevlitian Strategy?" *China Quarterly* no. 54 (April/June 1973): 345–53.

Blagadatov, A. V. *Zapiski o Kitaiskoi Revolutsii 1925–1927 gg* [Notes on the Chinese Revolution, 1925–1927]. Moscow: Academy of Sciences of the USSR, Institute of Oriental Studies, "Nauka," 1970.

Bland, J. O. P., and Backhouse, E. *Recent Events and Present Policies in China.* London: William Heineman, 1912.

Boorman, Howard L., and Howard, Richard C., eds. *Biographical Dictionary of Republican China.* 4 vols. New York: Columbia University Press, 1967–1971.

Borg, Dorothy. *American Policy and the Chinese Revolution, 1925–1928.* New York: American Institute of Pacific Relations, 1947.

Brandt, Conrad. *Stalin's Failure in China, 1924–1927.* Cambridge: Harvard University Press, 1958.

Brandt, Conrad; Schwartz, Benjamin; and Fairbank, John K. *A Documentary History of Chinese Communism*. Cambridge: Harvard University Press, 1952.

Bulletin d'École française d'Extrême-Orient 7 (1907): 442–54. (Contains an anonymous article on Sun Yat-sen, and abstracts of *Ko-ming Fang-lüeh* and *Ko-ming Hsien-feng*.)

Cantlie, James, and Jones, C. Sheridan. *Sun Yat Sen and the Awakening of China*. New York: Fleming H. Revell Co., 1912.

Cantlie, Neil, and Seaver, George. *Sir James Cantlie, a Romance in Medicine*. London: J. Murray [1939].

Canton, Municipal Government. *Kwang-chow Shih Shih Cheng Pao-kao Hui-k'an, 1923*. [Report of the Canton Municipal Government for 1923]. Canton: Municipal Government, February 1924.

Central Committee, Chinese Communist Party. "Second Manifesto of the Chinese Communist Party on the Current Situation, July 1923," In *Chung-kuo Kung-ch'an Tang Wu Nien Lai chih Cheng-chih Chu-chang*, pp. 48–53.

Chang, Chi. *Chang Po-ch'uan Hsien-sheng Ch'üan Chi* [The Collected Works of Mr. Chang Chi]. Taipei: Chung-yang Wen Wu Kung-ying She, 1951.

Chang, Fu-jui. "Hsin-hai Ko-ming Shih ti Fa-kuo Yü-lun" [Public Opinion in France at the Time of the 1911 Revolution]. Abridged translation by Ho Chen-hui in *Chung-kuo Hsien-tai Shih Ts'ung-k'an* 3 (August 1960): 45–77.

Chang, Kuo-t'ao. *The Rise of the Chinese Communist Party, 1921–1927: Volume One of the Autobiography of Chang Kuo-t'ao*. Lawrence, Kan.: The University Press of Kansas, 1971.

———. *Wo-ti Hui-i* [My Reminiscences]. Published serially in *Ming Pao Yueh-k'an*, from 1, no. 3 (March 1966) to 6, no. 2 (February 1971).

Chang, P'eng-yuan. *Liang Ch'i-ch'ao yü Ch'ing Chi Ko-ming* [Liang Ch'i-ch'ao and Revolution at the End of the Ch'ing]. Taipei: Academia Sinica, Institute of Modern History, 1964.

Chapin, Frederick L. "Homer Lea and the Chinese Revolution." A. B. honors thesis, Harvard University, 1950.

Chen, Eugene. "Sun Yat-sen—Some Memories," *China Weekly Review* 43 (December 19, 1927): 76–78.

Chen, Joseph T. *The May Fourth Movement in Shanghai*. Leiden: E. J. Brill, 1971.

Ch'en, Fu-lin. "Three Articles by Sun Yat-sen in the American Magazine *The Independent*." In *Yen-chiu Chung-shan ti Shih Liao yü Shih Hsüeh* [Historical Materials and Historical Studies on Sun Yat-sen], edited by Huang Chi-lu, pp. 317–44. (Reprints and translates into Chinese articles by Sun Yat-sen dated April and September 1912 and May 1919.)

Ch'en, Hsi-ch'i. *T'ung Meng Hui Ch'eng-li ch'ien ti Sun Chung-shan* [Sun Yat-sen before the Establishment of the T'ung Meng Hui]. Canton: Kwangtung Jen-min Ch'u-pan She, 1957.

Ch'en, Hsün-cheng. "Kuang-chou Shang T'uan Shih-pien," [The Canton Merchants' Corps Incident]. In *Ko-ming Wen-hsien*, 10: 1470–73.

Ch'en, Jerome. "Dr. Sun Yat-sen's Trip to Peking, 1924–1925." In *Readings on Asian Topics*. Scandanavian Institute of Asian Studies Monograph Series, no. 1 (1970): pp. 75–99.

———. "The Left Wing Kuomintang—a Definition." *Bulletin of the School of Oriental and African Studies, University of London* 25 (1962): 557–76.

———. *Yuan Shih-k'ai.* 2d rev. ed. Stanford: Stanford University Press, 1972.

Ch'en, Ku-t'ing. *Kuo Fu yü Jih-pen Yu-jen* [Sun Yat-sen and His Japanese Friends]. Taipei: Yu Shih Book Store, 1965.

Ch'en, Kung-po. *The Communist Movement in China: An Essay Written in 1924.* Edited with an introduction by C. Martin Wilbur. New York: Octagon Books, 1966.

———. "Wo yü Kung-ch'an Tang" [I and the Communist Party]. In *Ch'en Kung-po Chou Fu-hai Hui-i-lu Ho Pien* [Joint Edition of the Memoirs of Ch'en Kung-po and Chou Fu-hai]. Hong Kong: Ch'un-ch'iu Ch'u-pan She, 1967.

Ch'en Kung-po Chou Fu-hai Hui-i-lu Ho Pien [Joint Edition of the Memoirs of Ch'en Kung-po and Chou Fu-hai]. Hong Kong: Ch'un-ch'iu Ch'u-pan She, 1967.

Ch'en, P'eng-jen. "A Bibliography of Japanese Writings Concerning Mr. Sun Chung-shan." In *Yen-chiu Chung-shan Hsien-sheng ti Shih-Liao yü Shih Hsüeh* [Historical Materials and Historical Studies on Sun Yat-sen], edited by Huang Chi-lu, pp. 469–517.

———. "A Chronology of Sun Yat-sen's Visits to Japan (Preliminary Draft)," a supplement to his article, "A Bibliography of Japanese Writings Concerning Mr. Sun Chung-shan." In *Yen-chiu Chung-shan Hsien-sheng ti Shih Liao yü Shih Hsüeh*, edited by Huang Chi-lu, pp. 418–543.

———. *Sun Chung-shan Hsien-sheng yü Jih-pen Yu-jen* [Mr. Sun Yat-sen and His Japanese Friends]. Taipei: Ta-lin Book Store, 1973.

Ch'en, Tu-hsiu. *Kao Ch'üan Tang T'ung-chih Shu* [A Letter to All Comrades of the Party], December 10, 1929. Reprinted in *Chung-hua Min-kuo K'ai Kuo Wu-shih Nien Wen-hsien*. Supplement, *Kung Fei Huo Kuo Shih Liao Hui-pien* [A Compilation of Historical Materials on the Communist Bandits Ruining the Country] [classified]: "Most Secret." Vol. 1. Taipei: Chung-hua Min-kuo K'ai Kuo Wu-shih Nien Wen-hsien Pien-ts'uan Wei-yuan-hui, 1964. A translation of Ch'en's letter is in *Chinese Stuides in History* 3, no. 3 (Spring 1970): 224–50.

Cheng, Chao et al. *Sun Chung-shan Hsien-sheng Kan-i Lu* [Reminiscences about Dr. Sun Yat-sen]. Taipei: Wen-hsing Shu-tien, 1965. (vol. 132 in Wen Hsing Ts'ung-k'an.)

Cheng, Shelley Hsien. *The T'ung-Meng-Hui: Its Organization, Leadership and Finances, 1905–1912*. Ann Arbor: University Microfilms, 1962.

Cherepanov, A. I. *Zapiski Veonnogo Sovetnika v Kitae; iz Istorii Pervoi Grazdanksoi Revolutsionnoi Coiny, 1924–1927* [Notes of a Military Adviser in China: From the History of the First Revolutionary Civil War in China, 1924–1927]. Vol 1. Moscow: Academy of Sciences of the USSR, Institut Norodov Azii, "Nauka," 1964. An English "draft translation" by Alexandra O. Smith, edited by Harry H. Collier and Thomas M. Williamson. *Notes of a Military Adviser in China*. Taipei: [U.S. Army] Office of Military History, 1970.

Chesneaux, Jean. *The Chinese Labor Movement, 1919–1927*. Translated by H. M. Wright. Stanford: Stanford University Press, 1968.

——. *Sun Yat-sen*. Paris: Le Club Français du Livre, 1959.

——. *Les Syndicats chinois 1919–1927: répertoire—textes—presse*. Paris: Mouton, 1965.

Chi, Madeleine. *China Diplomacy, 1914–1918*. Cambridge: Harvard University Press, 1970.

Chiang, Kai-shek. *Soviet Russia in China: A Summing-up at Seventy*. New York: Farrar, Straus and Cudahy, 1957.

Chiang, Yung-ching. "A Comparison of Various Editions of *The Collected Works of Sun Yat-sen* and an Introduction to the New Edition." In *Yenchiu Chung-shan Hsien-sheng ti Shih Liao yü Shih Hsüeh* [Historical Materials and Historical Studies of Sun Yat-sen], edited by Huang Chi-lu, pp. 125–61.

——. "Development of Revolutionary Discussions in the Days of Hsing Chung Hui," *China Forum* 1, no. 2 (July 1974): 147–99. Chinese version, pp. 89–120.

——. "Hu Han-min Hsien-sheng Nien P'u Kao" [A Draft Chronological Biography of Mr. Hu Han-min]. *Chung-kuo Hsien-tai Shih Ts'ung-k'an* 3 (1960): 79–320.

——. "New Materials on Constitution Protection in the *Military Government Gazette*." In *Yen-chiu Chung-shan Hsien-sheng ti Shih Liao yü Shih Hsüeh*, edited by Huang Chi-lu, pp. 237–63.

——. *Pao-lo-t'ing yü Wuhan Cheng-ch'üan* [Borodin and the Wuhan Regime]. Taipei: China Committee for Publication Aids and Prize Awards, 1964.

China Weekly Review. Shanghai.

China Year Book, see *The China Year Book*.

Chong, Key Ray. "Cheng Kuan-ying (1841–1920): A Source of Sun Yat-sen's Nationalist Ideology?" *Journal of Asian Studies* 28 (February 1969): 247–67.

——. "The Abortive American-Chinese Project for Chinese Revolution, 1908–1911." *Pacific Historical Review* 41 (1972): 54–70.

Chou, Fu-hai. "T'ao-ch'u-la Ch'ih Tu Wu-Han chih Pao-kao" [Report of My Escape from the Red Capital, Wu-Han]. 1927. Reprinted in *Ch'en Kung-po Chou Fu-hai Hui-i-lu Ho Pien*. Hong Kong: Ch'un-ch'iu Ch'u-pan She, 1967, pp. 137–77.

Chow, Tse-tsung. *Research Guide to the May Fourth Movement: Intellectual Revolution in Modern China, 1915–1924*. Cambridge: Harvard University Press, 1963.

Chu, Samuel C. *Reformer in Modern China: Chang Chien, 1853–1926*. New York: Columbia University Press, 1965.

Ch'ü, Ch'iu-pai. *Chung-kuo Ko-ming chung chih Cheng-lun Wen-t'i* [Controversial Questions in the Chinese Revolution]. 2d ed. [Shanghai?]: Chinese Communist Party, June 1928. [First published in April 1927.]

Chung-kuo Kuomintang. "Ko-ming Cheng-fu tui-yü Nung-min Yün-tung Ti-i-tz'u Hsüan-yen" [First Proclamation of the Revolutionary Government on the Farmers' Movement]. In *Chung-kuo Kuomintang Chung-yao Hsüan-yen Hui-pien*, n.p.: Tang I Yen-chiu Hui, May 1929, pp. 347–51.

Chung-kuo Kuomintang Chou-k'an. Canton: Central Executive Committee of the Chung-kuo Kuomintang, 1924.

Chung-kuo Kuomintang Ch'üan-kuo Tai-piao Ta-hui Hui-i-lu [Minutes of the National Congress of the Kuomintang of China]. 1924. Reprint. Washington: Center for Chinese Research Materials, 1971.

Chung-kuo Kuomintang Ch'üan-kuo Tai-piao Ta-hui T'e Hao [Special Edition on the National Congress of the Kuomintang]. Canton: n.p., January 30, 1924.

Chung-kuo Kuomintang Chung-yao Hsüan-yen Hui-pien [A Collection of Important Announcements of the Chung-kuo Kuomintang]. N.p.: Tang I Yen-chiu Hui, May 1929.

Chung-kuo Kung-ch'ang Tang Wu Nien Lai chih Cheng-chih Chu-chang [Political Policies of the Chinese Communist Party in the Last Five Years]. 2d ed., n.p.: Central Committee of the Chinese Communist Party, October 10, 1926.

Chung-kuo Lao-kung Yün-tung Shih [A History of the Chinese Labor Movement]. Compiled by Chung-Kuo Lao-kung Yün-tung Shih Pien-tsuan Wei-yuan-hui. 5 vols. Taipei: Chung-kuo Lao-kung Fu-li Ch'u-pan She, 1959.

Chung-kuo Nung-min [The Chinese Farmer]. Canton: Farmers Bureau of the Central Executive Committee of the Chung-kuo Kuomintang, 1926. Photographic reprint edition. Tokyo: Tai-an, 1964. (This contains nos. 1–7, January to July 1926, and has been provided continuous pagination.)

Clark, Grover. "World Revolutionary Talk." *Peking and Tientsin Times*, January 19, 1924.

Dalin, S. A. "The Great Turn: Sun Yat-sen in 1922" [in Russian]. In *Sun Yat-sen, 1866–1966: Sbornik Statei, Vospomananii, Materialov* [Sun Yat-sen, 1866–1966: a Collection of Articles, Reminiscences, and Materials]. Moscow: Glav. Red. Vost. Lit., 1966, pp. 255–85.

Degras, Jane. *Soviet Documents on Foreign Policy.* Vol. 1, *1917–1924.* London: Royal Institute of International Affairs, 1951.

———. *The Communist International, 1919–1943: Documents.* Vol. 2, *1923–1928.* London: Oxford University Press, 1960.

Deitrick, James. The James Deitrick Collection. Special Collections. Stanford University Libraries.

d'Elia, Paschal M., S.J. *The Triple Demism of Sun Yat-sen.* Wuchang: The Franciscan Press, 1931.

Denham, G. C. "Anarchism and Communism in Canton and its Connection with the Labour Movement." GBFO 371/8040 [3215/2646/10]. (Covering letter dated Shanghai, 25 July 1922.)

Ermashev, I. *Sun Yat-sen* [in Russian]. Moscow: "Molodaia Gvardiia," 1964.

Eto, Shinkichi. "Hai-lu-feng—The First Chinese Soviet Government." *China Quarterly* no. 8 (October/December 1961): 160–83; no. 9 (January/March 1962): 149–81.

Eudin, Xenia Joukoff, and North, Robert C. *Soviet Russia and the East, 1920–1927: A Documentary Survey.* Stanford: Stanford University Press, 1957.

Far Eastern Review. Shanghai.

Fass, Josef. "Sun Yat-sen and Germany in 1921–1924," *Archiv Orientální* 36 (1968): 134–48.

———. "Sun Yat-sen and the May-4th-Movement," *Archiv Orientální* 36 (1968): 577–84.

———. "Sun Yat-sen and the World War I." *Archiv Orientální* 35 (1967): 115–20.

Feng, Tzu-yu. *Ko-ming I Shih* [An Unofficial History of the Revolution]. Reprinted in part in *Ko-ming Wen-hsien,* 52: passim.

Fischer, Louis. *Men and Politics: An Autobiography.* New York: Duell, Sloan and Pearce, 1941.

———. *The Soviets in World Affairs.* 2 vols. London and New York: Jonathan Cape, 1930.

Foreign Relations of the United States. See U.S. Department of State.

Friedman, Edward. *Backward Toward Revolution: The Chinese Revolutionary Party.* Berkeley: University of California Press, 1974.

Fuse, Katsuji. *Soviet Policy in the Orient.* Peking: Enjinsha, 1927.

Ganschow, Thomas William. *A Study of Sun Yat-sen's Contacts with the United States Prior to 1922.* Ann Arbor: University Microfilms, 1971.

Gasster, Michael. *Chinese Intellectuals and the Revolution of 1911: The Birth of*

Modern Chinese Radicalism. Seattle: University of Washington Press, 1969.

Gilbert, Rodney. "Dr. Wu Ting-fang Speaks Out Plainly." *North China Herald*, April 29, 1922, pp. 327–30.

———. "Military Operations in 1923." In *The China Year Book 1924/25*, pp. 914–19.

Glunin, V. I. "Comintern and the Formation of the Communist Movement in China (1921–1927)" [in Russian]. In *Komintern i Vostok; Bor'ba za Leninskuiu Strategiiu i Taktiku v National'no-Osvoboditel'nom Dvizhenii* [Comintern and the East: The Struggle for the Leninist Strategy and Tactics in the National-Liberation Movement]. Moscow: Glav. Red. Vost. Lit., 1969, pp. 242–99.

Great Britain. Foreign Office. FO 371. (The "general correspondence" series, the principal files concerning China, including dispatches, letters, telegrams, as well as interdepartmental correspondence, with a great deal of minuting by officials of the Foreign Office. Unless otherwise noted, these were the China files I consulted in the Public Record Office, London.)

Great Britain. Foreign Office. FO 405 confidential. *Further Correspondence Respecting China.* (Important documents printed for high-level circulation, then cumulated and bound semi-annually or quarterly.) Vols. 240, 241, 244, 245 and 247 cover the period January 1923 to June 1925.

Gruber, Helmut, *Soviet Russia Masters the Comintern.* Garden City: Anchor Press/Doubleday, 1974.

Hager, Charles B. "Dr. Sun Yat Sen: Some Personal Reminiscences." *The Missionary Herald* (April 1912). Reprinted as appendix in Lyon Sharman, *Sun Yat-sen,* pp. 382–87.

Hao, Yen-p'ing. *The Compradore in Nineteenth Century China.* Cambridge: Harvard University Press, 1970.

Harrison, James Pinckney. *The Long March to Power: A History of the Chinese Communist Party, 1921–72.* New York: Praeger Publishers, 1972.

Hirayama, Shū. "T'an-shang Chien Fei-li-pin so Kou Hsieh Tan Shih" [A Discussion of Borrowing the Weapons and Munitions Purchased by the Philippines]. In *Chung-hua Min-kuo K'ai Kuo Wu-shih Nien Wen-hsien,* Series I, vol. 9, *Ko-ming chih Ch'ang-tao yü Fa-chan—Hsing Chung Hui.* Taipei: Chung-hua Min-kuo K'ai Kuo Wu-shih Nien Wen-hsien, 1963, pp. 602–06.

Hofheinz, Roy, Jr. "Peasant Movement and Rural Revolution: Chinese Communists in the Countryside 1923–1927." Ph.D. dissertation. Harvard University, 1966.

Holcombe, Arthur N. *The Chinese Revolution: A Phase in the Regeneration of a World Power.* Cambridge: Harvard University Press, 1930.

Holoch, Donald, trans. *Seeds of Peasant Revolution: Report on the Haifeng Peasant Movement by P'eng P'ai.* Ithaca: Cornell University China-Japan Program, 1973.

Holubnychy, Lydia. "The Comintern and China, 1919–1923." M.A. thesis, Columbia University 1968.

Hsiang-tao Chou-pao [Guide Weekly]. Shanghai, 1922–1925. Page numbers from the Japanese reprint edition.

Hsiang, Ta-yen. "Annotations for the Newly Published Pieces of Dr. Sun Yat-sen's Holograph Letters to his Son." *China Forum* 2, no. 1 (January 1975): 206–21; Chinese text, pp. 145–63 with the four letters reproduced photographically.

Hsin Ch'ing-nien (*La Jeunesse*). Shanghai, 1920.

Hsin-hai Ko-ming [The Revolution of 1911]. Chung-kuo Chin-tai Shih Tzu-liao Ts'ung-kan. 8 vols. Shanghai: Jen-min Ch'u-pan She, 1957.

Hsiung, S. I. *The Life of Chiang Kai-shek*. London: Peter Davies, 1948.

Hsü, Leonard Shihlien. *Sun Yat-sen: His Political and Social Ideals*. Los Angeles: University of Southern California Press, 1933.

Hsü, Shih-shen. "Important Source Materials Not Printed in *Kuo Fu Ch'üan Chi*." In *Yen-chiu Chung-shan Hsien-sheng ti Shih Liao yü Shih Hsüeh* [Historical Materials and Historical Studies on Sun Yat-sen], edited by Huang Chi-lu, pp. 163–83.

Hsüeh, Chün-tu. *Huang Hsing and the Chinese Revolution*. Stanford: Stanford University Press, 1961.

——. "Politics in the Early Years of Republican China (Letter to Huang Hsing from Ch'en Ch'i-mei)." *Chinese Studies in History* 8, no. 3 (Spring 1974): 3–18.

——. "Sun Yat-sen, Yang Ch'ü-yün, and the Early Revolutionary Movement in China." *Journal of Asian Studies* 19 (1960): 307–18. Reprinted in *Revolutionary Leaders of Modern China*, edited by Hsueh Chün-tü, pp. 102–22.

——, ed. *Revolutionary Leaders of Modern China*. New York: Oxford University Press, 1971.

Hua, Tzu Jih-pao, comp. *Kwangtung K'ou Hsieh Ch'ao* [The Kwangtung Weapons Appropriation Storm]. Hong Kong: Hua Tzu Jih-pao, 1924.

Huang, Chi-lu. "Experiences in Enlarging and Collating the *Chronological Biography of the Father of the Country*." In *Yen-chiu Chung-shan Hsien-sheng ti Shih Liao yü Shih Hsüeh* [Historical Materials and Historical Studies on Sun Yat-sen], edited by Huang Chi-lu, pp. 101–05.

——. *Kuo Fu Chün-shih Ku-wen—Ho-ma Li Chiang-chün (Ch'u Kao)* [Military Adviser to the Father of the Country—General Homer Lea (Preliminary Draft)]. N.p., n.d.

——, ed. *Yen-chiu Chung-shan Hsien-sheng ti Shih Liao yü Shih Hsüeh* [Historical Materials and Historical Studies on Sun Yat-sen]. *Min-kuo Shih Yen-chiu Ts'ung-shu*. Vol. 2. Taipei: Chung-hua Min-kuo Shih Liao Yen-chiu Chung-hsin, 1975.

Huang, Philip C. *Liang Ch'i-ch'ao and Modern Chinese Liberalism*. Seattle: University of Washington Press, 1972.

Hummel, Arthur W., ed. *Eminent Chinese of the Ch'ing Period*. 2 vols. Washington: U.S. Government Printing Office, 1943–44.

Huston, J. Calvin. "The Recent Rise of Labor Unions and the Growth of Chinese Socialism in Canton under the Aegis of the Kuo Ming Tang." USDS 893.5043/1. Canton, June 28, 1922.

Iriye, Akira. *After Imperialism: The Search for a New Order in the Far East, 1921–1931*. Cambridge: Harvard University Press, 1965.

Isaacs, Harold R. "Documents on the Comintern and the Chinese Revolution." *China Quarterly* no. 45 (January/March 1970): 100–115.

Jansen, Marius B. *The Japanese and Sun Yat-sen*. Cambridge: Harvard University Press, 1954.

Jen, Yu-wen. "The Youth of Dr. Sun Yat-sen." In *Sun Yat-sen: Two Commemorative Essays* by Jen Yu-wen and Lindsay Ride. Hong Kong: Centre of Asian Studies, University of Hong Kong, 1970, pp. 1–22.

Johnson, Nelson T. Nelson T. Johnson Papers. Library of Congress, Washington, D.C.

Kao, Yin-tsu, comp. *Chung-hua Min-kuo Ta Shih Chi* [A Chronological Record of the Chinese Republic]. Taipei: World Book Co., 1957.

Kapitsa, M. S. *Sovetsko-Kitaiskie Otnosheniia* [Sino-Soviet Relations]. Moscow: Gospolitizdat, 1958.

Kartunova, A. I. "Blücher's 'Grand Plan' of 1926." Translated by Jan J. Solecki. *China Quarterly* no. 35 (July/September 1968): 18–39.

———. "Sun Yat-sen—a Friend of the Soviet People" [in Russian]. *Voprosy Istorii KPSS* 9, no. 10 (October 1968): 27–38.

———. "Sun Yat-sen and Russian Advisers; Based on the Documents from 1923–1924" [in Russian]. In *Sun Yat-sen, 1866–1966: Sbornik Statei, Vospominanii, Materialov* [Sun Yat-sen, 1866–1966; a Collection of Articles, Reminiscences, and Materials]. Moscow: Glav. Red. Vost. Lit., 1966, pp. 170–89.

———. "The Comintern and Some Questions on the Reorganization of the Kuomintang" [in Russian]. In *Komintern i Vostok; Bor'ba za Leninskuiu Strategiiu i Taktiku v National'no-Osvoboditel'nom Dvizhenii* [Comintern and the East: The Struggle for the Leninist Strategy and Tactics in the National Liberation Movement]. Moscow: Glav. Red. Vost. Lit., 1969, pp. 300–313.

Kasanin, Marc. *China in the Twenties*. Translated by Hilda Kasanina. Moscow: Central Department of Oriental Literature, 1973.

Kaufman, Paul. "Homer Lea." In *Dictionary of American Biography*, edited by Dumas Malone. 11: 69–70.

Kheifets, A. N. *Sovetskaia Diplomatiia i Narody Vostoka, 1921–1927* [Soviet

Diplomacy and the Peoples of the Orient, 1921–1927]. Moscow: "Nauka," 1968.

Klein, Donald W., and Clark, Anne B. *Biographic Dictionary of Chinese Communism, 1921–1965.* 2 vols. Cambridge: Harvard University Press, 1971.

Ko-ming Wen-hsien [Documents of the Revolution]. Compiled by Lo Chialun. 61 vols. Taipei: Committee for the Compilation of Materials on the Party History, Central Executive Committee of the Chung-kuo Kuomintang, 1953–.

Komintern i Vostok: Bor'ba za Leninskuiu Strategiiu i Taktiku v National'no-Osvoboditel'nom Dvizhenii [Comintern and the East: The Struggle for the Leninist Strategy and Tactics in the National Liberation Movement]. Moscow: Glav. Red. Vost. Lit., 1969.

Koo, V. K. Wellington. Interview with C. Martin Wilbur and Crystal Seidman, December 14, 1972. Chinese Oral History Project, East Asian Institute of Columbia University.

Krymov, A. G. [T'ing Sheng]. "The Last Trip of Sun Yat-sen," [in Russian]. In *Sun Yat-sen, 1866–1966: Sbornik Statei, Vospominanii, Materialov* [Sun Yat-sen, 1866–1966: A Collection of Articles, Reminiscences, and Materials]. Moscow: Glav. Red. Vost. Lit., 1966, pp. 289–309.

Kuo, Warren [Kuo Hua-lun]. *Analytical History of Chinese Communist Party.* Book One. Taipei: Institute of International Relations, 1966.

Kuo Fu Ch'üan Chi. See Sun, Yat-sen.

Kuo Fu Nien P'u Tseng Ting Pen [A Chronological Biography of the Father of the Country, Enlarged and Collated]. Compiled by Lo Chia-lun and Huang Chi-lu. 2 vols. Taipei: Committee for the Compilation of Materials on the Party History, Central Executive Committee of the Chung-kuo Kuomintang, 1969.

Kuo-wen Chou-pao (Kuowen Weekly Illustrated). Tientsin.

Kwang-chow Shih Kung-jen Tai-piao Hui Chüeh-i-an [Resolutions of the Conference of Workers' Delegates of Canton City]. Canton: Labor Bureau of the Central Executive Committee of the Chung-kuo Kuomintang, May 1924. Kuomintang archives, no. 447/155.

Kwangtung Nung-min Yün-tung Pao-kao [Report on the Kwangtung Farmers' Movement]. N.p., n.p., October 1926. (On microfilm from the Hoover Institution on War, Revolution, and Peace, Stanford, filmed from a copy of a 189-page printed book in the Library of Taihoku Imperial University, now the National Taiwan University.)

Lamont, Thomas W. *Across World Frontiers.* New York: Harcourt, Brace and Co., 1951.

———. Thomas W. Lamont Papers. Baker Library, Harvard University Libraries, Cambridge, Mass.

Landis, Richard B. "The Origins of Whampoa Graduates Who Served in the

Northern Expedition." Reprint from *Studies on Asia 1964* by the Modern China History Project. Far Eastern and Russian Institute, University of Washington, Seattle, Wash. Reprint Series No. 19.

Lawrence, Bonnie. "Sun Yat-sen, Ch'en Chiung-ming and the Coup d'État of June 16, 1922." M.A. thesis. Columbia University, 1971.

Leng, Shao-chuan, and Palmer, Norman D. *Sun Yat-sen and Communism.* New York: Frederick A. Praeger, 1960.

Leong, Sow-Theng. "Sun Yat-sen and Bolsheviks." *Transactions of the International Conference of Orientalists in Japan* 14 (1969): 39–53.

Levenson, Joseph R. *Liang Ch'i-ch'ao and the Mind of Modern China.* Cambridge: Harvard University Press, 1953.

Li, Chien-nung. *The Political History of China, 1840–1928.* Translated and edited by Ssu-yu Teng and Jeremy Ingalls. Princeton: Van Nostrand, 1956.

Li, En-han. "Historical Materials and Historical Studies for the Study of Sun Yat-sen in Southeast Asia." *Yen-chiu Chung-shan Hsien-sheng ti Shih Liao yü Shih Hsüeh* [Historical Materials and Historical Studies on Sun Yat-sen], edited by Huang Chi-lu, pp. 291–305.

Li, Huang. "Autobiography." Manuscript translated by Lillian Chu. Chinese Oral History Project, East Asian Institute, Columbia University, 1970.

Li, Kuo-ch'i, "Te-kuo Tang-an chung Yu-kuan Chung-kuo Ts'an-chia Ti-i-tz'u Shih-chieh Ta-chan ti Chi Hsiang Chi-tsai" [Some Records in the German Archives Concerning China's Entry into the First World War]. In *Chung-kuo Hsien-tai Shih Chuan-t'i Yen-chiu Pao-kao.* No. 4. Taipei: Chung-hua Min-kuo Shih-liao Yen-chiu Chung-hsin, 1974, pp. 317–43.

Li, Lu-chao. Letter to C. Martin Wilbur, October 25, 1974.

Li, Yün-han. "Comments on Biographical Writings Concerning Sun Yat-sen." In *Yen-chiu Chung-shan Hsien-sheng ti Shih Liao yü Shih Hsüeh,* edited by Huang Chi-lu, pp. 199–231.

———. "Dr. Sun Yat-sen and the Independence Movement of the Philippines (1898–1900)." *China Forum* 1, no. 2 (July 1974): 201–24. Chinese version, pp. 121–40.

———. *Ts'ung Jung Kung tao Ch'ing Tang* [From the Admission of The Communists to the Purification of the Kuomintang]. 2 vols. Taipei: China Committee on Publication Aids and Prize Awards, 1966.

Liao, Chung-k'ai. *Liao Chung-k'ai Chi* [Collected Writings of Liao Chung-k'ai]. Peking: Chung-hua Shu-chü, 1963.

Liew, K. S. *Struggle for Democracy: Sung Chiao-jen and the 1911 Revolution.* Berkeley and Los Angeles: University of California Press, 1971.

Lim, Edith Roca. "Singapore and the 1911 Revolution." M.A. thesis. Columbia University, 1974.

Linebarger, Paul. *Sun Yat-sen and the Chinese Republic.* 1925. Reprint. New York: AMS Press, 1969.

Liu, F. F. *A Military History of Modern China, 1924–1949.* Princeton: Princeton University Press, 1956.

Lo, Ch'i-yüan. "Pen Pu I Nien Lai Kung-tso Pao-kao Kai-yao" [Abbreviated Report of the Past Year's Work of this (Farmers) Bureau]. *Chung-kuo Nung-min* no. 2 (February 1926): 147–207; no. 3 (March 1926): 231–50.

Lo, Chia-luen. *The Pictorial Biography of Dr. Sun Yat-sen.* Taipei: Historical Archives Commission of the Kuomintang, 1955.

Lo, Hsiang-lin. *Kuo Fu yü Ou Mei chih Yu-hao* [Sun Yat-sen and his European and American Friends]. Taipei; Chung-yang Wen Wu Kung-ying She, 1951.

———. "The Story of the Founding of the Hsing Chung Hui." *China Forum* 1, no. 2 (July 1974): 131–45. Chinese version, pp. 79–87.

Lo, Jung-pang, ed. *K'ang Yu-wei: A Biography and a Symposium.* Tucson: University of Arizona Press, 1967.

Loh, Pichon P. Y. *The Early Chiang Kai-shek: A Study of His Personality and Politics, 1887–1924.* New York: Columbia University Press, 1971.

Lü, Fang-shang. "A Brief Account of the Homer Lea Papers." In *Yen-chiu Chung-shan Hsien-sheng ti Shih Liao yü Shih Hsüeh* [Historical Materials and Historical Studies on Sun Yat-sen], edited by Huang Chi-lu, pp. 417–68. (This contains reproductions in English of twenty-two communications from Sun to Homer Lea and Mrs. Lea between March 24, 1910 and February 11, 1922.)

Lu Hai Chün Ta-yüan-shuai Ta-pen-ying Kung-pao [Gazette of the Army and Navy Generalissimo's Headquarters]. In *Chung-hua Min-kuo Shih Liao Ts'ung Pien.* Series 3, no. 1. 12 vols. 1922–1925. Reprint. Taipei: Committee for the Compilation of Materials on the Party History, Central Executive Committee of the Chung-kuo Kuomintang, 1969.

Lynn, Jermyn Chi-hung. *Political Parties in China.* Peking: Henri Vetch, 1930.

McCormick, Frederick. *The Flowery Republic.* London: John Murray, 1913.

MacFarquhar, Roderick L. "The Whampoa Military Academy." [Harvard] *Papers on China* 9 (August 1953): 146–72.

MacMurray, John Van Antwerp. JVA MacMurray Papers. Princeton University Library, Princeton, N.J.

McVey, Ruth T. *The Rise of Indonesian Communism.* Ithaca: Cornell University Press, 1965.

Mao, Ssu-ch'eng, comp. *Min-kuo Shih-wu Nien i-ch'ien chih Chiang Chieh-shih Hsien-sheng* [Mr. Chiang Kai-shek before 1926]. 1936. Reprint ed. said to have been edited by Ch'en Pu-lei. 2 vols., n.p., n.d.

Marcosson, Isaac F. "The Changing East: Sun Yat-sen and South China." *The Saturday Evening Post* 195 (November 25, 1922): 20–21, 98–105.

Mast, Herman, III, and Saywell, William G. "Revolution Out of Tradition: The Political Ideology of Tai Chi-t'ao." *Journal of Asian Studies* 34, no. 1 (November 1974): 73–98.

Maybon, Albert. *La République chinois.* Paris: A. Colin, 1914.

Mif, Pavel. *Chin-chi Shih-ch'i chung ti Chung-kuo Kung-ch'an Tang* [The Chinese Communist Party in Critical Days]. Moscow: Sun Yat-sen University, 1928.

Mirovitskaia, R. A. "Mikhail Borodin (1884–1951)" [in Russian]. In *Vidnye Sovetskie Kommunisty—Uchastiniki Kitaiskoi Revolutsii* [Outstanding Soviet Communists—the Participants in the Chinese Revolution]. Moscow: Akad. Nauk SSSR, Institut Dal'nego Vostoka, "Nauka," 1970, pp. 22–40.

———. "The First Decade" [in Russian]. In *Leninskaia Politika SSSR v Otnoshenii Kitaia* [The Leninist Policy of the USSR with Regard to China]. Moscow: "Nauka," 1968, pp. 20–67.

Mitarevsky, N. *World Wide Soviet Plots.* Tientsin: Tientsin Press, [1927].

Munholland, J. Kim. "The French Connection that Failed: France and Sun Yat-sen, 1900–1908." *Journal of Asian Studies* 32 (1972): 177–95.

Muntjewerf, A. C. "Was There a 'Sneevlietian Strategy'?" *China Quarterly* no. 53 (January/March 1973): 159–68.

Nicolaevsky, B. "Russia, Japan, and the Pan-Asiatic Movement to 1925." *Far Eastern Quarterly* [later *Journal of Asian Studies*] 8 (1949): 259–95.

North China Herald and Supreme Court and Consular Gazette. Shanghai.

Papers Relating to the Foreign Relations of the United States. See U.S. Department of State.

Peffer, Nathaniel. "One of Asia's Three Great Moderns. The Enigma of Sun Yat-sen, Maker of the Chinese Republic, Without Honor Save in History." *Asia* (August 1924): 591–94, 657–58.

Pei Fa Chan Shih [A History of the Northern Punitive War]. 4 vols. Taipei: Ministry of Defense, History Office, 1959.

P'eng, Pai. "Hai-feng Nung-min Yün-tung Pao-kao" [Report on the Peasant Movement in Hai-feng]. *Chung-kuo Nung-min* no. 1 (January 1926): 59–69; no. 3 (March 1926): 251–69; no. 4 (April 1926): 351–81; no. 5 (May 1926): 489–524. (Pagination comes from the Tokyo, Tai-an reprint edition of 1964). See also Holoch, Donald, trans.

Persits, M. A. "The Eastern Internationalists in Russia and some Questions of the National-Liberation Movement (1918–July 1920)" [in Russian]. In *Komintern i Vostok; Bor'ba za Leninskuiu Strategiiu i Taktiku v Natsional'no-Osvoboditel'nom Dvizhenii* [Comintern and the East: the Struggle for the Leninist Strategy and Tactics in the National Liberation Movement]. Moscow: Glav. Red. Vost. Lit., 1969, pp. 53–109.

Price, Frank W., trans. *San Min Chu I. The Three Principles of Sun Yat-sen.* Shanghai: China Committee of the Institute of Pacific Relations, 1927.

Rea, George Bronson. *The Breakdown of American Diplomacy in the Far East.* N.p., n.d. [Shanghai, 1919?].

————. *The Case for Manchoukuo.* New York and London: D. Appleton-Century Co., 1935.

Reid, John Gilbert. *The Manchu Abdication and the Powers, 1908–1912.* Berkeley: University of California Press, 1935.

Reinsch, Paul S. *An American Diplomat in China.* Garden City, N.Y.: Doubleday, Page & Co., 1922.

Restarick, Henry Bond. *Sun Yat-sen, Liberator of China.* New Haven: Yale University Press, 1931.

Reynolds, Carol Tyson. "Sun Yat-sen and the Constitution Protection Movement, 1917–1918." M.A. thesis. Columbia University, 1971.

"Saggitarius." See Woodhead, H.G.W.

Schiffrin, Harold Z. *Sun Yat-sen and the Origins of the Chinese Revolution.* Berkeley and Los Angeles: University of California Press, 1968.

————. "Sun Yat-sen's Early Land Policy: The Origin and Meaning of 'Equalization of Land Rights'." *Journal of Asian Studies* 16 (August 1957): 549–64.

————. "The Enigma of Sun Yat-sen." In *China in Revolution: The First Phase, 1900–1913,* edited by Mary Clabaugh Wright. New Haven: Yale University Press, 1968, pp. 462–74.

Schurman, Jacob Gould. Jacob Gould Schurman Papers. Cornell University Libraries, Ithaca, N.Y.

Schwartz, Benjamin. *In Search of Wealth and Power: Yen Fu and the West.* Cambridge: Harvard University Press, 1964.

Seng, Png Po. "The Kuomintang in Malaya." *Journal of Southeast Asian History* 2, n. 1 (March 1961): 1–32.

Sharman, Lyon. *Sun Yat-sen, His Life and Its Meaning: A Critical Biography.* New York: John Day Co., 1934.

Sheridan, James E. *Chinese Warlord: The Career of Feng Yü-hsiang.* Stanford: Stanford University Press, 1966.

Shieh, Milton J. T. *The Kuomintang: Selected Historical Documents, 1894–1969.* New York: St. John's University Press, 1970.

Shisō No. 396 (1957, no. 6): 79–93.

Snow, Edgar. *Journey to the Beginning.* New York: Random House, 1958.

Sokolsky, George. "A Visit to Hong Kong and Canton." *North China Herald,* April 24, May 1, and May 8, 1926. Reprinted as a twelve-page booklet. London: The China Express and Telegraph [June 10, 1926].

Sokolsky, George E. The George Ephriam Sokolsky Papers, 1923–60. Special Collections Library, Columbia University Libraries, New York, N.Y.

(Contains scrapbooks of journalistic writings in China under several pseudonyms, and other memorabilia.)

———. "The Reminiscences of George Sokolsky." Manuscript, dated 1956 and 1963. Oral History Collection, Columbia University, New York, N.Y.

Soulié de Morant, George. *Soun Iat-senn.* Paris: Librairie Gallimard, 1932.

Su, Hsi-wen. *Kuo Fu Sun Chung-shan Hsien-sheng Hua Chuan: A Pictorial Biography of Dr. Sun Yat-sen.* Translated by C. M. Faure. Hong Kong: Chung-wai Wen-hua Shih-yeh Yu-lang Kung-ssu, 1965.

Su-ch'ing [pseud.]. *Kung-ch'an Tang chih Yin-mou Ta Pao-lu* [Conspiracy of the Communist Party Exposed]. Canton: San Min Chü-lo Pu, n.d. [preface dated August 27, 1924].

Sui, Hsüeh-fang, and Hsü, Ta-kang. *Sun Chung-shan Hsien-sheng Ku Chü* [Mr. Sun Yat-sen's Former Dwelling]. Shanghai: Jen-min Ch'u-pan She [1958?].

Sun, Yat-sen. *China and Japan: Natural Friends—Unnatural Enemies: A Guide for China's Foreign Policy.* Shanghai: China United Press, 1941. (The earlier edition of *The Vital Problem of China,* attributed to Sun Yat-sen.)

———. "China's Present and Future: The Reform Party's Plea for British Benevolent Neutrality." *Fortnightly Review* 61 (March 1, 1897): 424–40.

———. Four letters to H. C. Andersen, June 19, 1919 to c. May 1921. In Hendrick Christian Andersen Papers, Library of Congress, Washington, D.C.

———. *Fundamentals of National Reconstruction.* Taipei: China Cultural Service, 1953. (Contains many separate writings of Sun Yat-sen in appendices.)

———. "International Development of China," *Public* 22 (December 6, 1919): 1134–35.

———. *Kidnapped in London: Being the Story of My Capture by, Detention at, and Release from the Chinese Legation, London.* Bristol: J. W. Arrowsmith Ltd. [1897]. Photographic reprint. Foreword by Kenneth Cantlie. London: China Society, 1969.

———. *Kuo Fu Ch'üan Chi* [The Collected Works of Sun Yat-sen]. Rev. ed. 6 vols. Taipei: Chung-kuo Kuomintang Central Executive Committee, 1961.

———. "Letter to Chicherin, August 28, 1921." In *Soviet Russia and the East, 1920–1927,* by Xenia Joukoff Eudin and Robert C. North. Stanford: Stanford University Press, 1957, pp. 219–21. Also in *Current Digest of the Soviet Press* 2, no. 43 (December 9, 1950): 20–21; and in *Labour Monthly* (December 1950): 558–60.

———. Letter to Paul S. Reinsch, August 26, 1922. Paul S. Reinsch Papers. State Historical Society of Wisconsin, Madison.

―――. *Memoirs of a Chinese Revolutionary: A Programme of National Reconstruction for China*. 1918. Reprint. Taipei: China Cultural Service, 1953.

―――. *San Min Chu-i* [The Three Principles of the People]. *Kuo Fu Ch'üan Chi*, 1: 1–250. Translated by Frank W. Price. *San Min Chu I. The Three Principles of Sun Yat-sen*. Shanghai: China Committee of the Institute of Pacific Relations, 1927. Translated by Paschal M. d'Elia, S. J. *The Triple Demism of Sun Yat-sen*. Wuchang: The Franciscan Press, 1931. Abridged and edited version by the Commission for the Compilation of the History of the Kuomintang. Taipei: China Cultural Service, 1953. (This version is unreliable.)

―――. *Sun Chung-shan Hsien-sheng Shou-cha Mo-chi* [Reproductions of Mr. Sun Yat-sen's Handwritten Letters]. N.p., n.d.

―――. *Sun Chung-shan Hsien-sheng Yen-chiang Chi* [Collected Speeches of Mr. Sun Yat-sen]. Shanghai: Chung-kuo Kuomintang Chung-yang Chih-hsing Wei-yuan-hui, 1925.

―――. *Sun Chung-shan Hsien-sheng Yen-shuo Chi* [Collected Speeches of Mr. Sun Yat-sen]. Compiled by Huang Ch'ang-ku. Shanghai: Min Chih Shu Chü, 1926.

―――. *Sun Chung-shan Hsien-sheng yu Shanghai Kuo Jih-pen chih Yen-lun* [Speeches of Mr. Sun Yat-sen in Shanghai and Passing through Japan]. Recorded by Huang Ch'ang-ku. Canton: Min Chih Shu Chü, 1925.

―――. *Sun Chung-shan Hsüan Chi*. [Selected Works of Sun Yat-sen]. 2 vols. Peking: Jen-min Ch'u-pan She, 1957.

―――. *Sun Wen Hsüeh Shuo* [Memoirs of a Chinese revolutionary]. In *Kuo Fu Ch'üan Chi*, 2: 1–98.

―――. *10 Letters of Sun Yat-sen, 1914–1916*. Stanford: Stanford University Libraries, 1942.

―――. *The Cult of Dr. Sun: Sun Wen Hsueh Shu*. Translated by Wei Yung. Shanghai: The Independent Weekly, 1931.

―――. "The International Development of China: A Project to Assist the Readjustment of Post-Bellum Industries." Undated manuscripts, c. February 7, 1919. In Hendrick Christian Andersen Papers, Library of Congress, Washington, D.C.

―――. "The International Development of China," *Far Eastern Review* 15 (March, June, August 1919); 16 (April, June, October, November 1920).

―――. *The International Development of China*. 1920. Reprint. Taipei: China Cultural Service, 1953. (First printing, Shanghai: The Commercial Press, 1920).

―――. *The True Solution of the Chinese Question*. Eleven-page pamphlet. N.p., n.d. [New York, 1904]. (There is a translation into Chinese in *Kuo Fu Ch'üan Chi*, 6: 220–26.)

―――. *The Vital Problem of China*. 1941. Reprint. Taipei: China Cultural

Service, 1953. (Probably written by Chu Chih-hsin, this work was first issued in English under Dr. Sun's name in 1941 as *China and Japan: Natural Friends–Unnatural Enemies.*)

Sun, Yat-sen and others. *Kung-jen Ju-ho Ch'iu Kuo* [How Should the Workers Save China?]. N.p. [Shanghai?]: Min Te Shu Chü, [1928?].

Sun Yat-sen, 1866–1966: Sbornik Statei, Vospominanii, Materialov [Sun Yat-sen, 1866–1966: A Collection of Articles, Reminiscences, and Materials]. Moscow: Glav. Red. Vost., Lit., 1966.

Tan, Chester C. *Chinese Political Thought in the Twentieth Century.* Garden City, N.Y.: Doubleday, 1971.

T'an-ho Kung-ch'an Tang Liang Ta Yao-an [Two Important Cases of Impeachment of the Communist Party]. N.p.: Kuomintang Central Supervisory Committee, September 1927. Reprinted in *Ko-ming Wen-hsien*, 9: 1278–86.

T'ang, Leang-li. *The Inner History of the Chinese Revolution.* London: George Rutledge and Sons, Ltd., 1930.

Teng, Chia-yen. "Ma-ting Yeh Tsung-li Shih Chi" [A True Account of Maring's Visit to the Leader]. In *Ko-ming Wen-hsien*, 11: 1409–11.

Teng, Chung-hsia. *Chung-kuo Chih-kung Yün-tung Chien Shih* [A Brief History of the Chinese Labor Movement]. First published in Moscow, 1930. Many editions. N.p.: Hua Chung Hsin Hua Shu-tien, April 1949.

Teng, Ssu-yü. *Dr. Sun Yat-sen and Chinese Secret Societies.* Reprinted from *Studies on Asia, 1963.* Lincoln: University of Nebraska Press, 1963.

Teng, Ssu-yü, and Fairbank, John K. *China's Response to the West: A Documentary Survey, 1839–1923.* Cambridge: Harvard University Press, 1954.

Teng, Tse-ju. *Chung-kuo Kuomintang Er-shih Nien Shih-chi* [Historical Records of the Kuomintang of the Past Twenty Years] as reprinted in part in *Ko-ming Wen-hsien*, 52.

The China Year Book. Edited by H. G. W. Woodhead. Shanghai: North China Daily News and Herald. Approximately annually from 1912 to 1939.

The National Revolutionary Army, A Short History of its Origins, Development and Organization. In FO 405/255 confidential. *Further Correspondence Respecting China,* October to December 1927. No. 6, enclosure 2. Also in FO 371/12440 [F8094/87/10]. Translation of a Russian paper seized on April 6, 1927 in the Soviet military attaché's office, Peking.

Ti-i-tz'u Kuo-nei Ko-ming Chan-cheng Shih-ch'i ti Nung-min Yün-tung [The Farmers' Movement during the Period of the First Revolutionary Civil War]. Peking: Jen-min Ch'u-pan She, 1953.

Tikhvinsky, S. L. "On Sun Yat-sen's Attitudes toward Soviet Russia (1917–1925)" [In Russian]. *Voprosy Istorii* no. 12 (1963): 71–85.

———. *Sun Yat-sen and Problems of Solidarity of the Peoples of Asia.* Moscow:

Twenty-sixth International Congress of Orientalists, Papers Presented by the USSR Delegation, 1963.

——. *Sun Yat-sen: On the Occasion of the Centenary of His Birth (1866–1966)*. N.p.: Novosti Press Agency Publishing House [1966].

——. *Sun Yat-sen: Vneshnepoliticheskie Vozzreniia i Pracktika* [Sun Yat-sen: His Views on Foreign Policy and His Practice]. Moscow: "Mezh. Otn," 1964.

Ting, Wen-chiang. *Liang Jen-kung Hsien-sheng Nien P'u Ch'ang-pien Ch'u Kao* [A Chronological Biography of Mr. Liang Ch'i-chao, Preliminary Version]. 1958. Reprint. Taipei: World Book Co., 1959.

Tong, Hollington K. *Chiang Kai-shek*. Rev. ed. Taipei: China Publishing Co., 1953.

Ts'ai, Ho-shen. "Chin Nien Wu I chih Kwangtung Nung-min Yün-tung" [The Kwangtung Farmers' Movement on May First This Year]. *Hsiang-tao Chou-pao* no. 112 (May 1925): pp. 1030–36.

Ts'en, Hsueh-lu. *San-shui Liang Yen-sun Hsien-sheng Nien P'u* [A Chronological Biography of Liang Shih-i of San-shui]. Reprint. 2 vols. Taipei: Wen-hsing Bookstore, 1962.

Tsou, Lu. *Chung-kuo Kuomintang Shih Kao* [A Draft History of the Kuomintang]. 2d ed. Taipei: Commercial Press, 1965.

——. *Hui-ku-lu* [Reminiscences]. 2 vols., Nanking: Tu-li Ch'u-pan She, 1946/47.

Tsui, Shu-chin. "The Influence of the Canton-Moscow Entente upon Sun Yat-sen's Political Philosophy." *The Chinese Social and Political Science Review* 18 (April–October 1934): 96–145, 176–209, 341–88.

——. *Sun Chung-shan yü Kung-ch'an-chu-i* [Sun Yat-sen and Communism]. Hong Kong: Asia Press, 1954.

Tung-fang Tsa-chih (The Eastern Miscellany). Shanghai.

U.S. Department of State. *Papers Relating to the Foreign Relations of the United States.*

U.S. National Archives. Microfilm 316. *Records of the Department of State Relating to Internal Affairs of Russia and the Soviet Union, 1910–1929.* (This contains decimal file 861.44, biographical data on Soviet officials.)

——. Microfilm 329. *Records of the Department of State Relating to Internal Affairs of China, 1910–1929.* (This contains decimal file number 893.

——. Microfilm 339. *Records of the Department of State Relating to Political Relations between the United States and China, 1910–1929.* (This contains decimal file numbers 711.93.)

——. Microfilm 340. *Records of the Department of State Relating to Political Relations between Russia (and the Soviet Union) and Other States, 1910–1929.* (This contains decimal file number 761.93, Russian relations with China.)

——. Microfilm 341. *Records of the Department of State Relating to Political Relations between China and Other States, 1910–1929.* (The number 793.94 covers China's relations with Japan.)

Waln, Nora. *The House of Exile.* Boston: Little, Brown, 1942.

Wang, Chien-min. *Chung-kuo Kung-ch'an Tang Shih Kao* [A Draft History of the Chinese Communist Party]. Vol. 1, *Shanghai Shih-ch'i* [The Shanghai Period, 1921–1927]. Taipei: Wang Chien-min, 1965.

Wang, Ching-wei. "Tui Chung-kuo Kuomintang Ti-erh-tz'u Ch'üan-kuo Tai-piao Ta-hui Cheng-chih Pao-kao" [Political Report to the Second National Congress of the Chung-kuo Kuomintang]. Reprinted in KMWH, 20, 3851–70.

Wang, Gungwu. "Chinese Politics in Malaya." *China Quarterly* no. 43 (July/September 1970): 1–30.

——. "Sun Yat-sen and Singapore." *Journal of the South Seas Society* [Chinese title, *Nan-yang Hsueh Pao*] 15 (December 1959): 55–68.

Wang, Y. C. *Chinese Intellectuals and the West, 1872–1949.* Chapel Hill: University of North Carolina Press, 1966.

Wang, Yü-chün. *Chung-Su Wai-chiao ti Hsü-mo: Ts'ung Yu-lin tao Yo-fei* [The Prelude to Sino-Soviet Relations: From Yurin to Joffe]. Taipei: Academia Sinica, Institute of Modern History, 1963.

Whiting, Allen S. "A New Version of *San Min Chu I.*" *Far Eastern Quarterly* 14 (1955): 389–91.

——. *Soviet Policies in China, 1917–1924.* New York: Columbia University Press, 1954.

Wieger, Léon, S. J. *Chine moderne.* Tome 5, *Nationalisme, xénephobie, antichristianisme.* Tome 6, *Le Feu aux poudres.* Hsien-hsien [Hopei] n.p., 1924, 1926.

Wilbur, C. Martin. "Forging the Weapons: Sun Yat-sen and the Kuomintang in Canton, 1924." Mimeographed. New York: East Asian Institute of Columbia University, 1966.

——. "Problems of Starting a Revolutionary Base: Sun Yat-sen and Canton, 1923." *Bulletin of the Institute of Modern History, Academia Sinica* [Taipei] 4, pt. 2 (1975): pp. 1–63.

Wilbur, C. Martin, and How, Julie, Lien-ying. *Documents on Communism, Nationalism, and Soviet Advisers in China, 1918–1927.* New York: Columbia University Press, 1956.

William, Maurice. *The Social Interpretation of History, a Refutation of the Marxian Economic Interpretation.* New York: Sotery Publishing Co. [c. 1921].

——. *Sun Yat-sen Versus Communism: New Evidence Establishing China's Right to the Support of Democratic Nations.* Baltimore: Williams & Wilkins Co., 1932.

Woo, T. C. *The Kuomintang and the Future of the Chinese Revolution.* London: George Allen & Unwin, 1928.

Woodhead, H. G. W. [Saggitarius]. *The Strange Apotheosis of Sun Yat-sen.* London: Heath, Cranton Ltd., 1939.

Wright, Mary Clabaugh, *China in Revolution: The First Phase, 1900–1913.* New Haven: Yale University Press, 1968.

Wright, Stanley F. *The Collection and Disposal of the Maritime and Native Customs Revenue Since the Revolution of 1911.* Shanghai: Inspectorate General of Customs, 1925.

Wu, John C. H. *Sun Yat-sen: The Man and His Ideas.* Taipei: The Commercial Press, 1971.

Wu, P'ei-fu. *Wu P'ei-fu Hsien-sheng Chi* [The Collected Works of Mr. Wu P'ei-fu]. Taipei: Ta Chung Shu-chü, 1960.

Young, Earnest P. "Yuan Shih-k'ai's Rise to the Presidency." In *China in Revolution: The First Phase, 1900–1913*, edited by Mary Clabaugh Wright. New Haven: Yale University Press, 1968, pp. 419–42.

Yu, George T. *Party Politics in Republican China: The Kuomintang, 1912–1924.* Berkeley and Los Angeles: University of California Press, 1966.

Yü, Fei-p'eng. "Huang-p'u Chün Hsiao K'ai-chuang chih Hui-i-lu" [Reminiscences on the Founding of Whampoa Military Academy]. In *Ko-ming Wen-hsien*, 10: 1452–55.

Yung, Wing. *My Life in China and America.* New York: Henry Holt and Co., 1909.

Yuriev, M. F. *Revolutsiia 1925–1922 gg. v Kitai* [The 1925–1927 Revolution in China]. Moscow: "Nauka," 1968.

Index

INDEX

343n11, 344n21, 359n23, 363n62, 366n88,
393n1
Ho Shih-chen, 194
Hofheinz, Roy, cited, 354n114, 355n117
Holcombe, Arthur, N., cited, 314n3
Holoch, Donald, cited, 353n105
Holubnychy, Lydia, ix, 326n7, 327n15,
329n23, 333nn28, 33, 334n36, 335n42,
336n52, 337n67, 342n9, 351n93, 352n99,
353n101, 369nn25, 29, 370n34
Hong Kong: Sun in, 7, 12, 13, 14, 36, 101,
127, 143–44, 222, 283, 309n31; College of
Medicine, 12, 36; Sun's expulsion, 15,
18, 55, 73–74, 123; Sun's request for
loans Hsing Chung Hui in, 42; bond
sales in, 42, 47; fund raising in, 52–53,
101; ordinance forbidding Chinese to
celebrate Sun's inauguration (1921),
101, 163; Sun's request for loans, 146,
336n57; labor unions in, 220
Hong Kong and Shanghai Banking Cor-
poration, 144, 250, 252
Hong Kong Telegraph, 109, 133
Hong Kong University, Sun's speech,
144, 336n59
Hotung, Sir Robert, 143, 156, 340n96
Hou, Binko, 310n46
How, Julie, *see* Hwa, Julie How
Howard, Richard C., cited, 302n58 and
passim
Hsia Hsi, 349n66
Hsiang Ta-yen, cited, 302n62
Hsiang-tao Chou-pao, cited, 343n12,
365n82
Hsiao Fu-ch'eng, 52
Hsiao Yao-nan, 332n19
Hsieh Ch'ih, 190, 233, 236, 237, 239–40,
247, 357n8, 358n10
Hsieh Tsuan-t'ai, 295n7
Hsieh Ying-pai (Tse Ying-po), 221,
344n15, 355nn121, 122, 356n124,
357n134, 358n20
Hsin Ch'ing-nien, 326n4
Hsing-ch'i P'ing-lun (*Weekly Critic*), 30
Hsing Chung Hui (Society to Restore
China's Prosperity), 17, 296n17, 303n7;
financial support of Sun, 13–14, 40, 42,

44; organization in Hawaii, 13–14, 40,
44; power struggle, 14–15; in Hong
Kong, 14, 42; in Indochina, 61
Hsiung, S. I., cited, 333n32
Hsu Ch'ien (George), 280, 281, 332n18
Hsü, Leonard Shihlien, cited, 362n61,
354n110
Hsü Ch'ing-ho, 358n20
Hsü Ch'ung-chih, 30, 167, 197, 260, 261,
268, 275, 276, 361n43
Hsü Ch'ung-ch'ing, 344n15
Hsü Shih-ch'ang, president of Republic,
125–26
Hsü Shih-shen, cited 304n22, 341n2
Hsüan Chung-hua, 349n66
Hsüeh Chün-tu, cited, 82, 294n4, 295n10,
297n27, 298n29, 316n25
Hu Ching-jui, 53
Hu Han-min, 18, 26, 29, 37, 45, 46, 64, 80,
94, 190, 192, 236, 247, 256, 260, 266, 268,
276, 305n30, 343n15, 349n65, 358nn16,
20, 360nn33, 37, 365n82
Hu I-sheng, 62, 64, 356n132
Hua Tzu Jih Pao, 360n40
Huang, Philip C., 293n4
Huang Ch'ang-ku, 367n9
Huang Chi-lu, viii, 237, 295n5, 311n50,
312n59, 359n28
Huang Chü-su, 353n104
Huang Fu-sheng, 52
Huang Hsin-ch'ih, 345n30
Huang Hsing, 20, 43, 45, 64; and Sun, 18,
22, 23, 49, 58, 70, 90; in Japan, 78, 82, 85,
306n42, 312n62, 315n11; in United
States, 89
Huang Hua Kang uprising, 45, 305n25
Huang Huan-t'ing, 221, 356n124
Huang Lung-sheng, 180
Huang Ming-tang, 64
Huang Ta-yuan, 52
Huang Yao-t'ing, illustration 2
Hughes, Charles E., 103, 184, 320n77,
340n95
Huichow (Waichow), 31, 175, 344n19;
1900 revolt in, 18, 40, 57, 60, 308n7
Hunan, 31, 168, 315n12; Sun's invasion of,
119, 157; army, 167, 176, 258

INDEX

Sheng Shih Wei-yen, 16
Shensi, 152
Sheridan, James E., cited, 365*n*79
Shieh, Milton, J. T., cited, 345*n*28
Shih Ts'un-t'ung, 242
Shih-yeh Chi hua (Sun Yat-sen), *see International Development of China*
Shidehara, Baron, 368*n*16
Shihlung (Sheklung), 176
Shortridge, Samuel M., 340*n*95
Siam: fund raising in, 46, 47, 52, 53; Sun in, 61, 71
Sih, Paul, x
Simon, Stanislas, 66
Singapore: Sun's expulsion from, 18, 66, 74; bond sales in, 42; fund raising in, 43, 44, 45, 47, 52, 64; Sun in, 43, 44, 45, 63, 67, 74, 309*n*30, 310*n*41, 42; illustration 2
Sinkiang, 97, 98, 152
Sino-French War (1884–85), 12
Sino-Japanese War, 200
Sino-Soviet Treaty, *see analysis under* Republic of China
Skliansky, E. M., 152, 153
Smith, Adam, 16
Smith, Alexandra O., 337*n*68
Sneevliet, J. F. M., 31, 118–20, 121, 124, 130, 133, 148–50, 151, 153, 194, 207, 209, 224, 237–38*nn*14, 15, 332*n*22, 328*nn*, 332–33*nn*
Snow, Edgar, cited, 303*n*4, 314*n*3
Social revolution, 8, 176, 216–17, 219–20, 288
Socialist Youth Corps, 121, 150, 221; members in Kuomintang, 173, 174, 196, 214, 218, 222, 232–33, 238, 240, impeachment of, question of, 237–41; Young Men's Socialist Society, 221; Third Congress, 238
Society to Restore China's Prosperity, *see* Hsing Chung Hui
Sokolsky, George, 99, 100, 115, 323*nn*65, 68; cited, 314*n*4, 326*n*5, 6, 342*n*3, 352*n*97
Soong, Ailing, 301*n*50
Soong, Ch'ing-ling, *see* Sun Yat-sen, Mrs. (Soong Ch'ing-ling, Rosamonde)

Soong, Charles Jones, 303*n*4
Soong, T. V. (Sung Tzu-wen), 211, 277, 279, 342*n*3, 369*n*29
Soulie, George, cited, 309*n*19
South Africa, funds from, 307*n*51
Soviet Russia: and Manchuria, 81–82, 97, 98, 103, 117, 164; Karakhan Manifestos (1919 and 1920), 114–15; New Economic Policy, 119, 120, 124; postwar relations with Germany, 124; China policy, 164–65; and customs crisis, 187–88, 189 relations with Chinese Republic: recognition of, 112, 116, 118, 121, 124, 324*n*77; Sino-Soviet Treaty (1924), 229–32, signature, 230, 242; recognition of Soviet Russia by Republic, question of, 229–32, 238, 242
Soviet Russia and Sun, 33, 112–24 *passim,* 130–224 *passim,* 229–42 *passim,* 289; question of alliance with Canton government, 32–34, 38, 113, 119–20, 131, 123–40, 148–53, 155–57, 158–59, 160, 165, 174, 328*n*19; Sun's proposal for alliance between China, Russia, and Germany, 109–11; Sun's sympathy for Russian Revolution, 112–13, 115, 119, 179, 287; military and financial assistance, Sun's requests for, 113, 117–18, 120, 136–40, 148–53, 155–56, 160, 173, 208–09, 211–12, 248, 287, 343*n*10, 352*n*97; mid-*1918* to mid-*1922,* 113–24; *1917–18,* 114; Sun invited to, 116–117; mid-*1922*–December *1922,* 130–35
Spencer, Herbert, 16
Stalin, Josef, 280
Stanford University Library, 85, 91, 318*n*32
Stoianovitch, K. A., 207, 343*n*12
Straits Settlements, *see* Malay States
Strikes, *see under* Labor movement and unions
Stuart, Clifford, 87
Stubbs, Sir Edward, 143, 163, 336*n*57, 347*n*47
Students, Chinese, 242; contributions to Sun, 46; in Japan, 58; "returned," 76; overseas, 232–33
Su Hsi-wen, cited, 295*n*11

Studies of the East Asian Institute

The Ladder of Success in Imperial China, by Ping-ti Ho. New York: Columbia University Press, 1962.

The Chinese Inflation, 1937–1949, by Shun-hsin Chou. New York: Columbia University Press, 1963.

Reformer in Modern China: Chang Chien, 1853–1926, by Samuel Chu. New York: Columbia University Press, 1965.

Research in Japanese Sources: A Guide, by Herschel Webb with the assistance of Marleigh Ryan. New York: Columbia University Press, 1965.

Society and Education in Japan, by Herbert Passin. New York: Bureau of Publications, Teachers College, Columbia University, 1965.

Agricultural Production and Economic Development in Japan, 1873–1922, by James I. Nakamura. Princeton: Princeton University Press, 1966.

Japan's First Modern Novel: Ukigumo of Futabatei Shimei, by Marleigh Ryan. New York: Columbia University Press, 1967.

The Korean Communist Movement, 1918–1948, by Dae-Sook Suh. Princeton: Princeton University Press, 1967.

The First Vietnam Crisis, by Melvin Gurtov. New York: Columbia University Press, 1967.

Cadres, Bureaucracy, and Political Power in Communist China, by A. Doak Barnett. New York: Columbia University Press, 1967.

The Japanese Imperial Institution in the Tokugawa Period, by Herschel Webb. New York: Columbia University Press, 1968.

Higher Education and Business Recruitment in Japan, by Koya Azumi. New York: Teachers College Press, Columbia University, 1969.

The Communists and Chinese Peasant Rebellions: A Study in the Rewriting of Chinese History, by James P. Harrison, Jr. New York: Atheneum, 1969.

STUDIES OF THE EAST ASIAN INSTITUTE

How the Conservatives Rule Japan, by Nathaniel B. Thayer. Princeton: Princeton University Press, 1969.

Aspects of Chinese Education, edited by C. T. Hu. New York: Teachers College Press, Columbia University, 1970.

Documents of Korean Communism, 1918–1948, by Dae-Sook Suh. Princeton: Princeton University Press, 1970.

Japanese Education: A Bibliography of Materials in the English Language, by Herbert Passin. New York: Teachers College Press, Columbia University, 1970.

Economic Development and the Labor Market in Japan, in Koji Taira. New York: Columbia University Press, 1970.

The Japanese Oligarchy and the Russo-Japanese War, by Shumpei Okamoto. New York: Columbia University Press, 1970.

Imperial Restoration in Medieval Japan, by H. Paul Varley. New York: Columbia University Press, 1971.

Japan's Postwar Defense Policy, 1947–1968, by Martin E. Weinstein. New York: Columbia University Press, 1971.

Election Campaigning Japanese Style, by Gerald L. Curtis. New York: Columbia University Press, 1971.

China and Russia: The "Great Game," by O. Edmund Clubb. New York: Columbia University Press, 1971.

Money and Monetary Policy in Communist China, by Katharine Huang Hsiao. New York: Columbia University Press, 1971.

The District Magistrate in Late Imperial China, by John R. Watt. New York: Columbia University Press, 1972.

Law and Policy in China's Foreign Relations: A Study of Attitudes and Practice, by James C. Hsiung. New York: Columbia University Press, 1972.

Pearl Harbor as History: Japanese-American Relations, 1931–1941, edited by Dorothy Borg and Shumpei Okamoto, with the assistance of Dale K. A. Finlayson. New York: Columbia University Press, 1973.

Japanese Culture: A Short History, by H. Paul Varley. New York: Praeger, 1973.

Doctors in Politics: The Political Life of the Japan Medical Association, by William E. Steslicke. New York: Praeger, 1973.

The Japan Teachers Union: A Radical Interest Group in Japanese Politics, by Donald Ray Thurston. Princeton: Princeton University Press, 1973.

Japan's Foreign Policy, 1868–1941: A Research Guide, edited by James William Morley. New York: Columbia University Press, 1974.

Palace and Politics in Prewar Japan, by David Anson Titus. New York: Columbia University Press, 1974.

The Idea of China: Essays in Geographic Myth and Theory, by Andrew March. Devon, England: David and Charles, 1974.

Origins of the Cultural Revolution, by Roderick MacFarquhar. New York: Columbia University Press, 1974.

STUDIES OF THE EAST ASIAN INSTITUTE

Shiba Kōkan: Artist, Innovator, and Pioneer in the Westernization of Japan, by Calvin L. French. Tokyo: Weatherhill, 1974.

Insei: Abdicated Sovereigns in the Politics of Late Heian Japan, by G. Cameron Hurst. New York: Columbia University Press, 1975.

Embassy at War, by Harold Joyce Noble. Edited with an introduction by Frank Baldwin, Jr. Seattle: University of Washington Press, 1975.

Rebels and Bureaucrats: China's December 9ers, by John Israel and Donald W. Klein. Berkeley, University of California Press, 1975.

Neo-Confucianism and the Political Culture of Late Imperial China, by Thomas A. Metzger. New York: Columbia University Press, 1976.

Deterrent Diplomacy, edited by James William Morley. New York: Columbia University Press, 1976.

House United, House Divided: The Chinese Family in Taiwan, by Myron L. Cohen. New York: Columbia University Press, 1976.

Cadres, Commanders and Commissars: The Training of the Chinese Communist Leadership, 1920–45, by Janes L. Price. Boulder, Colorado: Westview Press, 1976.

Contemporary Japanese Budget Politics, by John Creighton Campbell. Berkeley: University of California Press, 1976.

The Medieval Chinese Oligarchy, by David Johnson. Boulder, Colorado: Westview Press, 1976.

Escape from Predicament: Neo-Confucianism and China's Evolving Political Culture, by Thomas A. Metzger. New York: Columbia University Press, 1976.

Sun Yat-sen: Frustrated Patriot, by C. Martin Wilbur. New York: Columbia University Press, 1976.